Apostolic Networks in Britain

New Ways of Being Church

STUDIES IN EVANGELICAL HISTORY AND THOUGHT

A full listing of titles in this series appears at the end of this book

STUDIES IN EVANGELICAL HISTORY AND THOUGHT

Apostolic Networks of Britain

New Ways of Being Church

William K. Kay

Foreword by Densil Morgan

MILTON KEYNES · COLORADO SPRINGS · HYDERABAD

First published 2007 by Paternoster

Paternoster is an imprint of Authentic Media
9 Holdom Avenue, Bletchley, Milton Keynes, Bucks, MK1 1QR
1820 Jet Stream Drive, Colorado Springs, CO 80921, USA
OM Authentic Media, Medchal Road, Jeedimetla Village,
Secunderabad 500 055, A.P., India
www.authenticmedia.co.uk
Authentic Media is a division of IBS-STL UK, a company limited by guarantee
(registered charity no. 270162)

13 12 11 10 09 08 07   7 6 5 4 3 2 1

British Library Cataloguing in Publication Data

A catalogue record for this book is available from the British Library.

ISBN 978-1-84227-409-5

Typeset by Anne E. Dyer.
Printed and bound in Great Britain for Paternoster
by Nottingham, Alphagraphics.

Series Preface

The Evangelical movement has been marked by its union of four emphases: on the Bible, on the cross of Christ, on conversion as the entry to the Christian life and on the responsibility of the believer to be active. The present series is designed to publish scholarly studies of any aspect of this movement in Britain or overseas. Its volumes include social analysis as well as exploration of Evangelical ideas. The books in the series consider aspects of the movement shaped by the Evangelical Revival of the eighteenth century, when the impetus to mission began to turn the popular Protestantism of the British Isles and North America into a global phenomenon. The series aims to reap some of the rich harvest of academic research about those who, over the centuries, have believed that they had a gospel to tell to the nations.

STUDIES IN EVANGELICAL HISTORY AND THOUGHT

Series Editors

Though it is the smallest of all your seeds, yet when it grows, it is the largest of garden plants (Matthew 13.32)

For Peter and Jenny, Paul and Carol

Contents

Foreword

With the world-wide Pentecostal movement now having come of age, it is good to have William Kay's analysis of Apostolic Networks in Britain. A century ago Pentecostalism was virtually an unknown phenomenon, but by now this vibrant form of Christianity has not only transformed faith in the southern hemisphere but has made a significant impact on religion at home. This informed, scholarly and soundly-researched study of the different strands within the British Pentecostal movement will be indispensable for those who want to know more about current spirituality and the religion of the recent past. With Pentecostalism now entering its second century, this study will enlighten us all.

D. Densil Morgan,
Professor of Theology,
University of Wales, Bangor,
2006.

Preface

Apostolic networks in Britain are at the heart of this book. These networks are collections of churches linked with each other and linked with an apostolic figure. In almost every case the networks are organised quite differently from denominations, and deliberately so, since the networks have conceived of themselves as avoiding the worst features of denominations by returning to a New Testament pattern.

This book is in five parts and begins by setting the scene for the emergence of the networks. The assumption here is that it is impossible to understand the networks properly without appreciating their historical origins and the ideas which helped form them and which stimulated their founding. The first chapter deals with the theological ideas that lie behind the networks and the preachers who articulated them. The second chapter explores the relationship between the networks and the charismatic renewal movement of the 1960s and the way that the networks came out of this movement and then began to arrange themselves into two broad groupings.

The second and longest section of this book tells the story of 12 separate networks in Britain. Actually it tells the story of slightly more than 12 groups because some of the networks broke into mini-networks but, in essence, the second section gives an account of the founding and development of the main networks and shows how they surmounted the obstacles in the way of their small beginnings and how, in some cases, they became strong and influential. Each of these accounts runs, as it were, in parallel with the others and without much cross-referencing between one network and another.

The third section of this book follows events and trends which crossed the networks and, in one way and another, applied to all of them. All the networks were formed within the same social and economic context and affected, to a greater or lesser extent, by what was happening in Britain from the period after about 1970 when the networks began. All networks, for instance, were affected by the 'Toronto Blessing' that hit the British churches in the early 1990s. All the networks were touched by the cell church movement and responded to it with varying degrees of warmth.

The fourth section begins an analysis of the networks and explores their theology, their relation to mission and their sociological characteristics. The rationale here is that it is not possible to appreciate the theological distinctiveness or the missionary effectiveness or the sociological shape of networks without first appreciating their historical development. Three chapters concentrate upon the analysis showing, for instance, that networks probably need to be viewed as new sociological animals that do not properly fit the old sociological categories.

The final section provides a quantitative account of the networks based upon a questionnaire to over 231 people and it deals with the factual and statistical elements of the networks including such matters as the age of leaders within the network churches and their beliefs, attitudes, and theological orientation.[1] This section of the book addresses some of the topics raised earlier and, in particular, concludes by evaluating the networks in terms of the broad classification that was given to them in part one. The section closes with a reflective chapter that looks backwards on what has gone before and forwards to what might happen in the future.

---

[1] Added to this were a further 85 usable online responses to some questions.

Acknowledgements

This book could not have been written without the help of a very large number of people. I'm grateful to the Arts and Humanities Research Board (now Arts and Humanities Research Council) for the grant that enabled me to begin the research project of which this book is a major product. Equally I am thankful to colleagues within the School of Theology and Religious Studies at the University of Wales, Bangor, for their encouragement and for comment during a research seminar on work in progress. Similarly, two of the chapters were first presented as papers at research gatherings, one at the International Society of Empirical Research in Theology (held at Bangor in 2006) and the other at the European Pentecostal Theological Association gathering at the Iso Kirja, Finland, in the summer of 2006. Other discussions were held at the St Deiniol's Symposium organised by Leslie Francis and Mandy Robbins. Feedback from all these presentations have been incorporated into the relevant chapters. Also important were scattered and intense discussions with attenders at the annual Charismata gathering at High Leigh.

The Arts and Humanities Research Council enabled the University of Wales, Bangor, to employ Anne Dyer as my research assistant and I am grateful to her for all the work that she carried out in relation to the distribution of the questionnaire, to her skills in databasing and to her capacity to extract information from a wide variety of sources as well as to the interviews she carried out both by herself and with me.

Many of the administrators of the apostolic networks described in this book kindly provided lists of addresses enabling contact with respondents to be established. Equally, a large number of interviewees gave a huge amount of their time (and in some cases excellent lunches) to allow me to begin to piece together the intricate story of their individual networks or the interaction between networks and other agencies. Heartfelt thanks are due to: Stuart Bell, Matt Biddlecombe, Richard Britton, Peter Broadbent, Peter Butt, Tony Cauchi, Steve Chalke, Gerald Coates, John Coles, Ian Coffey, David Damp, Ruth Dearnley, Gareth Duffty, Colin Dye, Roger Forster, Stephen Gee, Frank Green, Michael Harper, David Heron, David Holden, Alan Johnson, Keri Jones, Gerald Kelly, Peter Kerridge, Katei Kirby, Jeff Lucas, David Matthew, Andrew McNeil, Robert Mountford, Marlon Nartey, John Noble, Rachel Orrell, Hugh Osgood, Wesley Richards, Alan Scotland, Adrian Thomas, Steve Thomas, David Tomlinson, Colin Urquhart, Terry Virgo, and Nigel Wright for answering my sometimes persistent questions by e-mail, phone or, more often, in person. Details of tape-recorded interviews are footnoted in the subsequent text.

I'm also grateful to a variety of other people who helped in other ways. Allan Anderson provided me with an introduction to the Vineyard network in the UK, Barry Cooper provided information about church planting in New Frontiers International, David Hilborn was helpful about the byways of the Evangelical Alliance, Edna Jones (widow of Bryn Jones), wrote supportively to me, Huw Lewis of the Jesus Fellowship answered my questions thoughtfully. David Holden invited me to two days of prayer and fasting with New Frontiers International. David Matthew entrusted me with his precious set of *Restoration* magazines for well over a year. John Noble generously gave me a set of *Fulness* magazines while Michael Harper provided me with copies of *Renewal* and *Theological Renewal*. Mike Thompson gave me a copy of his thesis on New Frontiers. David Littlewood lent me books and tapes by Martyn Lloyd-Jones. Ewen Robertson let me read his pre-publication dissertation on Covenant Ministries International and Russ Spittler shared his memories of John Wimber. Andrew McNeil lent me audio tapes capturing Wimber at the peak of his powers. Noel Stanton answered my questions and provided access to information on the Jesus Fellowship and Andrew Walker, my friend at King's College, London, my half-time employers when I began this project, listen to my enthusiasms and provided creative insights in response to them.

All of those who were interviewed also subsequently checked the text of the interview or the account of their network elicited from the interview and made corrections to matters of fact and, in some cases, persuaded me that my interpretation of events needed to be re-assessed. Catherine Henderson was meticulous in scrutinising the chapter on Bryn Jones.

The library at the University of Wales, Bangor, efficiently dealt with my inter-library loans; the library at Mattersey Hall proved a treasure house of relevant books; and the Donald Gee Centre for Pentecostal and Charismatic Research, and its archivist David Garrard, accessed the most esoteric of items. To all of them my thanks are due.

Finally my thanks are due to my wife, Anthea, who put up with interminable discussions about the merits or otherwise of apostolic networks and whose critical skills were exercised at various stages in the production of this text, even while on holiday. Without her gracious contribution, this book would never have been completed.

Part I

Beginnings

Chapter 1

The Charismatic Movement and its Spin-offs

Even as early as the 1930s, perceptive observers could see that the Pentecostal movement was spreading around the world. Donald Gee published *Upon All Flesh: a Pentecostal world tour* in 1935. Gee's travels had taken him to see the revival 'first-hand on every one of the five continents' with result that he was able to weave together fragmentary documentary accounts with his own personal impressions of the flourishing growth of Pentecostal congregations in many cultures and climates.

By the mid-1930s, the Pentecostal churches had put down roots all over Europe and been most successful in the Protestant countries of the north, in Scandinavia, in the United Kingdom and in Switzerland. They were less successful in Germany and France and almost non-existent in Italy, Spain, Portugal and Greece. Bit by bit they had fitted into the theological and institutional space made by the free or nonconformist churches (which is why they did not flourish where there was no nonconformity) and had worked out their doctrine and practice. They believed in a baptism of the Holy Spirit that followed conversion and by which the Christian entered a world of charismatic gifts that distributed power inside the church across congregations and, outside the church, strengthened the work of evangelists through miracles of healing confirming the preaching of the Gospel.

By and large Pentecostal churches were isolated from the rest of the Protestant community simply because a theology that presumed the activity of the Holy Spirit in contemporary prophecy, healing or glossolalia was completely unacceptable. For the low-church Protestant - the Brethren, the Salvation Army, Strict Baptists and others - charismatic gifts were almost always relegated to the first few centuries of the church age.[1] Indeed, charismatic gifts were thought to be given precisely for the establishment of

---

[1] John Wesley was very emphatic about the continuation of miracles in the church in the first centuries. See his *Journal* entry for 2 January, 1749. He postponed a journey to Holland in order to answer a book by Dr Conyers Middleton that questioned miracles in the NT and as recorded by the Fathers. At the opening of Vol. 10 of the Jackson edition of Wesley's *Works* (*The letters of the Rev. John Wesley, A.M., sometime fellow of Lincoln College, Oxford* 14 vol. set, edited by John Telford. London: The Epworth Press, 1960, [the 'Jackson edition' from the name of its first editor in 1854] is Wesley's reply to Middleton in which he not only defends the continuation of miracles in the church but suggests that Middleton does not know the Fathers as well as he claimed! (I am grateful to Dr Herbert McGonigle of the Nazarene Theological College, Manchester, for this information.)

the infant church but to be unnecessary for the period beyond the lives of the original apostles named in the gospels. In other lines of argumentation, charismatic gifts, and indeed any belief in miracles, was suspicious because miracles and credulity were part of the panoply of Catholicism. The Reformers in their polemic had often sounded like incipient rationalists who wished to establish their doctrinal case by reason rather than by an appeal to the supernatural.[2] And for more liberal and often upper class Protestants, those influenced by the Enlightenment and German 19th century biblical scholarship, Pentecostals were primitives occupying a pre-critical mindset and, to boot, probably cultic.

Although Pentecostals at the start of the 20th century had seen the restoration of charismatic gifts to the church as a divine event of huge significance, the rest of the church and, indeed, the rest of society had largely ignored them or, when it had deigned to notice them, scorned them – as the tabloid newspaper reports of George Jeffreys' campaigns only too clearly showed.[3] The entrenchment of atheistic communism within the old Russian empire, the rise of dictatorships in Germany and Italy and, eventually, Spain, as well as massive unemployment across much of Europe appeared to diminish the relevance of Christianity. Who cared what the Pentecostals thought? And, when war came in September 1939, the church in many parts of Europe was soon fighting for its life.

When eventually peace came, it was evident that the 1939-45 war had wounded Europe deeply and torn the remaining fabric of Christendom. It is true that the churches survived as institutions and, on the western side of the Iron Curtain, were slowly able to take advantage of democratic liberties to evangelise and build. On the communist side of the curtain, Christianity was suppressed with varying degrees of severity and thoroughness. Where the Catholic Church was strong, as in Poland, Christianity was able to fortify itself against the encroachments of atheistic government but, in southern Russia, Pentecostals, like Baptists, were excluded from the protection given to the Orthodox Church and often imprisoned.

During the 1950s democratic Europe slowly recovered material prosperity. The habits of churchgoing had been disrupted by military service and, according to Brown, Christian Britain died in the 1960s, though there is evidence that the decay had begun earlier[4], probably in the

---

[2] G. R. Evans, A. E. McGrath, A. D. Galloway, *The Science of Theology* (vol.1), (Basingstoke, Marshall Morgan & Scott, 1986), p.120f; C. E. Gunton, S. R. Holmes, and M. A. Rae, (eds), *The Practice of Theology: a reader*, (London, SCM, 2001), e.g. p.72f.

[3] E. C. W. Boulton, *George Jeffreys: a ministry of the miraculous*, (London, Elim Publishing House, 1928).

[4] Arnold Toynbee in the Reith Lectures of 1952 described Britain as a 'post-Christian society'; see R. Manwaring, *From Controversy to co-existence*, (Cambridge, CUP, 1985), p.79. C. G. Brown, *The Death of Christian Britain*, (London, Routledge, 2002).

1920s following the 1914-18 war. Yet, although the churches began to record declining attendance, fewer marriages and baptisms and a downturn in the number of ordinands, these negative figures were offset by the rejuvenating power of large-scale evangelistic crusades where Billy Graham preached.[5]

While institutional decline could be detected at one end of the Christian spectrum, evangelistic life could be detected at the other. Both these trends took place when social attitudes were also beginning to melt. The hierarchical and orderly society of the 1950s with its short haircuts, philosophy of duty and deference, and its gradual accumulation of material goods began to give way to the volatile 1960s. The adjustments were largely generational because those born after 1945 found themselves being able to vote for the first time in the early 1960s. Political power began to change hands and the younger generation that came into prominence could amplify its fashions and opinions through rapidly growing broadcasting networks, particularly television but also local radio, resurgent cinema and the vast sales of recorded music. The basically conformist attitude of Bing Crosby and even Frank Sinatra began to give way to the anti-war protest songs of Bob Dylan ('The Times They are A-Changin', 'Blowing in the Wind') and the wilder fringes of drug-fuelled self-indulgence in the Rolling Stones ('I cant get no satisfaction').

The 1950s were marked by the Cold War, a stand-off between communism and capitalism, but in 1962 the Cuban missile crisis almost led to nuclear conflagration. Bertrand Russell's *Has Man a Future?* was published in 1961 and depicted apocalyptic dangers facing the entire human race.[6] Such fears, together with shifts in power between the generations, created a predisposition to question the wisdom of old political leaders and to mock their instinctive conservatism. Whether these fears catalysed change within the church is impossible to say, but undoubtedly an awareness of the nuclear threat increased the urgency of evangelistic preachers. A sermon by George Jeffreys at the Royal Albert Hall in 1955 hinted at the connection between the atom bomb and biblical eschatology.[7]

Outside Europe, change was slower, and in South Africa it was resisted. Apartheid was introduced in 1948 precisely in order to prevent any alteration to the pattern or balance in society, and the doctrine of racial segregation was supported by many of South Africa's churches.[8] Yet, David du Plessis, a South African Pentecostal was significant in helping to

---

[5] Manwaring, *From Controversey to co-existence,* (1985); B. Graham, *Just as I am,* (London, Harper Collins, 1998).

[6] B. Russell, *Has Man a Future,* (Harmondsworth, Penguin, 1961).

[7] Tape in the Donald Gee Centre, Mattersey.

[8] Nico Horn, 'Power and Empowerment in the Political Context of South Africa', *Journal of the European Pentecostal Theological Association,* (2005), pp.25, 7-24.

renew Roman Catholic/Protestant relations and diffuse the charismatic movement.

i. David du Plessis (1905-87)

The Pentecostal movement had taken root in South Africa after 1903. In 1918 at about the age of 13, David du Plessis was baptised in the Holy Spirit while a member of the Apostolic Faith Mission (AFM). He became a pastor though he had earlier been a street preacher and an apprentice printer within the denomination. After ordination at the age of 25 he began to edit the denomination's magazine *Comforter/Trooster* and in 1936 became its General Secretary. In the same year the unconventional British evangelist, Smith Wigglesworth, was working in South Africa and du Plessis was his interpreter for Afrikaans congregations.

One morning Wigglesworth arrived in du Plessis's office, pinned him against a wall and prophesied to him. The exact words of the prophecy are a matter of debate, particularly as du Plessis himself did not speak about the matter until about 1951, but their general import is clear enough.[9] Wigglesworth said, 'young man, you have been in Jerusalem long enough. The Lord says you have to go to the uttermost parts of the earth'. In its expanded version, as reported by du Plessis, he added 'through the old-line denominations will come a revival that will eclipse anything we have known throughout history... it will eclipse the present-day, 20th-century Pentecostal revival that is already a marvel to the world... this same blessing will become acceptable to the churches'.[10]

In 1947 du Plessis was in Switzerland preparing for the first Pentecostal World Conference to be held in Zürich in May that year. Du Plessis asked AFM leaders' permission to extend his leave of absence so as to continue working for the conference. The leaders refused and so du Plessis took the 'bold and prophetic' step of resigning as their General Secretary.[11] He sent a telegram to his wife telling her to sell everything and to come to Basle. From 1949 until the 1958, he served as organising secretary (though with a break between 1952 and 1955) for the Pentecostal World Conferences and in this way had his finger on the pulse of global Pentecostalism. He gradually grew in stature to the extent that his authority and influence quite outweighed his lack of any official position within one denomination or

---

[9] D. Cartwright, *The Real* Wigglesworth, (Tonbridge Wells, Sovereign World, 2000).
[10] D du Plessis, *A Man called Mr Pentecost*, (Plainfield, N J, Logos International, 1977), p.19.
[11] R Spittler, 'David Johannes Du Plessis', S. Burgess, and E. van der Maas (eds), *New International Dictionary of Pentecostal and Charismatic Movements,* (Grand Rapids, Zondervan, 2002).

another. Consequently, he was free to act and speak as he felt prompted by the Holy Spirit and without obligations to ecclesiastical politics.

He was sensitive to the intricacies and divergences of opinion on church government and mission held by various national groups of Pentecostals. For instance, Sweden strongly supported the independence of the local church and resisted the type of legal arrangements by which American Assemblies of God constituted itself. Du Plessis wanted to remain above these differences and independent of them. As result he consciously lived a simple life and rarely took a paying job in a denominational context for a prolonged period of time. Between 1949 and 1951 he worked at the Church of God school in Cleveland and for two years after this with the Far East Broadcasting Company and then as interim pastor for the Stanford Gospel Tabernacle, which belonged to Assemblies of God in the United States. He became an American Assemblies of God minister in 1955 and between 1956 and 1959 was organising secretary for the Voice of Healing Fellowship.

He increasingly saw himself as divinely called to bring the Pentecostal message to the mainline churches and he did so by waiting for invitations and trusting God that doors would open; he had no systematic policy of dissemination nor any official status as a Pentecostal spokesman. But in 1952 he spoke to the International Missionary Council in Germany and, as are result, became known as 'Mr Pentecost', a title which encapsulated his emerging role. In 1954 he attended the World Council Assembly and by the end of the decade he was speaking on Pentecostalism at major theological centres in the United States. His influence reached to the Roman Catholic Church and he was received by Pope John XXIII just at the time Vatican II was starting its deliberations.

Du Plessis's profile within the ecumenical movement grew at the same time as it diminished in the eyes of the Pentecostal movement. But, when yet another movement, the charismatic movement, began at the very start of the 1960s, du Plessis was poised to enter the completely new situation created by the outpouring of the Holy Spirit on the established denominations. He had been for all his life a 'card-carrying Pentecostal' but he now also had unofficial credentials with the more traditionally liberal ecumenicals. When Episcopalians, Methodist, Lutherans, Anglicans and others began to ask how they should understand the Holy Spirit, it was only natural that du Plessis should be invited to speak at large consultative conferences and conventions. He was a natural raconteur and had a way of presenting contentious issues with humour and originality. Spittler sees him as a prophet, while Michael Harper saw in his ministry a model for his own.[12]

---

[12] Spittler, 'David Johannes Du Plessis' (2002). Interview with Michael Harper, 17 September, 2004.

ii. Michael Harper (b 1931) and the Fountain Trust (1964-1980)

There was an evangelical awakening at Cambridge during the 1950s and Michael Harper, a law student in 1950, was converted to Christ and switched to theology.[13]   After his degree he trained for the Anglican ministry at Ridley Hall and was ordained in 1955 on the crest of the wave generated by the 1954 Billy Graham crusade to London. Britain appeared to be heading for revival and the Anglican church seemed to be healthy. After marriage and a first curacy, Harper moved to the premier evangelical Anglican church in Britain, All Souls Langham Place, where the minister, John Stott, had already gained a reputation for spirituality and intellectual evangelicalism.

Harper's attachment to the Anglican church was such that he has described the difference between himself and John Stott by saying that Stott was an Evangelical first and an Anglican second whereas, for Harper, the priorities were reversed – he was an Anglican first and foremost.[14] While studying the Bible in 1962 Harper began to see the place of spiritual knowledge in Pauline theology. His own praying became less formal and more experiential, and the change this brought about radically enlarged the power and relevance of his preaching which now evoked more than a polite hearing.

At the same time a friend spoke in tongues as result of attending a meeting in London addressed by David du Plessis. Harper heard about this and, while reading *Trinity* magazine, learnt of Episcopalians in the United States who were attending prayer meetings where charismatic gifts like tongues, healing and prophecy were freely expressed. Although Harper saw this as a sovereign activity of Holy Spirit within the historic denominations, he considered speaking in tongues to be undignified and unnecessary but, as he re-read the New Testament, he saw for the first time that that Pauline teaching, far from forbidding glossolalia or brushing it under the carpet, actively encouraged it. By 1963 Harper had received glossolalia himself and began moving swiftly in a direction that seemed to him to be prompted by the direct impulse of the Holy Spirit.

He arranged a meeting in London for David du Plessis and found himself at the centre of a flurry of telephone calls, tape recordings and invitations. A growing demand for tapes and writings led to a conflict of interest between All Souls and the new burgeoning ministry. So John Stott and Michael Harper parted company, and Stott was to become one of the most persistent advocates of a theological position that effectively marginalised

---

[13] M. Harper, *None Can Guess*, (London, Hodder & Stoughton, 1971).

[14] Interview with Michael Harper, 17 September, 2004.

charismatic gifts. Harper, while remaining an Anglican priest, left parish work to found the historically important Fountain Trust in 1964.[15]

Despite its enormous impact, the Trust had no capital funds or investments. Money was generated by conferences and gifts though, when *Renewal* magazine was successfully launched in 1966, the Christian public could more easily target their donations. Even so, the Trust never solicited membership fees or attempted to set up regional groups. It did not become a parachurch agency seeking permanency. It simply tried to encourage the renewal of denominational churches, including Roman Catholic ones, all over Britain. *Renewal* circulated widely and provided news, analysis, teaching and comment on individuals and congregations who welcomed contemporary charismata. The 1971 Fountain Trust's five day conference in Guildford Cathedral in July attracted a congregation of at least 2000 for preaching and celebration (*Renewal* 34). Despite the reservations of classical Pentecostal over the inclusion of Roman Catholics, the Trust continued its mission of teaching about the Holy Spirit across a wide Christian spectrum. In other words, the Trust was not overtly Protestant in outlook despite Harper's own narrowly evangelical and narrowly Anglican theological origins. This was, perhaps, a sign of things to come because, after a lengthy journey and with much heart-searching, Harper was to leave his beloved Anglicanism in the 1990s and to join the Orthodox Church.

Pentecostals thought that the charismatic renewal might result in a mass transfer of members from the mainline denominations into the classical Pentecostal fold. That this did not happen was due partly to the work of the Fountain Trust which never drew sharp lines around church polity. Yet in its own gentle way the Trust helped to reshape the Anglican structures and re-form modes of worship by making them more relaxed, informal, spontaneous and meaningful. The cultural gap between Pentecostals and Anglicans also helped to explain why few people jumped the divide between them. Pentecostalism was more working-class in its orientation than the Anglican church and, somehow, few people could bring themselves to leave the hallowed and ancient stone buildings of Anglicanism for the backstreet halls of Pentecostalism. Here and there, as in Tunbridge Wells, where the Pentecostal churches were open and young, charismatics did transfer. In the main, after the initial surprise, Pentecostals began to criticise the failure of charismatic groups to re-adjust their

---

[15] It is worth recalling Hocken's comment, 'By the middle of 1964 then, there was a common awareness in Britain of the arrival of this new Charismatic movement. What many participants thought of as its beginning – the visits of Maguire, Christenson and du Plessis with the Spirit-baptism of Harper – were not in fact the origins, but the major instruments by which the previously somewhat scattered streams came visibly and consciously into one movement' P. Hocken, *Streams of Renewal,* 2nd Edn, (Carlisle, Paternoster, 1998), p.132.

doctrine. Pentecostals, for instance, found it difficult to see how people who spoke in tongues could also baptise infants whereas, for fs and Roman Catholics, spirituality and church tradition were separable domains.

Behind Michael Harper's thinking was a belief that revival could spread across England. He had read Edwin Orr's book on the second evangelical awakening while at Cambridge and knew that revival could burn cross-denominationally across the whole UK. He was not yet clear about how the flow of events that were carrying him along might change the religious landscape. He was unclear whether the charismatic outpouring was the beginning of a renewal of the church in its historic institutional forms or whether the Spirit would produce deep structural change, even doctrinal change, that might draw together previously opposing branches of Christianity. Nor was it obvious how the renewal of the church might catalyse social change, especially if renewal turned outwards from the church in all its manifestations to become a flaming evangelical revival.

Renewal magazine, and subsequently *Theological Renewal* – its more heavyweight offspring born in 1976 - explored these issues although always with a tendency to answer theological questions with both/and rather than either/or. Charismatic gifts could operate within a liturgy *and* the liturgy could remain intact.[16] The Spirit was really given at infant baptism or adolescent confirmation *and* there was subsequent 'release' when people spoke in tongues.[17] Women might certainly prophesy and take a governing role in church life *and* be submitted to the authority of male ministers. In this way the renewal could flourish in diverse ecclesiastical settings and be interpreted as being supportive of all theological traditions apart from the most secular and liberal. Consequently, the renewal, as it extended a common experience of prayer and spontaneous praise, could be a force for Christian unity.

Such ecumenical hopes were, however, contrary to the radical thinking of a group of men who, from the late 1950s onwards, associated with Arthur Wallis (who became part of the Advisory Council of the Fountain Trust[18]) or those, in a circle focused on the theology of the Puritans and Reformed Christianity, who gathered round Martyn Lloyd-Jones.

iii. Arthur Wallis (1923-88)

Wallis' vision for a great revival was powerfully described by his book *In the Day of Thy Power: structural principles of revival* in 1956. He saw this

---

[16] A. Bittlinger, 'A function of Charismata in Divine Worship' *Theological Renewal*, 1, (1975), pp.5-10.

[17] S. Tugwell, *Did you receive the Spirit,* (London, DLT, 1971); 'Is there a Pentecostal experience?', *Theological Renewal*, 7 (1977), pp.8-11.

[18] A. Wallis, 'Springs of Restoration 2, *Restoration*, (September/October, 1980), pp.6-9.

revival as coming through the spiritual preparation of Christian believers but initiated and enacted entirely by the sovereign power of God himself. Early in 1958 Wallis began to pray with David Lillie and convened a meeting in Exmouth in May where he began to put forward his vision for the church, a vision arising out of the pages of the New Testament and without reference to historical accretions and the accumulated weight of ecclesiastical tradition. What he advocated was a church that is pure and organic but which functions not only as a temple for the presence of God but as the body of Christ where every part contributes to the unity of the whole and where each member, far from being weak, useless, helpless and perpetually sinful, is justified by faith, full of the Holy Spirit and sure of his or her own destiny in the purposes of God. Such a church was not part of an organisation run by ecclesiastical bureaucratics but, rather, was an organism that grew as it worshipped and evangelised. Such a church, in Wallis's opinion, rejected the twin difficulties of Brethrenism, which discounted the charismatic gifts of the Holy Spirit as valid expressions of the grace and power of God today, and of Pentecostalism, which might overemphasise certain spiritual experiences at the expense of others and create doctrines around particular charismatic gifts. And such a church began from the presupposition that the simplifications of the Reformation – the overturning of Catholic practice and medieval theology – were entirely welcome and, indeed, part of the divine purpose for humanity.

Wallis was important because he began to articulate a more radical theology of the Holy Spirit than that implied by charismatics elsewhere. For many of the most theologically aware charismatics, the reconciliation of their own dogmatic position with the assumptions of classical Pentecostalism became pressing. Initially, Pentecostals seemed to have all the answers (as Michael Harper's early books imply) but, gradually, a divergence between Pentecostal and charismatic doctrine appeared. Despite *Theological Renewal*'s irenic stance, its articles could to be seen as accommodating the *status quo* and muting the more radical voices within the debate.

This is nowhere more evident than in a group to which both Michael Harper and John Stott belonged. In 1977 the Fountain Trust and the Church of England Evangelical Council published a joint statement entitled *Gospel and Spirit*. The tract runs to a dozen pages and deals with six areas of contention. The first concerns the relationship between Christian initiation and baptism in the Spirit and, while accepting that all Gospel blessings are given in Christ, affirms that initiation is a unitary work with many facets and many overlapping concepts. These facets and concepts may be logically separated but essentially belong together since they express a single reality of the believer's incorporation into Christ. Consequently there is a need to avoid trying to stereotype the work of the

Holy Spirit or the experience of individual Christians into a one, two or three-stage experience.

Similarly the term 'baptism in the Spirit' should not be used to such a way as to question the reality of the work of the Spirit in regeneration. Nor should speaking in tongues be singled out as the universal or indubitable evidence that the Spirit has been given since this identifies the Giver of the charismatic gift with the presence of only one of the gifts.

In relation to particular ministries, the personal authority of the original apostles now belongs only to Scripture as found in the Old and New Testaments and under which all churches and church leaders stand. Latter-day ministries may parallel some aspects of apostolic functions – indeed modern apostles are not ruled out by such considerations – but their activities and statements must continue to be evaluated by the standards laid down by the first apostles and set forth in Scripture.

A year later Wallis wrote an article for *Theological Renewal* setting out his concern at what seemed to him to be the fudging of the issues or the surrender of important truths.[19] 'I believe there are basic issues involved that we must see clearly and hold to tenaciously. Otherwise we shall be surrendering the heart of what God has restored to us in these past years'. He argued that, even if it is theoretically true that the believer possesses every blessing in Christ on conversion, in practice this is not so because 'a thing may be true as far as divine purpose and intention is concerned, without necessarily being true in human experience'. And he instanced the statement of God to Joshua 'I have given into your hand Jericho' well before the city actually fell.

Wallis then presented his critique of John Stott's influential book *The Baptism and Fullness of the Holy Spirit* that had been published in 1964. Stott had contended that 'the revelation of the purpose of God should be sought in its didactic, rather than its historical parts' and therefore felt justified in basing expectations about normal Christian experience on the epistles rather than the book of Acts. Wallis pointed out that the writing of the epistles and the activities recorded in Acts were largely contemporaneous. 'It is surely inconceivable that the Holy Spirit is declaring the norm in the Epistles, and at the same time doing something abnormal, or at least different, in so many of the situations to which those Epistles were addressed'. By implication Stott's method for establishing doctrine and Christian norms was deficient.

Wallis went on to draw a distinction between having the Spirit at regeneration and receiving the Spirit in an empowering and gifting operation that, in Acts, is defined by the notion of Spirit baptism. He drew a parallel between ordinary Christians and Christ himself upon whom the

---

[19] A. Wallis, 'A Fresh look at the baptism in the Holy Spirit', *Theological Renewal* 73 (1978), pp.29-36.

Spirit descended at his baptism in the River Jordan by saying that '[to say that] Jesus receive[d] the Spirit at his baptism is not to imply that he was devoid of the Spirit for the first 30 years of his life'. In other words Wallis argued from Scripture for the distinctive Pentecostal, and as it became, Restorationist emphasis that later resulted in the formation of the house churches. For Wallis, baptism in the Spirit *could* validly be an experience subsequent to conversion and doctrine *could* validly be deduced from the book of Acts.

iv. Martyn Lloyd-Jones (1899-1981)

A Welsh-speaking Calvinistic Methodist would not be the obvious choice for a distinguished London pulpit. Westminster Chapel had been the premier Nonconformist congregation, a 2,500 seater 'Nonconformist cathedral', since 1865 but it was a difficult place to work because the size and acoustics of the building were extremely demanding. The minister was expected to preach three times a week and, by the mid-1930s, Campbell Morgan, the incumbent, was showing signs of strain. At the same time Martyn Lloyd-Jones had shown himself to be a prince among preachers. Lloyd-Jones had trained as a physician at Barts and had given up a glittering medical career to enter the ministry in 1925. The London Presbytery of the Calvinistic Methodist church accepted Lloyd-Jones in 1936 and youthful ministry in west Wales, as well as his quick mind and habits of scholarship, had resulted in early recognition of his gifts.

He drank deep at the well of Puritan theology and almost single-handedly stimulated a renewed interest in their lives and theological achievements.[20] At the same time he tenaciously held a doctrine of scripture that cherished inerrancy. There was a proposal to install him as the Principal of the Calvinistic Methodist college at Bala, though according to Davies many ministers in north Wales regarded him as too much of a fundamentalist for the role.[21] By a series of invitations and meetings which he took to be providential he moved to London in 1939 and was closely associated with the founding of what became known as Universities and Colleges Christian Fellowship as well as with London Bible College, now London School of Theology.[22]

By the 1950s Lloyd-Jones was the most famous London preacher and the large seating area of Westminster Chapel was regularly filled for his verse-by-verse expositions of biblical books. 'His preaching always took the form of argument, biblical, evangelical, doctrinal and spiritual... when it

---

[20] J. I. Packer, *Honouring the People of God*, (Carlisle, Paternoster, 1999), ch 5.
[21] G. Davies, *Genius, Grief and Grace*, (Glasgow, Christian Focus Publications, 2001), p.346.
[22] I. Randall, *Educating Evangelicalism*, (Carlisle, Paternoster, 2000).

came to the awesome thing that he had to declare at that point about our glorious, self-vindicating God, the doctor would let loose the thunder and lightning with a spiritual impact that was simply stunning'[23].   As an acknowledged leader of evangelicalism, Lloyd-Jones was able to address his sermons to a wide audience and, though he was most at home with biblical exposition, his talks often presciently diagnosed contemporary trends when other Christians had failed to detect subtle changes in the life of the church or the nation.   In this mode he became almost prophetic, especially when he drew far-reaching parallels between his own time and that of turning points in church history.

By the mid-1960s Lloyd-Jones lamented the parlous condition of British evangelicalism.   He saw that, in Victorian times, it had been collected together by societies and conferences out of disparate denominations. There were Anglican evangelicals, Methodist evangelicals, free Church evangelicals and others whose commitment to evangelical truth was far greater than their commitment to the historical distinctives of their denominations but who, often because they could see little point in changing one flawed denominational set-up for another, remained within their denominational homes while complaining about the sub-biblical practices of their leaders.   Such a body of believers could never act unitedly nor exert their proper influence on society.   And the one taboo topic for evangelicals was always the nature of the church itself for, if they discussed it,   they   would   risk   destroying   the   fragile   consensus   their interdenominational societies and associations had so carefully laboured to achieve.

In 1963 Lloyd-Jones addressed the Westminster Fellowship of ministers. He analysed their contemporary situation and warned that there were two positions, that of the Roman Catholic church and that of the Reformers: 'there they were and everybody recognised them'.   Comparatively recently, all this had become fluid – 'everything is once more being queried' and 'blatant unbelief is manifesting itself now in the official churches'.   Across the Atlantic, in United States, there was already evidence of a new soft evangelicalism that took a less trusting attitude to the early chapters of Genesis and miracles.   Bastions of evangelical orthodoxy showed signs of crumbling and, outside the church, the moral condition the British society was shameful.   Evangelicalism itself was largely confined to London and the southeast of England and within the major northern cities there were few large or thriving evangelical congregations.

Going back to first principles, he questioned the value of specialist societies and associations and asked whether evangelicalism 'should ever

---

[23] J. I. Packer cited in Davies, *Genius, Grief and Grace*, (2001), p.346.

be based on anything but the church'.[24] Shunning sociological or conventional definitions he contended that the church 'is a gathering of men and women who have believed the preaching of the Gospel' who form a spiritual society with the Holy Spirit as their companion.[25] Such a society not only preaches the Gospel but practices church discipline.[26]

Having defined the nature of the church by strict evangelical criteria, Lloyd-Jones turned to the subject of schism. He agreed that schism is sinful because it is the division of the church over non-essentials. But according to his definitions, to leave a denominational tradition that failed to conform to evangelical criteria was not schismatic because such non-evangelical bodies never truly belong to the church in the first place. In Lloyd-Jones's mind and in his writings it is clear that the Roman Catholic church can, as an organisation, never be considered as within the real circle of believers. It is a false church and the Reformers whose memory he honoured, by leaving it, were never schismatics. The tragedy lay not with the sundering events of the Reformation but with the condition of the Roman church that had necessitated such drastic action.

At the National Assembly of Evangelicals organised by the Evangelical Alliance in London 18-19 October, 1966, Lloyd-Jones was asked to give the opening address on evangelical unity. The leaders of the Alliance were familiar with his views but had asked him to present them publicly, perhaps to stimulate discussion and bring known differences into the open.[27] They could hardly have expected the impact of his impassioned oration.

His diagnosis of the position of evangelicals had not changed. Evangelicalism was based in societies and specialist groups but not in one united church. The situation that had led to the formation of the Evangelical Alliance in 1846 was the defection of John Henry Newman to Rome with all that that implied for a drift in a Catholic direction. A similar threat to evangelicals had come into being in 1948 with the formation of the World Council of Churches. The upheavals of the 16th century after the Protestant Reformation were being replicated in the middle of the 20th century. Evangelicals therefore faced the dangers of a world church inimical to their views.

So, rather than being content merely to comprise the evangelical wing of individual denominations, evangelicals should start afresh 'and discover what the New Testament church is really meant to be'.[28] As evangelicals,

---

[24] D. M. Lloyd-Jones, *Knowing the Times*, (Edinburgh, The Banner of Truth Trust, 1989), p.172.

[25] Lloyd-Jones, *Knowing*, (1989), p.179.

[26] Lloyd-Jones, *Knowing*, (1989), p.182.

[27] I. H. Murray, *D Martyn Lloyd-Jones: the Fight of Faith* 1939-1981, (Edinburgh, Banner of Truth, 1990), p.522.

[28] Lloyd-Jones, *Knowing*, (1989), p.251.

they put doctrine before fellowship but they needed to become a living body of people who could together declare the realities of Christ's sacrificial death and physical resurrection. 'We are not only the guardians and custodians of the faith of the Bible; we are the modern representatives and successors of the glorious men who fought the same fight, the good fight of faith, in centuries past'.[29] Consequently he was able to assert that he believed that God was calling evangelicals into a new communion, a new evangelical church, that, like the churches of the Reformation, would emerge from the corrupt and compromised church of the day.

The power and passion of his appeal electrified the hearers but, at the end of his address, John Stott, who was chairing the meeting, stood up to argue against the proposition. In his view history was against the proposal and, in any event, the godly remnant must exist within the church and not outside it – a piece of logic that assumed evangelicals could never start afresh because the institutional forms of the church are inviolable. Stott's intervention, which went beyond the duties of a chairman, flattened further discussion and, although the conference completed its planned course, nothing subsequently occurred to advance the launch of a new pan-evangelical church-based movement.

There is one further important area of doctrine that was addressed by Martyn Lloyd-Jones and which contributed to the eventual emergence of apostolic networks. Lloyd-Jones preached a series of sermons at Westminster Chapel between 1964 and 1966 on the baptism in the Spirit. He argued at length for an experience of the Spirit beyond that of regeneration and different from that of assurance. He built his case from a consideration of the New Testament evidence and made the point that it was absurd to consider that Christian doctrine should only be adduced from Acts or only adduced from the epistles. Rather it should be taken from both together as correlations were found between them and as they were echoed in church history.

He established the principle that there are gradations in the Christian life and did this by reference to the life of Apollos. He pointed out that Apollos was clearly a Christian when he first visited Ephesus and was helpful to the churches but that, after speaking with Priscilla and Aquila, he understood Christianity more accurately and ministered more powerfully. The point was that it was possible to advance in the Christian life beyond the initiatory stage. Moreover, the Ephesian disciples in Acts 19 were deficient in their Christian experience until Paul arrived to instruct them about the Holy Spirit and to pray for them.

Although Lloyd-Jones did not support the Pentecostal position over tongues as initial evidence for Spirit baptism, the fact that he was unwilling to wrap every aspect of the Christian initiation into one single regenerative

---

[29] Lloyd-Jones, *Knowing*, (1989), p.255.

package, opened the way for a theology of subsequence that was compatible with the Pentecostal view that a Christian should first undergo the new birth of John 3 and then, after this, receive power for service in the form of the baptism in the Spirit and that, even if these two events were only separated by a short interval of time, they were nevertheless theologically distinct with the result that it was unfortunately possible to receive the first without enjoying the second.

v. Conclusion

Although it would be completely misleading to attribute the charismatic movement to the ministry of one man, David du Plessis is a key and seminal figure in the acceptance of charismatic gifts by mainline denominations, both Protestant and Roman Catholic. Moreover he acted as a model for the ministry of Michael Harper. Harper was a communicator, a networker, a conference organiser and a teacher and once he moved out of the shadow of All Souls, Langham Place, acceptable to every style of ecclesiology. After he set up the Fountain Trust, he multiplied the resources available to budding charismatics and, in *Renewal*, he took a consistent line in favour of the reality of the baptism of the Spirit and charismatic gifts. Arthur Wallis, in Britain, also played a crucial part not only by defending the reality of a baptism in the Holy Spirit as a post-conversion experience but also by defending a radical theology of the church that largely ignored or denied the ecclesiastical forms and practices that had grown up in two millennia of church history. By making the argument that he did, Wallis strengthened the case for a restoration of New Testament order that was centred upon the purposes of God rather than the lessons of church history or the ecumenical aspirations of committees and councils, especially the World Council of Churches.

Martyn Lloyd-Jones, drawing on Puritan theology while being a member of the Welsh Calvinistic church, came to similar conclusions. His dramatic sermon to the evangelical Alliance in 1966 was effectively a call to re-start the church, an evangelical church, asking evangelical believers to come out of all the various denominations that contributed to the evangelical movement. If Wallis wanted to start a new church from scratch, Martyn Lloyd-Jones wanted to inaugurate a pure evangelical church by persuading denominational evangelicals to live under new leadership. Wallis was clearer about the kind of church he wanted, Lloyd-Jones was clearer about the need to leave behind the compromises of 'mixed' denominations.

Both men saw the baptism of the Holy Spirit as essential to Christian life at a time when the forces of secularism were eroding the vitality and reputation of Christianity and where social and moral standards were in steep decline. They saw a western society, and certainly a British society, whose core values were drifting further and further away from the

Christianity that had shaped it for centuries. Both believed that only an extensive revival would be sufficient to halt and reverse the social and religious trends that alarmed them, and both saw the baptism in the Holy Spirit an essential power animating the revival and sustaining a revived church.[30]

Among those who met with Arthur Wallis and who attended Westminster Chapel to hear the preaching of Martyn Lloyd-Jones was Terry Virgo, whose story is told in chapter 4.[31]

---

[30] Lloyd-Jones preached a series of sermons on revival at Westminster Chapel in 1959, in I. H. Murray, *The Fight of Faith*, (1990), p.609.

[31] T. Virgo, *No Well Worn Paths*, (Eastbourne, Kingsway, 2001).

Chapter 2

Restorationism until 1980

Apostolic networks in Britain grew out of the charismatic movement that took place in the 1960s and 1970s. The process has been compared to three waves of spiritual life.[1] The first wave, it is said, took place at the beginning of the 20th century when the pentecostal movement came into being. Initially, and in many places, the message of the baptism in the Holy Spirit and charismatic gifts was rejected by established churches with the result that the pentecostal movement began to form its own denominational groupings, starting in the United States at the end of the 19th century and continuing up through until about the mid 1920s.[2] Where Protestant groupings received the pentecostal message, pentecostal churches grew more vigorously, usually by transfer growth. Where evangelicals rejected the pentecostal message, as was the case in Germany, the pentecostal movement was smaller and marginalised. In Britain, where nonconformity was diverse and respected, the pentecostal movement grew reasonably well, though not as well as it did in Scandinavia or in the United States.

The second wave is the charismatic renewal that brought the pentecostal experience into the old denominations. This new spiritual movement took place around the world within denominational groups that had previously rejected the pentecostal movement 40 or 50 years before. Many of the same phenomena were to be found. There were home prayer meetings, there was spiritual excitement, lay Christians were empowered, there was prayer for healing and there were prophecies. The charismatic movement functioned interdenominationally and, within this chapter, those who were committed to it are labelled 'renewalists' since they wished to renew denominational churches from the inside but not to alter the structures or doctrines that had been so carefully constructed over many years.

Apostolic networks grew out of the charismatic movement, though they also occasionally drew upon pentecostals, or those with pentecostal backgrounds (like Bryn Jones), and the networks began as churches that met within homes – hence they were called 'house churches' – before moving to schools and hired halls before eventually buying their own buildings. So they moved from being 'house churches' to being a 'new

---

[1] Attributed to C. P. Wagner in S. M. Burgess, and E. M. van der Maas, *International Dictionary of the Pentecostal and Charismatic Movements*, (Grand Rapids, Mich, Zondervan, 2002), p.1181.

[2] W. K. Kay, *Pentecostals in Britain*, (Carlisle, Paternoster, 2000).

churches' and eventually, as they became configured under apostolic ministry, they became 'apostolic networks'. Those who supported the vision of the networks are labelled 'restorationists'.

The story of these churches in Britain has been told by Andrew Walker who traces their theological beginnings and their evolution from the 1970s to the early 1990s.[3] He examined their theology and ethos, and interviewed many of their leaders who, at that point, were young men with high hopes but relatively few solid achievements. Walker told the story of them collectively though he divided them into two basic blocks, R1 and R2. R1 was the more exclusive, organised, authoritarian and radical of the two groups and R2, centred largely in London, was more flexible, more expressive and more willing to work in conjunction with other Christian groups and agencies. His story outlined both the initial unity and the 1976 split between the two groups. Most of the main characters within Walker's account were well-known figures within the apostolic movement although only a few of them ended up in charge of their own networks and with recognised apostolic roles.

The present book introduces restorationism as a whole and pays greater attention to the groundwork of Arthur Wallis and Martyn Lloyd-Jones before giving each large network its own chapter so that its history can be followed through from its origins till about the year 2005.

i. R1, R2 and the Charismatic Movement

As we have said, the emergence of apostolic networks of house churches took place during the 1970s and 1980s. The distinction between R1 and R2 is essentially sociological rather than theological though, as we shall see, there were eventually theological differences. Although the analysis of apostolic networks through theological or sociological categories is helpful, it would be foolish to ignore the personal dimension driving many of these differences. Apostolic networks are, by definition, centred around the guiding ministry of an apostle. There are no time-honoured procedures or traditions. Nor is there a bureaucratic or legal basis for the network; everything is vested in the apostle and the charismata of the apostle. Naturally, the totality of the ministry of the apostle, including the expression of charismatic gifts, will be mediated by the apostle's personality. This is not to deny the reality of the Holy Spirit in relation to charismatic gifting but simply to recognise that gifting must be embodied within named individuals. Such a recognition justifies the concentration on the lives of key apostolic figures.

---

[3] *Restoring the Kingdom* was published in 1985, in 1988 and the revised and expanded fourth edition was printed in 1998.

There is also a difference, whether you call it sociological or theological, between the restoration movement at large and apostolic networks in particular. The restoration movement was built on a big idea, the idea that the church needed to be restored to its primitive glory. The idea implied far-reaching ecclesiastical change and, though it could embrace Catholics, tended to be much more compatible with a general Protestant desire to subject the church to the authority of Scripture and to return to the pattern laid down in the New Testament. The essential presupposition was that the church was in need of restoration just like a painted masterpiece might be in need of restoration after the grime of centuries had obscured its colours and lines. So restorationists turned to the bible and to the pattern of church history for an understanding of themselves and their role.[4] The charismatic movement was less radical in its theology and outlook and came to express itself by the term 'renewal', which was a concept that did not imply drastic doctrinal change, as the Protestant Reformation did, or intense evangelistic activity, as revival did. Renewal was more inward and personal and less threatening to religious hierarchies.

It is doubtful whether, without the flurry of activity and excitement that the charismatic movement of the 1960s and 1970s brought in its train, apostolic networks could have come into existence. Without the flexibility and mobility created by the charismatic movement, the restoration movement might have veered rapidly into marginalised sectarianism. The restoration movement took place inside the charismatic movement and was, in the early stages, indistinguishable from it. Only gradually, when the charismatic movement began to recede, was it apparent that something ecclesiologically new and different had been built beneath the waves. Apostolic networks had been constructed. We could say that apostolic networks came to understand themselves as the permanent structures of restoration, the means by which it could be expressed and sustained.

For those involved in restorationism, apart, perhaps, from Arthur Wallis and David Lillie, there was no grand plan or heavenly vision. Gerald Coates conveys the idea of a retrospective discovery of the significance of what had been done by the restorationist pioneers. Indeed, to use his language, they became aware that they were pioneers rather than settlers and did not know exactly where the journey was taking them. This is not to say there was a muddle in their forceful theology but it is to claim there were counterbalancing themes. Restorationists wanted to throw off formality and legalism while carrying forward the great idea of a renewed and unified

---

[4] There is a chart (*Restoration,* November/December, 1983, p.40) attached to an article by David Matthew showing the spiritual decline of the church in the 7th century and its gradual ascent after the Reformation through the Moravian and Methodist revivals to the Salvation Army and eventually the 20th century pentecostal and charismatic movements leading quickly to the return of Christ and the restoration of all things.

church; the first idea might lead to separatism, while the second was formally non-sectarian.

Geography also might play its part in the shaping of apostolic networks. London and the southeast were more than a train ride away from the north of England. There were sub-cultural differences between the big, pluralistic, densely populated stretches of prosperous southern suburbia and the poorer, more industrial heartlands of the north. Although the subtle cultural differences between the various parts of England might filter into the consciousness of leaders of the various networks, geographical proximity, at least in the early stages, was in another way practically important in the setting up of networks. Leaders had to visit the congregations they 'covered' and they could obviously do this much more easily if the distances between the congregations were small. As we shall see, some networks began by forming clusters of connected congregations that were relationally linked to the apostle.

ii. R1 until 1980

The course of the growth of R1 can be traced in the pages of *Restoration* magazine, a publication that was launched in 1975 and quickly assumed both a national profile and an international readership.[5] The magazine publicised the activities of the R1 preachers and the spread their teachings, advertised their meetings, demonstrated their understanding of history and theology and gradually distilled a distinctive essence. The first issue was edited by Bryn Jones with his brother Keri and sent out free of charge to various people including ministers of Elim Pentecostal churches. The address list of the mail-out indicated, perhaps none too subtly, that members from classical Pentecostalism might be drawn to the new style of church life.

The restorationist message was broadcast by preaching, writing and cassette tapes – then a relatively new invention. *Restoration* appeared every two months and on nearly every occasion listed the public places in England where restorationist preachers would be speaking. So, for example, in January 1979 there were 10 occasions when restorationist preachers were speaking in public meetings. Some were are held in school halls, others in town halls or concert halls and some at large centres like Church House Bradford. In February 1979 there were 15 meetings of this kind, and so on.

---

[5] *Restoration* was published bi-monthly until August 1992. In January 1993 it was published monthly free of charge. *Covenant News* replaced the news functions of *Restoration* but in the Summer of 1995 a new magazine, *Restore* was started with the task of interpreting what the Holy Spirit was doing – this was during the period of the 'Toronto Blessing'.

Restoration also advertised its own productions and sold these by mail-order through Harvest Time publications. There was a rapid dissemination of bible study materials, tapes of preaching or singing and books. There were even videos of meetings. A subculture of restorationism was rapidly established, and quickly funded its own growth. Most effective and most impressive, however, were the Dales Bible Weeks that were organised from 1976 in the beautiful surroundings of north Yorkshire and the Downs week in Sussex that was started in 1979. This was where Bryn Jones, David Tomlinson, Terry Virgo and other preachers were powerfully able to teach, preach and prophesy to the crowds who attended.

Arthur Wallis traced the springs of restoration to Brethren ecclesiology and to the desire for revival, and he could go back to the 1950s for these twin tributaries.[6] He could also see that the Restoration movement had flowed out into the wider Christian world through the Bible weeks of the 1970s. There were a series of these starting in a modest way with conferences for leaders. More than 100 attended Herne Court, Kent, on the theme of 'the apostolic commission' in 1965 for a leaders' conference arranged by Wallis, Lillie and Campbell McAlpine. In 1967 Maurice Smith organised Westwatch at which Roger Forster, Graham Perrins, Hugh Thompson and Gerald Coates were participants. When the Abinger Convention in Dorking, Surrey, came to an end Wallis, Campbell McAlpine, Jean Darnell and Denis Clark were invited by Fred Pride (who had previously organised Abinger) to speak at a charismatic and prophetic convention in the grounds of the Elim Bible College, at Capel, Surrey. The convention grew year by year until a marquee seating nearly 2000 people was erected. After six years (1970-75), the core group of preachers, which included Bryn Jones, felt that the event was diluting its distinctive message

By the start of the 1970s Wallis and like-minded leaders had come to accept that 'denominationalism was a major barrier to what God was wanting, and that denominational structures not only obscured the vision of the 'one body', but could never be a suitable receptacle for all that God wanted to bestow'.[7] This was the kernel of restorationist belief, but they also had differences clustering around eschatology. Some were premillennialist and believed that Christ would return before the glory of his reign was seen on the earth and others were amillennialist and believed that the church would gradually grow in power and splendour until the millennium came into being. The theological differences affected planning for the future. Those who were premillennial could anticipate a continuation of the *status quo* until cataclysmic events changed the current world order. Amillennialists were much more positive about the future and anticipated that the mustard seed of the kingdom of God would gradually

---

[6] A. Wallis, 'Springs of Restoration 2', *Restoration*, (September/October, 1980), pp.6-9.
[7] Wallis, 'Springs', *Restoration*, (September/October, 1980), p.6.

grow as divine authority became increasingly visible in the political and social governance of the world. In this scenario the church was the vanguard of the kingdom, the invincible army of the coming king.

At a meeting in Wallis's home in February 1972 he and five others (Peter Lyne, Bryn Jones, David Mansell, Graham Perrins and Hugh Thompson) met for a workshop on eschatology. During their time together Bryn Jones prophesied that 'seven shall be your number, and thrice shall you meet'.[8] They invited John Noble to join them and, as they prayed and fasted together, they were gripped by a sense of 'mutual destiny' and by shared recognitions of each other's ministries as prophets and apostles. Later that year they entered into a covenant relationship with each other and agreed to bring encouragement, direction and if necessary correction to each other's lives. The first fruits of this cooperation were seen in the burgeoning bible weeks: Capel had been successful, but the Dales weeks exceeded all expectations.

The 'magnificent seven' did meet three times and then decided to double their number by including seven other leaders, most of whom worked in the southern part of England. There has always been controversy about whether the transformation of the 'magnificent seven' to the 'fabulous fourteen' was mistaken. Bryn Jones thought so.[9] The new men were George Tarleton, Gerald Coates, Barney Coombs, Maurice Smith, Ian McCullogh, John MacLaughlin and Campbell McAlpine. The relationships between the original seven had been open and frank, which was part of their purpose, but such directness exposes fundamental differences of opinion or theology, and there had been little chance for these differences to be resolved or subsumed into larger unities. When the group doubled in size, these unresolved tensions within the original seven were reflected in the larger group. Not only were Bryn Jones and John Noble prone to clash but there were also divergences in working practice and theological emphasis among the others.

Gerald Coates had written *Not Under Law* (which sold 20,000 copies) and *That You May Not Sin* (later reprinted as *Free From Sin*) and these featured in heated discussions between the brothers, as also did the morality of one member of the group and the way the Londoners had handled it.[10] The differences went beyond morality to lifestyle. Walker points out that there was a puritanical streak in Arthur Wallis and, perhaps, Bryn Jones or, at least, the residue of the old holiness teaching which was averse to trips to the pub or fashionable clothing or jokes in questionable taste.[11]

---

[8] Andrew Walker, *Restoring the Kingdom*, (Guildford, Eagle, 1998), p.76.

[9] Brian Hewitt, *Doing a New Thing,* (London, Hodder & Stoughton, 1995), p.17.

[10] Gerald Coates, *An Intelligent Fire,* (Eastbourne, Kingsway, 1991), pp.101.

[11] Walker, *Restoring,* (1998), p.90.

In October 1976 Arthur Wallis sent a letter (probably with the consent or at the instigation of Bryn Jones[12]) to the southern restorationist leaders listing eight concerns. It suggested that 'some of the London Brothers might be motivated by an ambitious, jealous and worldly spirit. Because of the strains and stresses, it was explained that it would be impossible to work together'.[13] There were also references to theological issues as well as to the dispute over law and grace and the extent which grace had toppled over into license. Wallis also felt too much was claimed for apostolic authority and disliked the remnant theology (which was premillennialist) of Graham Perrins. To this was added the hint that the Londoners were being led astray by demonic forces[14].

The effect of the letter was to break the unity that had been achieved and to wound the London brothers. Coates describes 'feelings of hurt and rejection'[15] and Noble said that 'I don't believe what happened was right'.[16] Apart from the emotional upset, *Fulness* magazine (started in about 1972) which had been distributed among many restorationist churches, was now suddenly dropped because 'it was the publishing platform of the brothers with whom Arthur and Bryn couldn't work'.[17] Actually, a case can be made for saying that the split really occurred after 1975 when Bryn Jones announced to a gathering of the leaders that he was setting up new journal called *Restoration*, a journal that appeared to be set up in direct competition with all that was taking place in the south.[18] Be that as it may, there were attempts two or three years later to reconcile the restorationist leaders with each other when a small group from London met with Bryn Jones and Arthur Wallis.[19] Although Wallis admitted that his perceptions of what was going on might have been inaccurate and Noble and Coates might have mellowed, the damage had been done.[20] Things were never the same again.

Leaving the Denominations

It is unclear when restorationist leaders, especially those associated with Bryn Jones, came to believe it was morally and theologically right for

---

[12] Hewitt, *Doing*, (1995), p.140.

[13] Coates, *An Intelligent Fire*, (1991), pp.101, 102.

[14] Walker, *Restoring*, (1998), p107; even, according to Walker, to the point of associating with people who have long hair: this seems to have been one of the worries of the influential Ern Baxter.

[15] Coates, *An Intelligent Fire*, (1991), pp.100.

[16] Hewitt, *Doing*, (1995), p.188.

[17] Coates, *An Intelligent Fire*, (1991), pp.102.

[18] Walker, *Restoring*, (1998), p.103.

[19] Hewitt, *Doing*, (1995, p.138), gives 1978 as the date of the split and this must be a mistake unless he is referring to the subsequent failure to achieve full reconciliation.

[20] Coates, *An Intelligent Fire*, (1991), pp.102.

Christians to leave the historic denominations. There is an article by Hugh Thompson in November/December 1978 in *Restoration* pointing out that the church ought not to be a mixed religious body containing immoral practices or heretical doctrines. Restorationists knew, as Thompson admits, that the lessons of church history warned against every purificatory group that withdrew itself from existing denominations to establish an incorruptible new beginning. Yet he was also clear that, when Christ first came, he refused to establish a revamped Judaism but put in place a separate body that bypassed the chief priests, temple worship and Mosaic religious rituals. By the same token, restorationism might argue the case for a new body, especially if there was an eschatological imperative driving these changes.

In the same year Terry Virgo made the same case using different reasoning. For many converts the charismatic movement

> has often resulted in a mushrooming of non-church activity. Instead of this new energy being welcomed into local churches, many have shut their doors to charismatic gifts, forcing people into an unscriptural situation. While remaining loyal to their churches on Sunday, many attend mid-week meetings for charismatic fellowship. Hence energies are squandered and the church fails to benefit. If these groups are without proper oversight, they become open to error, so that the whole strategy of God for the church to contain and oversee this life is frustrated.[21]

The implication was that the divine impetus of the charismatic movement was being wasted in unproductive little meetings that failed to harness the energies of renewed Christians.

Less than a year later David Mansell in a provocatively entitled piece 'Unity – is it possible?' was asking why the charismatic movement was in decline and arguing that without commitment, relationship, authority, submission, apostles, prophets and the full range of New Testament ministries, the church was merely an organisation rather than an organism expressing a common life (July/August 1979). Later that year Arthur Wallis explained his fundamental premise: only a revived church is capable of sustaining revival. For him this was the great issue and the ultimate rationale for a new basis for church life. Only revival would save the world and only a revived church could carry spiritual fire into a darkened and irreligious society.

A little later the widely respected but non-restorationist Michael Harper published an article in *Restoration* (January/February 1980) that outlined prevailing problems in British society. Entitled 'Day is Dying in the West', his gloomy prognosis saw a society in mortal danger. 'The massive

---

[21] Terry Virgo, 'The Church: God's only answer', *Restoration,* (November/December, 1978), p.13.

defection of people from the churches in the past fifty years is a clear vote of no confidence in the church, its message and its leadership' that led him to expect 'accelerated decline' in the West. In an assessment of the mainline churches, he was honest enough to say, 'at the present time I see no hope of any substantial change in the condition of the historic churches, corrupted by their compromises and defeated by their doubts'. From an Anglican, as Harper then still was, this was a painfully direct diagnosis that, because it came from an insider, was all the more persuasive. The implication, though not one that Harper drew, was that Christian hope lay with the new churches. He predicted that 'in the coming years more and more people, particularly young people, will be turning in this direction'.

Restorationists and Renewalists

Subsequent research has shown how the tension between renewalists and restorationists goes back at least to 1966 when Hugh Thompson wrote a letter to *Renewal* magazine (July/August 1966, 4, 7) arguing that it is wrong to give assent to the 'unqualified inference that the mixed multitude of the Church of England is "the church"'.[22] The Advisory Council of the Fountain Trust included Arthur Wallis and the minutes of their November 1971 meeting reported that 'not very much progress had been made since the last meeting with those who roughly speaking take the "come out" line' though, according to Millward, it is doubtful whether other members of the Council appreciated the radical nature of Wallis' ecclesiology. In April 1972 Wallis is reporting that, in addition to the exclusive house churches, there were other house churches 'with an open attitude to other ministries'.[23] Michael Harper and Tom Smail attended the Capel Bible Week later that year to see for themselves but, although Smail reported that some of his prejudices had been displaced, he also found several unhelpful features. In 1973 Smail and Harper met the house churches in Capel during the Bible Week but there was no meeting of minds. In autumn 1974 *Renewal* made a further attempt to encourage the two sides to understand each other by commissioning articles from David Watson and Arthur Wallis and publishing them together in the same issue.

In an even-handed editorial Harper (*Renewal* August/September 1974) accepted that there were church situations where the Spirit had been quenched even if there were also undisciplined and exclusive little groups calling themselves house churches. David Watson explained his decision to

---

[22] See J. C. Millward, 'Chalk and Cheese? An Account of the Impact of Restorationist Ecclesiology upon the Baptist Union – with Particular Reference to those Churches in Joint Fellowship with the Baptist Union of Great Britain and New Frontiers International', (Brunel University, unpublished PhD Dissertation, 2003).

[23] Fountain Trust Advisory Council Minutes, 13 April 1972.

stay within the Church of England by reference to the doctrine of the remnant and by pointing out that Jesus lived according to the same principle and did not distance himself from the synagogue and the temple of his day, however corrupt they were. Wallis argued that the cause of the problems lay in the human structure of the denomination and by repeating his view that denominations had no biblical warrant with result that 'denominational loyalty... only weakened the unity of the body as a whole' (*Renewal* August/September 1974, 52).

Set out in this way, it was obvious that the two positions were irreconcilable. Michael Harper resigned from his directorship of Fountain Trust in April 1975 to devote himself to an international role in the charismatic world. He had hoped that Tom Smail would work out a theology undergirding the charismatic movement that might allow the two sides to continue to work together. In the event this did not happen despite valiant attempts, including the addition of David Mansell to the Advisory Council, and further discussions throughout 1977 to establish common ground. That year the Fountain Trust leadership tried to persuade Wallis onto the new Consultative Council, which he eventually agreed to in April 1978, but, by then, dialogue could make little progress – and the only progress that might have occurred would have been a respectful acknowledgement of each other's strengths. Whether this kind of rapprochement could have been obtained in the light of the hardening of positions on both sides is doubtful and, in any case, Smail was less of a diplomat than Harper. In 1980 the Fountain Trust disbanded.

Meanwhile the Dales and Downs weeks demonstrated that the Restoration movement offered a powerful and workable style of Christianity. The big meetings and the upsurge of worship, particularly as new songs celebrated 'taking the land for Jesus', contrasted with the meditative aspects of the charismatic movement to be found in Anglicanism or within the small prayer groups attached to congregations that had opened their doors to charismatic phenomena. At a local church level the restorationist groups were both more holistic and more purposeful than most charismatic and pentecostal groups. When Church House Bradford opened in 1981, its premises included a restaurant and a sports area as well as a recording studio. The governmental structure of restorationist churches anticipated fully committed and active church members working to an evangelistic or missionary target set by the leaders. Voluntarism disappeared. The church became an army rather than a scattered flock of sheep grazing on a comfortable hillside.

More than this, the language of restorationism presumed that restrictive traditions and arcane rituals could be swept away. Even if these rituals were embodied in the work of committees or procedures for administration, they might still be obstructing progress. A Methodist chairman who had always run his circuit in a particular way would never have survived the winds of

Restoration; a pentecostal treasurer who had always calculated finances on a limited and perhaps penny-pinching budget would have been smartly moved aside; an Anglican who practised infant baptism uneasily while acceding to requests for baptism by immersion, would have been told to scrap the infant variety; a member of the Brethren who had assiduously avoided voting and political activity on the grounds that Christians should be 'in the world' but not 'of the world' would have been brought up with a jolt and told to exercise his or her democratic rights, especially in relation to moral issues; any Christian who had been caught up in the dress codes of the 1930s or 1950s where women were prevented from wearing trousers or jewellery would have been told that he or she was under grace and not under an arbitrary holiness law.

Eschatology

More psychologically vital than the attractive practicalities of the Restoration movement was eschatology. As far as many Anglicans were concerned, eschatology was unknown territory – a subject that was rarely preached about and not often thought about. By contrast most pentecostals held a highly developed eschatological scheme. They had adopted their eschatology from the dispensational system developed by Darby and the Brethren and later encapsulated within the Schofield Reference Bible.[24] Most expected a fixed sequence of historically future events – often illustrated by complex prophetic wall charts – that culminated in a period of tribulation under the Antichrist before the return of Jesus to rescue his people and to establish his thousand year rule upon the earth, the millennium. Even if pentecostals expected the church to escape the scourge of the Antichrist, the outlook was essentially gloomy and pessimistic. Who knew when the pain of tribulation had reached such a pitch that the church needed to be divinely rescued? Even if the gospel was about to be preached across the world, darkness was beginning to fall.

Whatever variation there was among them in 1972, restorationists rapidly developed a preferred postmillennial eschatological scheme. This removed many of the prophecies of pain and persecution from the timeline of current events. Postmillennialism allowed restorationists to diffuse the blessings of the millennium into the present age of the church and to argue and preach that the reign of Christ upon the earth, which many pentecostals had placed within the millennium, could be seen here and now. So restorationism exchanged stoic pessimism for charismatic optimism. They believed that the kingdom of God was going to advance against all opposition and that the kingdom had an earthly and political dimension and was not simply a distant spiritual benefit or an internal blessing to be

---

[24] Kay, *Pentecostals,* (2000).

invisibly enjoyed by the believer. Bryn Jones put it like this, 'we do not believe that Christ will return for a feeble, cowering people. We reject such a possibility unequivocally. Rather we believe that God is actively restoring his church in order to use it as a tool to extend his rule across the nations...we are a prophetic people, bringing the present world order into submission to God's order and rule. That is our task prior to the return of Jesus.'[25] The mood was positive - aggressive even - and demanded action.

When Terry Virgo reviewed *The Puritan Hope*[26] in 1980 (January/February, p 11) showing that the Puritans expected a worldwide revival before the return of Christ, he was reminding readers that the tradition of revival before the return of Christ was older than the 19th century tradition of Darby and the dispensationalists. 'This book provides an opportunity for a new generation, many of whom have been raised on negative eschatology ... to learn that their forefathers had a far greater vision'. In effect, he was telling his readers to sweep away the false boundaries to Christian hope and expect the power of God to make an impact on this generation in this country at this time.

The psychological implications of this theology were noticeable in conversation with restorationists. Caution about the future was replaced by confident expectation that the power of God was going to be revealed in greater and greater measure, and events in the world could be interpreted in the light of theologically fuelled hope. I can remember discussing the 1981 Falklands war with restorationists before the outcome of the conflict had been decided. They had a confidence that all was going well even when events were balanced on a knife edge.

The creation of a completely new set of churches required a completely new basis for unity. It was not sufficient to place all the churches on a shared doctrinal basis (as was done by the 'fundamental truths' of the pentecostal churches) or to ensure practical unity on a quasi-legal platform as a consequence of the shared ownership of property or even, as was the case with many Christian groups, to look for unity among ministers at an annual or bi-annual conference where decision-making took place. The restorationist answer to the issue of unity was bound up with apostleship. As early as 1979 David Matthew had argued that 'the most significant element in [the] unity ... was a recognition of apostolic authority'. The apostle became himself a symbol and guarantee of unity. Churches came 'under apostolic authority' or 'related' to the apostle or 'came into relationship' with the apostle. This flexible concept allowed different churches to connect themselves to the apostle in ways most suited to their own circumstances.

---

[25] Hewitt, *Doing*, (1995), pp.30, 31.
[26] Iain H Murray, *The Puritan Hope*, (Edinburgh, Banner of Truth, 1985).

Apostles and Churches

Over and above the relationship between the individual congregation and the apostle was a covenant relationship between the apostles themselves. Arthur Wallis pointed out after 1972 when the group of seven apostolic and prophetic ministers entered into 'a covenant relationship, agreeing to be committed to each other's welfare in every way', that the networks avoided competition and worked towards a common goal. The mutual accountability created by this covenant was never translated into a legal document or a constitutional instrument: it remained a personal transaction between gifted individuals. But it gave a sense of national coordination to the ordinary member as well as a reason to delight in the variety of the whole restored church.

By the end of the 1980s the restorationists were in many cases calling their congregations 'community' churches. In September/October 1980 and in March/April 1981 the term is in evident use. In every case the community was a named geographical area with the implication that the church belonged to that area, drew from that area, served that area and was creating a new community within that area. Old people, married couples, singles, toddlers and everyone could be included within its arms. Theologically and sociologically the church conceived in this way was a recognisable unit suited to apostolic leadership just as 'the church in Corinth' was, in New Testament times, a single church despite its various sub-groups and in all its manifestations under the apostolic leadership of Paul. In other words, the appellation 'community church' solved the problem of the extent of an apostle's authority: it was geographically defined by the place name on the notice board. In this way apostles could keep out of each other's territory and prevent potentially dangerous clashes.

Shepherding

Transatlantic influences on R1 appeared before the end of the 1970s. The shepherding movement grew out of the association of four popular charismatic bible teachers in 1970 who were later joined by Ern Baxter to form 'the Fort Lauderdale Five'. The five circulated their views in *New Wine* magazine, held conferences, sold videos and books and taught that every believer needed to submit to a shepherd who would take personal responsibility for his or her spiritual development. Every believer needed to become a disciple and every disciple needed a shepherd/teacher. Independent charismatic groups were to be gathered up together under shepherds, and shepherds themselves were to submit to translocal ministries, particularly to apostles. More details are given of the whole saga in chapter 15.

In Britain, discipleship was certainly part of the fabric of R1. An issue of *Restoration* (July/August 1980) on the subject of discipling carried on its cover a picture of a runner being encouraged by his coach. The coach was the discipler, helping the runner to achieve the best possible performance. So discipling was seen as a way of receiving specialised mentoring to develop one's own spiritual potential. David Tomlinson wrote, 'discipleship is learning in the context of the yoke. The lack of the yoke has been a sad feature of much individualistic evangelicalism, where people learn what they want, when they want, if they want'. In the end, he said, the personal relationship was the key so that, in the context of a good relationship, discipling might take place safely for the purpose of fostering spiritual maturity.

iii. R2 until 1980

Although the designations R1 and R2 are helpful, they were only made with the advantage of hindsight and as a way of identifying the orientations of two groups of restorationist networks. R2 was always the more open group although this does not mean that its doctrines and expectations were any less influential than the R1 group centred round Bryn Jones. During the 1970s R2 was to be found in the south of England and several of its key representatives were in the London area. Its development can be partially traced in the pages of *Fulness* magazine although, unlike *Restoration* magazine, *Fulness* was not dated precisely and carried fewer photographs of events and fewer advertisements for books and other products. *Fulness* was more of a teaching magazine than a tool for creating identity.

Relationships

Fulness actually began in 1968[27] but, by 1972 or 1973, it was published three times a year and then, after issue 10, it expanded to four times a year and continued in this way right through until 1980 or 1981. Because it is undated and because the frequency of publication changed after issue 10, it is not possible to place individual articles with chronological precision. Yet, in about 1973 (in volume 8) it is concerned with praise, worship and creativity in the church. This in itself is indicative of the open R2 mindset. There is a focus on self-expression and dance. Issue 10 is concerned with relationships as the missing ingredient of friendship within the life of the church. Artificial Christianity, in the form of shallow relationships and perfunctory worship, must be replaced by Christians who are 'real' with each other. Gerald Coates wrote on 'reality in relationships' saying 'if we go through the veneer and disillusionment stages we shall come into reality'

---

[27] See *Fulness* 16, p.15.

(page 7) and John Noble wrote 'friendship is not a means to an end, it is the end. God started all this to make us, not simply friends but family-friends' (page 10).

The idea of real relationships was all part and parcel of the restorationist emphasis. By this restorationists meant that Christians should be honest with each other or, to use a biblical term, should 'walk in the light' and thereby strengthen congregational life. They were against politeness for the sake of politeness and the vicar's 'wet fish' handshake at the door of the church and wanted to share their lives together even if this meant doing ordinary things like watching television, eating fish and chips in the street after youth meetings or going on holiday together. It meant dropping the façade of holiness and, equally, it meant avoiding dressing up in smart clothes to go to church which, although common among evangelicals at the time, could be seen as a symbol of a pretence. The marriage bond was the relationship *par excellence*. For restorationists, especially those with young children, the good management of marriage was an indicator of spiritual maturity. The pressures of family life, in the light of the Pauline stipulation that the 'overseer... must manage his own family well' (1 Timothy 2:4), registered spirituality. In this way the nuclear family could be seen as a testing ground to prepare for promotion to a leadership position within the wider family of the church; marital relationships that could not bear the strain of this expectation were soon exposed. This, in turn, led to preaching and teaching about marriage that blew away the cobwebs of conventionality and shone light into dark places.

In issue 10, Barney Coombs wrote about the creation of an All Saints' Night that had developed from the ministers' fraternal in Basingstoke. As his own ex-Baptist congregation grew in leaps and bounds and the churches of the other ministers remained static or declined, Barney came to realise that he was a threat to them all. His answer was this: 'if others have made a circle to exclude us, we will make a bigger circle and include them'.[28] His All Saints Nights welcomed all the Christians in the town and he shared the platform with ministers of all the other denominations.

Charismatic Gifts

In issue 9 the radically charismatic side of restorationism became visible. Biblical passages were used to sketch out the role of the New Testament prophet, although biblical texts were also used to see what sort of temperament a prophet might have. In other articles prophecy was linked with music to show how to break old barriers in worship. John MacLauchlan wrote about the prophet as a person with a sense of history who has a particular role in relation to other leaders and he based this idea

---

[28] I heard him say this.

upon the function of the prophet in the Old Testament. 'We find that the prophet and his ministry are grounded in history... he sees the sweep of the purpose of God, and lives in it by faith'.[29] Equally, according to Hugh Thompson, 'each prophet has a personality and style which is quite his own' but 'it follows from all this that the prophet cannot afford the luxury of glorious isolation... he must deliberately yoke himself to men of God of another type of personality and ... different ... ministry'.[30] While, according to Graham Perrins, 'we... see that the coming of the Holy Spirit has baptised the whole realm of music, singing and dancing into an even deeper realm of prophetic worship and praise!'.[31] MacLauchlan argued that, 'we may expect the prophet to be clearly involved with communicating vision and direction' and that the prophet, in the New Testament, would be expected to impart 'foundational revelation'.[32]

So the prophet was a crucial person who contributed to the direction of the church, to its aims and practical goals, and to week-by-week worship and also to the foundations of every new congregation. More even than all this the prophet should speak to the world. As Coates put it,

> The New Testament prophet differs only from the Old in that he is set amidst the apostles, the teacher, the pastor and the evangelist. They give him a platform upon which to speak... I believe the prophet will proclaim increasingly that the kingdom of this world is going to become the kingdom of God.[33]

Indeed, according to David Mansell, every activity of the church could be performed prophetically whether prayer, worship, exhortation or healing – all could show that the kingdom has come in power.[34]

Speaking prophetically to the world had been on the agenda since the Festival of Light in 1971. This was an unprecedented demonstration of public revulsion at the slippage in moral standards in national life. A packed meeting in Westminster Hall, London, in September 1971 was followed by the lighting of more than 300 beacons and bonfires in towns all over the country and then, two weeks later, a large public rally in Trafalgar Square where 35,000 people heard the one-time sceptic Malcolm Muggeridge address them before they marched to Hyde Park and 90,000 people rallied in a Festival to Jesus: 'fellow celebrants of the Festival of Light... I look around with pride and joy at all these faces, all these banners and this mighty turn-out and pray with all my heart that it may be the

---

[29] *Fulness* 9, page 5

[30] *Fulness* 9, page 7

[31] *Fulness* 9, page 10.

[32] *Fulness* 9, page 11.

[33] *Fulness* 9, page 13.

[34] *Fulness* 9, page 16.

beginning of a continuing process of moral and spiritual regeneration'. Among those present on the platform with Malcolm Muggeridge was the young Gerald Coates, the archetypal R2 apostle.[35]

Iconoclasm

In keeping with the iconoclastic nature of prophetic restorationism Maurice Smith wrote on 'who's got the right biblical pattern?' and argued that 'God is a God of infinite variety... let us avoid a pattern-church like the plague and learn to move forward into all that God is doing today with all its tones and shades'.[36] At the same time, and by contrast, John Noble could say that 'Jesus is delegating his government to men so that the local church becomes a microcosm of the kingdom of heaven on earth' and he compared this picture of church government with the type that is 'political and man-pleasing'.[37] He placed denominational and restorationist congregations in opposing realms and imaginatively viewed the restored church in a position of political and economic importance. The church was the instrument of divine government and a microcosm of the social forms of the future. Such high theology infused the activities of new churches with significance and vested its ministers with leading roles in the dramatic struggle between good and evil. Even so, George Tarleton, picking up a theme that was common to restorationism, argued that the local church is 'the entire redeemed community living in the worldly community in a given area' with the result that the church ought to be *all* God's people in a town manifesting unity.[38] The only way to achieve this unity was to stop fighting under doctrinal banners.

Equally iconoclastic, from the standpoint of historical theology, is MacLauchlan's resounding 'no' to a reader's question, 'is there such a thing as original sin?'. MacLauchlan argued that sin is always external to human beings and originates in the environment because the whole world is under the domination of the devil. Christ rescues believers and makes it possible to submit to God's rule but human nature remains unchanged. Those passages in the Bible that refer to the 'flesh' are concerned with our natural humanity which, when it is dominated by sin, is by definition sinful. Whether this view was held by other R2 preachers is uncertain – and there were those like Terry Virgo who definitely did not hold it – but the inclusion of such an article demonstrates how far some restorationists were prepared to travel from standard evangelical doctrine and the tenets of the Reformation, let alone from the writings of St Augustine.

---

[35] Coates, *An Intelligent Fire,* (1991), p.83

[36] *Fulness* 11, page 5.

[37] *Fulness* 11, page 7.

[38] *Fulness* 11, page 12.

Iconoclasm was also behind John Noble's booklet *Forgive Us Our Denominations* (c. 1971) in which he made the case for a new beginning for the church, the whole church, without denominational apparatus,

> Almost everyone agrees that the denominational divisions are not of God. Loud 'amens' come from every quarter when we talk of the need to be one in Christ. Yet no one will take the initiative; no one is willing to make the first move; we remain boxed up in our neat little brick parcels labelled with a tag of our pet doctrine.

Although Noble's tone is that of a man who speaks more in sorrow than in anger, he believes that the church at the end of the age will be united and not defiled by schism. 'God is even now raising up men of vision within his body, equipped with a message that will purify the church and make her ready...' is his final clarion call, but it is the title of the booklet that resonates. Our denominations are a cause for repentance, not of pride, and the echo of the Lord's Prayer makes the point memorably.

If iconoclasm implies breaking things up, it was a demolition to make way for a new and better form of church. Gerald Coates preached a sermon to a thousand people at Friends' Meeting House, London, entitled 'Pioneers and Settlers' and contrasted two kinds of people. The settlers want, above all else, to maintain the *status quo* and are afraid to take risks, challenge the traditional pattern or upset their families. They want only a quiet conscience. The pioneers are people of risk: they risk making mistakes in their desire to sweep away the rubble of contemporary culture to clear a highway for God: 'so God is raising up a pioneering minority in order to bless the majority'.[39] It was to pioneering that R2 apostles called their people, and it is no coincidence that Pioneer Team became the name of the restorationist stream with which Coates is still most closely associated.

By about 1977 *Fulness* was being read in about 50 countries (editorial, volume 18) and large-scale events organised in the south of England like Kingdom Life 78 attracted speakers from Norway and the United States. Kingdom Life the following year drew crowds of up to 2,000 people for evening events and began with a march through the streets of Cobham. The dual combination of challenging what was old and replacing it by an alternative continued. Gerald Coates in his booklet *Not Under Law* argued that 'the church is in the main run by a group of frightened men' who, instead of preaching a gospel of grace, practise a gospel of coercion and that 'law, with its rigorous approach to life, is as damaging as permissiveness'. As far as he was concerned, there were Christian Pharisees who spent their time taking offence at the behaviour of others while

---

[39] Coates, *An Intelligent Fire,* (1991), p.95; see also *Fulness* 14.

congratulating themselves that only they knew how to live properly. 'These people need offending. Their gospel is bad news'.[40]

Attacking legalism had a centrifugal effect and there had to be counteractive forces that joined and bound Christians together. By 1979 (volume 23) *Fulness* was discussing the theology and practice of 'covering', the technical term given to the authoritative mentoring of one Christian by another that continued to be advocated by influential sources.[41] Noble and Coates wanted to avoid, on one side, the extremes of individualism and, on the other, the demands of a clear-cut structure where everybody knew who they had to approach and on what basis. So even though 'covering should come as a result of recognition and respect' it also 'should be developed wherever and however God's people come together'. Covering, in their view, flexible and natural though it should be, was not optional. Even in places where there is no obvious group of functioning restorationist Christians, an attitude of humility, a willingness to be 'covered', could be cultivated to help fellowship germinate.

Yet, as one reader pointed out, committed and covenant relationships might damage a marriage or disrupt a family. Coates and Noble admitted that this could happen but they did so without surrendering the principle. They certainly recognised the unique and fulfilling nature of marriage while protecting their theology of committed relationships outside the home since it was through these that 'God is building us together not as a mass, but one to one, and family to family, community to community, and eventually nation to nation'. In their conception, the personal commitments that began to spring up and flourish between Christians tied together a large and international network that expressed the totality of the church, God's people upon the earth.

Apostles and Unity

The other force binding Christians together it is found within the burgeoning ministry of the apostle. It is the apostle who is at the apex of the covering pyramid that rests over every group of believers. In describing the situation like this, there is a danger of being overcritical. Although there were tendencies within restorationism to place apostles at the top of the local church structure, the R2 group were quickly conscious of the dangers of sectarian apostleship and the possible exploitation of 'ordinary' Christians within an authoritarian system. Noble and Coates give their views at length in *Fulness* 24:

---

[40] Outlined in *Fulness* 21.

[41] The Fort Lauderdale Five continued to be influential despite their retractions on discipling. The South American pentecostal church continued to be regarded as worth emulating.

What is an apostle? The word itself, simply translated, means 'sent forth' or 'sent out'. One could foresee an apostolic prophet or teacher in the light of that meaning. We know that evangelists evangelise, teachers teach, prophets prophesy and pastors pastor or shepherd, but the apostles don't apostle. In that sense there is no defined apostolic ministry. The apostle works through the gifts of prophet, evangelist, teacher and pastor and is more often part of a team – an apostolic team.

The early church apostles were sent into virgin territory, a situation which no longer exists in Great Britain, or indeed in the rest of the Western world. Towns are littered with so-called Christian churches. We have to re-evaluate and overhaul our idea of the apostolic ministry and how it will operate in the light of so many believers already existing all over the country. We must learn to build community without becoming sectarian.

A prophetic voice has already been raised directing God's people to a new order of things. The proliferation of house fellowships and the renewal taking place within the institutional church straddles the globe. Prophets have knocked down cherished religious ivory towers, and men who can structure lives and families into powerful communities are beginning to emerge. We need to pray that these men will make the sacrifices necessary in order that what is on their hearts might become reality.

There are contrasting implications to be drawn from this explanation. First, apostles are not defined simply as church planters: the primary feature of apostles is that these are people who have been sent by God and, if these are men or woman whose ministry is primarily prophetic or evangelistic, they may still be apostolic. Yet, second, they retain the idea of an apostle as a church planter while acknowledging that church planting in an already Christianised world, cannot operate in a pure form. Third, there is a prophetic strain in their thinking that is dismissive of 'cherished religious ivory towers'. There is a tension here between the inference that church planting is essential and the understanding that people who come into new churches may perforce come out of old churches. Without wanting to attack the institutional church and set themselves in deep opposition to it, they want to reserve the right for new apostles to build new communities – a 'community' is a suitably broad and embracing term that implies a common life as well as a common mind – without being hemmed in by pre-existing religious boundaries and sensibilities. A community has one further advantage: it helps to create a 'sacred canopy' for those who live inside it, a shelter for their beliefs against the secularising winds of the contemporary world.

Fulness shows that the leaders of R2 were self-analytical enough to deal with perennial topics. By 1981, as Gerald Coates noted, 'criticism breeds defensiveness, defensiveness breeds insecurity, and insecurity breeds exclusivism'.[42] Restorationists had had their share of criticism and were in danger of relapsing into exclusivism. To guard against this they needed to continue to reach out to other Christians. They also needed to avoid pseudo-spirituality where, at the slightest excuse and because of encouragement from conveners of meetings, congregations might, like dogs let off the leash, plunge into a spate of visions, prophecies and interpretations of tongues that were of little value and high on the embarrassment scale. Where democracy was encouraged, other difficulties arose. Unanointed leaders would conduct meetings on the basis that it was 'their turn' and committees would assemble to debate trivia as a way of allowing everybody have their say. Indeed, Coates could admit, 'frankly I am pretty bored with many meetings I go to... the round of singing/preaching/singing is enough to bore anybody after a while'. Such a treadmill arose from the perpetual desire to put on fresh meetings, to the disease of 'meetingitis' where the cure for every spare moment was yet another meeting, and all of them starting with the same weary songs. Moreover, where congregations *had* accepted apostolic covering of some kind, the apostle was often tempted to insulate a congregation from other ministries than his own; the result of this was that the congregations under his care became unbalanced and only reflected his own emphases. The solution was for covered congregations to continue to be open to a variety of ministries so as to grow fully-rounded.

In the welter of change, the prayer of Jesus in John 17 was a key text for several restorationist leaders. Their critics accused them of dividing the church by setting up new denominations and falling into the trap of all previous schismatics. The prayer of Jesus for the unity of his church in John 17 appeared to forbid sectarian and schismatic tendencies but some of the restorationist preachers proclaimed the necessity of abolishing all the old shibboleths and abandoning the old traditions in order to meet together as one people on a common middle ground where a new and divinely-ordered unity might be created.[43] So the dilemma was whether the restorationist preachers were calling people out of old traditions into a new (but, in the end, equally invalid) tradition. Or, as was claimed, were they bringing about a new eschatological unity that would allow for relational harmonies in a purified church? In the short term John Noble and Gerald Coates dealt with a question on this topic in volume 28 by maintaining the need to hold on to 'our doctrinal understanding' while continuing to talk with those who saw things differently. So in the end they recoiled from attacking existing

---

[42] *Fulness* 28.

[43] I heard preachers make precisely this point in the late 1970s and early 1980s. They interpreted divisiveness as a necessary precondition of John 17 unity.

denominations in a way that would have come all too naturally to the fiery Bryn Jones of R1.

The final volume of *Fulness* appeared soon afterwards and, in March 1982, a new magazine, *Dovetail*, was launched. *Fulness* had a circulation of less than 4,000 but its international readership and pithy articles carried well beyond its own sphere.

iv. Conclusion

The early charismatic movement carried with it hopes for spiritual unity. It appeared to be another form of the ecumenical movement, but one that could be attributed very directly to the work of the Holy Spirit rather than to human efforts. The charismatic movement carried hopes of unity between Catholics and Protestants as well as within the range of Protestant denominations. That these hopes were unfulfilled may be attributed to their initial naiveté or to the struggle between renewalists and restorationist. The struggle was not driven by personality clashes or arcane liturgical disputes: it arose out of two very different visions of the church and two very different interpretations of the purpose behind the outpouring of the Holy Spirit. It is a nice historical judgment to decide whether the charismatic movement would have been better served without restorationism or whether restorationism, had it been presented differently, could have made a greater impact by carrying a larger number of charismatics with it.

The restorationist publications in the two decades of the 1970s and 1980s allow the reader to retrace the preoccupations and tensions within restorationist praxis. There was a sense in which the key restorationist figures 'made it up as they went along'. Their honesty and self-analysis enabled them to adjust their thinking as they bumped into unforeseen realities. Bryn Jones comes across as the ultimate idealist who was not prepared to compromise his large vision of restorationism with the contours of the ecclesiastical landscape in Britain and abroad. The other restorationists were more pragmatic and more willing to reconceive their own role within the larger body of church.

Once restorationism broke free of the charismatic movement, restorationist preachers were no longer bound by an umbilical chord to denominational tradition. They were able to move in whatever direction they felt the Spirit was propelling them. Equally they were open to the blandishments of other spiritual movements of a less well defined type. The doctrines of the shepherding movement, which would never make much impact upon the traditional denominations, could break into restorationism and mingle with it for better or worse. As we shall see, a similar mingling occurred when the Toronto blessing of the 1990s and the long running cell church movement came alongside restorationism. Restorationism was therefore never static or pure but combined with, drew itself away from or assimilated what it believed to be other Spirit-borne concepts and pressures that rolled in from beyond the horizon.

For those who remember the heady promises of the 1970s and 1980s, the confident claims and enthusiastic triumphalism of the songs and marches, the following chapters reveal how everything turned out. As we shall see in parts II and V, some of the networks and some of the apostles came much closer to fulfilling their ideals than others. Some of the apostles retained their original ideals while others modified them and sailed in different directions.

The chapters that follow tell the story of individual restorationist networks. They begin with the R1 group (Bryn Jones, Terry Virgo, Barney Coombs and Tony Morton) and follow this by the R2 group (Roger Forster, Gerald Coates/ John Noble). Other networks that cannot be easily fitted into either category come next (Stuart Bell, Colin Dye, Noel Stanton, John Mumford, Colin Urquhart and Hugh Osgood).

Part II

The Networks

Chapter 3

Bryn Jones and Covenant Ministries International

'He was a genius for communication,' Wesley Richards

i. Bryn Jones, the Man

A young man from the valleys of Wales, Bryn Jones, was beginning his spiritual journey while Arthur Wallis was putting together elements of the restorationist vision by combining Brethren ecclesiology and Pentecostal experience. At some time in 1956 Bryn met Arthur Wallis who was to become 'a strong example, a fellow-worker, a fellow-soldier, a covenant brother and, for me, deepest of all, a father in God'.[1]

Bryn Jones was born to a poor but godly home in 1940.

> We lived in a terrace of eighty houses with a pub at the bottom of the street. We had an outdoor loo: no lock on the door, hold it with one foot, torn-up *Daily Herald* for loo paper. We had coal fires, because we had cheap coal, but no bathroom. The tin bath had to be ready for when Dad came home.[2]

Both his mother and his grandmother were devout and active Christians and his great-uncle had been an elder in the Apostolic Church. His mother would kneel by her bed to pray morning and night

> She seemed to be on her knees an awful long time. I used to think, 'what on earth is she praying about for so long?' And I always thought that it was probably about me![3]

A friend invited him to the local chapel and then, on the way home, challenged him to read Acts chapter 2. He opened his mother's bible, was struck by the verse 'whoever calls on the name of the Lord shall be saved', prayed aloud to God to save him, broke down into tears, and felt God's presence fill the room. The next day he told the minister of the chapel what had happened to him. Soon afterwards his minister took him out to confess his salvation in public by joining the veteran preachers in the chapel's

---

[1] D. Matthew, *Arthur Wallis, 1922-1988: a tribute*, (1988), p.2 quoted in J. Wallis (ed), *Arthur Wallis: Radical Christian*, (Eastbourne, Kingsway, 1991), p.142.

[2] W. Richards, 'Everything you wanted to know about Bryn Jones', *Restoration*, (March/April, 1989), p.29.

[3] Brian Hewitt, (1995), *Doing a New Thing*, (London: Hodder & Stoughton, 1995), p.8.

open-air meetings. A year later, in 1957, he was baptised in the Holy Spirit and joined a small Assembly of God congregation at Pen-y-Waun.

Here he heard what might be seen as typical old-time valley holiness preaching. Television is wrong and women should not use washing machines because it makes them idle![4] It was also a world of miracles, healings, prophecy and all-night prayer meetings. In Bryn's assembly they met on at least three nights a week and prayed for revival and Bryn was at every meeting until he was told by his pastor to stay home on at least one night to help his mother. His father worked in the coal mines and when his younger brother, Keri, wanted to go to a Bible College his pastor told him that the colleges were too liberal. 'What should I do? My pastor told me not to go to college and my father told me not to go down the mines'. With advice of this kind reaching the brothers, it was hardly surprising that Bryn was only apprenticed to the National Coal Board for the year 1956-57; he then went by faith, that is without any guarantee that fees would be paid, to Swansea Bible College.

> The three years I spent at Swansea were tremendous. To be honest, I didn't receive a deep grounding in theology; it wasn't that sort of college. And although it had a heart for world missions, its strength wasn't missiology. What I did learn however, was a deep devotion to God and the power of corporate prayer during my three years there, I cannot recall a single day when we had less than three hours prayer together.[5]

The college was set up in magnificent grounds by Rees Howells whose extraordinary life is described by Norman Grubb.[6] Howells was the archetypal man of prayer and faith and the several acres of lands and buildings where the college was housed were all bought by money that was 'prayed in'. Among his student contemporaries was Reinhard Bonnke, later to become an international healing evangelist and who held the largest public gatherings Africa has ever seen, and his friend Ivor Hopkins who was later to join his apostolic team. Bryn himself, on more than one occasion, had visions of the Holy Spirit in fire or rain falling on Britain.[7] The deluge inspired the young man's subsequent restorationist preaching.

On leaving Swansea Bryn spent three years in Cornwall's Methodist chapels preaching and praying for the sick before going to France for nine months and Germany, with Bonnke, for six weeks. In 1964, having married Edna whom he had met at Swansea Bible College, he sailed to British Guyana where he and Edna spent 2½ years evangelising and pioneering

---

[4] Interview with Keri Jones, 2 February, 2006.
[5] Hewitt, *Doing,* (1995), p.10.
[6] N. Grubb, *Rees Howells Intercessor,* (Cambridge, Lutterworth, 1952).
[7] I have referred to Bryn Jones by his first name to distinguish him from his brother Keri. Other chapters more frequently use surnames for the main protagonist.

'New Testament' churches. He already felt a call to the nations of the world to preach the gospel and to plant churches and those early years confirmed his gifts.

> The Pentecostal men, whom met in my early days, used to drum it into me that Pentecost was an experience not a denomination. 'We are a movement,' they would say, 'not a denomination'. They were fiercely non-denominational.[8]

This non-denominationalism was enhanced by reading Roland Allen's account of the expansion of the early church through apostles and prophets. Allen's book, *Missionary Methods – St Paul's or Ours?* put the issue sharply and, as far as Bryn was concerned, it had to be the apostle Paul who was right and the latter day bureaucratic machinery of denominations or missionary societies that was wrong.[9] During this time he remembers speaking with a Muslim mufti who asked him, 'how many gods have you Christians got?' And when Bryn said, 'one of course', the mufti had contradicted him saying, 'You have a Baptist God, a Salvation Army God, a Pentecostal God'. Returning to Cornwall in 1967 for a further year of pioneering, his intellectual position began to clarify and consolidate: missionary methods should be strictly biblical; churches should be united outside denominationalism so that the 'many gods' taunt might be removed; new churches should be planted by authoritative apostles and prophets. Keri Jones, now a qualified school teacher, joined him in Cornwall with John Spiller and the ministry that came to be called 'Harvestime' was formed.

The charismatic movement was beginning but, according to Keri, Bryn had gone through all the spiritual experiences associated with it years before in his days with the Pentecostal churches. In 1969 Bryn moved to Bradford where he was to have his greatest impact. He continued to be a speaker in demand at inter-denominational and charismatic events. Once described as a 'performance preacher' he could certainly a lift an entire conference with his eloquence and biblical passion. Terry Virgo, no mean preacher himself, was to describe the series of sermons preached by Bryn at Capel some years later as 'excellent'.[10] Gerald Coates went a step further and described them as 'one of the finest things I'd ever heard'.[11] But it was not just his preaching that made Bryn such a formidable person or such a natural leader. In debate and conversation he was a lucid thinker and a persuasive speaker. He had clarity of purpose and a single-minded

---

[8] Hewitt, *Doing,* (1995), p.14.

[9] Roland Allen's book was first published in 1912 and is still in print. He also read Watchman Nee (*Restoration,* [March/April], 1989, p.30).

[10] Terry Virgo, *No Well Worn Paths,* (Eastbourne, Kingsway, 2001), p.105.

[11] Gerald Coates, *An Intelligent Fire,* (Eastbourne, Kingsway, 1991), p.101.

determination to sweep aside any sort of objection rooted in self-interest or unbiblical tradition. His own concept of restoration was, as we shall see, wider and more politically and socially engaged than either Arthur Wallis' or that of the early Pentecostals. He could, so his critics said, be abrasive and dogmatic even though he attracted loyalty and admiration.[12]

In Bradford was an assembly that had once been the spiritual home of the legendary Pentecostal evangelist, Smith Wigglesworth. There was also an Apostolic Church there that had been formed by the first wave of Pentecostal outpouring at the start of the 20th century. In this variegated religious landscape, at the time when Bryn arrived, there was also evidence of the ministry of Wally North, a kind of proto-apostle, who had established a congregation of believers in Bradford as part of his own proto-apostolic network.[13] North looked for a man to put in charge of the congregation and found Peter Parris, a man who had once regularly attended Westminster Chapel where Dr Martyn Lloyd-Jones preached. Peter Parris was unable to rescue the situation in Bradford and so sold the premises and brought the remnant, about 30 people, into his own home. North leaned towards the organic ecclesiology of Austin-Sparks while having Brethren views about the self-governing nature of each congregation. Peter spoke several times at the remnant group and David Matthew, a school teacher of similar views who lived practically next door, attended a set of meetings in Peter's house. At that time a nearby group of Brethren elders were dealing with a messy divorce in their assembly and wanted advice. So they asked Peter to sit in on their discussion to give his perspectives and Peter asked if he could bring Bryn Jones. So Bryn came and they had a friendly evening together, ranging far beyond the set subject. Bryn wanted to know whether they believed in elders and, of course, they said 'yes' and then Bryn asked whether they believed that all elders were equal to which, again, they replied 'yes'. Bryn made it plain that he was not sure about this and thereby sowed seeds for the future. He held the view that it was important to have a 'first among equals'.

Bryn, meanwhile, had become the focus for a small group of (mostly) Baptists who had been ejected from the church because they embraced charismatic things. Bryn invited Keri (who was a school teacher in nearby Dewsbury) to pastor the ex-Baptists and others. So by 1974 there were three groups in Bradford all relating in one way or another to Bryn: the Brethren group, the group associated with Peter Parris and the small group

---

[12] As was evident from conversations circulating in Pentecostal circles in the 1970s.

[13] Wally or Walter North was also a strong Holiness preacher who, according to Andrew Walker was a pastor in Bradford from 1952-65 who later itinerated successfully in the north of England to create a number of inward-looking pentecostalised holiness fellowships whose numbers dwindled once North moved to Scotland (Walker, *Restoring the Kingdom* (4th edn), (Guildford, Eagle, 1998), pp.44-46).

of charismatic ex-Baptists. Gradually Bryn encouraged the groups to join together, for example at baptismal services. By now they had become secure with apostolic ministry and there was open talk of apostles, but how did apostles manifest themselves?

In 1975 - once the Brethren group had become charismatic with tongues and prophecy - Bryn called all the elders together and asked, 'What was the point in continuing as three different groups?' All the elders of the different groups came back after a week and said they were happy to join together. So they then talked to their wives and came back a week later by which time the wives were also happy. If David Matthew had to characterise the groups he would say that the Brethren group was the Word group; Peter had the relational group; and Keri's group was the noisy worship and praise group. In October 1975 the three groups became one - this became known as 'The Merger'. Only the Brethren group had a building but this had been damaged by subsidence. So having sold that, they hired the Bradford City Centre Library Theatre for Sunday meetings and about 150 adults met together with their children. They established house groups and Bryn was recognised in an apostolic role and publicly prayed for Keri, Peter and David as elders.

Keri and Peter were full-time ministers from the start.[14] David was still teaching in school but on Bryn's suggestion, and with the congregation growing, left his job in Easter 1976 to join the team. That is how the Bradford centre, which became the symbol of Harvestime, came into being; the participants felt they were on the crest of a wave as the components of the new and thriving church fitted naturally and successfully together. Truly, they thought, God's Spirit is doing a new thing. They revelled in this but were by no means sectarian and, as an indication of their openness, gladly attended Fountain Trust meetings. Shortly afterwards they looked round the derelict Church House building and bought it later that year. It took 12 months to repair and became a large-scale complex with an ability to interface with the community on many levels.[15] The refurbished Church House became the first bricks-and-mortar indication that restorationism was more than a theological idea, and it made both charismatics and Pentecostals sit up and take notice.

Arthur Wallis invited a group of men (Peter Lyne, Bryn Jones, David Mansell, Graham Perrins and Hugh Thompson) to meet in his home in February 1972 to discuss the prophetic future of the church in the light of turbulence in the Middle East. The 1967 Six Day War had brought eschatology and Israel to the notice of biblical thinkers. In the event, the six

---

[14] Peter Parris was involved on Bryn's behalf with one group of charismatics in the USA in the late 1970s and eventually went over there to live.

[15] The building was eventually sold in 1990 (or thereabouts) when the Abundant Life Centre, also in the Bradford area, was built.

men found themselves bonded together by the Holy Spirit. This was a turning point for Bryn Jones who found himself committed to a group of radicals like himself who shared the same directive and prophetic experience of the Holy Spirit, the same belief in a restored church and an intuitive understanding that their coming together was providential. This was the start of their emphasis on covenant with all the privileges and responsibilities that attached to it.

In the summer Bryn and Keri oversaw the organisation of Bible weeks. The first of these were small and held in Wales in the early 1970s. Then, in the early 1970s, a conference in the grounds of the Elim College in Capel, Surrey, was successful and seminal; it attracted 2000 participants by the end and Bryn was one of the star speakers though, by about 1974, he felt that the message it expounded was mixing up restorationism and renewalism to the detriment of both. It was here, however, that Ern Baxter first sounded a trumpet note for restorationism. Keri put it this way, 'Baxter was important since he had the ability to enunciate the message we carried on a broad platform and caused everything to connect'.[16] In 1975 a bigger and entirely restorationist venture in the Lake District was launched by Bryn and Keri, the same year in which they launched the influential *Restoration* magazine, and this was followed in 1976 by the first Dales week at Harrogate.[17] The week offered a platform for a large number of apostolic ministers. In 1979 at the Great Yorkshire Showground in Harrogate there were 4000 people of whom 50% were newcomers and 75% were under 30 years of age (*Restoration* November/December, 1979). Dales was unquestionably attractive to young people, many of whom had been converted or renewed through the charismatic movement. No wonder that the Bible weeks offered fun-filled activities for children and seminars on family life. This was direct and relevant Christianity presented quite distinctly from the staid expository preaching of Keswick and other long-established Christian summer camps that catered for an older generation. Charismatics of various varieties came, although Bryn never accepted that the denominations were in God's plan and thus believed that God had no wish to renew and support them; his commitment was to people. Anyone though, denominational or otherwise, could book in to the event but they were then exposed to the full weight of restorationist theology through the preaching.[18]

As a further complication, Bryn was in demand in the United States and his linkage with congregations over there led to a parallel network being formed, or partially formed, between 1978 and 1983 centred on New

---

[16] Interview with Keri Jones, 2 February, 2006.

[17] By 1982, the magazine had a circulation of 12,000, (*Restoration*, July/August, 1982, p.5). The last issue was published in August 1992.

[18] Gareth Duffty organised all the Bible weeks from beginning.

Covenant Church in St Louis, Missouri. Eventually Bryn moved with his family to the United States for about five years although he came backwards and forwards and continued to regard the United Kingdom as his primary base.

ii. Bradford and Harvestime

Meanwhile the Bradford congregation grew although the leaders were anxious not to take on too many people too easily.[19] Richard Syms replaced Peter Parris and in due course there were a further three working elders. David Matthew compiled a commitment class for newcomers and tithing was strongly taught.[20] Tithing ensured that congregational members gave 10% of their income to the church in a pattern that dated back to the financial arrangements supporting Old Testament ministry.[21] Alongside tithing, church members received teaching about the blessings of material prosperity: in an article entitled 'God wants you to prosper' Bryn pointed out, 'Jesus became *poor* so that we might be *rich*. Does that refer to money and possessions? Yes, it does'. This wealth however was not to deflect Christians from setting their hearts on the kingdom of God.[22] Tithing resulted in a constant flow of income to the leadership at Church House, and the amounts at their disposal were increased by gifts and tithes of tithes from associated churches. The money was ploughed back into the expanding corporate ministry.

From 1976 to about 1990 there was a steady upward trend of growth both in Bradford and within the Harvestime apostolic network. For instance in September 1980 the International Christian Leadership Programme (ICLP), set up at Bryn's instigation by David Matthew, was launched with a one year course.[23] The three summer camps associated with Bryn attracted about 20,000 people in 1986, and almost all well-known restorationist leaders could be seen on the platforms publicly identifying with these occasions.[24] Expansion within the restorationist churches took

---

[19] The congregation was eventually renamed Abundant Life Church, (*Restoration*, November/December, 1987).

[20] Interview with David Matthew, 15 December, 2004.

[21] In theory the method ensured that the priests and Levites enjoyed an income equal to that of the rest of Israel; eleven tribes gave a tenth of their income to support the twelfth but, of course, the twelfth tithed to God. Further details are given in Leviticus 27 and *passim*.

[22] B. Jones, 'God wants you to prosper', *Restoration*, (September/October, 1986), pp2-4. Original italics.

[23] Interview with David Matthew, 15 December, 2004.

[24] *Restoration*, (November/December, 1986), p.14. The camps were at Shepton Mallet (South and West Bible Week with Tony Morton), Plumpton (Downs with Terry Virgo), Harrogate (Dales) and Builth Wells (Wales Bible Week).

place against the background of denominational decline. By 1987, it was estimated that restorationist numbers in the UK as a whole had grown from 20,000 to 75,000; indeed by 1987 there were some 20 Bible Weeks a year in the UK catering for 100,000 people.[25] In the previous decade the Church of England had lost 200,000 people.[26] Restorationism was bucking the secularising trend and felt itself to be the answer to Britain's – indeed the world's – problems and needs. The cry that God had finished with denominations seemed all too obviously confirmed.

In 1985, *Restoration* magazine carried articles (two by Bryn and one by Keri) on the role of the apostle and prophet and the difference between them.[27] Bryn laid out his understanding of the apostle as the master builder, the planner, and the man with a strategic grasp of the situation and the church planter appointed by God. Alongside the apostle was a prophet whose task was to keep the vision moving forward, to uncover blockages and to motivate God's people. In the final analysis, the apostle has the greater authority and, probably, greater patience and endurance. This emphasis upon apostolic and prophetic ministry was crucial to the development of Harvestime since it demonstrated the theological rationale for the leadership structures within Bryn's orbit. More or less at the same time as these theological concepts were being put in place, Bryn was looking at the enormous political and environmental problems facing the world. As a reader of *Marxism Today* (who nevertheless admired Mrs Thatcher's stance on moral issues) he kept in view a sharp left-wing critique of capitalism.[28] Islam was on the rise, genetically modified crops might cause catastrophe, the nuclear threat to human existence continued and South Africa still insisted upon apartheid – 'legalised racism' in Bryn's words.[29] The kingdom of God in all its multi-dimensional glory would one day establish the rule of God across the world and the apparently insoluble political and environmental problems facing humanity would be resolved. Only a powerful and properly constructed church, one that was right in line with the divinely ordained biblical pattern, could hope to carry forward God's purposes. This mindset explains why Bryn insisted so uncompromisingly upon the restored church. He did not see restorationism as a theological luxury or an interpretive quirk but rather as the divine response to a dark and threatening world situation.

---

[25] *Restoration*, (May/June, 1987), p.19. Some of these e.g. Spring Harvest were never anti-denominational.

[26] *Restoration*, (May/June, 1987), p.27.

[27] *Restoration*, (September/October, 1985), pp.22-23; 30-34; *Restoration*, (November/December, 1985), pp.24-27.

[28] *Restoration*, (March/April, 1989), p.32.

[29] *Restoration*, (March/April, 1989), p.32.

Apostolic teams were made up of a core group who worked with and were part of various local church leaderships in various locations across the nation, and in other nations. Each team member had, by definition, a wider role than that of a local church leader but also had a local church base.[30] The welter of activity was increased in 1987 by Bryn's announcement of a 13 year plan that necessitated the relocation to the Midlands of what was now to be called Covenant Ministries. By 1989 Bryn was working with twenty men 'on a broad front' with a core team of eight with whom he spent a great part of each week 'exploring the Word, planning strategy and praying for revival'.[31] He had, to the surprise of many outside his immediate circle, ended the Dales summer camps in 1986. In their place he instituted Restoration 'Days of Destiny' at the Royal Welsh Showground in Builth Wells in 1987 and Dayspring, which offered an Easter camp at Prestatyn (Denbighshire), Scarborough (Yorkshire) and Brean Sands (Somerset) on consecutive weeks in 1988.[32] As it turned out, though, only two Easter camps ran, but they attracted 4,500 people.[33] In later years summer camps were held in Wales and attracted around 5,000 people for a week of ministry.[34]

The 15 years during which Bryn and Keri Jones, David Matthew and others had been in the Bradford area had resulted in the pioneering of 20 new churches with 'a total of 30 full-time leaders and 4,000 committed people stretching from Liverpool to Hull'.[35] Indeed the Bradford congregation itself had grown in the period from 1975 to 1986 from 150 people to 650 adults worshipping in their own million-pound building; there were planted-out congregations at Leeds, Wakefield, Keighley, Skipton and York.[36] The move to the Midlands would bring the team's activities, with the possible exception of the training college, into a single large complex. In the new premises, it would be easier to concentrate on church-planting and evangelism; the training of ministers could be expanded from 20 to 50 students. By 1989 building work on Nettle Hill, a seven acre farm near Coventry, had received planning permission and was

---

[30] Watchman Nee had influenced the team's thinking about separating work and church life.

[31] *Restoration*, (May/June, 1989), p.40.

[32] *Restoration,* (November/December, 1987), p.21.

[33] *Restoration*, (July/August, 1988), p.19.

[34] *Restoration*, (November/December, 1990), p.33. Gareth Duffty remembers hiring the Welsh National Opera lorry to scour the area for chairs. Setting up the camp was a lengthy and exhausting business.

[35] *Restoration*, (November/December, 1987), p.17. Liverpool is on the west coast and Hull on the east coast of England.

[36] *Restoration*, (September/October, 1986), p19; *Restoration*, (March/April, 1989), p31. The Bradford congregation owned their own building and none of the apostolic team had any control over it (*Restoration* July/August, 1989, p.35).

making good progress. Team offices for Harvestime Publishing were to be located nearby, and the total project was expected to cost £1.5m. The interconnected ministries founded by Bryn were all separable: the publishing house was a limited company with a board of directors and Covenant Ministries was a charity with its own trustees.[37] Yet they were also coordinated and individually focused, and evangelism was by no means forgotten. Church-based GO! Teams of young evangelists in red Peugeot 205s had been assembled to work in Solihull, Birmingham, Coventry, Worcester, Prestatyn, Wrexham, Newport, Chepstow, Cowbridge, Woodford, Basildon and Chelmsford.[38] In addition to the publishing, training, and church-planting ventures, there was also Dales TV, an independent television production company. At the congregational level all this was grown out of 55 churches in the UK and over 20 in the United States that related to Bryn, Keri and the apostolic team. Further afield, there was also involvement with a Bible week in Norway and connections with South Africa.[39]

In terms of plant, equipment, impact and numbers of affiliated churches, this was the high watermark of Bryn Jones's ministry. It is true that the hugely successful Bible weeks in the Dales had closed down but the alternative weeks in Builth Wells, Wales, continued to be well attended and there was every reason to expect that the whole network would thrive and prosper as it burst forth in all directions. Yet this did not happen and the 1990s were a period of numerical contraction, though Bryn himself was in the UK for most of the decade.[40] The reasons for this cannot be attributed to any individual factor. We can isolate four: the corrosive effect of continual criticism of Bryn Jones as well as a series of problems with his health; the closure of the big Bible weeks in the Dales; the financial effort and structural disruption brought about by the move from Bradford to Nettle Hill; the splitting up of the apostolic team into several sub-groups with the consequent creation of separate mini-networks in the late 1990s.

iii. Criticism and Health

Bryn's ministry attracted criticism that he faced head-on. There were those who have circulated myths about the restoration movement in an attempt to discredit it. It was never true that Bryn had preached at a major celebration while smoking a cigar or that one of the country's leading apostles was a secret drunkard. Nor was it true that a Bryn Jones had supported or been

---

[37] *Restoration*, (July/August, 1989), p.35.
[38] *Restoration*, (September/October, 1985); *Restoration,* (November/December, 1987), p.17.
[39] *Restoration*, (March/April, 1989), p.31.
[40] Personal letter from Edna Jones, his widow, 6 June, 2006.

party to the hierarchical form of submission 'insisted on by the Fort Lauderdale men, where everyone submits upward'. Every man and woman is responsible directly to the Lord, so far as Bryn was concerned, and the church should submit first to one another and then to the eldership. Nor should Bryn be seen as a pope. 'I am not a pope, nor one of the Popes. We are a team of men – apostles, prophets and teachers – working together'. And as for TV programmes criticising the Bradford church, it would have been fairer to have interviewed, by way of balance, one of the 600 adults who had remained in the church rather than a couple who had felt aggrieved and left nine years before. Nor should the apostolic team be seen as imposing its uniform will upon the many local congregations within the network. On the contrary, local congregations reflect the outstanding characteristic of the leadership, and this varied from place to place - some being strong on teaching, some on evangelism and some on lively worship. And as for the destruction of church unity through restorationism, that was ridiculous. 'There simply isn't any unity to destroy'.[41]

Off-setting criticism was public recognition. The main public recognition given to Bryn Jones took place at Stoneleigh on one occasion when Bryn went there and Terry Virgo called him up onto the platform and publicly applauded him before 20,000 people. 'Bryn shouldered the knocks' was Alan Scotland's verdict, meaning Bryn took much of the criticism and flak that was been directed at the house churches. In this way he shielded the house church movement from attack.[42]

A new front was opened up when *Restoration* (May/June 1991) began to attract criticism by entering the bitter disputes over Israel's role in biblical prophecy. Evangelical Christians, especially those on the political right, had been among the staunchest supporters of the modern State of Israel in the belief that God's restoration of the Jewish people to the land had been in fulfilment of prophecy and a staging post along the way to the Second Coming of Christ.[43] Bryn, typically, confronted the political and theological right and pointed out that 'more than 300 resolutions have been passed by the United Nations over the last 43 years, Israel continues to ignore the world community, protected by the USA vote in the Security Council'. While condemning Palestinian acts of terrorism he drew attention to the massacres in Lebanon in Sabra and Shatilla. Indeed, 'although God loves the Jews, their rejection of Christ means they have forfeited any rights to being included as God's people'. Alan Scotland wrote an article entitled 'Israel: the last bastion of apartheid?' where he argued the ugly separation of races in South Africa was now to be found in Israel's treatment of the

---

[41] This paragraph and its quotations are based on an interview with Bryn Jones in *Restoration*, (May/June, 1989), p.39.
[42] Interview with Alan Scotland, 15 November, 2004.
[43] E.g. Deuteronomy 30.1-5.

Arabs. In an article on the people of God, David Matthew argued that the Jews 'are not the people of God' but that a redeemed community made up of Christians and Jews constitutes the new 'Israel of God'. David Mansell talked about 'debunking the myths of Israel' arguing that the Genesis promises given to Abraham about land are not eternal but were fulfilled in the time of Solomon's reign and are not relevant for today. In any case, if the promises given to Abraham are irrevocable, so also is the Levitical priesthood – a position that no Christian could accept. All this implied that 'Christians can no longer turn a blind eye to Israel's faults while condemning them in others'. Following up in the January/February 1992 issue of *Restoration* Mansell emphasised Abraham's justification by faith prior to the giving of the rite of circumcision; faith was vital, circumcision contingent. It did not help that an interview with the deputy head of the Palestine Liberation Organisation was carried in July/August 1991. This provoked further negative feedback and at least one letter in June 1992's postbag spoke of shock and disgust at the magazine's line.[44] None of this deflected *Restoration* from pursuing its social and political themes and in June 1992 the majority of articles were devoted to an onslaught on racism. Bryn saw the opening up of debate, 'what justice is there for the Palestinians – and what security for the Jews?' as belonging to the magazine's 'prophetic voice'.[45]

Together with the Bible weeks in the Dales, *Restoration* had been the main carrier of the restorationist message. Its high quality production values, its advertising of books, conferences, tapes and meetings, and its capacity to convey distinctive theological motifs globally, gave Bryn Jones an outlet for his intellectual and spiritual energies. With the loss of the Bible weeks and with the gradual depletion of income from the churches connected with him, it became more difficult to sustain *Restoration*. It had not regularly carried advertising for groups outside the Covenant Ministries circle and, because it was discounted within churches, it tended not to make a profit. By 1992 the financial pressures, together with the editorial pressure to collect printable material from busy preachers, became too much. Even though the magazine was bi-monthly, a new format was needed. So, from January 1993, *Restoration* became monthly and was available free of charge. Although it might appear to be more expensive to distribute it free of charge, the smaller print run appeared to save money. In the discussion with David Matthew and David Mansell of what happened, Bryn and Keri Jones took the view that, although the work of restoration is by no means complete, the magazine had seen many of its goals achieved.[46] Praise and worship had been revitalised; the church was now seen more as a covenant

---

[44] Various, 'Postbag', *Restoration* (June, 1992), p.40.

[45] *Restoration*, (August, 1992), p.37.

[46] *Restoration*, (August, 1992), p.35-37.

community than a congregation; there was a greater understanding of the nature of God's kingdom; there was now widespread recognition of apostles, prophets, evangelists, pastors and teachers in God's church. The magazine had had a major impact in the UK that had led to the pioneering of hundreds of churches and the prophetic voice of the magazine had had a 'healthy polarising effect'. The new magazine, also called *Restoration*, would 'inform, provoke and stimulate action' on policy matters connected with inner cities, family lives, secular jobs and the international scene. While evangelicals might be offended at the social consciousness of restorationism, restorationism was a bigger concept than the reformation of the church in the image of the New Testament. It concerned the transformation of the world itself. 'We want to apply medicine to the world's wounds, and we want are equip believers for a mighty revival'.[47]

To what extent the new version of *Restoration* was an in-house magazine rather than one aimed at 'the whole church for the whole world' is hard to assess.[48] To what extent cancellation of subscriptions made the magazine unviable is also hard to determine, though there were cancellations as a result of the Israel debate. Criticism of Bryn Jones personally may have had the effect of making him less willing to attend evangelical or inter-denomination events.[49] It may also have forced the Covenant Ministries group back into itself. What is less speculative concerns Jones's health. He suffered a minor stroke during the 1990s and also began to develop cardiomyopathy and was considered for a heart bypass operation because his heart was functioning at well below its proper efficiency. He was booked to go into hospital for surgery when, to the surprise of his medical team, his heart was found to be back up to a reasonable level and the surgery was cancelled. Sometime later in the 1990s he fell and had metal pins put into his ankle.[50] By this time he had put on weight and was forced to slow down. Though his mental capacity was never affected, his ability to sustain a preaching tour was impeded. He continued to preach right until the end of his life with the faith-based attitude that when his time was up, the Lord would take him.[51]

iv. Closure of Big Bible Weeks

The Dales Bible weeks – held over a fortnight at the Great Yorkshire Showground near Harrogate – demanded a huge effort and took about six

---

[47] David Mansell's words.

[48] This is the tagline printed beneath the title on the front cover.

[49] He declined to attend the 1990 event in Sheffield organised by Gerald Coates.

[50] Interview with Gareth Duffty, 5 May, 2005. The cancellation of the heart bypass surgery was deemed to be miraculous.

[51] Interview with Keri Jones, Bryn Jones's brother, 2 February, 2006.

months of the year to organise. Large numbers of people moved in the week before laying on the plumbing, repairing what was broken, installing toilets, collecting the children's workers, transporting the bookshop, the catering, the stage, the lighting, the sound system, the power supply and, at the end, handing back the venue in a better condition than before. After it was all over, it took 1½ days to dismantle.

Explaining the reason for the closure of the Bible week after 11 successful years Bryn said that it was to be replaced by a 'holy convocation of committed Christians' taking place at the Builth Wells Royal Welsh Showground.

> Although it will be open to all Christians, the thrust of the teaching will be geared to those who are already committed to Restoration of the church and who acknowledge the place and importance of the Ephesians 4 ministries today, including apostles and prophets... people have had every opportunity to weigh up what we are saying and to respond accordingly. They either received it or rejected it. Some have gone their own way while others have embarked on a pilgrimage similar to ours. Now we need to give our time and attention to instructing those who have responded to this message.[52]

A new emphasis was announced. The aim was to strengthen those who had embarked upon the restorationist pathway. Spring Harvest, the inter-denominational Bible weeks that manage to straddle restorationist and renewalist theologies, had started in 1979 and had begun to pick up high numbers of Christians. Bryn and Keri were never invited to preach at Spring Harvest and, although it is impossible at this juncture to work out how many people preferred the more interdenominational setting to his harder-edged restorationist message, there must be a suspicion that Bryn was right to concentrate upon core restorationists rather than providing a showcase of restorationism to a wide spectrum of charismatics and evangelicals. Undoubtedly, the Dales Bible weeks could have continued, but only about 4,500 attended the alternative events (like Dayspring). This suggests that Spring Harvest which, by putting on a series of events in several locations, managed to reach 80,000 people throughout the course of the summer would eventually have dwarfed the Dales and made it a more marginal platform.[53]

More to the point was the growing success of the Downs Bible weeks organised by New Frontiers. These also began in 1979 and built up slowly. They preached the restorationist message and were linked in the public

---

[52] *Restoration*, (July/August, 1986), p.22.

[53] It is true that the Restoration 1990 and Restoration 1991 events attracted crowds of more than 5000 (at Restoration 1991 they took in 5300), but these were not on the scale of the Dales weeks (*Restoration*, January/February, 1992, p.35).

mind with the Dales. When the Dales closed, the Downs continued and this made it much more difficult to re-start the Dales or for Covenant Ministries to put across its own unique and individual message within the restorationist sector. There was no obvious competition between the Dales and the Downs but, in the nature of things, once the Dales closed, the Downs became the main national camp where restorationists could gather. If Covenant Ministries appeared to be retreating to a Welsh heartland, New Frontiers was appealing to the wealthy commuters of south London. Leadership of restorationism looked as though it was passing to Terry Virgo with the result that undecided churches would find it natural to join with New Frontiers rather than with Covenant Ministries. A gradual drift of personnel and resources to the southern restorationists was, with hindsight, inevitable.

v. Disruption Moving South

To make the move southward, it was necessary to sell Church House in Bradford. With Bryn Jones' blessing, Paul Scanlon took over the work in Yorkshire and built up what became Abundant Life Ministries on a large campus less than a mile from the city centre of Bradford.[54] This meant allowing the churches that had previously been established to work together among themselves. Although the intention was to plant and network with churches in the proximity of Coventry, this did not happened, or did not happen to the same extent as had occurred in the 1970s when Covenant Ministries/Harvestime was first set up. Nettle Hill itself is set in farmland and could not become a congregational centre and, although there are links with the congregation in Coventry, it did not prove possible to repeat the runaway successes of previous decades. Having 'given away' a thriving congregation with associated building in the north of England, nothing comparable replaced it in the Midlands.

The ICLP (International Christian Leadership Programme) at Church House was moved to Riddlesden and then became Covenant College and then went to Nettle Hill. Although moving a college is exhausting and deters recruitment, the enterprise survived and has now bedded down with a cohort of residential students and three basic schools within it: a School of Ministry, a School of Worship and a School of Visible Voice (which is effectively an art school).

Additionally and relevant to future growth, there may have been disagreement between Bryn Jones and his brother, Keri, on how Covenant Ministries should relate to other groups. The result of 11 years of sounding out the message of restoration in the Dales and the wide circulation of *Restoration* was to produce other churches and groups that had moved

---

[54] See <http://www.alm.org.uk/church/> (accessed 7 June, 2006).

towards the position taken up by restorationists. However, rather than welcoming these developments, Bryn wanted to remain 'prophetically sharp' or to retain his 'distinctives'. Others, like David Matthew, saw that the non-distinctives would always be more important than the distinctives because the non-distinctives were shared by the common body of the church. Bryn's original commission was 'not to build on another man's foundation' and, in any case, he declared that it was impossible to 'serve two masters'. He wanted to 'start again on clear ground' to save himself from the hassle of extricating churches from their traditions and problems.[55] He eventually said to his team that he would no longer accept any pre-formed groups into his network, and this was faithful to his original commission.

vi. The Splitting of the Apostolic Team

David Tomlinson, based in the Middlesbrough area, had left Bryn Jones in 1980-81.[56] Paul Scanlon, remaining near Bradford, had become independent by the end of the decade and built up Abundant Life Church to the proportions of a megachurch. In the late summer of 1997 Alan Scotland was released with about 16 churches to set up Lifelink International.[57] This was all done openly and with the laying on of hands and prayer. At the same ceremony in Leicester Andrew Owen, now of Destiny Church, Glasgow, was released to what became a multi-faceted megachurch ministry stretching through a network of some six congregations to world missions.[58] All three men, Scanlon, Scotland and Owen were recognised as apostles and Robertson, researching the matter recently, concludes that 'although Bryn recognised these men as apostles, his hope was that they would remain within the 'fold' of CMI, under his fatherly apostolic oversight'.[59] There was some friction over their recognition, however, since Keri was not present on the occasion when this occurred.[60]

'Bryn felt he had a commission to be faithful to as opposed to a single vision'.[61] He was required to fulfil his commission to bring the message of restoration to his generation but he did not feel that he had a vision to set up

---

[55] Interview with David Matthew, 15 December, 2004.

[56] Interview with David Tomlinson, 4 May, 2005.

[57] <http://www.lifelinkinternational.org.uk/Default.aspx> (accessed 9 May, 2006).

[58] <http://www.destiny-church.com/index.htm> (accessed 9 May, 2006).

[59] A. Ewen Robertson, 'An Evaluation of Apostolic Ministry in Today's Church, with Particular Reference to the Offshoots of Covenant Ministries International', (University of Wales in partnership with Regents College: unpublished MTh dissertation: June 2006).

[60] Robertson, 'An Evaluation', (2006).

[61] Interview with Gareth Duffty, 5 May, 2006.

a network of Covenant Ministry International churches. Indeed he believed that his apostolic gift was expressed alongside or through his prophetic gifts. This meant that his default ministry was not one of administration or pastoral care but of prophetic insight. According to Alan Scotland he did not want to become 'an administrator of apostles' and was happier to let the different teams run their own operations.[62] As the 1990s unfolded and the Toronto blessing rolled across the restorationist churches, Covenant Ministries International welcomed the spiritual release brought by the blessing and encouraged it as a precursor to revival.[63] By 1995 when revival was nowhere to be seen, David Matthew found himself at odds with Bryn Jones over what had happened. Matthew expressed his reservations and Bryn had replied, 'I don't see, then, how you could be part of us'.[64] It was a parting of the ways and, although Matthew did not take any churches with him, his contribution to the editorship of *Restoration* (he had worked on it since 1979) and later to the training college was invaluable and his loss a diminution of the totality of the ministry.

The rationale for this, which was announced at the last Bible Week in Builth, was that Bryn was 'setting his sons in calling' by which meant that he was letting his spiritual sons stand on their own feet with sufficient resources to build their own lives and apostolic commissions.[65] That Bryn saw many of these apostolic figures as his own spiritual offspring is evident from the way he talked about them and by the age gap between himself and themselves. He was more than 15 years older than Gareth Duffty (who remained with him and later became the apostolic figure working from Nettle Hill), Alan Scotland, Andy Owen, Ian Rossol and one or two others in United States. The saddest goodbye was that between Bryn Jones and his brother, Keri, in about 2001. During Bryn's period of ill-health in the late 1990s, it had appeared that Keri would take over the whole network but, when Bryn recovered, the situation changed. At two CMI elders' conferences at Nettle Hill in September 2001 and January 2002, Keri agreed that Bryn should remain over the churches he had overseen prior to May 2000.[66] Keri returned to Cardiff where he had worked since the 1970s

---

[62] Interview with Alan Scotland, 15 November, 2004.

[63] I have used the term 'Covenant Ministries International' or CMI rather than Covenant Ministries though, as far as I can see, the new name simply recognised the existing international dimension of the work; it does not seem to have marked any new initiatives that Bryn made a public declaration at the last CMI Bible Week of the 1990s (1996) that he wanted to 'confirm' 'sons into their calling'. See A. Ewen Robertson, 'An evaluation of Apostolic Ministry within today's church with particular reference to Covenant Ministries International, (UWB and Regents Theological College, unpublished MTh Dissertation, 2006).

[64] Interview with David Matthew, 15 December, 2004.

[65] Interview with Gareth Duffty, 5 May, 2006. Confirmed by Ian Rossol.

[66] Robertson, 'An Evaluation', (2006).

with All Nations Church in a network of about a dozen congregations in Britain and many more overseas - three in United States, 18 in Norway, four in Canada, four in South Africa and two in India. Bryn died in May 2003.

vii. Reflection

The restorationist message that Bryn Jones preached led him to found organisations that engaged with contemporary problems. He believed that the kingdom of God upon the earth would see justice for the poor and the removal of tyrannical regimes like those that imposed apartheid. According to his theology, the millennium began at the crucifixion with the result that the historical working out of the kingdom of God would eventuate in the ultimate submission of earthly governments to the throne of Christ. By engaging in activities that advanced justice upon the earth, Christians were in line with the will of God and beginning to establish Christ's rule.[67] Both Bryn and his brother undertook masters degrees in Peace Studies at the University of Bradford and Bryn set up an Institute of World Concerns that was a kind of forum for all kinds of professional people. As he put it, 'justice is a foundational element of the throne' and according to Alan Scotland, 'he would put us in debt to help the poor... he had a big heart'.[68] When they moved to Nettle Hill, these conferences continued and invitations were issued to health workers, the financial sector, educators and carers. 'We must be properly positioned to make the most of every opportunity so that the world can see what a difference the people of God can make on earth', as one of the advertising leaflets put it. In the same vein Bryn began Help International.[69] There was a push to help Africa in 1986 and 1987, particularly when apartheid still suppressed the black population, and there was equally a desire to reach out to churches that were under the control of atheistic governments. Alan Scotland had gone to China at Bryn's request in 1996/7 to help the underground church there.

Whatever may be said about Bryn Jones's forthright stance on restorationist issues and his impatience with denominational minutiae, those who knew him well admired his generosity and drive. He may have been seen as sectarian by his critics but he would argue, 'we are not exclusive; we have been excluded' and he kept an open table welcoming all comers to his meetings. Wesley Richards characterised him as, 'a real rugby player who put his head down and moved the whole scrum forward. He was tough

---

[67] B. Jones, *The Radical Church*, (Shippensburg, PA, Destiny Image Publishers, 1999).

[68] Quoted by Alan Scotland (15 November, 2004)

[69] Help Africa *Restoration* (March/April, 1986), p.9-15 also *Restoration*, (July/August, 1986), pp.21-28; 1987 p.18; Help International and Help International details *Restoration*, (November/December), p.38 *Restoration* (January/February, 1992).

and he pushed hard for what he believed'.[70] Others put it this way, 'our certainties isolated us' and too much depended upon Bryn Jones's own ministry.[71] He could not be everywhere at once and he drove himself hard from meeting to meeting until his body let him down. Later, when it became evident that not everybody who was deemed to be an apostle had the same extraordinary capacity as Jones did, there were attempts to coordinate and spread the workload but organisationally this became too difficult.

Although there may be sadness that what he left behind is less substantial than it might have been, the individual ministries that have come into being as a result of his own encouragement are substantial. He once said, 'don't remember me but remember what I gave my life for', which seems a suitable epitaph.[72]

---

[70] Interview by telephone, 9 March, 2006.

[71] Interview with Alan Scotland, 15 November, 2004.

[72] Quoted by Gareth Duffty in an interview, 5 May, 2006.

Chapter 4

Terry Virgo and New Frontiers International

i. Terry Virgo, the Man

Terry Virgo was born in 1940 and came from a non-Christian home although, as was common in those days, his parents sent him to the local Anglican Sunday school.[1] Despite attendance there and at a Congregational Church youth club he 'never met God or anything spiritual in either of these churches'.[2] When he was 16 his sister came home one evening after having been converted and that night, kneeling in their own living room, he asked Christ to save him. When he heard John Stott preaching a few weeks later, he was transfixed by a wonderful presentation of the Gospel and he walked forward at the end of the meeting as a sign of commitment.

He was, by his own confession, an extraordinary mixture: he lived a double life by being in the church on Sunday and with the jazz club on Fridays and with lots of drinking and partying on Saturday. His father was a school caretaker and their house was in the grounds of the school. After an erratic academic career at Sussex Grammar School, he found himself occasionally repenting but without any idea how to sustain a positive Christian life. Aware that he was a living contradiction, he responded to a visiting preacher and offered his life for the mission field in an act that was as surprising to him as it was to his own minister.

However, for two more years, he continued to live inconsistently though, by now, he had a job in the civil service in London. Eventually, responding to a powerful sermon, and feeling the fear of God, he changed his circle of friends, pattern of life, gambling habits and preferred reading. During the daily two hours on the train to work he systematically read through a range of Christian books, threw himself into church life and began to work actively, though with great shyness and a sense of ineffectiveness. One Sunday in 1962 he attended the Pentecostal Church in Notting Hill; hands were laid on him by the pastor and, after doubts and inner arguments, he began to speak in tongues. After a week of turbulence during a retreat at his Baptist youth group he was asked to tell them what had happened to him.

---

[1] Much of this section is taken from: T. Virgo, *No Well Worn Paths*, (Eastbourne, Kingsway, 2001). Virgo had preached a seminar in 1998 at Stoneleigh entitled 'The Story So Far' that rehearsed many of the events later presented in greater detail in Virgo's book.

[2] T. Virgo, *No Well Worn Paths,* (Eastbourne, Kingsway, 2001), p.15.

So profound was the effect of his words that, with the pastor's approval, he laid hands on many of the young people who then received the Holy Spirit and spoke in tongues. That summer, he took part in an open-air meeting on the seafront at Brighton and felt that his embarrassment about speaking publicly for Christ had at last been conquered. His life became increasingly crowded with prayer and evangelism until, sensing that he was to be more available to God, and on the basis of prophetic utterances that he heard within a local Pentecostal Church, he gave up his secure job and, in 1963, launched out on what was effectively a full-time independent Christian ministry.

He spent two years working on a local housing estate. In the summer he organised children's meetings and, later, a regular Sunday school. He took the more radical step of moving onto the estate by becoming a lodger in one of the houses, learned to trust God for his material needs and, going door-to-door, he found out how to cope with discouragement and to share his faith with ordinary people. No church was planted and there were few conversions but, in retrospect, he felt that the time had shaped his character and consolidated his Christian commitment.

He steadily grew aware of a wider Christian world than that represented in his local Baptist church where he regularly worshipped. He heard Denis Clark preach, got to know Arthur Wallis and Campbell McAlpine, heard and admired the devotion to Christ shown by Willie Burton, the Pentecostal preacher who had planted numerous churches in the Congo, attended meetings where charismatic gifts were exercised, continued to read widely in Christian literature, listened to David Du Plessis speaking of Roman Catholics who had been baptised in the Spirit, and found himself being encouraged to attend Bible College by many of the people he met. Although he applied late in the summer and without any financial resources, he was accepted for London Bible College in August 1965 and offered a place for that September. Soon afterwards he was given a local government grant, the first ever to be awarded to a theological student by the county of Sussex.

For the next three years he lived as a student, though in digs, and gradually formed a pattern of Sunday worship. In the mornings he used to attend a new church at the offices of David Foot in Buckingham Street where Richard Bolt was a frequent preacher. The services were completely unpredictable when Richard Bolt preached but there was always a willingness to allow congregational members to contribute to the service in an extempore fashion following the New Testament pattern described by the words, 'when you come together, everyone has a hymn, or a word of instruction, a revelation, a tongue or an interpretation. All of these must be done for the strengthening of the church' (1 Corinthians 14:26). The atmosphere was enthusiastic and the services would often last all morning and the congregation would then eat their lunch together. On Sunday evenings Virgo would go to hear Martyn Lloyd-Jones preaching at Westminster Chapel and gladly learned from the rigorously inspired exposition of the great man. Lloyd-Jones was deeply Calvinistic in his theology and Virgo, through his private reading, had come to a similar position. What unsettled Virgo was his own understanding of the baptism in the Holy Spirit and speaking with tongues: arguments raged on the subject backwards and forwards both among the student body and within evangelical culture. One Sunday night he went to see Martyn Lloyd-Jones for advice and, instead of being warned off charismatic gifts, he was told that 'the great sin of the evangelical world was to put God in the box and tell him what he could and could not do'.[3]

He met his future wife, Wendy, also a student at London Bible College, during his time there and, in the summer that he left, they married and he moved to his first pastorate at Seaford, 16 miles from Brighton, where he began his ordained ministry in an Evangelical Free Church in 1968. By now Virgo had a clearer idea of the kind of church that he wanted. Spiritual gifts would be exercised freely in an atmosphere similar to the informality that he had enjoyed in Buckingham Street while, at the same time, there would be the expository preaching that Martyn Lloyd-Jones had exemplified. There would be an evangelistic Calvinistic theology coupled with a Pentecostal or charismatic theology of the Spirit. Little by little the new congregation became accustomed to longer and longer times of open prayer and, as a result of an electric charismatic prayer meeting on Friday nights, charismatic gifts began to be introduced to the Sunday morning meetings. The changes offended some of the older members but, having now an inkling of the glory of the church – the city set on the hill – there was no turning back. Healings followed and, as Virgo became more fully aware of the width of the charismatic movement, he was introduced to all the men who became leaders within British restorationism. He attended the 1971 gathering at Trafalgar Square for the Festival of Light and sensed that God was at work across the nation.

Yet, at a meeting at Torbay Court with denominational and house church leaders in attendance he felt part of neither.[4] In a powerful experience of divine revelation he sensed that he was being called to build a house for God though, as yet, the extent of the construction work was unclear to him. Meanwhile at Seaford the obstructive old elders were moved aside, in one case by death, and a new set of younger group of elders came in. Terry and Wendy, his wife, were, for the first time, offered a proper salary and able to buy a house. They began large-scale meetings in venues in the Brighton area and Virgo himself began to be invited to preach in churches further afield, in Heathfield, Lewes, Uckfield and Horsham. These invitations were

---

[3] Virgo, *No Well Worn Paths,* (2001), p.71.
[4] Virgo, *No Well Worn Paths,* (2001), p.89.

to preach for a weekend or a week and, bit by bit, a pattern emerged so that he was soon working with some 20 churches. This was a loose affiliation and had no name or formal structure. Virgo had by now begun to preach on the extent of divine grace and the result of this exposition was to remove the vestiges of legalism from the heart of renewed congregations. Grace arose from the generosity of God and lay behind copious miracles of healing and financial provision. It was grace that informed the New Testament Christian lifestyle and, once grasped, this led to a relaxed type of Christian community, even if alongside the message of grace was a realisation that the church was to be a place of holiness and powerful worship.

So, while the congregation at Seaford went through a series of sometimes painful transitions, these generated insights into the likely reactions of other congregations going through similar processes. The renewal of the concept of eldership helped to bring men into church life and made the church attractive to young married couples with families. Drawing upon the Seaford model, Virgo was able to help congregations and small groups connected with him to move in a similar direction. He began to formulate a big vision of the church as a whole, and he saw small charismatic prayer meetings gathering in homes and independent evangelical congregations as being equally open to the same divine purposes.

At the 1970 Capel (in Surrey) Bible week, 750 people were on the site by day and 2,000 came flooding in to the evening meetings. Terry Virgo was able to hear preachers like Ern Baxter who was 'able to paint a huge picture of the magnificent end-time church'[5] as well as Bryn Jones whose uncompromising restorationist emphasis was also rooted in eschatology.[6] Differences between the renewalist and restorationists came out into the open[7] and, though restorationists brought together their Magnificent Seven and even their Fabulous Fourteen, Virgo found that, when he joined them as they expanded to 20 people, there was little unity among them[8] so that it did not altogether surprise him that, even at great events like the one that took place at the Royal Albert Hall in the mid-1970s, nobody seemed to have a clear idea of what they wanted to achieve. Personality clashes as well as differences over the consequences of abandoning legalism could lead to 'very dismissive comments about the Bible and prayer meetings'.[9] Eventually when the 1976 split occurred between the northern and southern groups of apostles, Virgo found himself attracted to the purposefulness and

---

[5] Virgo, *No Well Worn Paths,* (2001), p.106.
[6] In 1973 and 1974, Briers, 'Negotiating with Babylon', (1993), p.30.
[7] Virgo, *No Well Worn Paths,* (2001), p.101.
[8] Virgo, *No Well Worn Paths,* (2001), p.103.
[9] Virgo, *No Well Worn Paths,* (2001), p.104.

moral stance of the R1 group. He became an associate of Bryn Jones who did him the service of first recognising his apostleship.

Equally significant to the eventual establishment of New Frontiers International was a trip that Virgo made to the United States with Bryn Jones. Before he left, Virgo had been asked to oversee a split-off of about 30 people in the Hove area but had told them to return to their churches and try to work out their Christian lives in an existing denominational context – which was precisely the position taken by renewalists. There was also beginning to be criticism of the new churches for stealing church members from the established denominations. During his preaching tour, he found himself being asked to give advice to all sorts of Christian groups who were in the positions similar to those in the United Kingdom: many of them had been renewed and some were independent and others nominally attached to other Christian denominations or organisations. How should they reconfigure themselves? While advising others he realised that his advice applied to himself. He must leave Seaford and move into the much larger population centre in Brighton and Hove. On his return to England, the charismatics whom he had advised to return to their own churches contacted him again and said that their situation was impossible. Despite appearing to confirm the criticisms that had been made of him, Virgo told them that he would be moving to Hove where he would take on the leadership of the congregation. In his last year at Seaford he had only been able to preach there on five Sundays. Evidently his ministry had outgrown the locality and become national and even international. He and his family relocated in 1978.

ii. The Downs Bible Weeks and Coastlands

One of the first things they did was to form a team that included an administrator because, in 1979 in Sussex, the first Downs Bible Weeks were launched. That year 2,900 people attended, cassettes were sold and the name Coastlands was adopted to give collective identity. Although it appeared that the name was intended to show that the churches were connected with the south coast of England, actually the name had been selected from Isaiah 42.4 in reference to far-off nations waiting to hear the gospel. Soon afterwards the congregation began to grow and one day the pastor of the old Clarendon mission church building, which had been erected in 1883 with a seating capacity of 500, contacted him asking if they might work together. Virgo agreed so long as the overall leadership remained in his own hands. Very quickly they moved in, began to flourish and spent nearly £250,000 renovating the building. Virgo began to appreciate that his ability to build congregations entailed an acceptance that his ministry was apostolic.

As this calling crystallised, Virgo became increasingly aware that the decision-making arrangements within traditional churches were unsatisfactory. Business meetings where the pastor's vote could be cancelled out by that of any backslidden member could hardly carry a spiritual vision forward. 'We began to see that Christ's instructions were not simply to go and have meetings but rather to go and make disciples'[10] and this implied that members needed to be committed to the over arching purpose of the community that they were joining. This, inevitably, led to wild rumours and the circulation of critical stories about the extent of authority demanded by leaders of the new churches so that, when Virgo was asked to preach at a Westminster Fellowship meeting for pastors, he found himself in a packed auditorium and facing a largely hostile barrage of questions. Because he had argued for the role of the apostle in today's church, he was accused of making himself equal with the apostle Paul. Because he did not know how many members in the church in Brighton were brand new Christians, he was called a liar. It was assumed that any church with a commitment course would have checked up on the previous religious affiliations of new people but, actually, Virgo was never personally involved in running the commitment course and with 350 members he did not know them all personally. Within the year a similar presentation to the Evangelical Alliance was made in a less hostile atmosphere though barbed questions about 'sheep stealing' hurt. In each setting Virgo had emphasised his belief that God wished to restore the whole church and not simply to bring about 'restoration churches'. He spoke about a fresh sense of sonship, grace rather than law, the priesthood of all believers expressed in open worship, the importance of friendship and the continuing role of the ministries of pastors/teachers, evangelist, prophets and apostles. His book *Restoration in the Church* was published in 1985[11] and puts all these ideas together into a connected discourse.

Coastlands was registered as a charity in April 1982 and, by then, its function had diversified. Virgo had already had numerous contacts with churches in the south of England. With the encouragement of the London Brothers[12] Virgo held celebrations that attracted more churches than had been reached simply by word of mouth. For instance, Allerford Chapel in Catford, South London, began to experience the gifts of the Holy Spirit and after an initial nine-day visit Virgo began to give two days to the church every two months spending the first evening with the leaders and the next with the whole church. Other churches had gone through the process of renewal under the influence of the Fountain Trust but found themselves unsupported by the Baptist Union and surprised by the unhelpful tone of

---

[10] Virgo, *No Well Worn Paths,* (2001), p.133.
[11] By Kingsway.
[12] Gerald Coates, John Noble and others.

denominational officials. Ray Lowe 'had become frustrated that there was little in the way of meaningful relationships within local Baptist life, and had been shocked when, at his accreditation interview, his inquisitors only seemed concerned about issues of "church meetings and money"'.[13] Not surprisingly Lowe was attracted to the friendly relationships that were fostered by restorationism, joined Coastlands, and later became one of the leaders in the youth work at the Downs Bible Week. Others, like John Colwell, were also becoming frustrated by the Baptist Union and by 1982 Colwell had also become involved with the network of Coastland leaders associated with Virgo. Colwell remembers that 'Coastlands was nothing that could be joined and had no hierarchy. There was no pressure to leave the [Baptist] denomination, and Terry wanted to work with everyone'.[14] Yet, despite his attraction to the direct and purposeful leadership of Virgo, Colwell eventually left in 1993, just after Coastlands had changed its name to New Frontiers International, or NFI for short. Colwell was an exception, though, because many other Baptists who liked the small-scale Coastlands remained and participated fully. The patterns were varied, however, not only because congregations might leave the Baptist Union, become independent and then join NFI while remaining part of localised Baptist associations but also because independent churches might merge with Baptist churches and the combined new congregation be a member of both the Baptist Union and NFI. This was possible because the Baptist Union began to be less exclusive in its expectations of individual congregations and because NFI could be equally flexible. Whereas the Baptist Union learnt to be less legalistic, NFI always understood itself as primarily being defined by its relationship to Virgo and his message of grace.

By the end of the 1970s Virgo was working with between 20 and 30 churches of which 16 were situated in the southeast of England. At that stage only three had Baptist roots but over the next 10 years 'many more'[15] joined Coastlands/NFI and it is not surprising that they did so because Baptist churches have their own restorationist history stretching back to the Anabaptists of the Reformation. Additionally, a number of the Baptist churches who joined Terry Virgo had been influenced by Martyn Lloyd-Jones and the Baptist Revival Fellowship. They found in Virgo a preacher similarly committed to exposition of Scripture and with a similar reformed theology. Moreover, Baptist polity allowed each congregation to interpret Scripture for itself subject only to certain restrictions within its trust deed. Although each church that came into the NFI family did so as a result of its own unique circumstances, many that did so were able to testify to the

---

[13] Millward, 'Chalk and Cheese', (2003), ch 7.
[14] Millward, 'Chalk and Cheese', (2003), ch 7.
[15] Millward, 'Chalk and Cheese', (2003), p.227.

'profound relief'[16] they felt on leaving the formal structures of Baptist Associations and Fraternals, 'many of which were dismissive, whilst ignorant, of the Renewal'.[17]

Virgo continued to preach at the Downs and Dales Bible Weeks and in his sermons began to draw out a theology that could inform the relationship between the new restorationist churches and other Christians. Joseph was a visionary man who was criticised by his brothers but, eventually, provided food in a time of famine; David was a man of action who gathered a new army that rescued Israel; Nehemiah, broken-hearted at the disrepair of Jerusalem, came to rebuild the city against mockery and slander. In each case the heroic biblical figure represented an aspect of the vision and mission of the new restorationist churches. In 1980 Virgo preached at the huge Dales Bible Weeks but, in 1984, the Downs Week, which had been continuing successfully, extended to a second week with the result that Virgo dropped out of Bryn Jones's circle and ceased his contribution to *Restoration* magazine. Because of the hectic nature of their lives, it was a parting of the ways and, from that time on, Virgo concentrated upon his own hugely demanding schedule.

iii. The Development of New Frontiers International

The Downs Bible Week created a unity and a momentum among the participating crowds, but there was, as yet, no sense in which they were all bound together into one enterprise. Some churches were glad to say that they were 'covered' by Virgo but, after a prophecy about a herd of elephants crashing a new path through an impenetrable jungle, and a confirmatory but separate vision given to Wendy, his wife, about runners battling through obstacles to reach a vast stadium, and Virgo's own reading of verses that lit up to him as he considered a stream that flowed out into the distance as a mighty river, he acknowledged the need to form a new entity, with the result that the New Frontiers International was founded.[18] Each church would now add to its name that it was in association with NFI.

---

[16] Millward, 'Chalk and Cheese', (2003), p.228.

[17] Millward, 'Chalk and Cheese', (2003), p.229.

[18] The Charity Commission gives the date of the registration of New Frontiers International as December 1991 but New Frontiers (without the word 'international') had existed for some years before then. Smith (2003) suggests a start date of 1980 but this only makes sense if New Frontiers was by then using the Coastlands name for charitable purposes. The exact dates, however, are not very important because there is an almost seamless continuity between Coastlands and New Frontiers and between New Frontiers and New Frontiers International. (D. Smith, An account of the sustained rise of New Frontiers International within the United Kingdom, *Journal of the European Theological Pentecostal Association*, 23, (2003), pp.137-156).

Although the Bible weeks had begun to make New Frontiers attractive at
the radical edge of evangelicalism, there were certainly critics of what was
happening (as the Westminster Fellowship meeting showed). The uneasy
relations between charismatic evangelicals and Pentecostals and
restorationists might have resulted in serious anathemas had it not been for
the healing (in more senses than one) ministry of John Wimber (1934-98).
Wimber's complex background included Quakerism and the music
industry, and his earliest theological affiliations were with men who had
been influential within the Jesus Movement of the 1960s.[19] In 1981 or 1982
Wimber first came to England and spoke to Anglicans at Bishop David
Pytches's church in Chorleywood and at David Watson's church in York.[20]
The charismatic movement had peaked in the 1970s but was now either on
the wane or seeking a new direction. Wimber's laid-back style, humour,
common sense, theology of the kingdom of God and healing ministry were
immediately attractive to large numbers of Anglican charismatics. In his
doctrine of the kingdom, Wimber was able to argue that Christ's power is
both here and yet-to-come and this explained the potential for immediate
healing and the reasons for delay. If men and women were healed by the
power of the Holy Spirit when Wimber prayed for them, this was a
manifestation of the kingdom; if men and women were not healed, then this
confirmed that the kingdom was yet to arrive in all its fullness. By making
the kingdom of God central to his healing theology, Wimber was able to
avoid, consciously or not, the kind of disputes that Pentecostals and
evangelicals had had with each other over the exact role of the Holy Spirit
in relation to the new birth and Spirit baptism. Yet it would be wrong to
attribute great theological cunning to Wimber's characteristic doctrine
because, as he saw it, his emphasis sprang directly and simply out of the
commands of Christ to his original disciples 'as you go preach this
message, "The kingdom of heaven is near". Heal the sick' (Matthew
10:7).[21]

Wimber and Virgo met and became friends just prior to Wimber's
memorable conference at London's Westminster Central Hall in October
1984. The conference, as Stephen Hunt shows, attracted large numbers of
Anglicans who comprised 42.5% of total number in attendance. Baptists
were the second largest contingent with 23.5% and the house churches third
with 16%. Pentecostals comprised only a small minority with 4% and
evangelicals an even smaller group with 3.5%. Wimber's ministry was

---

[19] C. Wimber, *John Wimber*, (1999), chapters 1-3.

[20] S. Hunt, 'The Anglican Wimberites', *Pneuma*, 17, 1, (1995) pp.105-118 gives 1982
but Carol Wimber, *John* Wimber, (1999), p.159f, suggests the year before. Wimber also
visited Baptist churches, among those one pastored by Nigel Wright, now Principal of
Spurgeon's College, London.

[21] Wimber, *John Wimber*, (1999), p.161.

therefore directed very largely to Anglicans and made an immediately impact. In Virgo's words he 'renewed the renewal'.[22] Why Anglicans should find Wimber particularly to their liking, is difficult to determine. Perhaps it was because he was the antithesis of the sharp-suited caricature of the American healing evangelist: Wimber was almost invariably dressed without a tie and his self-deprecating humour as well as his preference for worship songs sung to country-and-western rhythms had natural warmth. This is not to say that Wimber lacked passion. Virgo remembers him 'thundering out' in Westminster Central Hall that God was saying 'give me back my church!' This was a message about the liberation of the church from bureaucratic control and liturgical tramlines. It was a message that could find an echo in many weary denominational hearts. But, in the 'new churches' beyond the denominational scene, NFI also found release in Wimber's encouragement to members of their congregations to expect charismatic manifestations. The notion of 'every member ministry' was democratising and served to counterbalance the restorationist emphasis on the Ephesians 4 ministry gifts. In fact Wimber did not believe that all these gifts were available to the contemporary church and, from that point of view, was not a restorationist. Equally, he was not, at that stage, a church planter or a man who ran his own denominational empire: rather he offered a service to the whole church and stood as an ecumenical model.

For several further years NFI put its administrative expertise at Wimber's disposal and he thankfully used it for huge meetings at the Brighton Conference Centre where, in several of the sessions, Terry Virgo was asked to preach. Virgo taught on the liberating grace of God and this immediately showed that the rumours about NFI being a legalistic and enclosed set of churches involved in the heavy shepherding were false. As a result the doors opened and Virgo was asked to speak at several key evangelical venues like Spring Harvest and London Bible College. Wimber changed the climate for Virgo and NFI and brought them in from the cold.[23]

Although Wimber found a ready hearing among charismatic Anglicans, Baptists were also receptive to him. Indeed, Baptists had been receptive to the Fountain Trust in roughly the proportions that they were receptive to Wimber. 'Attenders at Fountain Trust conferences were mainly Anglicans and Baptists in a proportion of 3:1'.[24] These proportions provide further grounds for thinking that Wimber picked up the mantle of the Fountain Trust after its demise in 1980. In its latter years, especially under Tom Smail's leadership, the Trust had become increasingly centred on Anglicanism with the effect that Baptists and other Free Church people

---

[22] Virgo, *No Well Worn Paths,* (2001), p.152.

[23] Virgo, *No Well Worn Paths,* (2001), p.157.

[24] Millward, 'Chalk and Cheese', (2003), p.64, quoting McBain, recalled a conversation with Michael Harper and Tom Smail in 1974.

found themselves and their concerns either marginalised or implicitly criticised.[25] Wimber, coming as he did from a completely different ecclesiastical milieu, was able to speak in terms that transcended the deep-seated divisions running through the evangelical world within the United Kingdom.

After 1985 Virgo began to sense that restoring the church was only half the agenda. Restoration was intended to prepare and equip the church for mission, whether in the form of church-planting at home or in the form of charitable aid and prolonged teaching ministry abroad. The Downs Bible Week ran for a final time in 1988 because it had finished its course. NFI was now becoming an 'armada' – the metaphor was one Virgo used to express the variety and freedom of the NFI group of churches which, while all sailing in the same direction, had different functions within the fleet. The Brighton church was the largest but the philosophy of decentralisation ensured that 'other churches took responsibility for certain specific areas'.[26] At Brighton the congregations rapidly grew, multiplying first from two to five and then, after three years, re-combining into one new large congregation with its own team of pastors and a new building at the cost of £3.7 million. Despite the sacrificial giving that funded the new building project, mission continued in outreaches to the homeless in Brighton and to the impoverished of Africa.

The combination of overseas work and work in the south of England created a potential weakness. Would it be possible to move in both directions at once? After the closing of the Downs Bible Week, NFI decided to hold a summer camp for young people in 1990, and the event was an enormous success. The young people wanted to hear about revival and were less interested in the sports programme. In the absence of the Bible week, NFI arranged weekends in major cities across the UK for Virgo to teach on the subject of the grace of God and a series of sermons was turned into the book, *Enjoying God's Grace*, which sold widely. Contact with the Thai preacher Dr Kriengsak, also made an impact by stirring up NFI leaders for world evangelism. The young people's conference had been such a success that the following year there was a desire to go for an altogether larger event at Stoneleigh, near Coventry, much nearer to the centre of England and Wales and when Kriengsak, while speaking at a Brighton conference, suddenly stopped and said he felt that he had a revelation that great blessing would be poured down upon the gathering near a place called C-o-v-e-n-t-r-y, this was all the confirmation that anybody needed. Virgo then travelled to China and later to Thailand to see what was being done there. On his return, and during an NFI elders' and wives' retreat, Virgo had a vision of southern England with a bow

---

[25] Millward, 'Chalk and Cheese', (2003), ch 3.

[26] Virgo, *No Well Worn Paths,* (2001), p.172.

superimposed over the coastline and the arrow pointing southwards. He understood that only by increasing the congregational base in England well beyond the south-east corner could the arrow be pulled back to its fullest extent and fired southwards across the rest of the world. That was the start of NFI's deliberate church-planting programme across the UK.[27]

Meanwhile, Gerald Coates worked hard to bring together the scattered restorationist leaders who had been first convened as a group of 20 in the 1970s. Three events were held in Sheffield in successive years. In 1988 just before 'Together for the Kingdom' news came of Arthur Wallis's sudden death. Those who gathered remembered the impact that he had on their lives, his prophetic vision of a revived and radical church and the courtesy of a true gentleman. The three conferences rekindled mutual affection but the recognisable differences of emphasis between those who met prevented them from formal collaboration. At about this time John Wimber came over to Britain with Mike Bickle from Kansas City and Paul Cain whose prophetic ministry everyone agreed was insightful and often astonishingly accurate. Cain prophesied at an NFI leaders meeting in Brighton and spoke about the enlargement of NFI and its mission to 'change the expression of Christianity throughout the world'.[28]

NFI began to grow rapidly and Virgo's ministry took him to Asia as well as to North America. The Stoneleigh annual event grew ever larger reaching about 14,000 in 1994, about 20,000 the following year and eventually 30,000 in 2001;[29] it also produced a huge annual offering that helped create a vital funding stream – by the end more than £1m was being given.[30] Additionally, all NFI churches were invited to give a tenth of their income to a central fund for purposes that were beyond the capacity of any local church. New church plants were started with assisted funding and NFI within the UK was progressively organised on a regional basis. Virgo himself worked with a team of itinerant and gifted men over several years (though not always the same men) in a pattern that echoed the numerous companions mentioned by Paul in his epistles and in the Acts. By changing the team several times over the years, it was possible to avoid the idea that the team had a special status. As the number of associated churches grew, team meetings became unmanageable so that, eventually, its numbers were reduced to 'a central hub for decision-making and administrative

---

[27] The adoption of churches peaked in the 1980s but, after that decade, when those churches that were going to be adopted had been adopted, growth was largely by fresh planting and only one or two congregations per year were added by any other method during the 1990s (Interview with Dave Holden, 27 April, 2004).

[28] Virgo, *No Well Worn Paths,* (2001), p.192.

[29] Interview with Dave Holden, 27 April, 2004.

[30] Interview with Dave Holden, 27 April, 2004.

purposes'[31] - although men with travelling ministries and regional overseers continued their efforts. As time went on, evangelists were financially supported to work with local churches to stimulate growth. Somewhat to Virgo's surprise he found himself being led to work with a congregation in Colombia, Missouri, and so from 1993 to 1995 he relocated his family. The NFI work in the UK had to learn to function without him and the fact that it was able to do so is indicative of its health.

Whilst he was in Colombia, the Toronto blessing reached the area where the church was situated and Virgo saw at first hand its beneficial effects on the elders with whom he was working. They and large numbers of people who had been hurt by the previous pastor now found a new sense of joy and hope and healing for their emotional wounds. NFI as a whole embraced the Toronto phenomenon as a genuinely refreshing work of the Holy Spirit though they did not see anything more significant than that in it. Meanwhile the figures indicating NFI growth continued to be encouraging. In 1990 there were 60 congregations in Britain[32] - all except five of these were south of Milton Keynes[33] - and a survey of NFI congregations in 1994 showed that they varied in size between 33 and 1,000 with an average of 188. Baptists continue to be attracted to NFI and the same survey showed that people joined NFI because of church care and oversight and that this reason was slightly ahead of joining simply for the sake of NFI values.[34] The Toronto blessing did not contribute to evangelism or to the establishment of church structures or the recognition of ministerial gifts. There were, however, five apostles in NFI and these continued to work regionally or internationally.[35] Simon Pettit, for instance, was invited to South Africa in 1990 and travelled all over the country as well as to Kenya, Malawi, Ghana, Nigeria, Zambia and Zimbabwe.[36] Structurally, within NFI, Virgo was not invested with legal control of the entire enterprise. On the contrary, authority was left with the elders of each congregation and the influence of Virgo and other apostles, while it was decisive to the general direction and theology of the family of churches, did not rest on constitutional tenets or an all-embracing trust deed. Influence stemmed from a shared theology of charismatic gifting and a recognition that Virgo,

---

[31] Virgo, *No Well Worn Paths,* (2001), p.219.

[32] D. Smith, 'An account of the sustained rise of New Frontiers International', (2003), pp.137-156: table 3.

[33] P. A. Charman, 'The Rival Kingdoms of the New Churches empowerment and enfeeblement', (University of Lancaster, PhD Dissertation, 1995) p.72.

[34] M. J. Thompson, 'An Illustrated Theology of Churches and Sects', (University of Brunel, unpublished PhD Dissertation, 1996), pp.55, 174.

[35] Thompson, *An Illustrated,* (1996), p.171.

[36] Tribute to Simon Pettit on by Wendy Virgo
www.newfrontiers.xtn.org/magazine/volume2issue10/article_index.php?id=290. (May, 2005).

and the other apostles, deserved respect because of what they had so obviously achieved with the endowment of the Holy Spirit.

To have attempted to enforce apostolic authority by written agreements would have been destructive of the NFI ethos. This ethos was most consistently expressed and established by the two days of prayer and fasting that were held for all the leaders three times a year.[37] On these occasions, there was nothing on the programme but blocks of two hours of prayer (with worship) with one hour blocks of rest or discussion. Drinks were served but no food of any kind. The days started early and finished late and prayer might take place in one large group or in groups of two or three where individuals prayed for each other. Virgo might speak to the whole meeting for a little while, but it was not a preaching occasion. Almost always, as the prayer 'warmed up' there were prophetic utterances and prophetic pictures that the leadership grasped, tested and interpreted. The prophecies were also taped and re-examined by the senior leaders afterwards. The effect of this process was to make the whole of NFI open to new ideas and impulses and, in prayer, to unite them all behind shared projects and enterprises. The denominational method of decision-making, with its committees, minutes, debates and votes, might produce a majority in favour of one proposition or another but could not create the kind of motivation and sense of ownership that this united charismatic flow could so effortlessly engender. If there was a secret to the success of NFI, it lay here.

Evangelistic growth was also facilitated by the transition from house groups to cell groups. House groups varied enormously depending upon the character and gifts of the leaders. Some would offer teaching, others extensive prayer and praise and others simply a chance to chat. Cell groups were designed to be evangelistic from the beginning but were equally focused on the discipling of new converts. Gradually NFI churches introduced the cell principle of replication and multiplication through the splitting of spiritual DNA. This, together with a recognition of the role of evangelists and the Alpha course that NFI enthusiastically embraced, continued congregational advance in NFI churches in Britain and overseas during the second part of the 1990s.

In addition to congregational growth, church planting moved up the strategic agenda. It was not just a question of mathematics – although clearly there was a mathematical tipping pointed when it was better to plant more congregations, even if some of these were small, and to let them grow than to put all one's efforts into the growth of a fixed base of churches – it was also a matter of feeling the leading of the Holy Spirit. David Devenish returned from a trip to Ephesus where he had begun to appreciate the

---

[37] This pattern had been in place since the early 1980s when 60-70 met together (David Holden, interview 27 April, 2004). By 2005, the numbers had risen to about 500.

dissemination of churches from a teaching centre out to other nearby cities. He returned home and began to carry out the Pauline plan in the Midlands. At the same time, within a large number of NFI congregations, there was a realisation that jobs, house moves, and, indeed, the whole sacred/secular divide, needed rethinking. It was better to resist promotion for the sake of the local church than to accept a promotion that led one's family into a spiritual wilderness. It was better still to move house with the express purpose of building up a new congregation in a fresh town or city than to move house just because a secular corporation wanted to deploy one's talents for commercial gain. The church expresses eternal values while the secular job has far less long-term importance.

The adoption of churches to NFI began to decline in the 1990s, and this added to the drive to plant new congregations.[38] It made sense to reach out to comparatively virgin territory. Apostolic teams were formed. Each had three or four people although some might have six or seven and, ideally, they included a mixture of gifts to provide a balance of ministry to bring a rounded new congregation into being. Apostolic team members would, if possible, be supported by the churches of which they were a part but, if resources did not stretch this far, then central funds could be brought to bear.[39] Fourteen or 15 of these teams operated regionally and in 2003 NFI had about 60 churches being planted in the UK, and there were more overseas.

During the 1990s teaching about spiritual warfare and territorial spirits floated around the Pentecostal and charismatic movement.[40] In essence, the teaching was that Christians needed to engage in spiritual warfare to bind the spiritual forces that were hampering the progress of Christianity in particular geographical regions or cities. A form of prayer, by the individual or in concert, was devised that was intended to restrict and destroy the power of dark angelic beings. Such a doctrine transformed prayer from being an intimate exchange between the individual and a loving God and turned it into the authoritarian (but ineffective) shouting match against invisible spiritual forces. It is to NFI's credit that, after an examination of the biblical basis for these practices, they resisted them and took the view that spiritual warfare should be conducted by the proclamation of the gospel

---

[38] Though it has to be said that members from 76 Baptist Union churches attended Stoneleigh in 2001 (Millward, 'Chalk and Cheese', (2003), ch 8). Virgo, *No Well Worn Paths,* (2001), p.337 reports that 30% of those attending Stoneleigh were not from NFI.
[39] Interview with Dave Holden, 27 April, 2004.
[40] C. P. Wagner, and F. D. Pennoyer (eds), *Wrestling with Dark Angels: towards a deeper understanding of the supernatural forces in spiritual warfare,* (Ventura, CA: Regal Books, 1990).

and the building of the church and that it was almost entirely by these means that spiritual darkness should be driven back.[41]

As NFI grew – and there were about 2,500 people from approximately 30 nations at their leaders' conference in 1998 – there was a general broadening of its sense of calling.[42] Simon Pettit's insistent appeal that they remember the poor initiated projects, especially Act 2000, that helped materially and psychologically disadvantaged people in several British cities. In 2000 George Verwer, from Operation Mobilisation, fired listeners with a missionary call while others, like Bill Wilson, brought the attention of street children in major cities to NFI's notice. These new responsibilities cost money and much of the money was raised at the growing Stoneleigh conferences which continued until 2001 when, responding to what they took to be the unexpected leading of God, NFI decided to end the sequence. Stoneleigh had demanded resources of time and energy in planning and administration but, more than this, there was a feeling that the time had come to dispense the blessings of the conferences more widely.

The whole story of NFI is much more than the story of the invention of a new kind of flexible postmodern Christian organisation. It certainly *is* flexible and its avoidance of the bureaucracy and hierarchy of traditional ecclesiastical structures has been firm and determined. It has not fallen into the trap of surrounding its charismatic leader with a bunch of minders who control a vast secretariat that administers every corner of the expanding empire. On the contrary, Terry Virgo's apostolic gifts have been used to produce other apostolic gifts and apostolic teams but always with the overriding intention of producing excellent local churches. Indeed, one of the great distinctives of NFI is that it has theologically set its face against parachurch organisations that deplete the resources of the local church and function in a freestanding way without being accountable to anybody but anonymous donors. The overriding importance of the local church is expressed again and again and is central to all that NFI does. So central, indeed, that, contrary to the dispensationalist theology held by many evangelicals, NFI has always espoused a belief in worldwide church-based revival before the return of Christ. This upbeat biblical expectation does not preclude the possibility of persecution or pressure upon Christians but it does state quite categorically that, whatever the statistics of secularisation might show, the church will exist and thrive whatever hostile forms the transmutations of political and social culture may throw up. Such hopes are countercultural and, in many instances, counterintuitive and, as an example of its countercultural values, NFI is quite clear that leadership within its churches ought to be male. This does not prevent women from baptising or

---

[41] David Devenish, *Demolishing Strongholds: effective strategies for spiritual warfare,* (Carlisle, Authentic Lifestyle, 2000).
[42] Virgo, *No Well Worn Paths,* (2001), p.275f.

teaching other women or administering Holy Communion. Nor is this exclusive male leadership intended to be in any way demeaning to women but is seen as obedience to the teaching of Scripture, however inconvenient that might be. Indeed it is through Scripture that NFI appreciates that not everyone will accept its considered position: it merely asks that the principled diversity within the church, which existed within the New Testament church from the earliest times, might not descend to factionalism and schism. Its current position is that it wishes to work with other groups and to invite them to embark upon the journey to which it sees itself to be summoned.

iv. Reflection

NFI has grown slowly and, during the 1970s and 1980s, it appeared to be one of the smaller apostolic networks. It appeared not to have the prophetic cutting edge of Covenant Ministries (chapter 3) or the all-round inventiveness of Ichthus (chapter 7). It lacked the public profile of Pioneer (chapter 8) and the strong community base of Salt and Light (chapter 5). Yet, during the 1970s and 1980s working practices and aims were formulated and sharpened. NFI always gave priority to expository preaching which, with hindsight, can be seen to have made it less vulnerable to the swings of evangelical and charismatic fashion. Its leader, Terry Virgo, grew from the grassroots of the movement and had himself carried out most of the functions that were later to be inherent within New Frontiers as a whole. He had discovered the value of personal prayer and fasting; he had conducted evangelism; he had worked with a traditional church and brought it through to renewal; he had undertaken full-time theological education and had a wide appreciation of the charismatic and evangelical scene; he could write as well as preach; he had raised money for buildings and projects; he knew about family life and living by faith; he had travelled widely from quite early on in his ministry. More especially, he had learnt about spiritual gifts and their value and had integrated charismatic worship into the functioning purposeful life of the church. He did not see charismatic gifts as an 'add-on' to the church but as part of its life and a means by which the grace of God could be demonstrated. Or, to put this another way, he realised the importance of harnessing the power of spiritual gifts rather than seeing them as simply an adornment to liturgical patterns. Virgo's strength in depth, then, informed his preaching ministry and made it ring true at each stage of the collective journey; he was no mere theoretical bible teacher expounding Scripture from a fixed pulpit.

The slow start and care in building up New Frontiers allowed personal relationships to become strong and not liable to break under pressure; one of the dangers of a network is that a whole cluster of churches can break off – if there is a fracturing of relationships between the apostolic figure and the leaders of a collection of congregations. Along with the relatively slow build, NFI demonstrated flexibility and non-exclusivity. Unlike Covenant Ministries, which tended to take a hard line with organisations outside itself, NFI was prepared to be adaptable, although there were always non-negotiable values and doctrines within its operation. This made it easier for churches to affiliate to NFI, particularly before the formal setting up of its collective identity had taken place. The overriding purpose of NFI has always been centred on the local church and this makes it attractive to congregational leaders of many kinds. Everything flows out of the local church. There is no denominational structure to join, no denominational officials in offices who hold the real power of the organisation and there is no hidden hierarchy of committees with diverse and competing policies. Stemming from the vision of Terry Virgo and of those he has gathered round him and who have worked with him over many years, there is a commitment to the local church wherever it is situated and through the local church to the world. National and international boundaries are no obstacle to the building of relationships and, more recently, the emphasis upon remembering the poor and on missions has added further impetus to the entire NFI project which, in the light of prophetic direction, is believed by NFI leaders to have worldwide significance (see chapter 18).

In all this the connection between a strong biblical teaching ministry and openness to the charismatic has been crucial. Word and Spirit have worked together. Pentecostal and charismatic trends and waves have been tested against this dual commitment. This is seen in NFI's resistance to the inflated claims made by those who propagate spiritual warfare as the key to worldwide revival. One of the effects of such claims is to degrade human relationships by classifying all kinds of disagreement as arising from spiritual opposition. It becomes impossible to say that two people disagree on an important matter but rather that one of them is right (i.e. the proponent of warfare with territorial spirits) and the other one is subtly controlled by spiritual forces that foster the disagreement. NFI was able to avoid this dangerous and foolish paranoia. By 2005 NFI was working with more than 500 churches worldwide and its essential mission was largely unchanged from what it had been in the 1970s: it had simply become bigger and more influential.

Chapter 5

Barney Coombs and Salt and Light

i. Barney Coombs, the Man

Barney Coombs (born 1937) grew up in a Brethren assembly.[1] His father, Sid, a survivor of World War I, was an elder and outgoing evangelist. All the front windows of their house were pasted with Bible texts and his dad gave out tracts three or four times a week. He took his evangelistic banner to racecourses, carnivals and pickers in the Kent hop fields and was never ashamed of the Gospel, even wearing an outrageous tie bearing the words 'Jesus saves'. At the age of seven Barney gave his life to Christ. When Sid went preaching he would ask his young son to announce a hymn and then later do a Bible reading and sing a solo or lead in prayer. In this way Barney became accustomed to standing up in front of a congregation.

On leaving school he joined the police cadets on his way, so he thought, to a career in the Metropolitan police. At that time, 1954, Billy Graham came to the Haringey arena where he preached night after night and brought the elements of religious revival to London. Coombs was struck by the way the young Billy Graham faced down his detractors and spoke authoritatively about Christ in the public sphere. Emboldened, Coombs spoke to nine other police cadets and these made a commitment to Christ.

Despite his Brethren background, Coombs on one occasion attended a Pentecostal Church in Slough where he appreciated the Spirit-filled atmosphere in what was to become a large and thriving church. In 1958 Barney married Jeanette and a young family was soon on the way. In 1965 he attended a conference at Herne Bay Court organised by David Lillie and Arthur Wallis on the Apostolic Commission and among the speakers was Willie Burton.[2] Later that year Barney was baptised in the Holy Spirit while kneeling down in prayer on his own and shortly afterwards noticed that his own preaching had become more authoritative. Later that year, having just come off duty, he read words of Isaiah 52 saying, 'Depart, depart...' and felt immediately God was calling him out of secular employment. He spoke to his pastor and explained that he was going to leave the police force and go into full-time ministry. Despite discouragement, he pressed ahead and attended Capernwray Bible School in the North of England and then moved

---

[1] Much of the information in this section is taken from B. Whitchurch, *The Journey*, (Oxford, Salt and Light, 2002).
[2] A. Wallis, 'Springs of Restoration 2', *Restoration*, (September/October, 1980), p.7.

to Basingstoke where, in 1966, he was asked to look after the town's Baptist Church until they found a minister. The previous pastor, Mike Pusey, had begun to usher in change and Coombs struggled to maintain harmony between factions within the congregation. Yet, with a few months, he was successful enough to be asked to stay on permanently.

Basingstoke had been a typical Hampshire market town. It had its own market square and the local farmers brought produce from the surrounding villages to sell. By the 1960s this pattern began to falter. Post-war local government planning saw the town as ripe for expansion, especially as rail links to London were rapid.[3] A ring road system was built, new housing went up and industrial estates containing business premises were quickly erected. The population soared (from 68,000 in 1961 to 104,000 in 1971) and the Baptist Church benefited from the growth and prosperity that these changes brought.[4] The old main street of the town now led to a large shopping complex, a multi-storey car park and a walkway to the railway station. Visitors could get off the train and go shopping or, conversely, residents could commute to London. The complicated ring roads produced estates each of which was self-contained with primary schools, a secondary school, land for churches, a pub and a mixture of private and public housing. Strategic thinking had gone into the planning of the town and that thinking was later to underwrite the strategic thinking of the church that Coombs was leading.

Christians from other denominations began to notice Basingstoke Baptist Church.[5] Bible studies and special events attracted visitors. The interior of the church building had to be altered to make way for the growing congregation. Charismatic gifts began to be exercised and the old-style Baptists who objected to what was going on found themselves marginalised. Coombs later wrote:

---

[3] The 1952 government Bill affected 32 towns round London, including Basingstoke, Swindon and Aylesbury. <http://www.crawley-online.eurobell.co.uk/inquiry/chapter two.html> (accessed 20 November, 2005).

[4] The population of Basingstoke and surrounding area reached 150,000 by 2001, <http://www.statistics.gov.uk/census2001/pyramids/pages/24ub.asp> (accessed 20 November, 2005). At the 1951 Census, the population of the area now covered by the Borough of Basingstoke and Deane was approximately 53,000, of whom about 17,000 lived in the town of Basingstoke. By 1961 these figures had increased to 68,000 and 26,000 respectively; by 1971 they had reached 104,000 and 53,000; by 1981 they had reached 131,000 and 75,000. Personal communication from Basingstoke and Deane Borough Council.

[5] In B. Coombs, *Snakes and Ladders*, (Tonbridge, Sovereign World, 1995), p16, Barney tells of how during this period he was invited to speak at international conferences in India, Kenya, Nepal, New Zealand, Canada, Japan, Eastern Europe and Nigeria. His reputation and that of his church was growing.

I first met Bryn [Jones] in 1967…from the moment we met, Bryn was always a great encouragement to me…a source of great strength…I well remember him confronting me to 'come out' and accept that God had deposited in me the grace to function as an apostle. In those days to admit to being an apostle was viewed as being proud, presumptious and arrogant.[6]

At about this time Combs came to know Arthur Wallis and Willie Burton, both of whom had had Brethren backgrounds and both of whom had little time for small-minded traditions. Elders were introduced into the government of the church and there was talk of new wine requiring new wine skins. At a church meeting convened along traditional Baptist lines the congregation voted out democracy so as to give Coombs significant freedom to restructure the church in any way he saw fit. Willie Burton, then 84 years old, came to preach to a packed congregation in the Baptist building to a congregation made up of most of the Christians in the town. He was a man who was unquestionably an apostle according to biblical criteria: he had planted churches by the score, evangelised a huge area of the Congo, seen miracles and yet, without bombast or hype, carried true authority. Who could argue against the 2,000 churches in the Congo that he had founded since 1915? He preached for two hours one evening while the congregation sat entranced by the stories and adventures he recounted.[7]

ii. The Basingstoke Community Churches

Other restorationist preachers followed – Gerald Coates, Campbell McAlpine, Jean Darnell – challenging evangelical, Baptist or Pentecostal expectations. Words of knowledge were given before healing prayer and on one occasion Jean Darnell stirred the whole congregation to prophesy. Meanwhile outreach activities continued. The youth group under Tony Gray grew, the town hall was hired for evangelism - admittedly by the Pentecostals - and great numbers of Christians took part and Barney (as he was always known) became a familiar and respected figure all over the town. In 1970 Peter Lyne from Bristol prophesied that the Basingstoke church would be an 'Antioch', by which he meant that the Basingstoke church would emulate the missionary-mindedness of the church in Antioch described in the Book of Acts.[8] This prophecy provided a sense of direction for the burgeoning congregation and behind the scenes Barney was working out a theology that saw the purpose of the church as being to advance the kingdom of God in the world. He accepted the discipleship teachings that

---

[6] Barnie Coombs, *A Tribute to Bryn Jones*, privately published (undated, presumed post-mortem) 2004.

[7] I was there.

[8] Coombs, *Apostles Today*, (1996), p.176.

began to circulate in charismatic circles in the 1970s but his own particular emphasis was upon spiritual fatherhood, mentoring and relationships. If one word was to summarise the Basingstoke church it was 'relationships' and it was a word that was set against 'office', 'committee' or 'denomination'. Quite quickly the Basingstoke Baptist Church left the Baptist Union and transformed itself into the Basingstoke Community Churches (BCC).[9] There was a subtle balance between the open welcoming nature of the new church and the non-negotiable authority of its leadership. Tony Gray once spoke of this balance as being found in the person of Christ, in a blend of compassion and authority that was distinctive of Christianity; Barney himself would speak of Christ as being 'full of grace and truth' and not simply full of grace, which would have been 'soft', or full of truth, which would have been uncompromisingly hard.

The 1974 musical, Come Together, was sung in Basingstoke and brought the church to the notice of charismatics well beyond the town. The appointment of elders a few years before had shifted the concept of ministry within the church from the traditional 'one man band' to a more collective expression. Even so it was impossible for the five men (Barney and four elders) to look after 300 people effectively. So, under the direction of the collective leadership, some members of the church began to meet together locally during the week and, at these meetings, the typical politenesses of church life were stripped away to allow more authentic relationships to emerge. Then, in the autumn of 1974, the customary Baptist mid-week meeting was abolished and further local groups were established, making a total of 12. Each of these groups was situated in precisely defined areas within Basingstoke, a relatively easy job since the town itself was divided into housing estates by the ring road. These 12 groups were responsible to a leader and the leader was responsible to one of the full-time elders. The leaders lived within the areas for which they had responsibility and the meetings took various forms: sometimes worship and prayer, discussion, relaxation, meals, breaking bread, evenings of games, a slide show or practical evenings of decorating. By this means members began to relate to each other seven days a week in the sharing of personal problems and family needs.[10]

Every Sunday morning the local leaders and the full-time central leadership met together to pray and share their concerns. Policies and strategies were worked out and, on major issues, the deacons were also involved. These deacons were appointed to the local groups so that each one had their own. By this means embryonic congregations were being brought into being, though each was linked to the others through the body

---

[9] The Basingstoke Community Church left the Baptist Union in 1977.

[10] Barnie Coombs, 'It All Fits Together', *Restoration*, (March/April, 1975), pp.18, 19.

of leaders or elders. It was this pattern that eventually became the characteristic Community Church structure.

Once a month the local groups came together for an All Saints night in one of the local churches and up to 500 people could gather at any one time. One night in the same week as the All Saints gatherings, the local church leaders met together, usually for a meal, and to be served by the young people of the Community Church. There might be 30 or 60 people at these meals and the leaders of other churches could not fail to be impressed by the resources and the style of their hosts. After the meal there was usually a speaker, sometimes Barney himself, who talked about future plans and dreams or shared recent theological insights. Barney was impressed by the discipleship message coming out of South America and began to broach the subject of covenant relationships with the other ministers. Barney's own theology of the church was implicit in what he was organising. He believed that the church existed at three levels: the universal, the church in the city or town and the church in the home. There was no other biblical variant. Consequently the jumble of denominational expressions appeared to him to be so much junk thrown up by the imperfect realisations of church history. It is not clear whether he made any serious attempt to join all the churches in the town together in a grand unity independent of their denominations, although that idea was certainly floated.

The All Saints nights mainly received ministry from restorationist sources. Terry Virgo was one such speaker, as was Arthur Wallis. From very early on Barney saw himself as a leader to whom people would join themselves. He was the young King David assembling an army around himself. Vic Gledhill, a onetime missionary in Nepal, became loyal to Barney, as did Ron Trudinger, an Australian who had spent time as a missionary among Australian aborigines. These men came with proven ministerial gifts and an ability to see the worldwide dimensions of the church. For this reason they were not going to be deflected from the larger purposes intuited by Barney. Vic had had experience of Operation Mobilisation whose teaching on discipleship and living by faith produced mental toughness coupled with a commitment to teamwork. Although the All Saints nights continued, in 1975 Bryn Jones and Arthur Wallis, at Barney's invitation, went to the church in Basingstoke to review its structure and function. This was understood to be an apostolic audit, a check-up on the spiritual health of the whole enterprise. Both Wallis and Jones were by this time persuaded of the inevitability of free-standing restorationism. They were not inclined to compromise their principles to achieve inter-denominational sweetness and light, and it is after the mid-1970s that the Community Church began to question the value of trying to work with all the ministers in the town. There were fewer meetings to which other Christians were invited and the BCC, after engaging in ministry trips to the still persecuted churches in Eastern Europe, made a surprising decision when, in 1976, Coombs felt a call to relocate to Vancouver, Canada, and work with a congregation there.

By then the Basingstoke Community Churches had firmly established their house groups and their six congregations. The apostolic work had been largely done. Vic Gledhill took over from Coombs and the openness of the early 1970s was replaced by a more austere face. A little later Vic left Basingstoke for Vancouver and Ron Trudinger followed to Winnipeg to lead a church there.[11] Faithful men like Tony Gray and Bruce Blow were left in charge and the church continued to grow so that by 1982 there were 500 to 600 committed believers in attendance, easily the largest Christian unit in the town.[12] A little later Dave Richards took over the oversight of the expanding network.[13] In 1976 a small number of churches in the Oxford area, at Witney and Kidlington, began to relate to the leadership of the Basingstoke church and the foundations were gradually laid for what became the Oxford Community Churches, which eventually had a structure and pattern very similar to the one established in Basingstoke (see below). Multiple congregations within a relatively close geographical range were able to share resources and support a joint leadership that coordinated the congregations without removing sensitivity to the needs of local areas. There now began to be quite clearly discernible levels of leadership. There were house group leaders, there were congregational leaders, there were elders who led groups of congregations and then, above these, were trans-local leaders who were apostolic or prophetic in function.

iii. The Kings' School

In 1981 the Basingstoke Community Churches opened their own school and named it The King's School. This was an indication of the numerical and financial strength of the church as well as of its kingdom theology. Actually there were several strands of reasoning at work. The church leaders believed, on the basis of Scripture, that the education of children is primarily the responsibility of parents – and in this they concurred with Roman Catholics – who may or may not choose to discharge this responsibility by making use of tax-funded institutions. In this instance there was no catalysing crisis among the children of the church especially because, as it happened, many of the schools in the town were staffed by committed Christians, a good proportion of whom actually attended the Community Church. There were active Christian Unions in most of the secondary schools in the town and yet, in the aftermath of huge national

---

[11] He subsequently returned to Australia for a couple of years.

[12] Basingstoke Community Church, *Restoration*, (January/February, 1982), p.34.

[13] Dave Richards was also known as the man who wrote the song 'For I'm building a people of power'.

educational reorganisation that had led to the formation of vast comprehensive schools with as many as 1800 pupils, parents of the town were concerned about indiscipline and falling standards.[14] In the 1960s small schools had invariably opened the day with a 'school assembly' which was in essence a miniature Christian service but, by the late 1970s when schools had swollen to proportions that had never been seen before in Britain, it was impossible to assemble all the pupils in a hall or gymn at the same time. School assembly became an entirely secular affair and religious education was also beginning to become multi-faith rather than distinctly Christian. Disquiet at these developments may have contributed to the decision to open a new Christian school but it may also have been connected with theological reasoning that argued for the Christianisation of culture as an adjunct or preparation to the coming kingdom of Christ.

The King's School made use of the original Baptist building and bought in Accelerated Christian Education (ACE) materials. Every child among the 70 or so enrolled could work through the materials at his or her own pace in an open cubicle and call on teachers for help. Although there was class teaching, much of the work was individualised, and had to be, because the age range of the pupils was wider than would normally be found in a school dividing pupils by year groups. School assemblies were held and the children were encouraged to worship in a meaningful way using the same songs and format as they were accustomed to during Sunday worship. Charismatic gifts could be exercised by children and the linkage between home and school was such that no parent felt uninformed and no child could get away with laziness. The younger children were catered for easily but science, language teaching and games presented a challenge to the organisers. They drew upon the goodwill and expertise within the congregation and, when the pupils left the King School to attend the recently founded Sixth Form College, most of them performed well academically.[15]

iv. The Development of Salt and Light

Coombs's work in Vancouver took place in a church that had grown rapidly through the years of the Jesus Revolution in the late 1960s and early 1970s. Coombs's theology of discipleship did not go down well with many of these ex-hippie believers and, in two years, 365 people left the church. Coombs admitted that he learnt a lesson in humility during this period.

---

[14] Circular 10/65 i.e. the tenth circular from the government in the year 1965 asked local education authorities to draw up plans for comprehensivisation. By the early 1970s these plans were being enacted.

[15] By 2004, the school had grown to 170 pupils aged seven to sixteen years and has an advantageous teacher/pupil ratio.

Weird stories circulated the city about what I was doing, yet no one ever came to ask me whether the stories happened to be true; all of which only served to further feed my ungodly self-righteousness. We were increasingly shunned by other leaders and churches in our region. It was heartbreaking and a constant uphill struggle to keep the sweet forgiving spirit.... after reading Proverbs 18.23 ['the poor man utters supplications, but the rich man answers roughly'] suddenly my eyes were opened; the light flooded in. I could see it all so clearly. I had come to Vancouver as a rich man and handled people roughly. People who were not walking righteously had been handed the letter of the law without the spirit of tenderness or compassion of Jesus... pride is a horrible, ugly thing.[16]

One of the influences upon him was Bob Mumford who was part of the Fort Lauderdale Five that, in 1977, convened a charismatic conference in Kansas City that gathered 50,000 people. The Fort Lauderdale Five issued their magazine, *New Wine*, that circulated widely across the world in charismatic circles and carried with it a teaching on discipleship, submission, spiritual gifts and even, at one stage, floated the idea of reconstructionism, the notion that a modern political party could be formed using elements of Old Testament jurisprudence. Coombs acknowledged the Fort Lauderdale Five offered an extreme answer to an extreme situation: the church in North America was highly individualistic and the Five wanted to replace individualism by discipled, servant-hearted Christians in tight structures. Coombs admitted 'we were infected by that' though 'we largely escaped the worst repercussions' of the controversies that arose.[17]

Coombs's work in Canada also stretched to Winnipeg where he was asked to help a struggling church, to Vernon in 1980 and later to a fellowship in Niagara Falls. Eventually the Vancouver church became West Coast Christian Fellowship in 1984. By 2005 there were 12 Salt and Light congregations in Canada, at least one of them with a Christian school and often carrying the word 'community' in their name. Equally, there was progress in the United States as, in 1987, a Mennonite congregation in Indiana was renewed by the Holy Spirit and joined the Salt and Light family. To some of the North American congregations Barney brought Vic Gledhill, whom he had put in charge in Basingstoke in 1976, and other reliable leaders from Basingstoke also followed. To build up the network in the way he wanted, Barney continued to need people he could rely on absolutely, and who shared his own concern to extend a relational church. There was never any expectation that the grouping would become a denomination and the language used to describe what was happening was connected with 'family'. The family grew in size, love and diversity and yet

---

[16] Coombs, *Apostles,* (1995), pp.17, 19.
[17] Whitchurch, *The Journey,* (2002), p.29.

the churches all shared the same 'genes', the same ethos and structural characteristics. By 2005 there were 16 churches in United States.

By 1982 Barney was confident enough to set up the Salt and Light Trust and this gave legal identity to the work in the UK.[18] In 1983 Barney was moved by orphans who had been bereaved of their parents by Idi Amin's despicable and brutal regime in Uganda. When the children were assembled into a choir that toured North America, the West Coast Fellowship responded and within a few months Barney was teaching in Kampala at a conference for pastors. There he formed strong relationships with some of them. In 1987 he set up Church Relief International as an agency of charitable help. Later, through Dr Ian Clarke, this led to construction of a new hospital in Uganda dedicated to the memory of Barbara Kelly, the wife of Ian Clarke's pastor. Barbara's sudden death triggered a wave of compassion in the Salt and Light churches in the UK and they took up an offering that helped to buy the plot and pay for the hospital in several acres of open land. Over the years the Oxford Community Churches, inspired by Dr Jan White, one of their members, set up a medical centre in Kampala and then, later, other clinics and then, in 2001, a hospice for terminally ill cancer and AIDS patients. Again money and personnel flowed through the relational bonds from one part of the Salt and Light network to needs in other parts.

Coombs found himself travelling from country to country looking after the growing network. There were connections in Zimbabwe, Kenya and India. The church in Africa is diverse and extensive with the result that churches of different types are affiliated to Salt and Light: it is by no means a network of clones. The church in India had been Bombay Baptist Church but, after being inspired by Salt and Light, planted out congregations across the city and ministered into six different language groups with a training programme in three of them. The setting up of Salt and Light ministries in Canada and the UK provided a legal and financial basis for the travelling ministry that took up so much of Coombs's time. Trustees were appointed in both countries and the purpose of the trust was 'to promote the advancement of the Christian religion and the advancement of education and relief of poverty'. Administrative tasks could be funded out of the legal entity but a bureaucratic centralised structure could be avoided. Having been based in Canada for nine years, Barney returned to the UK and lived in the Oxford area for a while after 1985.

In the early 1980s four Salt and Light leaders were brought together as the 'UK and Northern Ireland Council' and this group subsequently became

---

[18] Salt and Light Ministries was registered as a charity in Septemberember 1998. According to the Charity Commission website, Salt and Light Ministries has three working names: King's Bible College and Training Centre, Church Relief International and Euro Net. Donations to charities can be exempted from tax.

the 'Senior Council'. By the mid-1990s there was a realisation that the term 'council' not only gave the wrong impression but also gave an impression of a static organisation. So the Council was reformed into a 'team' that met three times a year in different Salt and Light locations where its members ministered to the churches, stayed in local homes and grounded their impressions of the work in close human relationships. Barney was the chair of the team until 1998 when aged 62, at a conference in Harrogate, he installed Steve Thomas as the leader of what now became 'The European Apostolic Team'.

Organisational development continued with the appointment of a North American Council under the chairmanship of Ron MacLean since 1996 and, subsequently, an International Apostolic and Prophetic Council that meets annually in different parts of the world. In 1996 Salt and Light ministries added publishing to their portfolio and by this means theological issues have been expounded in a series of booklets. The largest teaching operation within the whole network, however, has been the setting up of King's Bible College which was first launched in Canada in 1983 with about 30 students. After four years it moved to West Herts Community Church in Harpenden in the UK and then to the Borders district of Scotland where it stayed from 1991 until the year 2000. Barney's own home was next to the college both when it was at Harpenden and when it was in Scotland. After a break of a year the college came to Oxford and opened again in 2001. There, in the context of the close matrix of congregations that form the Oxford Community Churches, the college is able to service training needs of the entire network, including those felt by churches in North America.

Meanwhile, there are links between Salt and Light and the other prospering apostolic networks in the UK, especially in their shared desire to reach out into Europe and in their general willingness to let prophecy guide the strategic thinking of trans-local apostolic leaders. Terry Virgo has spoken at weekend camps (e.g. in 1995) and Salt and Light used the Stoneleigh location in 1996.

v. The Oxford Community Churches

The origin of the churches goes back at least to 1974. Steve Thomas, an Oxford graduate, was inducted as the Baptist pastor of Cote and, in about 1979, started to link up with Barney Coombs. Although a Baptist, Thomas did not find within the Baptist Union the apostolic support that he was looking for but, with Barney Coombs and others like Bob Mumford, he did. Praying together with Barney and these others, he began to feel divinely directed to cooperate with like-minded churches because they could achieve more together than separately. In 1978 the Cote congregation agreed to work with the congregation at Witney and in 1981 they made church plants to the south in Wantage and to the north in Chipping Norton. In the same year a group in Kidlington joined the matrix. The big step occurred when, from Witney, Cote and Kidlington, a church was planted in 1985 into Oxford itself. A powerful prophecy had been brought at a meeting in Kidlington asking, 'how can a city come out of a village?' The rhetorical question implied that with God's help the apparently impossible could be done. Oxford was and still is not only a traditionally Anglican city but also one that, because of its large international student population, is highly sophisticated and likely to be imbued with secular values.[19] The church plant in Oxford was achieved by first relocating key people from their villages into the city and, for a while, the new congregation hired and met in the cinema in George Street near to the centre. Out of Oxford came Abingdon and Bicester plants in 1992 and, in 2001, a fresh congregation was placed at Blackbird Leys, a large and reputedly rough housing estate in the south Oxford area. Since the Witney congregation had grown sufficiently to allow it to split into two parts, there were in just under 30 years 10 linked congregations that formed the Oxford Community Churches.

Steve Thomas had been released into a wider ministry in 1982 and was able to give drive and direction to church planting but, in addition to this, the cooperating churches were registered as a single charity under the then-existing charity law. This allowed the churches to pool their resources and pay their ministers out of a central fund. All the 10 churches gave part of their income into the central fund and all the ministers were paid out of it. If a minister needed to move from one place to another, he or she was not dependent upon the financial support of individual congregations: the community of congregations provided finance for a strategic deployment of resources. Or looking at this in a simpler way, the larger congregations subsidised the smaller ones. In addition to the 10 established congregations church planting is currently taking place in Carterton, Thame, Banbury and Swindon and there is a determination to move into a second cycle of church planting equalling the pioneering activities of the 1980s. By 2005, the community supported a total of 24 ministries (congregational leaders, children's and schools' workers, evangelists) of various kinds.

The churches' permanent building in Oxford is on a commercial estate and contains offices, a gymnasium, a canteen, space for the Bible School, several smaller meeting rooms and a thousand-seater auditorium. The churches in the villages and towns round Oxford can come in to the central church for worship at regular but not weekly intervals. This unites the separate congregations and enables a collective vision to be imparted. As a whole the churches have seven priorities: to bring people to Jesus; to make

---

[19] On the Anglicanism of Oxford see, for instance, R. Jenkins, *Gladstone*, (Basingstoke, Papermac, 1995), p.325, 326.

disciples; to multiply small groups or cells; to plant churches; to live in the power of the Holy Spirit; to redeem society and education; and to go to the nations across the world in church planting, aid and development. The underlying initial vision was shaped by a desire to reach across Oxfordshire, and the planting of churches has been achieved with an eye to the systematic coverage of the land within the county boundaries, the city of Oxford being more or less in the exact middle. More recently a tested prophetic pronouncement has added a second vision: the churches should share what they have with Europe where evangelical and charismatic Christianity is far weaker than it is in Britain.

The investment made by the community churches into education is demonstrated by the tenacity with which the King's School has been supported and developed.[20] The school has grown gradually out of early financial and practical difficulties – and with reason since the creation of an entirely new educational establishment is a massive undertaking – and now offers both primary and secondary phases. The primary phase covers children from the ages of five to 11 and a senior school from the ages of 11 to 16. The government league tables demonstrate just how impressive is the educational standard of the school. Some 93% of pupils gained five GCSE/GNVQ passes with the grades between A* and C, a percentage that would comfortably place the King's School within the top 10 schools in the county.[21] The school is independent and receives no financial help from the state. Everything is provided by the fees that parents pay and by a subvention from the central resource of the Oxford Community Churches. Tithing members of the churches pay a discounted fee. The curriculum is strongly influenced by Scripture and opportunities are given to children for the memorisation of biblical texts and the meditation upon them. This should not be taken to indicate that the other subjects normally provided by a secondary school are omitted. In addition to maths, English and science there is music, arts and craft, history, geography, PE, games and computer skills, and all the members of staff are committed Christians. In addition, because of the church's links with several countries outside Britain, pupils have a chance for direct and indirect involvement with Christian schools in Canada, Zambia, Uganda, Rwanda, Burundi, India, Norway, France, Germany and Kazakhstan. The school's rationale is based upon the notion that education is the responsibility of parents rather than of the state and that a good education along Christian lines will lead children to be ambassadors for God all their lives.

---

[20] The story is partly told in S. Baker, and D. Freeman, *The Love of God in the Classroom: the story of the new Christian schools*, (Fearn, Christian Focus, 2005), pp.67-78.

[21] See <http://news.bbc.co.uk/1/shared/bsp/hi/education/03/school_tables/secondary_ schools/html/931.stm, (accessed 16 January, 2006).

In addition to the school the churches offer Stepping Stones, a pre-school facility for the children from two and a half up to about the age of five. In an era when both parents may be in full-time paid employment, childcare facilities are valued by busy professionals and the community churches would like to expand their provision in this field.

A larger aim of the schools and the pre-school facility is to redeem education itself by transforming it from a secular mindset at the beck and call of secular regulatory authorities so that it can transmit godly knowledge and form virtuous character. Such a high aim demonstrates that the churches do not see their task as entirely defensive or protective but rather as being part of theological rationale that culminates in the reign of Christ.

About a hundred students at the university attended the Oxford church on Sundays. Within the university, the students are organised into cells by a married couple belonging to the Oxford congregation with specific responsibility for student care; in this way the students are directly linked to the Oxford congregation and not part of a free-standing parachurch agency. The cell philosophy within higher education is inspired by Fusion (which started in 1997), an offshoot from the new churches. Its website states:

> Fusion estimates that annually, around 8,000 - 12,000 churches send 25,000 – 30,000 Christian men and women to University for 3 or 4 years. The vast majority have not received any training or equipping on what to expect or the difference they could make.
>
> Fusion… is working to create a framework that connects churches and students across the UK. We are working to see churches active in student ministry, more who partner with us in preparing and sending their young people away to University, and a generation of students willing to serve God in their Universities.[22]

Its aim is to:

> To see thousands of Christ centred, active, caring, mission-focused groups springing up all over the nation's campuses – we call them Cells. There are now around 350 Cells in the UK – and with empowerment and support from local churches our prayer is that they will continue to multiply.

The cell principle is all of a piece with the strategy for allowing a radical Christian life to be lived within fast-moving student culture. It emphasises day-to-day discipleship while encouraging contact with down-to-earth church members living their lives outside the artificial world of essays, lectures, parties, libraries and the swirl of sexual relationships.

---

[22]   <http://web.fusion.uk.com/content.php?type=1&id=118&site_id=2>   (accessed   18 January, 2006).

So far as the Oxford Community Churches' attitude to cells are concerned, Steve Thomas says,

> there is no uniformity across the network. Our posture is to encourage what local churches feel they should be doing. A number of churches did go down that road though most have settled back to seeing that you need both - big and small meetings. A number are cell churches. A number have espoused the G12 principles of cell life, but the jury is still out on its effectiveness. Cell churches have brought evangelistic zeal. Only one area of Oxford has G12 cells. The end result of this is growth, but it is not clear whether growth is caused by cell, by being purpose-driven or by simply being an ordinary church. Really it is all to do with faith and vision.[23]

In effect the Oxford Community Churches have seen the cell principle as a method of church building rather than an end in itself. More important is the general direction of the whole Salt and Light enterprise in Britain. Steve Thomas takes up the story.

> About six years ago [2000] we had a very clear prophetic word which said to us 'you people of Salt and Light, go to Europe, it is time to take the values and principles that you have been building by for years and help brothers and sisters to build over there'. The prophecy had three thrusts: go and plant new works, and go and help people who are seeking to do the job there and go and make friends.
>
> So we have much more actively been trying to pursue that amongst ourselves as a team and pointing our churches in that direction too. Because we may think the church is struggling here in this country where 7% of the population or whatever has faith but with more like 0.1% in France it's a different kettle of fish. And even the most lively churches are small, much smaller... and divided among themselves... actually it takes you back 30 years.

Prophetic ministry is crucial to the way that Salt and Light set their course. They do not have constitutional debates and votes where, in a business meeting, 51% of the participants may vote for a proposition and so drag the other 49% kicking and screaming down a new policy path. Prophecies are given, written down or recorded and then pondered and revisited by the leadership who will be able to say, 'yes, this sounds like God'. In this sense prophecies are used in an equivalent way to that carved out by New Frontiers. At the annual conference of leaders and on two other occasions in the year when the senior S and L leaders meet there is an opportunity for prayer and for prophetic words and there is an expectation that the voice of God will be heard.

---

[23] Interview with Steve Thomas, 6 January, 2006.

New Frontiers and Salt and Light are male-led networks. 'As long you understand what we mean by that. Any ministry is open to women apart from eldership. Eldership is the one thing that we see as where the door is closed. Eldership is the main leadership of the church. We're constantly sending out couples. It's to do with how we see husbands and wives and headship and how that works. Everything else is well open to the womenfolk.' Women can minister. They can baptise and there is no professional exclusivity that keeps women at bay. Other networks take an alternative view of the role of women and 'we have huge respect for [them]'. It is not to do with one's view of the authority of Scripture but with how Scripture is interpreted. That is the sticking point.

Looking back over the last 30 years, it is evident that the apostolic networks have settled into mutually supportive relationships. There is friendship across the networks and a willingness, also, to work with conventional denominations. The networks themselves have made enormous progress since the 1970s but have not fulfilled the grandiose plans that Bryn Jones and others preached when the new churches came into being. The friendship among the new leaders ensures that there is crossover ministry and the sharing of ideas, some of which flow into them from the Evangelical constituency of which they are a part. Salt and Light is large enough for debates to occur among its leaders – 'it's not monochrome' – over such matters as postmodernism. 'On the one hand we need 21st century expressions of the Gospel and on the other hand we need positive, faith-filled clarity about what the Gospel is, and some of those discussions are going on at the moment'[24]. Equally, over the last 30 years, the networks have acquired their own historical perspectives. The Toronto blessing came and went and, so far as Salt and Light were concerned, it motivated them to evangelism and re-energised that allegiance to spiritual gifts and spiritual experience, but it did not fundamentally change their nature or their calling.

vi. Reflection

The biggest structural difference between Salt and Light and other apostolic networks probably revolves around the investment that Salt and Light has made in education. The effect of a schooling programme is to insulate the children of the community churches from secular and anti-Christian currents within the mainstream of society. On the evidence available so far this process does not produce an inward-looking movement but one that is stronger and more able to retain its young people. There are certainly financial costs incurred by an educational process but, where faith schooling is broadly supported by government policy, Christian schools of

---

[24] Interview with Steve Thomas, 6 January, 2006.

this kind may be able to draw upon public funding without having to compromise their Christian values and message. The post-1997 Blair government has been supportive of faith schooling of all kinds - Muslim, Sikh, Jewish and Christian – and, within limits, private Christian schools have benefited from this policy.

What is impressive about Salt and Light, as with other successful apostolic networks, is the overall stability of the entire operation. The same people have been working in its churches, sometimes in multiple capacities, for many years. They know each other and their children well. Intermarriage may occur between leading families and there are high levels of trust as well as a willingness to move either from one town to another or from one country to another as the leadership proposes.[25] Apostleship is governmental but not dictatorial.[26] Equally impressive is the pattern of clustered congregations each of which can support the others. This is almost unique to Salt and Light and has enormous practical benefits in terms of the coordination of leadership and the pooling of human and financial resources.

In recent years, the Salt and Light leaders have met together for teaching and prophetic ministry and key sermons and prophecies are now downloadable from the Salt and Light web site. Books and tapes are also available so that what is going on within the churches can be heard and understood by those standing outside the network. The sectarian tendencies in the heyday of the discipleship era in the 1970s have largely been forgotten. The theology of apostleship is no mere add-on to the theology of networks. Coombs is very clear about male and female roles and absolutely emphatic about the priority of the male in respect of leadership roles within the church. This is all spelt out in considerable detail in his book on apostles and is based upon an understanding of the eternal fatherhood of God 'I believe it is impossible to attack patriarchy without involving the Trinity: fatherhood is just that basic'.[27] While Coombs has no quarrel at all with the equality of men and women in the sight of God or in terms of redemption, his argument is that there is a difference in male and female functions within the church just as there is a difference in the functions of the three Persons of the Trinity. The issue transcends culture just as God transcends culture and no doctrine of God should be tailored to conform to the vagaries of contemporary opinion.

---

[25] For instance, families from Basingstoke moved to Milton Keynes with the express purpose of church planting.

[26] 'Neither do the scriptures support the democratic model for church government. The pattern that we see in the pages of a New Testament is one of consultative leadership, where the maximum room is given for discussion, dialogue and input, but the final decision rests with the leadership' (Coombs, *Apostles,* (1996), p.99).

[27] Coombs, *Apostles Today,* (1996), p.163.

All this places the role, character, gifting, authority and functioning of the apostle at the centre of 21st century ecclesiology. The apostle is one who makes the church grow, ensures that its congregational foundations are correct, carries ultimate responsibility for order and discipline, and ensures that every local expression under his care is healthy. This does not prevent apostles being subdivided into several categories including the original Twelve apostles of the Lamb - those chosen by Christ at the beginning of the church age - the 70 sent out by Jesus in Luke 9, equipping apostles spoken of in Ephesians 4, local apostles spoken of in 1 Corinthians 12:28, ethnic apostles sent out to particular groups of people, fathering apostles spoken of, for instance, in Titus 1:4 and serving apostles. Nor does it presume that all apostles must be miracle workers; rather they must demonstrate great patience and long-suffering in the pursuit of their calling. Even so, apostles are expected to outrank local church elders and able to make decisions that supersede whatever plans local elders might have, always bearing in mind that the interaction between local and trans-local authority requires wisdom.[28] And the normal method by which apostles help local churches is by conducting a review using questionnaires, interviews and other forms of information gathering. This review process is not dissimilar to the check-up that might be given by management consultants to a business that is struggling, although it must hastily be said that reviewing is in no other sense parallel to management consultancy.

The apostolic ministry reproduces itself. Barney Coombs met up with Steve Thomas and showed him by example and teaching how to function. Some ten years later, Barney 'released' Steve to a wider ministry. The term 'released' has become a technical one in new church and charismatic circles and it derives from the Greek word used in Acts 13.3 (*apoluo*) where Paul and Barnabas are sent on their way from Antioch for the first missionary journey. The concept is that the new ministry is set free to express itself in a place and a way that breaks out of the confines of the local church where it has up till then been established. By releasing Steve Thomas in this way, the network of churches within the Oxford area could more readily be knitted together and, later, Steve Thomas was in a position to ordain or release other ministries that emerged from the congregations he supervised.

This last factor is important because it shows that the apostolic networks have, against the odds, found a way to solve the problem of charismatic succession. Whereas denominations have long-established mechanisms for transitioning leadership – and this has given them their historic stability – in many cases apostolic networks have not yet been forced to move beyond the founding generation of apostles. Yet, as this narrative account of Barney Coombs' work reveals, there are instances where apostolic leadership *is* handed on, even when the original apostle is still alive and well. This is

---

[28] Coombs, *Apostles,* (1996), p.196.

highly significant and boosts the long-term survival expectations of all kinds of apostolic networks in their original relational form.

Chapter 6

Tony Morton and Cornerstone (c.net)

i. Tony Morton, the Man

Tony Morton, for reasons that will become apparent later, did not give an interview about the story of the Cornerstone network. Morton himself was born in about 1950, became a student at the University of Southampton and stayed on to train as a teacher. By the mid-1970s he was the acknowledged leader of a group of charismatic Christians within the Southampton area and, though he taught for a while, in 1975 he became the leader of a new Community Church in Southampton that was made up of three groups: students from Southampton University, some members of Millbrook Assemblies of God and the West End Evangelical Church. By 1977 the Community Church stood at 170 people but very quickly it grew and after roughly 10 years comprised about 500, a substantial congregation within the British context at that time.[1]

Morton began to relate to Bryn Jones and did so from around 1975 to 1980, at the same time as Terry Virgo and David Tomlinson. To relate to Bryn Jones was to imbibe faith and determination to make the new restorationist movement grow. His was an uncompromising vision to build a new kind of church whether by planting, by amalgamating small groups or by taking large congregations and redesigning them. The matter hinged on the creation of viable and loyal pastoral groups under the submissive leadership of local but not full-time (and therefore not paid) elders. There was a kind of spiritual pragmatism to Bryn Jones's mode of operation and it rubbed off on those who worked with him. According to David Damp's recollections, the expansion of the work in Southampton

> all began around 1980 when Tony Morton was prayed for and set apart as an apostle. The ceremony took place at a convent at Ilkley, West Yorks. A group of us went with Tony, some of us feeling uncertain why we had been invited and wondering what was going to happen. A group of recognised apostles and prophets including Bryn and Keri Jones, Arthur Wallis and David Mansell took charge of the meeting. Tony and Terry

---

[1] See J. Wallis, *Arthur Wallis: Radical Christian*, (Eastbourne, Kingsway, 1991), p.258.

Virgo were prophesied over and prayed for at length, given an apostolic charge and then sent forth to touch the world for Christ.[2]

This apostolic charge was taken straight out of the pages of the New Testament.[3] Those who were charged and sent forth poured their energies into their networks and, strengthened by prophetic encouragement, were prepared to surmount all the ministerial challenges thrown at them by later circumstances. The apostolic charge was personally significant as well as spiritually empowering and it is in the light of this commission that the next few years of Morton's ministerial career should be seen.

ii. Cornerstone

The apostolic team was rapidly set up and comprised four men: Tony Morton (young, charismatic and energetic), Arthur Wallis (the elder statesman who had been working in the north of England with Bryn Jones[4]) Peter Light (who had an administrative gifts, though he subsequently developed preaching gifts and a passion for Asia) and David Damp (who brought with him local knowledge and support). The team spent a lot of time in prayer, often going on 2-3 day retreats. They felt that the Lord wanted Cornerstone to be unique, not following the pattern of other national teams and streams though the presence of Arthur Wallis, when he moved down in 1982, was of huge significance since his insight and stature made him acceptable to all the other apostolic teams as well as to many denominations. The combination of gifts and ministries that the team represented made it easy for Southampton to be distinctive and, from the beginning, the approach adopted seems to have been less 'heavy' than Bryn's.

The minutes of the meetings of the early days from May 1982 give vivid insights into the first days of the new network. From the start there was a successful Bible Week in the summer modelled on the pattern of the Dales and the Downs. The New Forest Bible Week offered evening celebrations and daytime seminars and functioned with a turnover of £35,000 and offerings that averaged about £1,000 per night. Given that a schoolteacher

---

[2] David Damp (b 1929) became one of the team who worked with Tony Morton after 1982. Beginning as a charismatic leader in Gosport, David linked his congregation to Cornerstone and moved to Southampton in 1983. He retired from active team participation in 1997. David's written recollections were given to me on 11 January, 2006.

[3] 1 Timothy 1.18, 1 Timothy 4.14.

[4] Arthur Wallis had been in touch with the West End congregation when numbers of them had been baptised in the Holy Spirit at the Lakes Bible Week in 1975 (Wallis, *Radical Christian*, (1991), p.257). So Wallis had natural Southampton links.

might then expect to earn about £9,000 per year, the sums were healthy and indicative of good attendance and generous giving.

The financial arrangements of the network were based upon the proposition that churches should be 'encouraged to at least tithe from tithes into Cornerstone, and when a project or overseas ministry is imminent to consider raising an offering at celebration meetings'.[5] Cornerstone was the overarching organisational structure or network that held participating churches together and there were soon about a dozen of these. The Community Church in Southampton was the largest and gave £3,000 per month to Cornerstone but other support came from Gosport, Fareham, Teddington, Southfields, the Isle of Wight, Portsmouth, Andover, Romsey and Winchester to the extent that Cornerstone's monthly income was about £4,250, giving an annual income of about £51,000. Out of this Tony Morton and Arthur Wallis were paid at the same level as the city elders, a salary roughly equal to that of a head of department in a secondary school. Their salary was neither princely nor mean but it was more generous than what would have been given to many nonconformist pastors. There was certainly money to spare because Cornerstone rapidly invested in video and other equipment that was then relatively more expensive than it later became.

There was enough money in the budget to cover the cost of a magazine, *Life-Link*, with a print run of 35,000 for distribution to all the related churches. Additionally, the budget covered travel in response to a plethora of invitations. Cornerstone rapidly established its own identity within the area and offered not only leaders' days but also short-term conferences and a Foundations for Ministry training programme that attracted 16 students of various kinds in a hired building.

Morton made weekly visits to London with the aim of drawing in congregations in East Acton, Southfields and Teddington as well as Hounslow, Staines and Richmond. It was in London that he found himself working in a district that was so close to David Mansell that one Baptist Church found itself uncertain about whether to join with Cornerstone or David Mansell. This possible confrontation between two apostles over churches within sectors claimed by both was an unexpected source of possible disharmony that was quickly resolved, but it showed the potential for rivalrous clashes. Yet, in other Baptist churches, other ministers were spotted as being in need of revitalising and, if the Baptist pastor voluntarily stood down, as happened on at least one occasion, the network was ready to pick up the pieces. In one place a member of the Cornerstone team went into a church to give it a three-day checkout with Morton being invited in for the final day. This kind of spiritual auditing was believed to be an

---

[5] Minutes of Team Meeting in May 1982. The tithe of tithes rapidly became 'a contribution' i.e. an unspecified proportion.

essential function of apostolic ministry and any church which had been audited and which appreciated the advice and ministry that had been apostolically given, might well agree to commit itself to the apostle's network.[6]

In essence what was happening was that the growing Community Church in Southampton and the surplus generated by the Bible week – and later the two Bible weeks – was funding the Cornerstone ministry that was able to spread out in all directions. At first there was a concentration upon the home base or the immediate geographical area around Southampton which, because it was on the coast, could only spread north or west or east but, to the east lay the heart of the Coastlands network under Terry Virgo, and there was no call to spread in this direction with any vigour. As a result Cornerstone found itself expanding northwards and westwards, apart from working on the Isle of Wight, which was a short ferry ride away across the Solent. The southern part of Hampshire contains well established and well-heeled villages and towns that had been reached by the charismatic movement in the 1960s.

The ministry quickly began to work in Bridgwater, Yate, Havant, Isle of Wight, Andover, Winchester, Lymington, Fareham and Fulwell and, because of Tony Morton's visits to London, began to establish relationships with East Acton and other London congregations, some of whom were Baptist. The Baptists who had become unhappy with the Baptist Union because of its apparently anti-charismatic stance, found the New Churches far more attractive than Pentecostal denominations. As a result of rapid linkages, Cornerstone soon possessed a strong home base that funded the more extensive international ministry. Contacts with Nepal were no mere flash in the pan but were consolidated and, over the years, training, finance and ministry were given to the kingdom that, until tragedy struck, was one of the most open of those bordering northern India.[7] Even after political turbulence began at the turn of the millennium, however, c.net (as Cornerstone came to be called) continued its ministry there.

In February 1983 there was involvement – either continuing or new - with groups in Reading, Kidlington, Petersfield, Romsey, Totton, Taunton, Hayling Island and Teddington. Not all these congregations eventually ended up within the Cornerstone orbit (for instance Kidlington in Oxfordshire was drawn into the Salt and Light network). Where congregations were weak or badly led, Cornerstone offered a Foundation for Ministry course with the aim of enabling 'men and women who are clear on the call of God on their lives and want to take effective positions of leadership either full-time or with a secular job within one year of

---

[6] This is evident from the Team Meeting minutes, May 1982.
[7] King Birendra was killed by his son on 1 June, 2000.

completion of the course'.[8] Even without training, there might be elders in waiting within the groups and it became a mark of the maturity of the congregation that elders could be 'set' within them so that, by April 1983, the minutes record the 'recognition and setting in of elders would have to be done soon'. This was a formal process and recorded in the Cornerstone magazine on a full double page spread with photographs of the elders. By this means the local network was well and truly established. Not only might these churches run along lines broadly directed by Cornerstone but there would continue to be a financial flow from them to the Cornerstone umbrella. In December 1983 the minutes record that Fareham, Teddington, Gosport, Winchester and Portsmouth were all giving regular amounts to the central resource.

On their side, Cornerstone provided full-time leaders' seminars, a discipleship course, evangelistic outreach, a *Life-Link* magazine, young people's weekends, a full-time leaders' day and a wider leaders' day. Cornerstone provided what the small churches needed and gave them the opportunity to participate in much bigger events that they were incapable of mounting themselves. The New Forest Bible week and the South and West Bible week were both running by 1983 and a considerable amount of time was taken by the Cornerstone administrative staff in planning and in analysing each year's events so as to make improvements the following year. The Bible weeks demanded advertising, booking facilities, seminar speakers, a proper site, a copying machine to allow audiotapes of the meeting to be reproduced and sold, children's activities and a proper handling of deposits, stewarding, musicians, and the like.

While the administrative staff at Cornerstone dealt with the infrastructure of the Bible weeks, Tony Morton and Arthur Wallis travelled widely. By December 1983 Morton was to take a three-month sabbatical for preaching, travelling and writing and expected to visit the United States, Hong Kong and Spain (he was fluent in Spanish). Arthur Wallis anticipated going to China and South Africa and, indeed, did so and later wrote a book about the church in China that was one of the first to bring popular Christian attention to the details of spiritual renewal in that vast, populous and totalitarian state.[9] The finances continued to be healthy and a planting begun in France was sustained, though more on an inter-team basis, than purely under the aegis of Cornerstone: Terry Virgo and others joined and Cornerstone hired a flat in northern France to provide accommodation for an evangelistic group.

By 1984 prayer warfare seminars were being organised at Southampton, Taunton, Plymouth, Bristol, Torbay, Bournemouth, Portsmouth and on the Isle of Wight and feedback from the seminars was encouraged. Cornerstone

---

[8] Minutes of Cornerstone Team Meeting, 24 January, 1983
[9] A. Wallis, *China Miracle*, (Eastbourne, Kingsway, 1985).

itself was established as a charity to which covenant giving was possible and this enabled tax to be reclaimed on the money given, thereby raising its value by about 20%. By now a church in Hong Kong was tithing to Cornerstone and, later that year, the training of elders was formalised with a training course which had already been used by Coastlands (later to become New Frontiers). But in 1984, also, David Tomlinson's departure from Bryn Jones's circle was noted and the first tremors of a realignment among the networks were felt. Cornerstone, though, remained loyal to Bryn Jones and the magazine that he had launched, *Restoration*, which, despite its high quality and attractive articles, found itself likely to yield a deficit of nearly £12,000 for that year alone. Cornerstone agreed in September 1984 to take responsibility for underwriting the magazine to the tune of £3,000 per year, an amount equal to that provided by Bryn Jones's group and by Coastlands, even though both these groups were larger than Cornerstone. Cornerstone were able to publish and advertise in *Restoration* and to sell it within the churches but the high cost of subventing the magazine was registered (negatively?) at the leadership meetings. By now there were four people on the administrative staff and, from time to time, the account dipped into the red. This did not deter Morton from pressing on, particularly as the tax rebate generated by covenanted giving would cover the shortfall.

He wrote to the churches laying out the need for money for a series of projects: £3,000 for *Cornerstone News*; £3,000 for *Restoration*; £6,000 for the general fund; £35,000 for the evangelism fund; and £20,000 for a European base. Pioneering in London continued with Streatham, East Acton, Kingston and Weybridge. In Dorset there were churches at Wimbourne, Ringwood, the New Forest, Salisbury and Lymington. In Somerset there was a group at Minehead, Barnstaple, Bridgwater. In Hampshire there was a group at Fareham/Locks Heath while, abroad, there were connections with Germany, Colombia and, still, with Nepal. In 1984 the in-house magazine *Cornerstone* gave over its central pages to the photographs of ministry team so that everyone could see who they were and what they did. Later in the same issue there was also reference to the Community Church's primary school, King's School, an indication of how firmly rooted and substantial the congregation had become.[10]

In 1985 £3,500 was put aside for a school in Nepal while the evangelism team reported expenses of £1,200 a month. There were six people led by Billy Kennedy (who later became team leader of the Community Church in Southampton) and they worked especially in the summer months putting on evangelistic events. By March funds were coming in from all the expected 15 churches while evangelism was being vigorously pressed in six local areas. An international Bible week was planned the following year and reference was made to the appointment of elders in Southampton,

---

[10] The school began in September, 1982.

Winchester, East Acton, Salisbury, Jersey, Bridgwater, Fareham and Locks Heath. On the international scene there were visits to Spain, West Germany, Zimbabwe, Hong Kong and France.

Unexpectedly at the end of 1988 Arthur Wallis died. He had been active in preaching and, with hindsight, can be seen to have provided stability, a passion for prayer and what might have looked like an old fashioned concern for the minutiae of Scriptural exposition. During the six years that he had been with Cornerstone, he had been a regular and welcome speaker at all the main Bible events – though he took his share of teaching small groups as well. His absences abroad had never been for prolonged periods and his concern for integrity was noted and celebrated by Morton in a long tribute,

> Arthur's prophetic teaching brought an awareness and expectation to many thousands all around the world. His grasp of the Scripture plus his devotion to the Lord made him a popular speaker.... he made a platform for apostolic teaching to come forth... he was a man sent from God to envision the church, to challenge men's views on the end times, the nature of the church, spiritual gifts, ministries in the church, prayer, personal security in Christ... for many of us it seems hard to imagine the coming days without Arthur's wise and prayerful support...
>
> While filled with kindness and consideration he was always one to confront anyone, great or small, if he found them expressing self-interest instead of Christ.[11]

Meanwhile the evangelism continued and in 1988 Cornerstone led a 1000 strong March for Jesus in the city of Southampton while its evangelistic team worked that summer in Barking, Romford, Havant, Gosport, Eastleigh and Southampton itself.

By the time that the 1990s broke, Tony Morton, the senior leader of Cornerstone, articulated a vision of the kind of church that he wanted to see: 'a bold, honest church established and abounding in God's work, releasing ever-increasing numbers of truly anointed Ephesians 4 ministries'. He appreciated that the 1990s would be the period of social change whether in relation to public morality, medicine, education, family life, social welfare or the environment. For instance a pregnancy counselling service had been set up in Southampton in the 1980s and this flourished as a local community service, with many referrals coming from doctor's surgeries and local schools. It proved to be a model for other similar centres in the UK and abroad. In 1991 a new pregnancy crisis unit was established in Jersey. Morton had said, when reviewing what Cornerstone stood for, that 'we have concluded that the flexible approach is crucially important still... that this is the reason we have played down the Cornerstone image and

---

[11] *Insight*, 4, 1988, pp.2-5.

majored on being ministries in local churches'.[12] Although he reiterated commitment to raise up new leadership 'here and abroad', he wanted to maintain a family identity with annual leadership gatherings, joint events for children, youth and specialised issues and, instead of having a fixed team, to have a core council with others who were occasionally invited to join them on 'a fellowship or consultative basis'. By 1999 the *Community Church Handbook* could speak about Cornerstone (now called c.net) as, 'both a family of churches and a network of ministries' that had, within the United Kingdom, around 40 churches who were either partners or associates. Overseas there were many more. Their goals were to establish contemporary and dynamic local churches; to enable individuals to reach their potential; and to facilitate international and cross-cultural networking of churches and leaders.

The Community Church in Southampton prospered. They bought the famous Central Hall (Billy Graham had preached there on one of his first post-war visits to Britain) that served as an auditorium and an office complex. They offered a well planned teaching programme called School of Ministries that replaced the old Foundation for Ministry course.[13] They also offered a professional counselling and training service that was used by the social services as well as by the church itself. They continued to run King's Primary School[14] as well as Sanctuary, a house in the city that offered support to residents (some ex-prisoners) in transition to independent living. And, in an appealing project, they funded Miracle Street, described as 'an arrow fired out of the church' that performed classic street entertainment to communicate the gospel.[15]

Throughout the 1990s the network continued to press forward in its diverse and complicated way, though the underlying legal structure was simplified and unified. Those who knew him agree that Tony Morton was openhearted and with a consultative leadership style. He had a gift of being able to see to the heart of matter and to bring leaders who did not see eye to eye into accord.[16] Despite his openness Morton was hesitant about confronting people. Though the leadership of the Community Church had specific roles, the wider Cornerstone leadership team which grew to about 20 or 25 people was more loosely defined and most of its members were supported by their own congregations or itinerant ministries: they were not paid from a central resource. Morton's ministry took him away a lot though

---

[12] *Insight*, 8, 1990, p.6.

[13] Now led by Peter Butt.

[14] Only in the summer of 2006 was the King's School detached from the Community Church trust to stand on its own feet.

[15] <http://www.bbc.co.uk/hampshire/content/articles/2005/09/12/miracle_st_feature.shtml> (accessed 13 July, 2006)

[16] Interview with Peter Butt and David Damp, 11 January, 2006.

he was still financially supported by Cornerstone. In about the year 2000 he was diagnosed with cancer and faced up to the possibility of his own early death. He recovered and continued to minister at home and overseas. No one quite knows when he began to lose his dedication to his apostolic task. At any rate, he would return from some of his ministry trips exhausted and feeling undervalued. In June 2004 a moral failure came to light and shortly afterwards his marriage collapsed. He left for Spain where he had bought a house, started a new life and so disappeared from Cornerstone.

In October 2004 about 150 leaders from Cornerstone (now called c.net) gathered to decide what should be done. They met for two days 'in the light of Tony Morton's decision to step down from all leadership responsibility'.[17] So-called 'apostolic hubs' had been formed in Belgium, France, Germany, India, Nepal, Kenya, Uganda, South Africa and the USA. The leaders who gathered rejoiced in all that God had done over the previous 20 years. The international hubs, it was decided, 'will continue to operate but under new identities'; in effect they were set free to do whatever they wished. In Britain a steering group continued to meet to oversee the groupings of churches that were now forming in Hampshire, the Isle of Wight, Dorset, London, Surrey and East Solent. These groupings decided about their own futures in different ways. Some explored going into relationships with other networks and others found the 'emergent church' agenda attractive to them. The steering group was open to the continuation of relationships but such authority as Cornerstone had exerted now evaporated. Yet, as they realised 'if we are a relational network then there must be things that do remain'. These things are beginning to be clarified.

The first thing to say is that the Community Church at Southampton has survived and grown so that by 2005, there were 1,000 people who belonged to the church in five connected congregations. It was always a root from which the Cornerstone network grew and, under Billy Kennedy's leadership, it has concentrated on a variety of tasks within the city of Southampton and the surrounding area. The sheer diversity of its operations is amazing and its budget is impressive. All the activity over 25 years has paid off and this explains why in a short few months in 2006 it was possible to raise nearly £450,000 for the refurbishment of the building. As their 2005 Annual Report put it, 'we held our Members' Day at Central Hall. Against a background of the difficult events of the latter half of 2004, it proved a very significant day as we drew a line in the sand and were able to move forward positively into the year ahead'. In addition the international work continued in Africa, India, Spain, Germany, Canada, Albania and Malaysia – all places visited by members of the community church in 2005. Indeed the budget of the Community Church runs to £1.8 million.

---

[17] Press release issued after the event.

iii. Reflection

The situation at c.net always differed from that of the other apostolic networks within Britain. From the late 1980s onwards – perhaps from the death of Arthur Wallis onwards — c.net saw itself as being less structured or directed from the top than the other networks were. Tony Morton's style of leadership was to encourage other members of his team to do what they felt God was calling them to do. He was not so much a director as an encourager and, in bringing a large team together, he had the personal skills to ensure that relationships within the team remained sweet. In this respect Morton was different from Bryn Jones. He did not build up an organisation or set targets but encouraged the network to grow in an almost spontaneous way.[18] After his moral failure and after the shock and disbelief had given way to a sober realisation of what had happened, members of the team in Southampton, both within the Community Church and from the wider Cornerstone (c.net) team, began to recover. The ministry to projects abroad was able to continue through the same travelling preachers and, though the network at a distance unravelled, the network within the Hampshire area remained more or less intact. Two years after Morton had left, the church relations began to be (re)established with other networks or flagship churches in Britain.

The loss of the apostolic leader through moral failure is, in some senses, akin to the loss of a leader through a road accident. It is a sudden bereavement and those who look back on it find themselves asking whether there was anything they could have done to have prevented it. Indeed was there anything that Tony Morton could have done to prevent what happened? Should he have asked for help? Were there underlying problems with money, family relationships and burnout? Was the responsibility for the whole enterprise too great for one man to carry? Should he have organised the network in greater detail and clarified responsibilities more? Or was he right to emphasise the creative approach and the relaxed style? Only gradually will answers to these questions become accessible. Yet, the loss of the apostle by moral failure is worse than his loss through death in one respect: it may remove the confidence so vital to the success of any Christian enterprise. Confidence, like faith, helps to ensure that obstacles are overcome, finance flows, hope grows and that personal and working relationships remain intact. We can put this another way by saying that, if the apostle fails, those who have previously related to him must renew their

---

[18] Interview with Adrian Thomas, Peter Butt and David Damp, 12 July, 2006.

own faith in Christ. They must look – as they have done – beyond the servant to the Master.

Chapter 7

Roger Forster and Ichthus

i. Roger Forster, the Man

Roger Forster (born in 1933) went up to Cambridge to read mathematics in 1951. He was evangelically converted from agnosticism and a liberal Methodist background in his first term and applied himself to his Christian faith with extraordinary vigour and discipline. He combined personal evangelism with a wide reading of Christian classics including Chesterton on Francis of Assisi, Hudson Taylor on living by faith and Thomas à Kempis's *Imitation of Christ*. To this intense application to Christian reading was added vital religious experience. On one occasion while he was on his own, Forster experienced wave upon wave of divine love permeating his being. Thereafter he identified the baptism with the Holy Spirit with 'the Abba-father experience' rather than with speaking in tongues (though he himself did speak in tongues later), a position that typified his willingness to think originally about theology.

His disciplined life-style was reinforced by two years of national service in the Royal Air Force from 1954 to 1956. Through force of character and Christian commitment he made an impact on the RAF base where he was stationed. He put into practice the notion of 'organic church' that he had learnt from G H Lang who had been brought up amongst the Exclusive Brethren but now ministered more widely. Forster would meet with others for study and worship in the bar of a local pub. This willingness to put a religious congregation outside any obviously sacred space exemplified his radical mindset, especially in the 1950s. Attenders all sat in a circle and contributed to the service in a format that mirrored the Pauline description of a meeting in the early church (1 Corinthians 14:26).

When news of the unusual religious life within the RAF base spread to the local area, Forster was asked by the nearby churches and gospel groups to undertake itinerant evangelistic activities in the southwest of England and in Weston-super-Mare. In this way he developed a preaching style that was evangelistic, and this became fundamental to all he did; there was no more important task than proclaiming the gospel. In the 1960s to the 1980s he led a large number of university missions and was a popular speaker with students because of his engaging personality, creativity and informality.

It is this creativity that makes Forster hard to categorise. He went to see Martyn Lloyd-Jones in 1956 and the great man encouraged him in second blessing theology but distinguished it from Wesleyan theology of sanctification after conversion, which Forster would not totally exclude. When the charismatic movement broke out in the 1960s Forster found himself neither fully identified with it nor opposed to it. There was much that delighted him although he never found a body with quite his own willingness to throw out inessential traditions alongside a truly catholic appreciation of the wealth of the Christian heritage. He was committed to evangelical conversion, but never Calvinistic, and completely convinced about the necessity for Christians to do good deeds of every charitable kind. He was also temperamentally averse to complicated ecclesiastical hierarchy while being willing to collaborate with almost every mainline denominational variation of Christianity. His optimism was tested when various family members were faced with terminal cancer.

In 1965 he married Faith and in 1969 they settled in south London and joined the Honor Oak Fellowship. This was a unique independent congregation that had originally been Baptist. Theodore Austin-Sparks (1888-1971), who had had become its minister in 1921, decided to sever its connections with the Baptist Union in 1926 so that he could take his people in a new direction that stressed aspects of Keswick holiness teaching in the framework of Brethren ecclesiology or, to put this less theologically, so that he could stress unemotional self-denial in the context of a non-residential Christian community.[1] Yet Austin-Sparks was a devotee of Mrs Jessie Penn-Lewis, a scurrilous critic of pentecostalism, who believed that the church as a whole was being deceived by wicked spirits purporting to usher in evangelical revival.[2] Penn-Lewis's solution was to preach a 'special teaching' that seems to have been an extreme form of the believer's identification with Christ to secure sinless perfection.[3] Less idiosyncratic, but popular at Honor Oak, was Watchman Nee (1903-72), the Chinese Christian imprisoned and martyred by the communist government in his home country. Nee's own teaching, though partially explicable in the light of his ill heath and persecution, was that 'the outer man' needed to be broken to release the Spirit.[4] Such a doctrine, though it may be interpreted as an extreme quest for holiness, ran completely counter to the joyful reception of the Holy Spirit that marked the discovery of charismatic gifts in churches in the West; it was effectively an anti-charismatic stance.

---

[1] Andrew Walker, *Restoring the Kingdom* (4th edn), (Guildford, Eagle, 1998), p.63; G. Lie, 'T Austin-Sparks: a brief introduction', *Refleks 3, 1,* (2004), pp.48-52.

[2] Penn-Lewis, *War on the Saints,* (London, Marshall Bros., 1912).

[3] B.P. Jones, *The Complete Life of Evan Roberts, 1878-195,* (South Plainfield, N. J.; Bridge Publishing, 1995), p.161.

[4] <http://www.ministrybooks.org/books.asp?id=19&chapterid=0&sectionid=1&pageid=1> (accessed 6 October, 2005).

Despite his membership of the Honor Oak Fellowship, Forster was aware of the free-standing charismatic fellowship at Chard in Somerset in 1949. The conferences held by Chard in the 1950s and 1960s attracted a stellar list of independent Pentecostal and charismatic preachers including Willie Burton, who had established hundreds of independent Pentecostal congregations in the Congo, Cecil Cousen, who had belonged to the apostolic movement, Bryn Jones and Graham Perrins.[5] Forster had heard these men preach and realised, that whatever its merits, Honor Oak could not be his permanent spiritual home. In addition, Forster had been in touch with Michael Harper and had been at Cambridge with David Watson – both of them Anglicans - who were now becoming well-known charismatic figures. Moreover Forster had, in the 1960s, through his itinerant preaching, established at least five home groups which, though they came to little, showed him that it was possible to begin gathering converts into the nucleus of new churches.

In 1974 Forster sensed a call from God to establish a permanent itinerant team to evangelise London, especially south of the Thames. After carrying out an evangelistic campaign in the Peckham area under the Evangelical Alliance title 'The Power Project', Forster presented the prospect of continual evangelisation to the churches in the area, including Honor Oak, but none of them responded positively so, after prayer, Forster and his co-workers, Roger and Sue Mitchell, along with Faith met together in the front room their house and founded the Ichthus Christian Fellowship, along with 10 others.

ii. Ichthus

Ichthus came out of the rich and varied influences that had impinged on Forster. There were elements of Brethren ecclesiology, an acceptance of second blessing theology, a willingness to engage in spiritual warfare, a recognition that the church was big and varied rather than narrow and sectarian. Although the Forsters and Mitchells were committed to charismatic gifts within church life, Ichthus had not been founded simply to 'make room for the gifts', the *charismata*.[6] The implication of this was that Ichthus should engage in practical programmes of service (called Jesus Action) to the locality while training men and women within the community of the new body; projects have included an alcohol-free pub, a community centre, a pregnancy counselling service, an agency to help prostitutes and reading to the blind.[7] Forster understood the

---

[5] A. Sullivan, 'Roger Forster and the Ichthus Christian Fellowship: the development of a charismatic missiology', *Pneuma* 16, 2, (1994), pp.247-263.

[6] Interview with Roger Forster, 12 December, 2003.

[7] Ian Cotton, *The Hallelujah Revolution*, (New York: Time Warner Paperbacks, 1995).

interconnectedness of mission and training, and of community and good works. His philosophy could be summarised as being found in 'Words, Works and Wonders' and his original purpose was to reach out across the world from a church that has started in the front room of a house. So how could the intimacy of the home be retained when vision and membership multiplied?

In the early days Ichthus grew as a series of house groups until a three-fold structure emerged. The smallest unit continued to be the house group, or cell, which comprised a group of people no larger than those who could fit comfortably into the room of a typical house. Beyond this was the congregation. Clusters of home groups, often drawn from a well-defined geographical area, came together each Sunday, or at convenient times, for a service that would include preaching and sometimes Holy Communion. Beyond this again congregations would assemble, about every three months, for a large meeting where a national preacher might be heard. This soon led to celebrations emphasising healing and prophecy on both Saturdays and Sundays for their own people plus many from other churches. Every member of Ichthus therefore belonged to a small friendly group of people whose names and life histories he or she knew well and also to the two bigger groups where an altogether larger sense of identity was created. The celebrations would be marked by high quality vibrant music but they had the additional purpose of allowing the senior leaders of the growing network to be visible and accessible to newly-joined members.

By 1982 Ichthus had grown to around 400 people in two new congregations.[8] By the end of the decade Ichthus had grown to nearly 2,000 people in south London in 43 groups of various kinds. It had planted overseas congregations in Cyprus, France, Egypt and elsewhere in the Middle East. It was linked to about 120 churches in the UK.[9] All in all it became a model for others to copy, whether they were denominationally minded or orientated towards apostolic networks. In the 1970s when the shepherding controversy arose, pentecostals and charismatics could see that Ichthus managed to steer a course between extremes so that, though Forster accepted the need for church structures, he was always sure that the structures should serve the purpose of the church and should never degenerate into legalism or perpetuate an artificial and potentially abusive division between leaders and followers. Equally, Ichthus was able to say that denominations were valuable and God-given. At a time when restorationists were 'preaching the kingdom' and berating the persistence of denominational organisation, Forster, in his charming way, could stand on a

---

[8] <http://www.ichthus.org.uk/vision/> (accessed 6 October, 2005).
[9] Brian Hewitt, (1995), *Doing a New Thing*, (London: Hodder & Stoughton, 1995), p.108.

public platform and say 'let's have more denominations, not fewer; God created them and loves them'.[10]

There was one other way by which Ichthus marked its own theological position. Most of the other restorationists, and many pentecostals in practice if not in theory, restricted or forbade the ministry of women. This caution was based upon an exposition of the Pauline texts stressing male authority or 'headship' in marriage (1 Corinthians 11:3) and denying a teaching role to women (1 Titus 2:12) that, in settings where teaching was central, effectively prevented women from exercising any independent form of leadership, even in home groups. Anglicans had not, at this time, accepted the ordination of women with the result that no large segment of Christianity apart from the Salvation Army encouraged female ministry. Any calls to allow women into church leadership could be dismissed or resisted because they appeared to echo the secular agenda of the Women's Liberation movement. Yet, Ichthus from its founding days accepted the co-eldership of women. Faith Forster and Sue Mitchell preached at large gatherings and functioned within the leadership team alongside their husbands and with public recognition of their gifts.

In his attitude to the ministry of women, Forster was guided by a theology of gifting,

> We have opened up every level of ministry and leadership to allow women, including area and congregation leaders as well as house group leadership.[11]

Forster had been dismissed by some teaching charismatics as an evangelist and his own apostolic role had been challenged at the height of the shepherding movement by those who had fixed and authoritarian ideas about what constituted an apostle. He developed a theology of apostleship that was determined by the task that the apostle performs.

> What matters is [that] the purpose for which the apostle exists is actually attained – however it is going to be done. It is not important that we have men called apostles, but that we have people doing the work or 'apostle-ing'.[12]

And, of himself, Forster says, 'clearly I am involved in apostolic work since I function in planting and helping others to plant new churches'.[13] His

---

[10] Something he said at Summer Praise at Mattersey Hall in the 1980s. But see also Hewitt (1995, p.111) 'There are more than 22,000 denominations in the world. A few more won't matter'. John Noble's c. 1971 booklet *Forgive us our Denominations* (privately printed) was the most gracious expression of the anti-denominational tendency.

[11] Hewitt, *Doing,* (1995), p.120.

[12] Quoted in Sullivan, 'Roger Forster', (1994).

[13] Hewitt, *Doing,* (1995), p.120.

definition of an apostle is one who plants new churches. There is no extension of the apostolic concept beyond the strictly biblical data. If someone plants a church, that someone is an apostle. If someone claims to be an apostle but fails to plant a church, that person is not an apostle. The test is entirely practical. And the authority of an apostle is subordinated to this overriding task of planting churches. 'I believe that the authority that Christ gives to the apostles and to the church is first and foremost an authority over the devil. I don't want authority over the saints'.[14]

The core values developed by Ichthus were driven by evangelism and a knowledge of church history. Forster is clear 'the Marches for Jesus were born out of prayer'.[15] In May 1987 Forster together with Gerald Coates from Pioneer, Lynn Green of Youth with a Mission and Graham Kendrick, a member of the Ichthus fellowship and director of a music company, Make Way, led the first march.[16] They started in Smithfield market and marched around the City of London. They were joined in the rain by 12,000 people and sang and praised through the normally discreet and money-making streets of the financial districts of London as well as through the red-light area of Soho.[17] They did not march to protest but to celebrate and there was a carnival atmosphere as they smiled and worshipped Christ in the open air. The media did not know what to make of it all.[18] There was a background theology of pronouncing 'the defeat of the spiritual forces entrenched in the capital and the heart of the nation'.[19] More than this there was a sense that the church was being ignored in public life while politicians at both local and national level were riding roughshod over the sensibilities of Christians and caving in to the demands of secular pressure groups.

A second March in 1988 attracted 55,000 people and this time they walked along the Thames embankment to Hyde Park and passed the Houses of Parliament and Buckingham Palace. There was a deliberate symbolism in the route and Graham Kendrick's music, specially written in 1987, proclaimed:

> *Shine, Jesus, shine*
> *Fill this land with the Father's glory*
> *Blaze Spirit blaze*

---

[14] Hewitt, *Doing,* (1995), p.120.

[15] Interview with Roger Forster, 12 December, 2003.

[16] This was the first March for Jesus.

[17] This was an Ichthus march, though others joined.

[18] To one BBC interviewer who could not see the point of it all Gerald Coates retorted, 'don't accuse us of failing to do what we did not try to do', which shut the interviewer up.

[19] P. Ward, *Selling Worship,* (Carlisle, Paternoster, 2005), p.73 quoting Kendrick et al, *March for Jesus,* (1992), p.28.

> *Set our hearts on fire*
> *Flow river flow*
> *Flood the nations with grace and mercy*
> *Send forth your word, Lord, and let there be light.*

The desire for the light of Christ to spread across the human landscape while the fire of the Spirit burned in the heart of Christians could hardly have been expressed more clearly or strongly, and it echoed round the public spaces of central London.

Throughout this time, and to the present, the three levels of cells, congregations and celebrations continued in Ichthus. It is true there were apparent disadvantages in so many permutations of meetings. People had to work hard every Sunday because the congregations in almost every case used hired buildings that had to be kitted out with amplification equipment that was set out in the morning and packed up in the evening. It was not always possible to find good preachers for all the scattered congregations and there were times when trainee preachers did their not-very-good best from notes prepared by Roger Forster or one of the full-time leaders. To try to keep all the members together on the same spiritual journey the congregations worked to a common pattern of biblical readings and texts. Yet over against the practical demands of running so many interlinked congregations, the advantage of the congregation was that it could make a social and political impact upon its locality. Had the church dispensed with congregations, it would have amounted to a scattered collection of house groups with the occasional celebration. The congregational structure, despite the hard work engendered by keeping it going, gave Ichthus members a sense of normal church life while enabling the 'works' aspect of Forster's philosophy to operate. It also gave opportunity in the congregations for developing gifts of preaching, teaching, pastoral care and so on.

The ecumenical and inclusive stance taken by Ichthus benefited returning missionaries who, without a car, might be provided with one from the Ichthus stock, and these missionaries did not have to be in any way connected with Ichthus formally but simply to be generally evangelical. It cultivated a genuine servant heart that was demonstrated by the practical help given to old and disadvantaged people in South London as well as to a wide spectrum of Christians of all kinds. There was also emphasis on prayer and on providing accommodation for the homeless or drug addicts. During the summer months Bible teaching conferences were held to allow families to enjoy fun and sunshine in the Sussex countryside and, at set points in the rest of the year, training of all kinds was arranged. The theology that associated a person's function with his or her gifting ensured that church leaders were not selected from an elite group of educated white men. As a result the leadership of the church was multiracial as well as being of both genders.

In 1992 a process of restructuring took place. The 43 London congregations were reduced to 27 by a process of combining the small ones. The aim of this re-sizing was to ensure that the main Sunday meetings were large and strong; small congregations tended to put too much work on too few shoulders. Because South London was originally made up of separate villages, each one has an individual identity and a slightly different sociological or demographic profile. Each congregation roughly fits the pattern of its community and nobody has far to travel for worship on Sunday morning.

Matching this configuration of groupings is a collection of leaders. In 1993 there were eight full-time leaders with overall charge of the fellowship though Roger Forster was recognised as the 'first among equals'. There were several 'area committees' to coordinate each celebration, a necessary task since the celebrations might draw upon the personnel of a dozen congregations. The area leaders were usually also congregational leaders, though not all congregational leaders were area leaders. Some of the area leaders were Ichthus Christian Workers who had administrative or evangelistic gifts, and there were 30 such people in full-time service in the church. Each area committee met formally and minuted its discussions. Forster saw the minutes of each of these meetings and met the chairperson of one of the areas each week. Others of the full-time leaders met other area chairpersons.

Leaders of the hundred or more home groups normally had secular jobs and each leader aimed to have contact with every member of his or her group at least weekly and to offer fine-grain pastoral care. Considerable responsibility fell on these homegroup leaders because they attended six-monthly leadership weekends and were given the task of training new house group leaders. Though personally demanding, the role gave active Christians a chance to multiply their talents and develop their ministries. For all the demands made upon the leaders, however, the general style was not coercive. For instance, a married couple happy in a particular congregation would not be required to move to where a new and small congregation might be starting, and this would be especially the case when an old and established congregation might have facilities for children whereas a new and smaller congregation might not.

Forster did not have a sectarian mentality and he was open to charismatic currents flowing in the wider body of the church. He became involved with the Nationwide Initiative on Evangelism (NIE) which became Churches Together in England (CIE). When the Toronto blessing came to Britain in 1994, he accepted it at first but later became disappointed with its mode of operation and its results.[20] It was 'a disappointment not renewal 'and he became dissatisfied with the 'lack of love' conveyed by some of its practitioners. 'We need a stronger theology not just an experiential emphasis' was his summary.[21] Actually he thought that the church needed a cosmic worldview and new biblical thinking to accommodate the changing patterns of church life and structure. As far as he was concerned the charismatic movement was in the vanguard of eschatological events and still has a part to play. Forster's own eschatology is pre-millennialist but not pre-tribulationist, and he holds a theology of Israel that presumes it will be incorporated into the church rather than take its own separate path within the divine economy. Quoting Romans 11:17f he believes that the Gentiles have been grafted into the trunk of Israel and that in the future Israel will be grafted back into it and that the two groups, Jew and Gentile, will be one people within the fully formed world-wide church.

Spiritual warfare was also part of Forster's theology. He had reason to take such a position when his own son was diagnosed with cancer and expected to die. Gathering friends together they stood around the young man's bed in hospital and battled in prayer for his recovery. He did recover and, despite criticism from non-charismatic evangelicals for his stance on healing, Forster feels vindicated by the position he has taken. 'My boy is alive. Who do these people think they are when they want to confine healing to the first century of the church?'[22] After 2002, however, a more intense battle raged. Some Ichthus congregations showed an inclination to break away from the main body and to become independent. After a difficult and protracted period of discussion and argument, about half a dozen congregations did sever links with Ichthus and become separate clusters or joined with other networks.[23] This was painful and discouraging but, by 2005, Ichthus was making good its losses. In Forster's view the departing congregations were led by a disaffected 'middle management'. The younger and older leaders remained loyal to him.[24] By 2005 Ichthus comprised some 18 congregations and the leaders of these congregations together with their wives or assistants plus the pastoral worker from the central drug addiction unit meet together to form the body that has final and complete authority for the London church.

There are also 'link churches' over which Ichthus exercises 'no more due restriction than they are willing to give, by their invitation to us and by our service to them'.[25] There is a kind of apostolic relationship between Roger

---

[20] D. Hilborn, *Toronto in Perspective*, (Carlisle, Acute, 2001).

[21] Interview with Roger Forster, 12 December, 2003.

[22] Private conversation. Quoted from memory.

[23] Ex-Ichthus members formed T-Net with about 12 congregations.

[24] Interview with Roger Forster, 12 December, 2003.

[25] Personal email, 16 May, 2005.

and his wife and all the link churches but it is mediated through the leadership of the London church which is made up of the congregational leaders. There are also those within the group of congregational leaders who take on more specific roles for overseas work, link churches, leadership training, and so on. This forms a small caucus which meets informally with workers twice a month and acts as a kind of executive body of the full leadership group.

In essence, then, the 18 congregations and the drug rehabilitation unit are all joined together at the top in a body of elders who meet to discuss matters of general concern. A subgroup, a caucus, acts as a kind of executive body for this larger group and Roger and his wife act as a catalyst for the executive caucus and the big group of congregational leaders. While the big group has responsibility for the 18 London congregations, the more distant congregations need also to be looked after and these relate more directly to Roger and his wife or to selected London leaders within the caucus. It is a complicated set of arrangements that is necessary because of the diversity of the work and the values that inform it. This is not a top-down management system issuing orders nor is it simply a focus group responding to requests from the grassroots. There is an attempt to ensure mutual accountability between the congregational leader and the executive caucus. In Forster's words,

> The reason I emphasise the congregational leaders is so that they recognise they are the stewards of the vision and have responsible people in the movement and it's up to them to check out and for us to check with them the decisions and the directions in which we are going. When a small group takes over completely it can become an in-house or an old boy kind of relationship which is not really beneficial for the 18 congregation church.[26]

iii. Reflection

Ichthus is unique among the apostolic networks in having had wide-angle vision from the very beginning. This breadth of interest is attributable directly to Roger Forster: he had read voluminously in church history and reflected at length about new expressions of Christianity. Ichthus understood mission, training, evangelism, charismatic gifts, home groups, intercessory prayer and compassionate social action as all belonging together within the full orbit of the church. The church was understood by reference to the person of Christ. Where two or three were gathered together in Christ's name, the church existed and there was no need for symbolism, finely tuned hierarchy or complicated definitions of

---

[26] Personal email, 16 May, 2005.

apostolicity. Those who heard Roger Forster speak in the 1980s can remember his youthful enthusiasm and humorous presentation of vividly conceived and ambitious programmes for the many facets of Ichthus.

Ichthus has passed through intermittent periods of trial. While it is true that Covenant Ministries International suffered ruptures towards the end, these were at least partially contained within the purposeful theology of that network. Ichthus lost churches for reasons that do not appear to have been theological and the losses have been incurred as clusters of churches have left, not just one or two in isolated disagreements. It is perhaps for this reason that the present leadership arrangements of Ichthus are more complicated than those in other networks. The current arrangements constitute a balance between various leadership functions and so make splits far less likely in future.

Chapter 8

Gerald Coates and Pioneer

i. Gerald Coates, the Man

Gerald Coates (born 1944) grew up in a pleasant village near Cobham, Surrey, just over 20 miles from the heart of London. His home was stable and, like most of the children in his area, as was common at that time, he went to the Anglican Sunday school.[1] When he was 11, his cousin took him to a Christian camp where he found himself making a commitment to Christ. He went home, full of excitement, 'I have been born again, saved and converted!'[2] but his parents displayed polite indifference and let him get on with his newly found religious enthusiasm as a kind of hobby. The leader of the youth camp attended a Gospel Hall and was a member of the Plymouth Brethren. So Coates went to the Hall's youth group in Cobham throughout his school years. After leaving school and getting a job in a local departmental store, he continued to attend the youth group, became a leader there, helped to run summer camps and saw numbers in attendance grow. Despite this, he was conscious that his Christian life was marred by inconsistencies and uncertainties.

In May 1962 an accident provoked a crisis. Coates rode a friend's motorbike one Saturday evening weaving between the parked cars near where he lived, lost control of the bike when the front tyre burst, clipped the kerb and tumbled forward over the handlebars to hit his unprotected head on a large brick pillar. He was unconscious in hospital for a week and semi-conscious for week after that. Medics expected him to die but, when it was clear that he would survive, they thought he would be permanently disabled. In the event he was back to normal within nine weeks, a 'miracle boy'.[3]

His unbelieving parents began to pray while he was in hospital and, after a summer camp later that year and in a deliberate intensification of his Christian life, Coates formally joined the Gospel Hall, a Brethren assembly, where he stayed for the next six years. He attended Bible studies and prayer meetings, learnt a form of dispensational theology that ruled out apostles, prophets and contemporary spiritual gifts, got to know the members and respected their sincerity. At work he met his future wife, Anona, and the

---

[1] Brian Hewitt, *Doing a New Thing*, (London: Hodder & Stoughton, 1995), p.130.
[2] Gerald Coates, *An Intelligent Fire*, (Eastbourne, Kingsway, 1991), p.25.
[3] Coates, *An Intelligent Fire*, (1991), p.44.

two of them went to the Gospel Hall almost every Sunday and Thursday evening. They attended the 1966 Billy Graham crusade and their religious horizons began to enlarge. After water baptism, they were encouraged to attend Sunday morning meetings. Returning from holiday that year Coates found that the assembly had split and that the more gracious group were those who had left. He joined these and, together, they formed Ebenezer Chapel. After marriage and setting up home, he began to find himself occasionally in touch with the charismatic movement. After comic misunderstandings with proto-charismatics, Coates felt the ground shifting under his feet at Ebenezer. The elder there had decided that they should reunite with the assembly from which they had split. Knowing that the consolidated Brethren assembly would be firmly against pentecostal and charismatic beliefs, Coates and his wife found themselves excluded by the merger and without a congregation to attend. For two Sundays they wondered what to do and then began to meet in their own home with five friends. Cobham Christian Fellowship was born. The year was 1970.

ii. Cobham Christian Fellowship

At the start of the decade they know of no other networks or models that the Fellowship could copy. They were guided by their spiritual instincts and the emphasis, in keeping with the youthfulness of many members, was on friendship, counselling and prayer. By way of reaction to the limitations of 'church-ianity' they wanted to create a form of Christian living that avoided pretence and formality. Numbers grew and Coates changed his secular job to devote more time to look after the people under his care. He became a postman for two years, getting up early each day and then finishing work just after lunch. One morning while singing a hymn on his Royal Mail bicycle, he found himself speaking in other tongues; he was being drawn in a more overtly charismatic direction. And he was not the only one taking this journey. Through the newly founded *Buzz* magazine[4] Cobham heard about other Christians who were striking out for the promised land of what Coates was later to call non-religious Christianity. As part of this journey, they made a place for the arts and Coates would sometimes go to Arts Centre meetings in London – Cliff Richard was a member - as a way of linking up with Christians in the world of entertainment.

Although the Fellowship prospered, Coates, under the influence of Watchman Nee's teaching, never made any statement about his own financial needs. His wife and young children lived from hand to mouth until

---

[4] In 1987, Buzz magazine changed its name to 21st Century Christian. Some time later it merged with Today (a magazine which had previously been called Crusade) - and they together were called Alpha. With subsequent changes of ownership, the magazine Alpha then became Christianity and finally Christianity + Renewal.

the congregation picked up its responsibilities towards them and started to pay a regular salary. This did not change the character of the group since, as part of its communal ethos, financial help was also given to all sorts of other members. Financial distribution was an element in the strong community feeling that Coates' ministry had generated: people were constantly in and out of each other's houses, helping each other in spiritual and practical ways, and even going on holiday together. The new congregation began to acquire an enviable reputation and Coates found himself being invited to speak all over the place to explain how this new and fresh form of Christianity worked. One day, however, after a broader leadership team had been formed, the group began to insist that Gerald invest his time locally rather than being stretched by long overseas trips. At first he found this irksome, but he quickly saw this was the right thing to do. Even so, horizons were never limited especially as, after 1971, when participating in the effervescent Festival of Light[5], contact with other similar charismatic leaders was established and Cobham could begin to see itself as belonging to a large divinely caused upheaval within British Christianity.

In his autobiography, Coates never claims to be an apostle.[6] He writes of himself as a pioneer, prophet, visionary, messenger and even a pastor but never as a church-building apostle weaving together a network of congregations. He certainly functioned as a pastor and leader in his early days at Cobham and, one could argue, he provided evidence of apostolic gifts as he helped to create a large and thriving congregation but, in himself, he felt that he was a man to speak with intuition and insight under the inspiration of the Holy Spirit, someone to strip away pretence, challenge any vestiges of legalism and ridicule the unexamined traditions of evangelicalism or Brethren dispensationalism. He recalls a vision of himself driving a car down a winding stony road with high trees on each side until, at last, he saw an open expense of beautifully manicured grass where people were sitting in smart clothes undertaking Bible studies. Turning the wheel of his car he drove over the beautiful lawn and ruined the grass and scattered the people. He felt that it was his duty to disturb the religious facade of Christianity, and this has been a constant theme within his ministry. Sometimes he has set out to upset and, at other times, his intentions have been directed towards making a splash for Jesus in the secular world. Over the years he has been associated with numerous celebrations, events, marches, broadcasts and campaigns, all of them with

---

[5] The Festival of Light began place on 9 September, 1971 and ended with a rally in Trafalgar Square on 25 September. The 35,000 people who squashed into the square then marched to Hyde Park for a rally of 90,000 in a Festival for Jesus.

[6] Coates, *An Intelligent Fire*, (1991).

the aim of taking Christianity out of the comfortable enclosed space of the traditional church into the godless spaces of British culture.

In 1972 the musical, *Come Together*, was brought to Britain. It was essentially a composition for massed choirs highlighting the story of Jesus while, at the same time, speaking of the renewed church that spread its light across the world. 'Come together' was the call made to Christians to unite and drop their divisive differences.

> *God forgave my sin in Jesus' name,*
> *I've been born again in Jesus' name,*
> *And in Jesus' name I come to you*
> *To share His love as He told me to.* [7]

The music had its own Gospel-sound appeal and came to influence worship songs within the charismatic movement and new churches. Though *Come Together* went on tour, Coates hosted the striking production in London's Westminster Hall where 2500 people were crammed into the building and others sat on the steps outside. Unity among Christians made an emotional impact on Coates and offset the occasionally destructive themes within the kingdom preaching of other restorationists. For all his prophetic fire, Coates was a man to heal relationships; he was no natural sectarian.

After the success of *Come Together* Coates joined with Peter Hill, John Noble, George Tarleton, Dave Mansell and Maurice Smith to arrange other major meetings in London. One of them, held at the Friends' Meeting house in 1974, saw Coates preaching to 1500 people on the subject of pioneers and settlers.[8] The message was reprinted in *Fulness* (volume 14) and still reads well today. Although preaching and worship bring consolation and comfort, 'the current danger to the church in the West is not martyrdom, loss of material blessings, the dividing up of our families, the imprisonment of our leaders and the scarcity of the Scriptures, but rather the disease of insulated selfishness, an attitude of heart unable to love God and promote his glory'. There is a need for a fresh beginning and a fresh obedience to God, a need for a pioneering spirit. For, 'whatever else my opponents have called me, I don't recall one of them calling me a coward'. Lack of courage leads to compromise in behaviour and doctrine and eventually to sin. Ultimately Christians become either settlers who appreciate upper middle-class ways and the predictability of a punctual God or else they become pioneers who risk making mistakes, who want to bless the earth, deal a death blow to selfishness and play their part in a ground-

---

[7] Words by Carol Owens.
[8] A. Walker, *Restoring*, (1998), p.86. Walker refers to a 1974 meeting at Friends' House, and I am assuming that this is the same as the one addressed by Gerald Coates.

breaking prophetic community. 'God is raising up a pioneering minority in order to bless the majority'.

Progress continued on these two fronts. The local congregation continued to grow and there were almost 100 people meeting in Cobham by the mid-1970s.[9] Outside and beyond the local congregation large meetings were periodically convened and Coates found himself speaking at them. He interviewed Malcolm Muggeridge (1903-90) at the Royal Albert Hall before a crowd of 5,500 people and, on several occasions at other meetings in the same premier venue, he would find himself being overcome by the emotion and weeping over the state of the church.[10] His anti-legalistic message brought him notoriety, criticism and misunderstanding. When a local charismatic vicar in the Church of England with whom he had become friendly committed suicide as a result of an inability to cope with the conflicting demands of a congregation that contained charismatics and non-charismatics, Coates felt vindicated in his championship of the new churches. However much restorationists wanted to work with the traditional churches, there would always be those who resisted the essence of restorationism. It was better to work in a church setting that was unambiguous about its acceptance of charismatic gifts and non-ritualistic worship.

At the time events were harder to interpret. It was not clear whether the house churches would survive and prosper or whether the denominations would be renewed or would continue their cycle of decline. *Reformation Today* and *The Evangelical Times* published scathing criticisms of anything remotely charismatic while *The Evangelical Magazine of Wales,* in a misinformed article, took Coates to task for being antinomian – against any form of moral restraint on the behaviour of Christians. The Plymouth Brethren magazine, *The Witness*, added to the chorus of criticism.[11] It often appeared that non-charismatic evangelicals were surer about what they opposed than about what they stood for since, despite being outside the established church, they implied that it ought not to be disturbed. There is an historical paradox here in that nonconformist churches, while historically being critical of many aspects of Anglicanism, nevertheless appreciated the role of the established church as a bulwark against state-sponsored secularism. When Anglicanism was attacked by people other than themselves, they defended it.

Outside the Cobham congregation and on the wider restorationist scene, Coates became a member of the 'Fabulous Fourteen' in about 1973. The original seven had met in Arthur Wallis' home in 1972 and increased their number to include other men whose ministries had a high profile and were,

---

[9] Coates, *An Intelligent Fire*, (1991), p.96.

[10] Coates, *An Intelligent Fire*, (1991), pp.96.

[11] Coates, *An Intelligent Fire,* (1991), pp.148-152.

in so far as the theology was formulated, apostolic. There were tensions between the original seven and the new 'London Brothers' from the outset and these erupted around 'the handling of a case of immorality among one of the fourteen'.[12] As Coates dryly remarked, it was ironical that among the London group who stressed the grace of God to the extent of appearing antinomian, there was no case of immorality whereas, among the original seven, who tended to be more legalistic or at least more authoritarian in their understanding of Christian lifestyles, immorality occurred. In any event Arthur Wallis' letter to the southern restorationists ended the accord. Cooperation stopped overnight and despite attempts to restore (!) what had been lost, nothing was ever the same again.

The effect of this joining together with like-minded restorationists in the early 1970s and then the rift between them in 1976 was to ensure that the southern restorationists concentrated upon their own area and left the northern group, effectively under the powerful leadership of Bryn Jones, to advertise and organise their own large-scale events in the Yorkshire Dales. The pain of being criticised by non-charismatic evangelicals from one quarter and of being rejected by fellow restorationists from the other was salutary. It led the London men to initiate their own programme of events and establish their own priorities: relationships, friendships, exuberant free worship, evangelism, relevant prophecy, music, drama, the arts and social concern. In 1979 the summer camp, Kingdom Life, based in Cobham, was started and about 2000 people attended regularly. Whatever else might be going on in other parts of the country, Coates was determined that his own version of restorationism should continue to prosper.

As Andrew Walker points out in a full analysis of the theological and relational manoeuvres within 1970s restorationism, there were all kinds of ideas circling round at the time.[13] The alliance of the seven, and subsequently the fourteen, was expressed in a covenant that was intended to formalise relationships and prepare for a future extension of the kingdom. Some of these ideas were grandiose and others mere wisps of possibility. There were already differences between the northern and southern groups in terms of organisational ability, financial competence and structural sophistication; the north had the benefit of Bryn Jones' drive. Concerns about authority and control were expressed through the discourse of discipleship and 'covering'. Here the presumption was that every Christian needed to be 'covered', that is, to be under the authority of another Christian in an extendable ladder of submission and leadership with an apostolic figure, or group of apostles, at the top. For some of the

---

[12] Hewitt, *Doing,* (1995), p.130. Wallis' letter implied that the southern group tended to moral laxity but, some time later, it was a member of the northern group who was admitted to have committed adultery.

[13] Walker, *Restoring,* Chapter 3.

restorationists this kind of hierarchical thinking was all too parallel with the denominationalism they had previously escaped. For others it was a way of biblically binding the kingdom together in order to prevent the vision and energy generated by the large successful public occasions escaping into the ether (see chapter 15).

When Carlos Ortiz, the Argentinean, came to restorationist meetings at the Bonnington Hotel in London, he put forward doctrines about discipleship and shepherding that were in line with those already being implied.[14] When Ern Baxter, a powerful American preacher, began to expound the same ideas, this style of church government became distinctive of parts of the restorationist company though, significantly, never as deeply entrenched among the London Brothers, among whom was Coates, as it was among the subalterns of Bryn Jones. Yet the whole issue of authority in discipleship inevitably arose in connection with the appointment of new elders in new congregations, and it filtered down to the ministry of numerous house group leaders who might be elders, or ancillary to elders, but were at any rate vital to expanding congregations that did not have their own premises.

I can recall hearing Ern Baxter preach to a large collection of Christians drawn from many denominations. His message was simple but persuasive. The pillar of cloud and fire led the people of Israel through the wilderness. When the cloud moved on, the people moved on. Unless they remained with the cloud and the pillar, they would be lost in the desert. Christians today needed to move on with God and leave behind their old encampment so that they might reach the promised land. This demand for change was irresistible but, less well explained, was why Christians should think that the restorationists were anything to do with the moving of the fiery pillar. This was assumed. Indeed it was assumed that restorationists were at the forefront of the moving column and everybody else should run to catch up with them leaving behind the obstructive tradition which kept them so far from the land of milk and honey. For all its striking advocacy of change, however, it is doubtful whether Baxter said anything different from Coates in his pioneers and settlers sermon.

Again, according to Andrew Walker,[15] the underlying incoherence within restorationism was evident before the split occurred. Baxter's visits to Britain in 1975 and 1976 made an impact from the public platforms where he spoke. Many of his 'submission' teachings were rapidly disseminated and it is arguable that Jones used Baxter to buttress his own preferred solution to the practicalities of coordination and authority. Formal agreements were intended to unify the restorationist kingdom but faltered on the failure of John Noble to submit to Bryn Jones. The American Fort

---

[14] J. C. Ortiz, *Call to Discipleship*, (Plainfield, N.J., Logos International, 1975).

[15] Walker *Restoring*, Chapter 4.

Lauderdale Five, to which Baxter belonged, believed that a solution could be found if Bryn Jones and John Noble both submitted to Arthur Wallis and then if Arthur Wallis submitted to the American apostles. John Noble, together with Maurice Smith, went over to Florida and, in face to face meetings, was put under pressure by Baxter and Bob Mumford, to submit Arthur Wallis. John Noble demurred and Maurice Smith thought that Arthur's gifts lay in another direction. After this point blank refusal the American influence came rapidly to an end and Baxter played no further part in the British story after 1977. Consequently the apostolic split, when it occurred, was not simply about law and grace, or morality and immorality, but reflected irreducible personal differences; alpha males were very bad at submitting to each other.

With hindsight Coates thought the split had been beneficial: it was 'the great split forward'. It freed all the members of the Fabulous Fourteen from the quasi-covenantal restrictions that had previously begun to coordinate them. Although there were setbacks for the London Brothers – the southern magazine *Fulness* closed down in 1981 – they were able to concentrate upon holding their own events and building up their own networks.[16] In 1979 Kingdom Life was started and quickly attracted a good crowd to the meetings in its 2000 seater marquee. A drama group performed and Coates's attraction to music and the arts could flourish without criticism. Sheila Walsh, Britain's foremost female gospel singer, and her husband, stayed with the Coates family for four years and used their home as a base for singing tours and Sheila began to host the BBC series *The Rock Gospel Show*.

Although the Cobham Christian Fellowship continued to grow, Coates's attention was continually drawn to national and international events and engagements. He associated Christian music with a prophetic ministry, seeing each as being able to support the other. He understood the critics who said that the Christian music industry was full of ambitious independent people whose interests were more focused upon music than upon doctrine or worship. Equally he understood the music industry's suspicion of the restorationist movement which it took to be too much under the thumb of dictatorial apostles. Trying to bring both sides together he convened The Banquet in May 1983, a weekend in Wembley Arena that mixed gospel bands, teaching, worship, evangelism and attended by about 12,000 people. The meeting between show business, albeit a specialist section of the show business world, and restorationism was love at first sight. Many people came to Christ and were filled with the Holy Spirit, not

---

[16] The dates of *Fulness* are problematic because it was undated: it seems to have run from 1971-1981, though both these dates may be wrong by a year. Graham Perrins was the editor and Maurice Smith coordinated articles.

least some of the gospel musicians who had become detached from their roots. In 1985 The Banquet went on tour around Britain.

Coates's personality as well as his ministry made him an ideal subject for the secular media. If the colour supplements or religious broadcasters wanted to turn the spotlight on the new churches, Coates could be guaranteed to produce a provocative quote. In several instances journalists were simply exploitative: they took Coates out to lunch, appeared to be friendly and sympathetic, and then published damning pieces mocking his appearance, all he stood for and anything else they fancied.[17] On other occasions it was the religious media that got Coates into hot water. He gave an interview for *Redemption* magazine, at that time the official magazine of British Assemblies of God, and at a meeting over coffee in Harrods was foolish enough to express reservations about the fallibility of Scripture. Although he was quoted verbatim, the interview generated hundreds of letters and led to the cancellation of several speaking engagements. Clive Calver of the Evangelical Alliance had to smooth over the turbulence.

iii. Pioneer

Meanwhile, and away from fickleness of the media, Coates, guided by prophetic visions, was working with churches outside the Cobham area. A group in Plymouth became connected and many of its members moved up to Cobham. The Pioneer team continued to look after linked churches, plant new churches, train leaders and be at the forefront of changes in musical worship. Eventually, by the mid-1980s, Coates had been released from his local responsibilities. There were, by then, 100 Pioneer leaders who met at regular conferences, and Festival, a summer camp in Staffordshire for about 5000 ran from 1983-87.[18] More dramatic was the 1987 March for Jesus which took the gospel out onto the streets and asserted the presence of Christianity as a force in the land.[19] More sustained was ACET (AIDS Care Education and Training) that was heralded by Patrick Dixon's 1987 book *The Truth about AIDS*.[20] Pioneer Trust gave money to make ACET an institutional reality. By 1990 it had about 30 staff working in four major

---

[17] Val Hennessy of the *Mail on Sunday* was the most duplicitous (see Coates, *An Intelligent Fire,* (1991), p.182).

[18] Coates, *An Intelligent Fire,* (1991), pp.129.

[19] Though the March for Jesus, MFJ for short, has spread to the USA and its UK originators travel over to give advice on how to organise the events (Cotton, *The Hallelujah Revolution,* (1995), p.224).

[20] The book was issued in various versions. *The Whole Truth About AIDS,* was published by Thomas Nelson (1989), *The Truth About AIDS,* by Kingsway (1994); *The Truth About AIDS: and a practical Christian response* was published by ACET International Alliance, (2004).

centres in Britain that provided home-care for more men, women and
children suffering from AIDS than any other charity in Britain. It partnered
with Tear Fund and began a programme in Uganda and, at all these events,
Coates spoke on public platforms, helped to raise money and brought his
prophetic intuition to bear.

Prophetic intuition comes in different guises. Coates got to know the
elderly Malcolm Muggeridge in the 1980s. Muggeridge, an ex-*Guardian*
journalist with a distinguished career dating back to the 1930s, had become
disillusioned with left-wing solutions to political problems and eventually
disillusioned with the whole of western civilisation. He made eloquent
comparisons between the fall of the Roman Empire and the declining moral
standards of the West. When he came to Christ late in life, he saw more
clearly than most how the media were commercially and ideologically
driven and often, for these reasons, inimical to Christianity. Speaking of
journalism, he once wrote, in words that deliberately reversed the opening
of John's Gospel, 'in the beginning was the lie, and the lie was made news
and dwelt among us...'. Muggeridge understood almost uniquely among
intellectuals of his time how rotten and ready to fall was Soviet
communism. By spending time with the younger man he was able to give
Coates an insight into the values and purposes of the media and show him
how even cynical journalists might be persuaded to carry a pro-Christian
message. This was part of the agenda of the Marches for Jesus: they were
intended to attract publicity although, as the years went on, the media
ignored Christian marches and began to concentrate more on Gay Pride
marches, even if these attracted smaller numbers of people.

The Cobham congregation continued to grow, reaching 650 by 1990 and
1300 by 1995.[21] Ian Cotton gives an account of a service in the early 1990s:

> I remember well the first charismatic service I ever went to – held in a
> school hall in Cobham... by early evening the place was packed. The glam
> girls with glittering teeth gave out programmes; old men in Paisley shirts
> smiled benevolently on; fraught couples with flailing kids, young blokes
> with rings in their ears, best-behaviour eight-year-olds, infinitely-wobbly
> grandmas – all burst uproariously, come the start of the service, into the
> first to the evening's charismatic hymns, 'Shine Jesus Shine'... the hand
> went up, the forefingers pointing, the congregation swaying in a kind of
> third cousin of the twist; the noise, helped on by a 10-piece band, was
> quite startling until the end of the evening when Gerald Coates,
> microphone in hand, launched into an end-of-service winder-downer, and
> the band played moody, low-key music in the background.[22]

---

[21] Cotton, *The Hallelujah Revolution*, (1995), p.14.
[22] Cotton, *The Hallelujah Revolution*, (1995), p.6, 7.

As the original congregation grew, so did the network. Pioneer People expanded southwards and into London and northwards to Leeds and about 80 congregations belonged. The relationship between Coates and the leaders of individual churches remained low-key. They were friends, people he pastored, people he liked. He remained averse to hierarchical definitions and ranks. By the late 1988 and early 1990 Gerald, along with John Noble, David Tomlinson and Peter Fenwick could gather 1000 new church leaders for conferences on theological themes. In 1990 they met in Sheffield to consider the relational unity prayed for by Jesus in John 17 and, by this date, Coates estimated that there were about 1000 churches within the various networks and another 1000 that were still independent and part of nothing much bigger than themselves.[23] By underlining the message of Christian unity, Coates demonstrated a largeness of vision. His earlier impatience with liberal Anglicans and prissy knit-picking nonconformists led him to make pithy criticisms about the way they played around with Christianity. He recommended (tongue in cheek) that we should,

> strip all clergy and denominational leaders of ecclesiastical status and let those with God's gift get on with what they have to do... close all denominational headquarters overnight... even some of those who sound like eagles, on closer inspection live like parrots.[24]

He could see no point in institutional Christianity going through sacramental motions while perpetually compromising with the dominant secular-liberal culture of the day, and he never changed this view, but he did come to appreciate that not all Anglicans were by any means the same, and he formed a good friendship with Sandy Millar of Holy Trinity, Brompton, and later came to appreciate George Carey as Archbishop of Canterbury.[25] In the early 1990s he began to see that, even if denominations could not be renewed in their entirety, there were many people within them who had sufficient freedom to march in step with the Spirit. And this marching might even be literal in the sense that the Marches For Jesus brought groups of like-minded Christians together into purposeful networks.

In 1993, as a result of prophecy from Paul Cain, John Noble and Gerald Coates joined forces and the Team Spirit network founded by Noble came within the Pioneer compass. From the start Team Spirit was orientated towards the community. It comprised about 50 churches in the UK and overseas and, using Christine Noble's drama training, worked to incorporate the arts into the life of the church. This fitted well with part of the Pioneer vision and, in addition, the joining of networks was in accord

---

[23] Coates, *An Intelligent Fire,* (1991), pp.218.

[24] Coates, *An Intelligent Fire,* (1991), pp.186.

[25] Cotton, *The Hallelujah Revolution,* (1995), p.223.

with the John 17 prayer for relational unity within the wider body of Christ. From July 1997 onwards Gerald Coates organised meetings at Emmanuel Centre, Marsham Street, at the heart of London, calling the church to prayer for the revival that had failed to come 10 years previously.

By the turn of the millennium, when it was clear that revival had not arrived, Pioneer began to re-think its role and purpose until, in around 2006, it began to conceive of itself as a network of networks expressed through a National Churches Forum. The forum was made up of network leaders as well as key team members and its agreed purpose was, 'connecting, releasing and resourcing teams and churches for building strong vibrant communities of faith to reach the nations'.[26] The forum, facilitated by Billy and Caroline Kennedy, formerly of Cornerstone or c.net, appears to contain some elements of the c.net philosophy. The forum meets about four times a year and allows the various apostolic leaders to pray for each other, understand each other's problems and collaborate in a way that prevents duplication or competition. There are just under 20 leaders within the forum most of whom work with clusters of a dozen or so churches in small but viable networks. For instance, Chris Foster works with a group of congregations that make up River Church in Berks, Bucks and Surrey. Phil Collins works with the VIA team in the midlands as well as being part of the leadership team of Net, a team that serves about 70 churches mainly in the middle of England. John Noble works with Spiritconnect and a core of about 12 congregations in Britain as well as congregations in Norway and France.[27]

The forum helps to organise a symposium for leaders. This can bring together about 200 men and women who are key personnel in the networks but without obvious apostolic functions. The symposium has a communicative and training role.

Pioneer itself has been happy to encourage transmutations of church structures. There are now two things happening at once: in one direction local and senior leaders are looking after groups of congregations in an apostolic way while, in the opposite direction, groupings may be moving into the 'emergent' mode whereby Christians can express themselves by compassionate social action or in the arts or in other ways without retaining the conventional structures or titles of church life. 'Liquid' is a youth church that came out of Pioneer People while the Cobham Fellowship from which Pioneer originally grew does not now exist but those of its members who wish to can worship in a congregation in The Theatre, Leatherhead. The Leatherhead Revival Trustees are tasked to use the building creatively

---

[26] <http://www.pioneer.org.uk/Mobile/default.aspx?group_id=10832> (accessed 21 August, 2006); also sourced from a phone conversation with John Noble, 21 August, 2006.

[27] <http://www.spiritconnect.org/mainpage.html> (accessed 21 August, 2006).

and this has led to a constant coming and going that enables the Christian community or communities to interface with the secular community smoothly and naturally.

iv. Reflection

Pioneer was one of the early networks and its ability to readjust and re-focus itself is one of its strengths. It has always had a big public profile because of Coates' capacity to organise big events in London and the recent changes within Pioneer, after a period of consultation, are indicative of its willingness to settle back on congregational life without compromising its allegiance to the expressive arts or the communication of the gospel in social circles – like those of the broadcasting media – where most churches have no foothold.

This evolution of Pioneer from being what appeared to be a conventional apostolic network to being a network of networks with a variety of ministries and lifestyles allows everyone to find their own niche without an authoritarian organizational control system being put in place. Those who wish to move towards the emergent church end of the spectrum can do so and those who wish to be involved in charismatic congregational life can also do so. Christian music and connections with mainstream television or local radio are also possible. The leaders of the smaller networks have a chance to meet and pray and support each other as well as sparking off fresh initiatives. One thing that is perhaps absent (at least as it was done in the past) is church planting. Separate and distinct from what is going on within the forum or the Leaders' Symposium is a Roundtable convened by Gerald Coates that draws 45 senior leaders from across the streams and denominations.[28] At the Roundtable it is possible for Anglicans influenced by their 'fresh expressions'[29] initiative to rub shoulders with new church people in a way that can be theologically understood to be in line with Jesus's prayer for Christian unity in John 17.

---

[28] <http://www.pioneer.org.uk/Group/Group.aspx?id=15853> (accessed 21 August, 2006).

[29] <http://www.freshexpressions.org.uk/section.asp?id=14> (accessed 21 August, 2006).

Chapter 9

Stuart Bell and Ground Level

i. Stuart Bell, the Man

Stuart Bell's father was a Methodist local preacher. Stuart, born in 1951, travelled with his dad and became aware of the decline of the church in Britain. He made a faith commitment at the age of 14 and became part of British Youth for Christ under whose auspices he began to preach the Gospel. He held a mission in Lincoln, near where he lived, and saw 30 young people become Christians. He began to look after them though he had no idea of church planting. This all took place in the late 1960s as the charismatic movement began to gather speed and strength.

Among those with whom Bell came into contact were John Shelbourne and John Phillips, both ministers within the lively classical pentecostal (Assemblies of God) congregation in the city itself. When Bell came into an experience of the baptism of the Holy Spirit – the hallmark of the charismatic movement – he came into conflict with the Methodist church. Methodism at that time was staid and had no charismatic wing; indeed it is questionable whether it had an evangelical wing of any substance. Bell wanted to form a mission church attached to Methodism and he began meeting with about 40 young people in his own home. The local Methodists were not enthusiastic about these arrangements and so Bell set up an independent fellowship in the north of the city. This continued to attract young people, became known as Lincoln Free Church and, for seven years while Bell worked in a secular post, the congregation grew to about 150 people till it was a fully functioning charismatic fellowship with house groups. In about 1980 the question arose, what should the congregation become part of? The Baptists, particularly the Baptist Revival Fellowship, and the cathedral, in the person of Rex Davies, were both helpful.

Bell was delighted that his independent church had reached a stable and substantial size. When he had begun his evangelism such a congregation seemed beyond his wildest dreams. Yet he soon saw the need to make an impact upon the whole city and, from there, the whole region. He sent out a letter to other churches in the area and they met together to pray, and the phrase 'Humber to the Wash' began to be meaningful. The Humber is the great river running north of Lincoln while the Wash marks the division between Lincolnshire and Norfolk. The whole large flat area of mainly agricultural land and fenland is composed of villages, a few market towns, seaside resorts and the one cathedral city of Lincoln itself. For centuries it has been the home of many kinds of Methodism, containing as it does the birthplace of Wesley, and of moderate Anglicanism.

Gradually Bell found the most like-minded people in the area were John Phillips and John Shelbourne. These were men who had a large 'kingdom' sympathy for the whole church regardless of denominational labels or traditions. The Assemblies of God in Lincoln was being transformed in worship, in attitudes and in its willingness to mix and mingle charismatic streams with traditional Pentecostal theology. Bell brought his own congregation into Evangel Church, the building that Assemblies of God had bought from the Anglicans, and sited prominently near to the centre of Lincoln. Not without difficulties the combined congregation reached about 500 people. The ministry team contained not only Stuart but also the two Johns, and the musical inventiveness of Chris Bowater who was, by this time, becoming an international figure with songs that were sung all over the world.[1]

> During this early period we received help from Bryn Jones, a church leader based in Bradford. In many ways, he was one of the founding fathers of the New Church movement. He gave us some wise counsel, but following his advice did mean that we had to dismantle some of the existing church structures in order that the new church could emerge. This was a difficult process for some people.[2]

What happened next has a bearing on the style and operation of apostolic networks. Bell, whose experience of rejection and friction in the Methodist Church had made him cautious about denominational machinery, was happy to incorporate his congregation within the Assemblies of God congregation since this was done on the basis of the personal relationships with the two Johns.[3] But then the Assemblies of God congregation began to undergo a painful period of relationship with its own denomination – though this of course was unknown to Bell. The issue concerned the rebate given by the Inland Revenue to charities whose members had given by deed of covenant. At that time, all the Assemblies of God churches were part of the single Assemblies of God charity. Each church submitted to the General Offices of the Assemblies of God the amount that its members had given by covenant in the preceding year. All these figures were added together and

---

[1] There are now over 50 people involved in music and worship at New Life (S. Fox, *Grapevine: the story so far* (Lincoln, Ground Level, 2006), p.17). The merging of Lincoln Free Church with Evangel Church formed New Life Christian Fellowship, the current name of the congregation at the centre of Ground Level.

[2] Fox, *Grapevine*, (2006), p.16.

[3] As he later wrote, about Nehemiah 'far too many leaders find themselves "sifting" the rubble rather than "serving" the Kingdom. The frustration of red tape, denominationalism, constitutions and traditions can delay the rebuilding' Stuart Bell, *Rebuilding the Walls*, (Tonbridge, Sovereign World, 2003).

submitted to the Inland Revenue and then the Inland Revenue paid the rebate to the General Offices and the General Offices redistributed this money to the churches proportionally according to their giving. The problem arose when the Inland Revenue began to clamp down on the scheme, and all the more so if rebates given by the Revenue amounted to more than £1 million per year. Although many of the assemblies kept close records of the giving of their people, there were others that relied on the 'open plate' system whereby individuals put money in the collection without any paper-based record of their donations. As a result of the tougher government policy on charities, the Assemblies of God found itself being asked to give the Inland Revenue £4 million to make up for the 'inflated' rebates of previous years.

This produced consternation in the General Offices and face-to-face meetings between the Inland Revenue and denominational officials. While this was going on, the annual rebates were held in suspension. The assembly at Lincoln, which because it was a large assembly receiving a large rebate, found itself financially embarrassed by the failure of the system. It had come to rely on a large annual injection of finance at a fixed point in the tax year. Eventually, the dignified and retired general treasurer of the Assemblies of God found an old letter from the Inland Revenue showing that the tax authorities had previously given permission in writing for the open plate system. The demand for £4 million shrank to £300,000. Although this was good news, the protracted uncertainty irritated the church leaders in Lincoln. Moreover, the demand for £300,000 reduced the amount of rebate that each church received from the offices that year. Lincoln looked for a covenant scheme which could by-pass the General Offices and discovered to its horror that the previous amalgamation of the Assembly of God at Lincoln and the Independent Methodist group had no existence in law. Both groups had different trust deeds and, after legal advice, it seemed that only if the Lincoln assembly withdrew from the Assemblies of God could a new integrated church group be formed which would exist as a legal entity and to which covenant payments might be made.

The oversight of the Lincoln assembly took decisive action. They wrote to the members of their congregation to inform them that the church would be withdrawn from the Assemblies of God. There was no consultation or vote on the matter. This was quite contrary to normal practice within Assemblies of God congregations which, for all their Pentecostal theology, were remarkably prone to democratic procedures – indeed there were times when a resemblance between the creaking consultative processes of Assemblies of God and the trade union movement seemed all too apparent. This decision shocked Assemblies of God, particularly as the two Johns were much loved figures and John Phillips had for 24 years been on the Assemblies of God Executive Council and therefore enjoyed a high profile at scores of conferences and conventions. John Shelbourne had been a missionary in Congo and escaped under gunfire during the Mau Mau uprising; his concept of the church was altogether wider than that of most Pentecostal ministers.[4] The issue came to a head at the 1988 Assemblies of God annual General Conference. The two Johns were not eligible to retain their status as Assemblies of God ministers since they no longer ministered to an Assemblies of God congregation. Although the conference by a majority wished to retain them on the ministerial list – even if for understandable reasons their congregation was now independent, the required two thirds voting figure was not reached. They left and the break was complete.

The painful departure of the Lincoln assembly from Assemblies of God had other consequences. A small group of about 40 people within the congregation of 500 objected to the action of their oversight and claimed that they were the 'continuing assembly'. They claimed the building as their own. Although, eventually, this claim was resolved more or less amicably, the disruption and bad feeling created by the entire series of events coloured the thinking of the two Johns and Stuart Bell. They saw denominations as hidebound and crippled by quasi-legal regulations. Their vision of the church as a whole was freer, more ecumenical, more mobile, more locally directed and governed and more firmly based within a New Testament pattern of ministry that took no account of denominational officialdom.

ii Ground Level

The origins of Ground Level date back to the era of Lincoln Free Church before the merger. Stuart Bell had sent out letters to a number of evangelical churches in Lincolnshire asking their leaders to meet together and, slightly to his surprise, about 30 leaders came to the first meeting. They also found in a circle and talked and prayed together. A little while after this, when they began to think about making an impact on the local region of Lincolnshire, they realised that they had drawn people from further afield, from the Humber to the Wash. So this became the focus of their vision with the catchphrase 'we want to see a cell in every village, a congregation in every town, and a celebration in every city between the Humber and the Wash'. The vision was primarily evangelistically. They took on the name 'Ground Level' because they wanted to work at the local church level and wanted to avoid making inflated claims about themselves. They began to call preachers in the house church movement to come to minister to them and heard from Gerald Coates, Roger Forster, Dave Matthews, Barney Coombs and Terry Virgo. They learned a great deal from

---

[4] John Shelbourne was to die suddenly in the mid-1980s at the relatively young age of 55.

these people but decided that the pursue their own strategy. Early on they planted congregations in Grimsby, Horncastle, Market Rasen, Louth, Woodhall Spa and then, later, in Cleethorpes and Mablethorpe on the coast.

The leaders who had met together as Ground Level decided that they would set aside time annually for their churches together, and this is how Grapevine began. The name was chosen because it spoke of communication (in a phrase like 'I heard it on the grapevine... ') and also referred to the new wine of the Spirit.[5] They launched Grapevine by hiring the Agricultural Showground at Lincoln. They brought 60 leaders and their people into a summer camp for seminars and evening meetings, the first of which was held in August 1982. In this way, especially after the vision was more clearly articulated in 1983, the Humber-to-the-Wash idea was disseminated and given substance. Visitors came from further afield to the evening meetings while more local people enjoyed the holiday atmosphere generated by activities for children and seminars for adults during the day. The event had similarities with the Dales and Downs Bible weeks but the thrust of the ministry was more obviously evangelistic.

Year by year Grapevine grew as did Ground Level. In 1985 a company limited by guarantee was established.[6] Between 1980 and 1990 Ground Level grew to 15 churches. In 1990 in response to prophecies from Jean Darnell and Gerald Coates, the scope of the network was widened beyond the Humber and the Wash. By 1999, the number of associated churches had reached 58. The growth graph of core churches is almost a steady straight line, but this does not tell the whole story[7]. There are about three times as many churches that have *some* kind of relationship with Ground Level as there are in the core group. Many of these peripheral churches decline a more formal link for denominational reasons and others are the kind of churches that value their independence so greatly that they do not want to belong to anything bigger than themselves. Other churches take the opposite view; they belong to more than one network.[8]

An examination of the size of the Ground Level congregations shows that nearly all have grown. Of the 15 congregations that joined between 1980-1990, the largest proportion (11) had 25 adults in attendance. By the year 2000 the largest proportion (4) had 50 adults and three had risen to 300 adults. Similar patterns of growth are found in the congregations that joined after 1991. One of the ways in which this happens is through Alpha courses

---

[5] Fox, *Grapevine*, (2006), pp.19-31.

[6] It was registered as a company limited by guarantee having no share capital. It was also registered as a charity.

[7] Substantial offerings were given, rising to around quarter of a million points from 2004 onwards. The offerings largely supported mission and charity projects.

[8] A. E. Dyer, 'Research on Ground Level', (MTh Essay on empirical theology, University of Wales, Bangor, 2000).

(over two thirds of churches have made use of these) and the other is through on-the-job training of ministers. When the age and training of leaders are examined, the largest percentage (46%) are in the category of 40-49 years of age and of these just over half have received training within the Ground Level set-up. Of those of all ages who have been trained elsewhere about 43% have attended a theological college of some kind – a finding that reflects the original contribution to Ground Level of the denominational heritage. In such circumstances one might expect Ground Level to hold itself aloof from denominations in any form but, in practice, Ground Level has avoided sectarian attitudes. Over 90% of Ground Level leaders favour unity with other churches and nearly 70% want town-wide events where all the churches in a locality can cooperate for their common benefit. Such an openness is expressed by membership of the Evangelical Alliance and Churches Together. Around 85% of Ground Level congregations belong to one or both of these umbrella organisations.[9]

When the dynamics of sustained success are examined, it is evident that Grapevine functioned as the annual public expression of Ground Level; Grapevine provided ministry, fellowship and a sense of co-belonging, and Ground Level itself became the all-year-round existence of the summer event. Although the intention was only to create a regional network, in 1990 the network cast itself more widely. It is, however, concentrated in Lincolnshire and this is one of its strengths. It is possible to arrange meetings for local church leaders without requiring lengthy and expensive travel. About a third of the 85 or so churches are outside the Lincolnshire area and there are also warm, fruitful and long-standing links to networks in the United States (Grace Network headed up by Jack Groblewski) and South Africa (Francois Van Niekerk of Hatfield church in Pretoria). Grapevine itself attracts around 10,000 people annually.

The network expresses its relationship between member churches through the phrase 'partnership without ownership'. There is local autonomy and there are free relationships. There is no financial commitment or membership fee although nominal amounts are given by participating churches for general administration. There is an annual offering at Grapevine but the whole ethos of the network is guided by a desire to avoid tight guidelines – painful experiences with Methodism and Assemblies of God have seen to that. So the network has its own apostolic team and members of this are engaged in planting new churches as well as helping in the building of existing ones. There is a monthly meeting of the church leaders belonging to Ground Level and here about 100 people gather for a day of preaching and prayer. Some of the main (and usually full-time) leaders also meet three times a year residentially but the biggest gathering, which involves around 400 people, calls together those who are in

---

[9] Dyer, 'Ground Level,' (2000).

leadership of any kind within the Ground Level churches usually at the Hayes, Swanwick. This gathering lasts three days and is a kind of conference. All in all this interlocking set of meetings spread out in advance carefully across the calendar with the kind of precision that Methodist circuit preachers know all about, gives solidity to Ground Level aspirations. The main apostolic leaders know each other well and the residential event at Swanwick ensures that local church leaders (these could be house group leaders, or part-time ministers, or youth workers) and their wives are also knitted together. It is this ability to coordinate trans-local leaders and local leaders and to speak to the spiritual needs of each that contributes to the success of Ground Level. There are, within the network, churches belonging to a variety of denominations: Assemblies of God, Methodist, Baptist, and others. These take from the network the kind of help that their own denominational structures fail to deliver. Full-time ministers receive help and encouragement as they set about raising money, expanding their buildings, putting on events in their towns, and so on, while the local part-time leaders get a chance each month to hear good preaching and receive encouragement for the Sunday-by-Sunday ministry.

The network has sufficient flexibility to allow local church leaders to take their own decisions and its evangelistic priorities ensure that the sorts of disputes that can upset evangelical groups are put into perspective. The Toronto blessing was seen as valuable insofar as it contributed to the planting or growth of local churches. And the same may be said of the cell church movement which, in its way, has the potential to be even more divisive. Stuart Bell describes his own congregation as 'a church with cells rather than a cell church', a formulation that is nicely pragmatic. His youth group is divided into cells but the main congregation does not have a uniform structure: 'not all are in cells but many are'.[10] Though there is a cell group among the students and Lincoln University, this is a matter more of convenience than theological conviction.[11] Similarly, there is no commitment to spend time and money on building new Christian schools since none of the leaders within the local churches feels especially troubled by the schooling offered within the maintained sector. Nor is there a plan to launch into expensive Christian broadcasting even if, from time to time, interviews and programmes are put out on local radio or television.

Ground Level has its own general statement of beliefs but this is a not carefully crafted table of doctrinal propositions. Rather they cover, in a shorthand way, the authority of Scripture and the gifts of the Holy Spirit.

---

[10] Email from Stuart Bell, 25 October, 2005.

[11] About 30% of Ground Level churches organise their on-going weekly life around centrally planned events rather than by devolving planning to the cell or home level. Another 40% cannot differentiate between central planning and cell-led planning (Dyer, 2000).

The other articles are more aspirational and practical and include 'revival in our nation', 'servant leadership', 'creative worship' and simply 'the local church'. The pragmatic approach of Ground Level is found in this latter definition and, judging by recent attendance at Grapevine, the prospects for what amounts to a regional network appear to be good. By building up support over more than 20 years, the network is established in reality rather than rhetoric and the accessibility of its key leader, Stuart Bell, adds to the sense that Ground Level is, indeed, grounded in its constituent local churches.

iii. Reflection

Like several of the best networks, this has been a slow-burning success. Ground Level originally confined itself to a restricted area within Britain. Its outlook was evangelistic and the network was a support service for evangelism through church growth and church planting. The regional nature of the network turned out to be its strength since, once the regional base had been consolidated, the network was in a strong position to branch out overseas. It did so on the basis of a few close relationships between leaders and without turning in every direction in response to a plethora of invitations.

Like other networks Ground Level has a flagship congregation through which outreach activities can be funded, though the Humber-to-the-Wash vision grew at roughly the same pace as the big Lincoln congregation. Unlike other networks which ran successful summer camps for only a few years, Ground Level has persisted with Grapevine. On the occasions when leaders have wondered whether Grapevine was worth all the effort, charismatic gifts have encouraged them to continue. In 2006 Grapevine celebrated 25 years and, almost year on year, attendance has gradually increased. Though there are now congregations at a distance from Lincolnshire connected with Grapevine, the feel of the network remains local – and it is none the worse for that. There is a stability within the network and within Grapevine itself that augurs well for the future and a simplicity of approach that ensures the original evangelistic vision is retained. Stuart Bell's own leadership sets the tone, and his family's battles with illness have given a depth and compassion to his preaching that create many resonances.

Chapter 10

Colin Dye and Kensington Temple / London City Church

i. Kensington Temple

Kensington Temple, or KT as it was often known, is a thriving multi-ethnic Pentecostal Church in west London. It belongs to the classical Pentecostal stream, Elim, and grew out of the revivalist campaigning of George Jeffreys during the 1920s, although the 1,500 seater building itself was started in 1848. Jeffreys bought it from evangelical and missionary-minded Congregationalists in about 1930 and began to use it as his London base.[1]

The modern history of Kensington Temple begins with the arrival of Eldin Corsie in 1965. The building had remained intact and its congregation had declined but, with the arrival of Corsie and the transplanting of another congregation to the old building, a new start could be made. When the new members started to clean and renovate the place they found in the basement relics of the revivalist past. There were signboards carrying the words 'church full' and wheelchairs, leg braces and other medical impedimenta that had been thrown aside during the healing ministry of the Jeffreys brothers.

By the late 1970s Kensington Temple had become the foremost Pentecostal Church in the whole of Britain. Not only was it growing but its congregation was constantly turning over as people came and went from London in a flow of migrations and job changes, and this meant that its influence spread much further afield than London itself. Additionally, and unusually for classical pentecostalism, the congregation began to reflect the extraordinary diversity within the capital city. There were diplomats, lawyers, doctors and sportsmen as well as local people and students in attendance. By the mid-1970s Corsie was able to appoint twelve elders who each took an area of responsibility within the church as well as a sub-section of it for pastoral care. This was the beginning of the satellite congregation concept that KT was later to adopt.

In 1980 Wynne Lewis became the senior pastor at Kensington Temple. He built rapidly upon the foundations that had been laid and quickly appreciated the opportunities afforded by working within an enormously rich and varied capital city. Building costs in London were prohibitive,

---

[1] J. Hywel-Davies, *The Story of Kensington Temple,* (Eastbourne, Monarch Books, 1998), p.36.

even for large and prosperous congregations, with the result that it was not possible to build or hire vast halls to house the expected expansion of the congregation. The only solution was to see Kensington Temple ringed by numbers of daughter churches, and this became a conscious strategy. It was a strategy that could be carried out by utilising an unusual form of evangelism. Most of the ethnic groups within London had their own culinary preferences and it was possible to attract Chinese people through Chinese food, Portuguese people through Portuguese food, and so on. Kensington Temple began to arrange evenings of Bible teaching aimed at particular linguistic communities and to complete the evening by providing a meal of culturally appropriate food. As a result some but by no means all the daughter congregations could be based around particular linguistic networks of immigrants to London. Congregational leaders with the right linguistic backgrounds were appointed.

In this respect Kensington Temple was different from the other apostolic networks that began to emerge in the 1980s. Not only did it live within a classical Pentecostal milieu – and this connection became especially obvious when Wynne Lewis became the General Superintendent of Elim in 1991 – but also its network grew out of the concept of daughter churches and church planting. Within classical pentecostalism the daughter church was always expected to be smaller than, and subsidiary to, the parental church. Sometimes, it is true, the daughter churches grew more than the mother church but more often they did not, especially if the mother church was based in a larger centre of population with greater resources at its command. So its daughter congregations were always seen as likely to remain dependent upon the technical, financial and ministerial strength of KT. The pattern of mother-daughter churches, however, was not as well worked out as the pattern of relationships that existed within emerging apostolic networks. As a result the relationship between the ministers of the daughter congregations and the mother church was not laid down as the bond that held the whole growing structure together: after all, denominational systems had relied on statements of faith and ministerial conferences for coordination. Wynne Lewis, perhaps instinctively realising this, was determined to make himself available both to his own congregation and to the leaders of other congregations and would meet regularly with them for breakfast and a time of ministry, and in this way they had access to him. Yet as his own congregation grew, it became difficult to care pastorally for the growing numbers. So he ran the network 'like the managing director of a company'[2], with a touch of authority overlaying the relational links with the daughter congregations.

During the period of Wynne Lewis's leadership, the KT central congregation grew to perhaps 5,000 people whom it accommodated in a

---

[2] Telephone interview with Colin Dye, 22 September, 2005.

series of Sunday services running at intervals throughout the day. Lewis handed over to Colin Dye (b 1953) who had been associated with the church at least since 1972 when he had been baptised in water by Eldin Corsie. Under Dye the church continued to be expansive and unashamedly Pentecostal. In conversation with me Dye compared himself to the primitive Methodists who, in response to the failing power of 19th century Methodism, pioneered a return to their radical roots; Dye saw himself as essentially a primitive pentecostal reasserting uncompromising zeal for mission and powerful charismatic gifts.[3]

ii. Colin Dye's Leadership

Under Colin Dye, Kensington Temple began to have associated with it a trail of satellite congregations as well as daughter congregations. In some respects there was little difference between these two concepts but, in others, there was because the satellite congregation was one that tapped into the resources of Kensington temple without necessarily being founded by KT or related to its pastoral team in a strongly personal way. As the 1990s developed, congregations, and particularly African congregations of new arrivals in Britain, began to take advantage of the expertise and advice that KT offered without a great sense of loyalty to its vision or purpose. This is not to say these African congregations were disloyal or cynical but rather to indicate that, in the struggle to establish a foothold within immigrant African and multicultural communities in, say, north London where they found themselves, KT's open-handedness appeared to be part of the generally greater level of wealth that London afforded. The net result of all this was that the numbers of satellite congregations could go down quite as easily as they went up.[4]

At the same time the opportunities opened up by technology were vigorously pursued. Actually the word 'satellite' becomes confusing here because it can refer to the method of relaying broadcasting signals from satellites circling the earth or to congregations that circled round KT: many satellite congregations were satellite in both senses. On top of this, internationally experimental broadcasts were made to halls in Paris and Brussels while the main London congregation, in addition to its multiple meetings, could also collect more intimately during the middle of the week in homes and smaller venues. Some 300 of these care groups were set up and estimates of the total size of the London congregation(s) suggested that it might reach as many as 10,000 people, especially when the associated ethnic churches were added in.[5] Earlier, in 1986, Dye had formed the

---

[3] Interview with Colin Dye 16 January, 2004.
[4] Interview with Marlon Nartey, 10 December, 2003.
[5] Hywel-Davies, *The Story of Kensington Temple,* (1998), p.164.

International Bible Institute of London and this quickly grew to be one of the largest training centres of its kind in Britain. Although there was an emphasis on Bible study, discipleship and pastoral placement were also included. Bible students contributed to the church's music and evangelism and, during the 1990s, the KT congregation grew in leaps and bounds, especially by instigating several city-wide evangelistic crusades and by supporting the work of Morris Cerullo who annual conducted a Mission to London.

As the impact of the Toronto blessing was felt in London, KT welcomed both the laughing-falling phenomena and the hot prophetic streams that began to flow within pentecostal and charismatic culture, especially those that indicated that revival fires might begin to burn across the nation.[6] There was no logical or theological connection between the Toronto blessing and the prophetic impulses that began to be felt - although the openness to the Holy Spirit brought about by Toronto had affinities with openness to prophetic images and declarations. Yet, as Thomson has shown in a recent book, the majority of attenders at Kensington Temple, whatever their age, took the view that it was *not* for them to speculate about the return of Christ or the significance of year 2000.[7] As many as 73% of the whole church (from a survey of 2,973 members) took this view whereas only 8% of the church stood on the tip-toe of expectation and believed that Christ would return within 10 years. Of the Africans who attended the church, and they appeared to be the majority group, only 5% believed in an imminent Second Coming: indeed African members belonging to KT appear to be more interested in practical matters concerned with health and prosperity rather than with eschatological ones.

At some point in the late 1990s Kensington Temple began to use a large building in North Acton that could accommodate 4,000 people. The morning congregation still met in Kensington but the evening congregation went to North Acton where the whole KT family from all over London could assemble. Kensington Temple (KT) began to transform itself into London City Church (LCC).

This is part of a complicated story. The Elim Pentecostal Church in Britain is organised into regions, each of which has its own superintendent. Elim accepted Kensington Temple and its associated groups as a new region. By this means the churches planted out by KT became Elim churches and over the decade the churches grew, the biggest to about 500, and they functioned as churches in their own right, with ministers who were

---

[6] J. P. Gouverneur, 'The Third Wave: a case study of Romantic narratives within late twentieth century charismatic evangelicalism', (University of Sheffield, unpublished PhD Dissertation, 2004).

[7] D. Thompson, *Waiting for the Antichrist: Charisma and Apocalypse in a Pentecostal Church*, (Oxford, Oxford University Press, 2005), p.134.

ordained by Elim who managed their own finances and followed an independent path. While KT considered itself as a large multi-congregational church that might have an impact on the whole capital city, the planted churches did not understand themselves as *inter*dependent; they saw themselves as ordinary free-standing churches within the Elim set-up. They did not understand the concept of one membership and one philosophy. Some congregations that had been formed by KT did not buy into its city-wide vision. Some began to ask whether they were KT churches or Elim churches. When Wynne retired from the Elim general superintendency, the issue of identity sharpened.

Dye did not want to set up 'a denomination within a denomination' but he also came to the conclusion that a 'network inside a denomination is unworkable'.[8] The network appeared to make demands that conflicted with the denominational ethos, even if all the churches inside the network were also inside the denomination. The network empowered people but failed when it attempted to coordinate them. The denomination neither coordinated nor empowered but it did give individual identity, an identity perhaps stemming from the process of ministerial ordination, historical perspective and a clear doctrinal basis for faith.

These events raised theological questions about the nature of the church. On reflection Dye came to understand that the great big concept of the church operates at five levels. First there was companionship between two people gathered in the name of Christ. This was where it all began. Slightly larger than this, there was a cell which was a microcosm of the church and intended to be able to grow by dividing itself (as biological cells do). Larger than this again was the congregation to which gifted speakers and singers could minister and, above this, was a celebration were congregations might join together and, finally, there was a convocation where the church as a whole might speak to the nation.[9]

According to Thompson, whose study is specifically focused on eschatological themes, the congregation at Kensington Temple began to be prepared for a major push towards the year 2000. There was a drive to create 2,000 church-related groups by the year 2000 and the desire, at the same time, to buy or secure the building in North Acton which had been renamed London City Church Tabernacle. Yet, despite the high targets, congregational growth was slowing. This may have been due to the opening of specifically Nigerian churches in London that siphoned people away from Kensington Temple.[10] In any event, a meeting was held in Wembley Arena in October, 1998, and around 6,000 people were present. Dye spoke

---

[8] Telephone interview with Colin Dye, 22 September, 2005.

[9] Interview with Colin Dye, 16 January, 2004.

[10] For instance Kingsway International Christian Centre was started in 1992 and is located in Hackney.

of a vision that he had for growth of the church to avert divine judgement on London: 'the Lord showed me that we need to be 2,000 by the year 2000' though he added that 'there are now 800 churches and ministers and groups linked together as one body'. The idea of creating 1,200 extra groups in 18 months was astonishingly bold and, as it turned out, unachievable. The Wembley Arena event was a huge spiritual effort to generate massive expansion, but the strain proved to be too much and by January 2000 it was clear that LCC only had about 500 churches, fellowships and ministries connected with it. Dye's analysis was that there has been 'a failure to mobilise the members of LCC into effective discipleship'.[11]

More serious and symbolically devastating, however, was the loss of the North Acton building. There was not enough money available to buy the building and the church was outbid on the renewal of the lease. In Easter of 2000 LCC 'was forced to vacate the building, which housed its auditorium, administrative headquarters, and Bible College'.[12] Dye withdrew for a 40 day fast to look for answers and revitalise his vision. By the end of the year he was ready to throw himself into the most disciplined and structured of the cell church models, the so-called G12 model, that operated by a kind of pyramid system whereby the minister discipled 12 people in a cell group who then each began their own cell groups and discipled their own converts while remaining in relationship with their original leader. The new people then discipled a further 12, and so on and on. This model appeared to be a remedy for the turnover of people which in the 1990s had rendered KT/LCC vulnerable to alternative spiritual attractions on the church scene. Quite quickly the limited extent to which British people, as well as people with bi-cultural capacities like British Africans, British Chinese and British West Indians, would knuckle down to the demands of the cell system became obvious.

Indeed soon after adopting the G12 model, Dye came to realise 'too much accountability and not enough fellowship and community' characterised the Latin American style of cell church. He changed the 'tone' of cells to make them focus around the presence of Christ rather than a series of evangelistic tasks.[13] By 2001 there were 200 cells in the central church and 900 in the LCC network as a whole.[14]

Meanwhile the religious condition of London has subtly changed. Whereas, in the 1980s, Africans would get of the aeroplane at Heathrow

---

[11] Thompson, 'Antichrist', (2005), p.158, from which the quotations in this paragraph are taken; *Revival Times*, January 2000 <http://www.revivaltimes.org/index.php/10.htm> (accessed 8 July, 2005).

[12] Thompson, 'Antichrist', (2005), p.159.

[13] Telephone interview with Colin Dye, 22 September, 2005.

[14] <http://www.kt.org/about> (accessed 9 July, 2005).

and come straight to KT in large numbers for what was an increasingly expatriate African church, by the late 1990s Kingsway International Christian Centre (KICC) was first stop for African Christians. KT had now begun to attract Brazilians, East Europeans, Spanish and other visitors to London; it had become an international church rather than an expatriate church. Holy Trinity Brompton, pioneer of the Alpha course, as well as the Australian Hillsongs stream, were also equally acceptable destinations for charismatic Christians. Although it is sociologically tempting to do so, it would be wrong to see these different churches as simply competing with each other for the attentions of a fixed number of charismatics within a religious market. Rather, the number of charismatics has climbed upwards while their attitudes, preoccupations and values have subtly shifted first in one way and then in another as global economic trends and population migrations played upon the demographical harmonics of the great city.

iii. Reflection

KT/LCC became a network, but it did so from a different starting point from all the others. The mother-daughter relationship between an originating congregation and a planted congregation goes back many years, well before the vocabulary of apostolic networks was articulated. For this reason KT/LCC, which long had daughter congregations, took on the features of an apostolic network slowly and gradually since Elim, the classical Pentecostal denomination to which KT belonged, was cautious about recognising 20th century apostles. Pentecostals had recognised pastors, evangelists and teachers but, for theological and pragmatic reasons, apostles and prophets were rarer: it was difficult for apostles and prophets to function within any group of churches utilising constitutional procedures since prophets and apostles tend to become impatient with this form of rationality. (It is true that the Apostolic Church of South Wales managed to combine apostles and prophets with constitutional government but it did so by curtailing the free ranging role of these ministries).[15] The result of this is that in some forums KT's apostolic leadership co-exists (surprisingly easily) with Elim's constitutionally validated leadership.

KT/LCC is unique among the networks for other reasons: it is really a London network and not a national one. London is demographically, culturally and economically distinct from other parts of Britain. It is true that the large cities of Britain share characteristics of urban life but London, because of its numerous ethnic groups, soaring house prices, effective public transport system and bewildering variety, outfaces even

---

[15] *The Constitution of the Apostolic Church* (3rd edn, revised), p.13.

Birmingham.[16] Population flows and economic upturns and downturns may be reflected in the London congregations more easily than they are elsewhere and, in the case of KT/LCC, such effects are visible and make the task of pastoral care especially challenging. These challenges, as well as the bold and visionary plans of its leaders, help to account for the zig-zagging path that KT/LCC has sometimes been forced to take.

---

[16] For instance. it is not difficult to find children in London who are from Chinese, Arabic, and Latin American Spanish backgrounds who attend English primary schools, and Saturday Schools in their home language. http://ioewebserver.ioe.ac.uk /ioe/cms/get.asp?cid=4441&4441_0=5194> (accessed 12 September, 2006).

Chapter 11

Noel Stanton and the Jesus Fellowship

i. Noel Stanton, the Man

Noel Stanton was born in 1926 and had grown up on his parents' farm in Bedfordshire.[1] He had worked in a bank and was then conscripted into the Royal Navy. While serving in Sydney, Australia, he was approached by someone in the street who asked him where he expected to spend eternity. The question struck his conscience forcibly and shortly afterwards he gave his life to Christ. After attending All Nations Bible College, he acted as the delegation Secretary for the West Amazon Mission before returning to Bedford as an accounts clerk but, with his heart set on pastoral ministry, he became the leader of a small Baptist Church in Bugbrooke, an English village south of Northampton.

Stanton had been inspired by Arthur Wallis's book on revival, *In the Day of Thy Power*, and invited Wallis to lead a week's retreat, and this pattern of retreat, evangelism and Bible studies continued. In 1960 a tent crusade was held in the surrounding villages and 50 people came forward to commit their lives to Christ. Roger Forster led a Bible week that winter but, after nearly four years, the little chapel had hardly grown beyond its 80 or so members. By 1967, progress was still unremarkable. In the summer of 1968 Stanton began a Saturday night prayer meeting in the manse looking for the power of the early church though, if possible, without the gift of speaking in other tongues. Yet, after reading *The Cross and the Switchblade* about converted drug addicts in New York, Stanton laid down his theological reservations. By the end of 1968 he was praying for revival in Bugbrooke and at the annual meeting that year he told his congregation to ask God for the Holy Spirit. A little later he was praying in the manse when the Spirit came upon him in power and he spoke in tongues and praised God for hours.

A group began to meet in the manse for charismatic prayer meetings and shortly afterwards books and tapes from the Fountain Trust began to find their way to Bugbrooke. Visits from R2 restorationists leaders like Graham Perrins, Gerald Coates and John McLaughlin helped clarify how spiritual gifts might operate and contact with South Chard independent Pentecostal fellowship in Somerset resulted in highly enthusiastic meetings with

---

[1] Much of this whole section is taken from Simon Cooper and Mike Farrant, *Fire in our Hearts*, (Northampton, Multiply Publications, 1997).

clapping, dancing, shouting and tambourines that attracted young people but left Stanton feeling cautious.

In 1971 Gerald Coates came for a week speaking about the grace of God, seeing at least one miracle of healing, and encouraging an uncompromising yet non-legalistic form of Christianity. That summer 60 people went down from Bugbrooke to an old Bible College in the New Forest for a retreat. By then Bugbrooke itself had received ministry both from restorationist and from renewalist streams, that is, both from the ministries opposed to denominationalism and those that wanted denominations to be renewed. Bugbrooke valued its own independence, an independence dating back to its nonconformist heritage, though it was affiliated to the Baptist Union. So it remained where it was, looking for a path of its own. That summer it launched a crusade in August, and in the same summer the news of the Jesus people in California began to reach England. Leather jacketed young people began to come to Bugbrooke, guitars were heard within the previously staid chapel and a cavalcade through the village culminated in a music festival nearby. Local youth began to be converted. That September the nationwide Festival of Light began and a sense of spiritual excitement inspired people to try to move into the village to be near the thriving chapel. The cost of housing, however, was too high and so a Sharing Fund was set up to provide low-cost homes but, despite the enthusiasm, by Christmas, Stanton felt that compromise was preventing lasting growth.

ii. Bugbrooke

In 1972 Bugbrooke began to evangelise the drug scene in Northampton, talking to the bikers, hippies, Hells Angels and acid heads. Converts or potential converts began to come back to meetings at the chapel and trust was gradually built, especially when the chapel was prepared to go to court to testify on behalf of those whose crimes put them in danger of imprisonment. Meetings took place six times a week, gang members began to renounce violence, drug addicts began to be 'high on Jesus' and, despite setbacks of all kinds including fights in the manse car park and painful backsliding, there was steady progress. Alongside the counter-cultural converts, young professional people began to be drawn into the new fellowship and this led to the formation of a new culture that was neither the conventionally middle-class Christian culture of most congregations nor the drop-out culture of hippies. The radical nature of the Christian Gospel and the teaching of Watchman Nee, led to a reassessment of values: a rejection of traditionalism within the church and of anything that smacked of worldliness. By 1973, a new community was being formed. Michael Harper's book, *A New Way of Living*, describing communal living in the

Church of the Redeemer in Houston, Texas, struck a chord.[2] Two Jesus Homes in Northampton now operated and the concept of a common purse, of shared material possessions, was put into practice. Three types of community home were envisaged. There would be Jesus Family Homes for extended families, and Jesus Welcome Homes for front-line evangelism and the Jesus Central Home at Bugbrooke itself. There were now about 200 people attached to the chapel and the national media began to take notice as a 1974 Thames Television film told the story.

Building a community was painful and there was teaching on the cross that broke down old preferences and habits. While the contemporary church emphasised liberty, Bugbrooke needed ground rules to allow its community to function. That year, in 1974, they bought Bugbrooke Hall in 13 acres of parkland with a large deposit and an even larger mortgage. In the summer retreat, now for 170 people, they began to restructure the fellowship by breaking down into shepherding groups of up to 30 people and new leaders were selected, each one with pastoral responsibility for about 10 people. In community houses, elders had continuous responsibility. So, following the internal dynamics of the growing community, they restructured themselves on lines that were partially drawn from wider evangelical and charismatic principles. This was the era of shepherding as well as the era of liberty and Bugbrooke took hold of shepherding ideas while de-emphasising the libertarian streak that ran through some of the R2 congregations; it was counter cultural and counter-Christian cultural.

Once the Hall was in place, numbers quickly increased and they formed an odd bunch of ex-bikers, hippies, graduates and others, all of whom fell to work on the refurbishment of the buildings and grounds. Flats were built to give privacy to families and the building work led to flourishing and unlikely friendships. Some earned their money working for outside employers but others began to work for the Housing Association and a community Food Store that was established in the Hall. Ex-hippies established herb gardens and collections of books were pooled into a library so that, quite quickly, about 30 people were now in residence in New Creation Hall, as it was now called, and many others were in the Welcome Homes in Northampton or other homes bought by members of the community in the village. They became almost self-sufficient as musical instruments were learned, songs and poems were written, pigs were farmed and a common bank account was opened. Women also joined the community and there was formal teaching on the importance of celibacy.

Teaching about the kingdom of God filtered in from the wider church outside. The kingdom was understood as both present and future but the

---

[2] See for instance J. Hinton, (ed) *Renewal: an emerging pattern, Graham Pulkingham and others*, (Poole, Celebration Publishing, 1980), where there is extensive discussion of modern Christian communal living.

church of the present was a foretaste of the kingdom, and the Bugbrooke people began to see themselves as radicals for the kingdom of God. Their community became 'Zion', the city of truth that should shine out with holiness in love, a place to resist the encroachments of the world by acknowledging neither the lordship of Caesar nor wisdom of the Greeks, almost a new monastic movement of simplicity and non-violence. Stanton urged the assembled members at the annual summer retreat not to forsake their special calling despite the hard road ahead and, though some left after his sharp challenge, others joined.

The next year the community life deepened with mutual submission and mutual recognition of the gifts and qualities of members. Stanton moved into New Creation Farm and partially devolved his pastoral leadership to others. Meanwhile the Hall became so full that there were two portakabins in the courtyard and over 100 people were sharing in the common purse and in the farm as well as the health food[3] and building enterprises. People came from as far afield as Holland and Australia and in that year more than 300 people attended the annual retreat. Yet there were also troubles as the group was accused of being cultish and one member died in the open air of hypothermia. Members of the Bugbrooke community were disillusioned with the sloppy Christianity in the churches and some of the churches retaliated by circulating false rumours about the community. Even so in 1977 two more community homes were opened, one in Daventry composed of three houses in a row. Despite criticism, the value of 'shock troops' to the church at large – whether the Anabaptists of the 16th century or the desert communities in patristic times – were understood, and Stanton believed that a community lifestyle built on personal sacrifice could only be entrusted to those who had renounced everything. Covenant brotherhood, echoing the cry of the Scottish Covenanters, was esteemed and, when in November a builders' yard in Towcester was bought, expansion into a network of businesses escalated.

Over the following years the number of properties increased and the Bugbrooke community was constantly evangelising by putting on midweek meetings or Saturday evening gatherings in nearby towns. The old hotel, Cornhill Manor, a mile from Bugbrooke itself, was bought in 1978. A converted motel was bought in a village within reach of Coventry, Rugby and Warwick and renamed Harvest House and evangelism on university campuses took place. There were tensions at Warwick University within the Christian Union when the Bugbrooke folk were accused of being like Moonies and an article in a national newspaper implied that Stanton was the leader of the dangerous cult.

---

[3] Goodness Foods has a turnover of £10 million per year and employs about 70 people, all of whom are paid the same (BBC Working Lunch, 17/10/02).

To counteract this the community reached out across the evangelical spectrum, and drew up an orthodox statement of faith ('this church upholds orthodox Christian truth, being reformed, evangelical and charismatic; practising believer's baptism... we believe in God, Father, Son and Spirit; in the full divinity, atoning death, bodily resurrection of the Lord Jesus Christ; and in the Bible as God's Word'). Local church leaders were invited to ask questions and by then the financial structure had been formalised. Members shared their income through a common purse account and the surplus went into a community trust which was used to purchase property and capital goods. The accounts were open to members, audited by outside accountants and presented at an annual church business meeting. Those who left could receive back the capital they had invested. Even so, there was criticism in the Christian and the secular press. Stanton was too authoritative for *Buzz* magazine, which also did not like the absence of television, radio or pop music or recreational activities like going to the cinema. Greenbelt was similarly cold but, despite the opposition, by 1981 there were 600 in residence and 70 leaders so that Bugbrooke amounted to the largest Christian community in Europe. Even so, the opposition was discouraging and Stanton pressed for deeper spirituality although, for those in the community, the more subtle dangers of unthinking routine and dull order threatened religious vitality.

A fresh spiritual fire began to burn the following year and Stanton, in his unwavering public ministry and in private conversations in the Hall, did his best to motivate the entire community. It was a hard-working life. On Tuesdays there was a covenant *agape* meal.[4] On Wednesday servant groups drove all over the Midlands to meet people. On Fridays there was evangelisation and on Sunday there was worship with Holy Communion and Stanton preaching and an invitation for visitors to go back to the community houses for a late lunch and an afternoon of fellowship. In the evenings there were Gospel meetings in various parts of the Midlands. Shops had been opened in Leamington, Bletchley, Rugby and Leicester and the building services continued. A new road haulage business was started. Altogether about 150 people were employed in these commercial enterprises.[5] The inspiration of the big Korean churches helped the community to see that was no upper limit to what might be achieved. Their evangelists working in Birmingham spoke to glue sniffers, pimps and prostitutes, continuing the outreach to the unchurched margins of civil society. By May they had established a large house in the Birmingham area as well as one in Banbury. Church households were also established, where

---

[4] *Agape* is the Greek word for divine love.
[5] They have a turnover of about £15 million per year (Northampton Chronicle and Echo 7 July, 2000). By 2003, the figure had risen to £35 million per year.

the 'household' was a community house plus its non-resident members and friends.

Numbers continue to increase as better support networks were put in place for new members. Each one belonged to a specified group and a discipling band. Each had his or her own shepherd and a brother or sister assigned to them. A new household was established in Milton Keynes and in Yarmouth. Another went to the Glastonbury Festival. Revival meetings began in the chapel and lengthy periods of prayer followed. The community now had 150 servant groups as well as Fire Teams that would live in the area and stay for a few months to evangelise. Beachfire Teams would go to holiday resorts like Hastings, Blackpool, Weymouth and Brighton. Marquees were set up in each of the areas where they were working and, although they did their best, they were unable to bring revival to Britain. Whenever they went out into the public world like this, opposition would almost invariably raise its head either in the form of denunciatory religious pamphlets or secular articles. There was a misunderstanding with Evangelical Alliance[6] and then, despite their vibrant activity, they were rejected by the Baptist Union Council which refused to allow Stanton even to address them.[7] Nevertheless evangelism continued and 64 people were baptised in 1986, many of them from among the forgotten street children. Prophetic words gave encouragement as did the example of the early Salvation Army so that, in 1987, the Jesus Army was born.

iii. The Jesus Army

The Jesus Army is the campaigning arm of the Jesus Fellowship Church and the Army's intention is to go where others will not go. It marched from Hyde Park to Trafalgar Square and delivered a letter to the prime minister in Downing Street. With green combat jackets, a large golden 'Jesus Army' patch on the back and red epaulettes and a desire to declare war on homelessness, alcoholism, racism, abortion, hate, drug addiction, violence and crime, the Army was usually greeted enthusiastically. Later that year and in 1988 there was a further spiritual outpouring, similar to and in advance of the Toronto blessing, so that by the late 1980s there were 49 households with 900 adults in covenant and 200 children. When the large inter-church March for Jesus was held in April 1988, the Army sent 400

---

[6] Following investigations into the fellowship the Alliance cited the lack of good relationships with other evangelical churches, and the dangers of 'a single-mindedness of approach that inferred directive leadership to a strong degree' within their reasons behind the request for resignation.

[7] The Union cited the fellowship's lack of involvement with other Baptist churches and the group's expansion/recruitment in areas near other Baptist churches without consultation as the main reasons for their expulsion.

'soldiers' down to London to take part. By the 1990s, a giant marquee was put up at the Cornhill for bank holiday festivals three times a year and teams joined YWAM and British Youth for Christ. And at the beginning of the 1990s the whole community met together for a bumper celebration in Northampton. Stanton predicted a time of great victories in the midst of great pain. There was a big rally at Wembley and Stanton showed an interest in the prophetic movement exemplified by the Kansas City prophets. By 1991 the Bugbrooke people were gladdened by the optimistic faith of restorationist movement. Campaigns continued, the marquee was taken to Liverpool, and there was a feeling that the Jesus Movement of the 1960s might at last come to Britain in the 1990s. For those brought up within the Bugbrooke community, church-based Christianity seemed to be insipid, too well-behaved, too groomed and too disconnected from the tattooed, nose-ringed, hair-dyed 'underclass' who found their way into the Jesus Army. In 1992 as part of the restorationist surge 50,000 Christians filled the streets of London and it appeared possible that, at long last, there would be an awakening in Britain that would change the political and social face of the country. That this did not happen is a matter of historical record: there were victories of expansion and there was the pain of disappointment – as predicted.

By 1994 in response to a prophetic word, the Fellowship was seeing its mission as being to 'adopt the lost generation' and the 'young men and women from broken families, often living on the streets'. Here the idea was that a moral revolution should inform the fight against drug abuse, abortion, crime, promiscuity and selfishness. Generation J (for Jesus) should replace Generation X (the unknown lost generation whose parents were the wild children of the 1960s).[8] What Stanton had built within Britain looks set to last for a long time to come. One national coordinating body of 25 (or 20 with 5 members of an apostolic team) looks after 75 church households led by 200 pastors and their trainees and the Jesus Army of 3,500 members. There are around 24 congregations scattered in the big cities of Britain, and as many as 25,000 magazines and 100,000 street papers are distributed three times a year.

iv. Reflection

The Jesus Fellowship at Bugbrooke is different from all the other British apostolic networks because it centres upon community living and common ownership. The result of this is that the Fellowship can go through periods of isolation when it is the internal dynamics of the community that determine its direction and priorities more than the external forces and

---

[8] See S. J. Hunt, 'The Radical Kingdom of the Jesus Fellowship', *Pneuma*, 20, 1, (1998), 21-41.

factors of the outside world. There are periods when the community appears to be introverted and concerned with its own purification or holiness and then there are other periods of extraversion when, realising its separation from the rest of the Christian world, it reaches out only, on occasion, to be rebuffed. In phases where the internal dynamics set the trend for the coming year, this often happens during the annual retreats. In phases where external relationships predominate, it is through the ministry of visiting preachers or by meetings between community leaders and other Christians.

The community life offers emotional, psychological and spiritual support for its members. Some of these may find that the support becomes overbearing and, even, oppressive and it is these, presumably, who eventually leave. Yet the support system is also invaluable to aimless and vulnerable people whose tangled lives have led them to the streets and to drugs and crime before they find Christ and a new way of living. In other words, it is unlikely that the homeless or the aimless would make the transition from the streets to a settled Sunday congregation, however good and caring the ministry of this congregation might be. The leap from the uncertain streets of big cities to the ordered lifestyle of disciplined Christianity is simply too great to be made through the ebb and flow of weekly churchgoing. So the community is especially suited to providing a home for young men and women outside the normal orbit of Christian influence. At the same time, and inevitably, these young people may find the contrast between the freedom of their previous lives and the discipline of their new Christian lives too great to sustain with the result that, if they eventually leave the community, they may do so with bitterness and recrimination and with all the sense of psychological desolation that the ending of close relationships entails. Accusations of abusiveness and the misuse of authority may follow.[9]

The criticism of the Jesus Fellowship both in the national press and by Christian agencies has obviously hurt it. The Fellowship feels itself to be offering a unique, radical and committed form of Christianity suited to the current era. Its response to such criticism has often been shaped by prophetic utterances or visionary pictures. Charismatic gifts have helped to nurture the community and to erase discouragement. Moreover the theology of the kingdom of God, and of the church as an expression of the kingdom, has helped to produce a view of normal Christianity as being permanently

---

[9] Nigel Wright's chapter 'Restoration and the House Church Movement' in S. Hunt, M. Hamilton and T. Walter (eds), Charismatic Christianity: sociological perspectives, (Basingstoke, Macmillan, 1997), pp.60-76, sees an inevitability in this.   'Not surprisingly, the Fellowship's intense style and all-engulfing requirement of commitment lead to occasional allegations of abuse from disillusioned former members' (p.67).

in opposition to the world. In this respect criticism from the world is a badge of honour and an indication that the community is 'being persecuted for righteousness' and therefore approved by God. Looked at in this way, criticism will achieve the exact opposite of its intentions. If the world tells the community to embrace more competitive sport or television and less celibacy, the reaction of the community is to reaffirm its current practice – and to do so with a shout of triumph.

The community has formed and founded a complicated set of institutional and organisational components and has done so largely as a result of its common purse policy. Without the funds generated by the common purse, it would have been difficult to set up businesses. Without the businesses it would have been difficult to buy the properties, buses and marquees that are used in evangelism. There appears to have been no large strategy at the beginning. The network of homes and businesses grew up bit by bit in response to needs and successes. Stanton brought an uncompromising heart and mind to bear upon the development of the entire process and, in this respect, demonstrated great qualities of leadership. His willingness to listen to what was going on in the charismatic or restorationist movement, however, gave him access to theological debate on shepherding, prophecy or the Toronto blessing. He shared in the hope for a national revival that ran through the millennium-conscious churches of the late 1990s. As the Multiply Network – the name of the independent congregations connected with the Fellowship – shows, church planting is also within his plans.

Chapter 12

John Wimber and Vineyard

i. Beginnings

The account of John Wimber (1937-97) and the development of Vineyard congregations in the United Kingdom is not parallel with accounts of other networks discussed in this book. This is because the Vineyards in the United Kingdom were *prepared for* by Wimber's ministry (though he stopped short of calling himself an apostle) and then *initiated by* John Mumford who functioned, from the first, in a quasi-denominational framework that also avoided seeing what was being done purely in apostolic terms.

Wimber was born into a poor non-Christian home in 1934 and became a musician, playing his first gig in 1949 at the age of 15 while living in California. He put together a rock group called The Righteous Brothers and, when the drummer was converted, John, still a heavy smoker, began to attend a Bible study and in 1963 he and his wife, Carol, accepted Christ. A year later to Carol's consternation John was filled with the Spirit and launched into a period of intense evangelism. A short while after this, his own small son wandered into their neighbour's yard, where there were beehives, and was immediately badly stung by a swarm. John carried the child back to their house and began instinctively praying in tongues for the boy's healing - which rapidly took place.[1]

This was the era of Californian hippies, of 'flower power' and of the subsequent Jesus movement. In the mid-1960s, Chuck Smith began to pastor a small church that grew to be the influential Calvary Chapel. Although Smith had grown up in a Pentecostal denomination, he played down charismatic manifestations in public worship. He concentrated on teaching the biblical text with care and accuracy.

> When we started at Calvary Chapel in 1965 with only 25 people, I was determined that I would make those 25 people the most knowledgeable people of God's Word in all the harbor area. I began teaching them five nights a week ... We began to develop the fellowship, the koinonia, where we really became an integrated unit and began to minister to each other both in the physical and in the spiritual sense, praying for each other,

---

[1] C. Wimber, *John Wimber: the way it was,* (London, Hodder & Stoughton, 1999), p.76.

binding our lives together in prayer, helping out each other in a physical sense. [2]

One estimate put the total number of Calvary Chapel (Costa Mesa) baptisms performed over a two-year period during the mid-1970s at well over 8000. Additionally, over 20,000 conversions to the Christian faith took place during the same period... from humble beginnings more than 40,000 people now call Calvary Chapel their home church. Calvary Chapel has become the third largest Protestant church in America and the largest in California. [3]

In 1974 Kenn and Joanie Gulliksen started an offshoot of Calvary Chapel and called it The Vineyard. Wimber, meanwhile, worshipped at the Yorba Linda Friend's church, a Quaker congregation, and became co-pastor in 1970. The church grew to a hundred people. Wimber took a biblical degree at Azusa Pacific University and entertained a cessationist theology that ruled out charismatic gifts in the present age. After a crisis of conscience in 1974 when Wimber felt he was treating pastoral work merely as an occupation – he left it and was offered a job by Peter Wagner at the Charles E. Fuller Institute of Evangelism and Church Growth. He remained at the Quaker congregation while travelling extensively and working with 27 denominations, none of them Pentecostal or charismatic, as a church growth consultant. He began to apply the findings of church growth research that Donald McGavran and Peter Wagner had compiled. [4] While working at Fuller Wimber began to talk with Chuck Kraft and Russell Spittler as well as returning missionaries from Third World countries who spoke about dramatic healing and miracles. While both Wagner and Wimber heard the stories, it was Wagner who began to experience a paradigm shift that brought the power of the kingdom of God to the forefront of his understanding of church growth. The church should not grow simply by a series of cleverly devised programmes but by power encounters as the kingdom of light overcame the kingdom of darkness and as God set free those whom Satan had bound.

Not long afterwards John and Carol Wimber started a Bible study group in their own home and rediscovered spontaneous charismatic Christian worship. In 1977 Wimber was forced to spend the night in Detroit when his

---

[2]   <http://www.calvarychapel.com/?show=Resources.Ebooks.thephilosophyofministry ofcalvarychapel> (accessed 28 February, 2006) and, according to Jackson, B. Jackson, *The Quest for the Radical Middle: a history of the Vineyard,* (Cape Town, Vineyard International Publishing, 1999) p.85, the church had been 'birthed in revival', spiritual gift followed after Sunday morning services.

[3] Quoted in Jackson, *The Quest,* (1999), p.37.

[4] E.g. D. McGavran, *Understanding Church Growth,* (Grand Rapids, MI, Eerdmans 1985); C. P. Wagner, (ed) *Church Growth: the state of the art,* (Wheaton, Il: Tyndale House, 1986).

flight schedule was deranged by a snowstorm. After reading Psalm 61 he woke up and felt that God spoke to him saying, 'I've seen your ministry and I'm not very impressed and now I'm going to show you mine'.[5] The Bible study group in the Wimbers' home prospered but, though painful, they judged it wisest to leave the Quakers whose elders did not want a 'tongues outbreak'.[6] Within a few months their home group had become about a hundred people. By the summer of that year it had reached 200 and the Wimbers formally joined their new congregation to the Calvary Chapel network.

For nine months in 1977 Wimber preached his way to the new congregation through the healing-packed gospel of Luke. Jesus preached the kingdom of God and demonstrated it by healings. Nothing similar happened for Wimber until one unexpected morning when a member of the congregation immediately recovered after prayer.

> Do you see it, Carol? We teach the Word, then God does the work. Like TELL and SHOW or SHOW and TELL! I think I get it![7]

A spate of healings followed together with openness to the Holy Spirit until, on Mother's Day 1980, when the church had grown to about 700 people, in response to the prayer 'Come, Holy Spirit', young people began to speak in tongues, cry out, fall over, praise and be healed. Wimber agonised over what had occurred but felt that this was from God. Power evangelism – the title of first Wimber's book, was initiated.

When Wimber first arrived in England in 1981, he was a successful pastor of a congregation of at least 400 people and had worked as a church growth consultant for several years. He had wide experience of different denominational structures and policies; he had himself been attached to two denominations; he had been a successful evangelist and pastor; he had experienced dramatic healings following his preaching; he had a well-worked out theology of the Holy Spirit within a bigger theology of the kingdom of God[8]; he saw the kingdom of God as being manifested now/not yet, with the result that healings are an expression of the present kingdom of God while failure in the realm of healing belongs to the 'not yet' dimension; he was an accomplished musician whose style of worship was supported by original songs; he had a relaxed West Coast personality. His visit to Britain was a resounding success, particularly among charismatic Anglicans who warmed to the self-deprecating humour and unthreatening renewal ministry. St Andrew's Chorleywood, where Bishop David Pytches

---

[5] Jackson, *The Quest,* (1999), p.61.
[6] C. Wimber, *John Wimber*, (1999), p.120.
[7] C. Wimber, *John Wimber*, (1999), p.134.
[8] Based largely on the exposition of G. E. Ladd, e.g. G. E. Ladd, *Jesus and the Kingdom*, (London, SPCK, 1966).

was the minister, and St Michael le Belfrey at York, where David Watson had been in charge since 1965, were specially and miraculously affected.

ii. After 1981

Between 1982 and 1986 Wimber taught his famous, controversial and well-attended Signs, Wonders and Church Growth (MC510) course at Fuller.[9] He was now putting into practice what he had learnt about the Holy Spirit and had joined this to his expertise in the theory and practice of church growth. Church growth was partly a theological discipline, partly missiological and partly anthropological and organisational. It was certainly intellectually robust. While these ideas were being verified in practice, Wimber found himself at the centre of an argument among the pastors of Calvary Chapel, some of whom disliked his emphasis on contemporary spiritual gifts. Wimber left with Smith's blessing and joined the Vineyard of which, in 1982 with Gulliksen's consent, he became the leader. He therefore found himself, without foreseeing the path, the leader of a small and distinctive denomination dedicated to church planting and open to spiritual gifts. In 1983 Wimber had a vision and heard God asking him to start 10,000 churches.[10] Vineyard Ministries International was formed to facilitate Wimber's international conference activity, to be a distributing company for the Vineyard's music and teaching tapes and to oversee the planting of congregations. Wimber's visits to Britain continued to take place while the 'back story' unfolded in the United States.

Before the first visits to England in 1981 Bob Fulton dreamt that Vineyard would be planting churches abroad. On reaching Britain, the team told David Watson about the dream but he said 'No – that is not what this is about at all' and he asked Wimber to agree not to plant any churches in England.[11] Instead Wimber agreed to equip existing British churches with power so that they could do the planting for themselves. Watson was thoroughly evangelical and equally thoroughly Anglican. It took other Anglicans to persuade Wimber to change his mind.

John (b 1952) and Eleanor Mumford were Anglican curates who had attended Vineyard meetings in California and had liked them so much that they had moved their whole family out there (1985-87) to learn from Wimber. Mumford had expected that he would return to the Anglican church to apply his insights. On several occasions he asked Wimber's permission to plant in the UK and, on each occasion, was denied. In 1984 Watson lost a long-running battle with cancer and died. Wimber had been

---

[9] Among those who attended the course was John Coles, who went on to lead the New Wine network, Hunt, (1995), p.112.

[10] Jackson, *The Quest,* (1999), p.93.

[11] Jackson, *The Quest,* (1999), p.259.

true to him and had even flown over to the UK specially to pray for him. In 1986 Wimber gave Mumford permission to begin planting Vineyards. Mumford returned and planted a large Vineyard in southwest London. Other ex-Anglicans like Rick Williams, Martin Smith and Chris Lane joined the British Vineyards.

The expansion of Vineyards in Britain must be understood against complicated pressures and needs arising out of the religious situation within the United States. First, Vineyard's own natural growth resulted in the need for structures and relationships to be gradually redefined. This was particularly so once the Association of Vineyard Churches (AVC) saw itself more clearly as a church planting movement with responsibilities in many nations. Second, there were pressures and conflicts within the United States over issues relating to prophecy, and later, the Toronto blessing, that impacted the North American Vineyards. These impacts inevitably rippled across the international structures and values that Vineyard came to articulate as well as more directly upon Britain. Third, Wimber himself was in declining health from the period when he had his first angina attack in 1986 until he was diagnosed with cancer in 1993; although he made far-reaching decisions right up until his death in 1997, Wimber gradually retreated from the scene.

With regards to natural growth, the Association of Vineyard Churches doubled in size in United States in the 10 years from 1988 to 1998. What had been a largely Californian movement spread across the country. At the same time and in the same 10 year period Vineyard began working in other countries: it was in three in 1988 and by 1992 was in eight, and by 1998 in 52. That decade, when North American and international Vineyards are added together, saw an increase of nearly 400%, from 236 churches in three countries to 819 churches in 52 countries. There can have been few other such rapid phases of ecclesiastical growth within the whole 2,000 years of church history, and, without the conflicts that accompanied it and without the gradual diminution of Wimber's energies, the AVC's progress might have been even more spectacular.

Moreover the growth in the number of Vineyard congregations was by no means a foregone conclusion. In 1988 the AVC pastors assembled at Anaheim for a week to discuss their organisational links. They were intent upon agreeing a constitution and bylaws so that they could transform themselves into a denomination. Wimber understood that religious movements often consolidated their initial gains by legal enactments and formal agreements so as to preserve benefits for future generations. The meeting of pastors was divided on the subject. Some, particularly the original Calvary Chapel pastors, thought that it was important to remain entirely relational and informal. Others were prepared to concretise their practice into quasi-legal formulae for the sake of the future. At the end of the week, when the pastors were prepared to sign the document, Wimber met with the board and admitted that he felt that God had spoken to him telling him to back down. The pastors left the conference slightly dazed but without any constitutional encumbrance.

Second, in the same year Wimber began to be influenced by prophetic ministry coming from Kansas City Fellowship. The Kansas City Fellowship was an independent and radical church that gave great prominence to prophecy and a restoration model of the Christian history. The Kansas City Prophets were introduced to AVC in 1989 at a spiritual warfare conference where prophetic words were given to the whole Vineyard movement. It has to be said that some Vineyard ministers accepted what was proclaimed while others were dubious.[12] Among the prophetic utterances given to Vineyard were those announcing a new breed of Christian champions would be raised up and that Vineyard itself had been sovereignly brought into being by God, that prophetic and apostolic ministries would come into maturity in the 1990s, that worldwide movements of prayer would be raised up, that the Holy Spirit would be imparted to the church for power evangelism, that there would be signs in the heaven, that those who did not abase their hearts in humility would be cut down by God and that the Vineyard was going to increase tenfold. In addition individual prophetic words were given. Paul Cain, the most prominent of the Kansas City Prophets, told John and Eleanor Mumford that the revival would 'probably find its starting point... when the Lord will just start to move throughout London and throughout England'.[13]

The predicted revival did not arrive and Wimber went through a period of intense criticism as a result. Much of this was public and in the form of polemical books, tracts or articles by scholars of non-charismatic persuasions.[14] In November 1990 at the AVC board meeting conflict over the desirability of organising for the next generation resurfaced. In Jackson's words,

---

[12] 'It should also be noted that those Vineyard leaders who had to deal with problems related to instances of prophetic abuse have called the credibility of many of these stories into question. Their opinion is that some of the prophecies were bogus...' Jackson, *The Quest,* (1999), p.175.

[13] Jackson, *The Quest,* (1999), p.208.

[14] There was an article in *Christianity Today* (August, 1986). J. R. Coggins, and P. G. Hiebert (eds), *Wonders and the Word: an examination of issues raised by John Wimber and the Vineyard Movement*, (Winnipeg, MB, Kindred Press, 1989), was more critical; John Armstrong wrote unsympathetically about Wimber in *The Standard* (May, 1991), a journal connected with the Baptist General Conference, and this was followed by M. S. Horton (ed), *Power Religion: the selling out of the evangelical church?*, (Chicago, Il, Moody Press, 1992). M. Percy, *Words, Wonders and Power*, (London, SPCK, 1996), though more nuanced and without personal animosity was also negative in his assessment and showed that Wimber was attracting scrutiny in Britain too.

The issue on the table was whether the Vineyard would choose to become an organised, cohesive movement which would make room for and take pastoral responsibility over hundreds, even thousands of new churches, or whether it would become a completely loose fellowship of churches with no organisational ties or structures for church planting, missions and pastoring.[15]

In the event, the board decided on the organisational option. Some of the pioneering pastors resigned almost immediately. The Kansas City Fellowship, which joined itself to Vineyard in 1989, left in 1996. Wimber himself would eventually apologise to his pastors for leading them into the prophetic era and it is possible to interpret the Vineyard's change of direction and fresh philosophy of ministry as a reaction against the untested and, in some cases, untestable utterances of the Kansas City prophets.[16] Such an interpretation is too simplistic since the AVC continues to be open to charismatic gifts. Rather it has become a new kind of denomination, one that Wimber, calling on sociology rather than theology, defined in terms of 'centred sets', a term that describes groups that have joined together around core values because people agree on the direction they want to go and roughly speaking on how they want to get there. There can be disagreement on the non-core values without any threat to the stability of the whole group. In making this choice to be a 'centred set', Wimber was deliberately avoiding the alternatives of becoming a 'bounded set' that specifies definite beliefs and practices and that thinks sharply in terms of an 'in' or 'out' group. Equally, AVC was not to become a 'fuzzy set' without any organisational centre.[17]

Once the denominational option had been selected, the planting of British Vineyards could go ahead more easily. Britain, and the other countries where Vineyard now had a presence, knew what sort of values and styles should be propagated. *Some* kind of structure both within each country and between countries could be put in place and the purpose of that structure, whether in dealing with the pressures of the outer fringes of the charismatic movement or in handling disagreements among leaders, was plain to see - as the preceding turbulence over AVC's direction and its reaction to prophecy had so graphically shown. Structure laid down an agreed method for resolving conflicts and coping with crises.

Third, Wimber's health suffered a series of hammer blows. He was diagnosed with cancer in 1993 and his son was diagnosed with cancer a year later. In 1995 he suffered a stroke. The cancer treatment had left him with damaged saliva glands so that it was difficult for him to speak. He did his best and continued to write in AVC publications but, as the Toronto

---

[15] Jackson, *The Quest,* (1999), p.231.

[16] Jackson, *The Quest,* (1999), p.234.

[17] Jackson, *The Quest,* (1999), p.244.

blessing gathered speed in the mid-1990s, a series of criticisms of Wimber, his methods, his churches, his theology and his person were unleashed upon him.[18] His wife Carol describes some of the 'vicious attacks' including those who told him that his illnesses were the result of divine retribution. But he could hardly have expected being attacked in a public restaurant and pursued by a man screaming 'Antichrist! Antichrist!'[19]

The only consolation was that the debilitation produced by cancer and heart problems ensured that Wimber understood that his days, however they might be stretched out by medication, were numbered. If divine healing did not occur, he would die. And if he was going to die, he must do what he could to ensure that the Vineyard succeeded in surviving and avoiding the mistakes of earlier revival movements. He felt that the Lord said to him, 'you must die before you die' meaning that before he died physically he must efface himself from his constitutional positions within the different branches of the Vineyard.[20] It must learn to stand without him. Perhaps for this reason in 1995 the Vineyard International Consortium (VIC) was set up with a membership of all the national leaders, and national leaders were those ministers who oversaw 30 or more Vineyards in their own countries. The consortium was a relational group and Wimber was its head until his death. Afterwards Bob Fulton, his brother-in-law, was chosen as leader, and more recently John Mumford was chosen, and the group continued to function without any international bureaucracy that had power to control. This was done by the simple expedient of ensuring that money was not creamed off to employ international staff. In America, Vineyard churches gave 3% of their income towards the Vineyard movement and similar figures were chosen by each nation where Vineyard worked. Consequently, each national Vineyard leader is also the pastor of a local congregation. The Consortium gave space for friendships to be built and, when some years later, potential problems occurred because two national Vineyards were planting churches in a third country, it was agreed that no one should be bound by a regulatory framework. The newly planted Vineyards would cooperate with each other in the new nation simply because they shared the Vineyard values, its DNA and its style, rather than because they were obliged to do so by ecclesiastical bylaws – though it is true there were such bylaws.[21]

---

[18] The published critiques were one aspect of the criticism he faced.

[19] C. Wimber, *John Wimber*, (1999), p.171.

[20] He was leader of the Anaheim Vineyard (which he handed over to Carl Tuttle), of the Association of Vineyard Churches and of Vineyard Ministries International.

[21] Interview with Andrew McNeil, 27 February, 2006.

iii. Vineyard in the UK

In a discussion of 'the Anglican Wimberites' Stephen Hunt identifies a series of factors that made Wimber's ministry attractive to charismatics in general and to Anglicans in particular.[22] Wimber's six-day 'Third Wave' conference held at Methodist Central Hall, Westminster, in October 1984 attracted a large attendance, the largest contingent of which (42.5%) was Anglican. Baptists amounted to 23.5% and Pentecostals to a mere 4%. Evangelicals Methodists, Roman Catholics and others accounted for lower percentages still. The main attenders, therefore, of the big conference were Anglicans even though the conference had been convened by Douglas McBain, a leading Baptist charismatic.

The conference involved meetings and workshops on topics like inner healing, deliverance, spiritual warfare and their connection with church growth. The conference fell at a propitious time. The charismatic movement had reached its zenith in the previous decade and was looking around for direction. Conflict remained in the air between charismatics who stayed inside their denominational homes and charismatics who mutated into restorationists. Wimber came with what appeared to be an answer to many of these concerns. He was not attacking denominational charismatics but, because of the setting up of the Vineyard in California, could hardly fail to recognise the process whereby newly charismaticised converts joined newly founded congregations. It was not that Wimber offered a mediating position but rather that he offered something for everybody. There was spiritual warfare (outward and aggressive) and there was inner healing (quieter and more introverted); there was church growth; there was a relaxed attitude to the 'stay in/come out' debate among charismatics. Among Anglicans, too, the Wimber's impact was sustained when about 1,200 clerics signed up to the Vineyard's mailing list so that future conferences and celebrations could easily be notified to likely attenders.

Another appeal of Wimber's ministry was that charismatics who debated with conservative Anglican evangelicals about the theological conundrum of 'how God speaks today' could find in kingdom theology an answer: God speaks by acting in power, and it is this that raises debate about the authority of Scripture beyond disputes about texts and propositions. Conservative Anglican evangelicals were not traditionally dispensationalist and had no built-in theological bar against the miraculous. When they saw miracles, as they believed they did during that London conference, their temperamental reservations could melt. Moreover there had been healing ministries within charismatic Anglican churches for several years. Colin Urquhart was known and respected. Wimber's approach, which completely

---

[22] S. Hunt, 'The Anglican Wimberites', *Pneuma*, 17, 1, (1995), 105-118.

lacked the hype of the independent televangelists, accorded with British predispositions.

After the conference, a 200-strong set of Vineyard teams fanned out from Greater London to 35 different centres in Britain. Churches from several denominations (including Anglicans) accepted preaching and teaching. The model of ministry that the teams adopted was that, when they prayed for people who were ill, they also expected revelatory words of knowledge or wisdom to help diagnosis or in counselling. Such revelations might be imparted to praying individuals or the leaders of meetings without prolonged preparatory hours of spiritual wrestling. Moving in the Spirit was activated by faith, and young people in jeans and t-shirts could exercise charismata as well as any clerically attired ordinand or Bishop. What the teams did was not too far removed from traditional Anglican beliefs. After all, the Anglican Confirmation Service during which the local Bishop lays his hands on young Anglicans who are affirming their faith, is one where young people are intended to receive the Holy Spirit. The Spirit is imparted by the laying on of the Bishop's hands in a ceremony that is squarely modelled on New Testament practice. Wimber's practice of laying on hands for the receiving of the Spirit (for healing) was therefore quite in line with three centuries of Anglican practice.

When after 1986 Vineyard moved into church planting, the ground had been prepared. Vineyard congregations in the UK grew rapidly and steadily between 1986 and 1996. There was one congregation in 1987, three in 1988, four in 1989, 10 by 1992, 17 by 1994 and 32 by 1996. This is exceptional growth for British culture and, even more astonishing, is the way that the growth was achieved. Very little of it was by the adoption of congregations that slipped their moorings from older established denominations so as to connect with Vineyard. Of the 32 Vineyards in existence by 1996 only five were adoptions. All the rest were planted out from existing congregations. The Vineyard in southwest London, the first in the country, gave away people to create a nucleus for its new plantings, and the same can be said of Riverside Vineyard at Twickenham. In these densely populated urban areas the Vineyards were able to meet in schools and other hired buildings and to draw in young families and professional people in relaxed settings. They copied Californian culture by making their casual style of dress an explicit expectation and this made their congregations attractive to young people. They expressed a concern for the poor and, in worship, made use of Vineyard music that appealed to the taste of Generation X. According to Peter Versteeg 'rejection of 'religion' by Vineyard believers, ultimately leads to a religiosity in which the emotional life of individuals is sacralized'.[23] In any case 2002 there were over 75 Vineyard congregations in the UK and by 2006 this had grown to 85.

From his years as a church growth consultant, Wimber understood cycles of church growth. He appreciated how, in United States, the cohort of churches founded in the 1940s had served their own generation with a style of 'being church' that entirely suited the cultural norms of the era. The new generation required a new style of church, a new way of doing and being church, that took into account clothing, music, sport, typical family relations, and other features of contemporary life. It was not that Wimber was deliberately targeting the young but rather that he was creating a church scene where the young would feel at home, where they would not be out of place or embarrassed and where the church would address their hopes and needs. He understood, also, that it was young congregations which planted out from themselves. Once the church settles into a comfortable middle age, it was much less likely to take risks or to disturb its 'primary group', a term that he invented for the core cluster of people – often members of the same family – within a congregation. The implication of this was that young congregations could rapidly plant out a new congregation and the new congregation could plant out another new congregation but, eventually, when the first congregation having lost key personnel was weaker than it had been previously, it needed to recover, and the same was true of the second new congregation. As a result church planting on this model functioned in cycles and periods of recuperation were eventually necessary. The growth of the Vineyard within Britain reflects this pattern since, although there was an increase in the number of Vineyard congregations right through the 1990s, at the turn of the millennium there was a slowing down and even, in 2002 a slight net decline.

Vineyard churches UK worked by in-house, on-the-job training and 'vision casting'. This is supplemented by short-term residential training. Rick Williams took charge of the planting task force and gathered people together for three weekends per year. Regional or national leaders send promising church-planters to these training sessions. Otherwise training is provided within local churches and this is coupled with 'vision casting' where prophetic utterances and other charismatic gifts seek to unveil the mind of God for direction and tactics. The approach prioritises charismata over planning committees.

Coordination is achieved by an annual meeting. Every year there is a residential national leadership conference lasting four or five days. Here there is Bible teaching as well as the casting of vision. At the start only about 25 people attended and John Wimber or Bob Fulton would come

---

[23] P. Versteeg, 'Draw Me Close: An Ethnography of Experience in a Dutch Charismatic Church', Vrije Universiteit Amsterdam, PhD Dissertation, 2001.

through to preach. Now each country makes its own arrangements and preachers are invited in as the national leaders think fit. Conference attendance in Britain has grown so that in 2006, 500-600 local leaders are expected.

The concept of a 'centred set' continues to be expressed among the British Vineyards. Similar values are instilled within each of the congregations and each congregation is autonomous. The values hold them all together (though there is also a creedal statement). The network is small enough in Britain for many of the pastors to know each other personally and for the churches within the region to be linked together under the supervision of a Council and to be joined electronically by access to a shared password-controlled web portal that holds a wealth of theological, financial, administrative and pastoral resources. By these means a common vision for church planting and for the 'feel' of Christian life is maintained. Each autonomous congregation reaches out in relationships to its kindred congregations as well as to nationally and locally recognised leaders. Local autonomy ensures that each congregation is financially self-governing although each is asked to contribute 5% of income to a national fund, of which 1% is sent to the Vineyard International Consortium. There is no giant national headquarters full of office staff running the organisation. Wimber had wanted his administration lean and mean and the British churches follow his lead. All its national leaders pastor local churches.

John Mumford is the national director of Vineyard Churches UK and was installed into that position publicly by Wimber in March 1996 at the Vineyard National Leaders' Conference. Wimber's philosophy of ministry, dating right back to the early 1980s, saw leadership in terms of function rather than office.[24] What mattered was what a man or woman did for God rather than the badge they wore. So far as Wimber was concerned, somebody might function as an apostle in one situation and as an evangelist in another. Equally someone might once have been an apostle but later have subsided into eldership. The name tag was not important and, as a result, Wimber never held the view that apostles were brought into existence by irrevocable callings. His notion was more flexible and less hierarchical – although he clearly believed that leaders should lead and pastors should be in charge of their churches. Yet he was less hierarchical in the sense that he did not anticipate that certain ministerial offices always pulled rank over other ministerial offices to produce elite classes of governing Christians. When he recognised John and Eleanor Mumford, however, he was doing something more than being pragmatic. He recognised in them an ability to lead and transmit Vineyard values.

---

[24] As his tape series, 'Church Growth Leadership: Wimber interprets Wagner', (1984) indicates.

The Vineyard system of oversight in the United States made distinctions between three levels of leadership: the local pastor, the regional overseer and the national director, but it also made distinctions between those who were people-orientated and those who were task-orientated. Among those who reach particular goals were church planters, evangelists, educational specialists and worship leaders, and these people could operate at the regional or national level. Such a matrix of analysis recognised the distinctions between trans-local ministries and local ministries and between pastoring ministries and other forms of ministry.[25] The UK adapted the system of leadership and government used in the US.

In Britain until the end of 2001 Vineyard Churches UK were managed by a board that had no leadership functions. After the 1st January 2002 the board became a Council and the Council was required to focus on leadership and strategic direction and vision while leaving various task forces to manage their own responsibilities. The Council leads churches by exercising spiritual, trans-local authority although it is not of itself a decision-making body. This Council is made up of national leaders who meet together and can make decisions by voting if necessary. At the same time Vineyard wishes to underline the notion that spiritual authority is different from structural authority: 'if we have spiritual authority, we don't need a legal authority. And if we don't have spiritual authority, we certainly don't want legal authority'.[26] The Council works with a group of trustees who have a responsibility for the legal and financial propriety of Vineyard Churches UK and whose task is to protect the reputation of the churches and to ensure integrity. Trustees also operate at the local church level and, although Vineyard Churches UK have adopted what is effectively an episcopal form of government, they have done so while paradoxically recognising the autonomy of the local church. The local church and the local pastor draw upon the services of the national leadership – of the episcopacy - because they recognise that this leadership expresses their own deepest values, and not because they are obliged to do so.[27]

The national Council is not always in session and an innovative method of helping pastors spiritually has been invented. Each pastor has an overseer, a senior figure who is another Vineyard pastor, who will have up to six pastors to look after. (This is equivalent to the regional overseer in the States). This ensures that there is always someone to whom the pastor can relate. Care and thought have been given to the way that pastors and

---

[25] Jackson, *The Quest,* (1999), p.340.

[26] <http://www.vineyardchurchesuk.com/> (accessed 3 March, 2006).

[27] If a Vineyard pastor dies or resigns, a replacement is found by consultation between the local leaders (usually the trustees) and the national leadership but not by one or other acting independently of the others. Because so few Vineyard churches are adopted, there is exceptional loyalty to the fellowship.

overseers interact because some pastors are independent and other overseers tend to take the 'call me if you need me' stance. The best relationships between pastors and their overseers are to be found when they have a similar perception of the frequency with which they should interact. Vineyard works hard to make sure pastors and overseers connect synergistically. The overseers work as 'mentors' and 'coaches' (two words that feel at home in a Vineyard setting) and there are 25 of them for the 85 churches. Lastly at the local level the pastor leads by providing direction, vision, teaching and care and local trustees facilitate the achievement of this mission and give advice in financial and legal matters.

iv. Reflection

Vineyard is the only one of the networks considered in this book that originated outside the United Kingdom. The network came into existence as Wimber's ministry passed through a transition from its beginnings in church growth and interdenominational renewal until it reached the more unbounded condition of becoming a free-standing collection of international networks. Yet, because Wimber delegated the running of Vineyard in the UK to John Mumford, Vineyard in the UK is a genuinely apostolic operation. There has been church planting and the churches formed in this way have been linked together through their relationship with a recognised apostolic figure. Because of Mumford's own ecclesiology, Vineyard is content to utilise episcopal concepts rather than apostolic ones – though the difference between these two concepts may be undetectable to the naked eye. Where Mumford has been precise in his organisational distinctions, however, is in the connection between the autonomy of the local church and the authority of the episcopal figure overseeing the local church. Here the paradox of autonomy and oversight is well understood but made workable by an emphasis upon shared values.

The growth of Vineyard in Britain has been rapid and comparable to that achieved by any of the other networks. Its attractiveness to young people and its distinctive musical tradition have resulted in lively congregations while its openness to charismatic gifts and its concern for charitable enterprises have resulted in well-rounded congregations. The lessons in cultural sensitivity learned by Wimber in California in the 1970s have turned out to be transplantable to Britain, and there is every likelihood that Vineyard will continue to grow. Its existence demonstrates that networks can come into existence in a variety of ways and need not follow a predetermined sequence of stages. There must be forces that draw collections of free congregations together and, equally, there must be at least some capacity to plant new congregations. Beyond this, the balance between newly planted and existing congregations will vary between networks and over the course of time.

Chapter 13

Colin Urquhart and Kingdom Faith

i. Colin Urquhart, the Man

Colin Urquhart (b 1940) was brought up in a non-Christian home. He enjoys singing and so went to join the choir in his local Anglican church where he began to hear about God and started to ask questions that his parents were not able to answer. At his request they bought him a book of prayers and he used to kneel down to say these prayers each night. He asked God to speak to him. Sometimes he would fall asleep on his knees. God's glory began to be revealed, though he did not realise this at the time. At the age of 13 he knew he wanted to be ordained. This was reaffirmed when he was 17. So he went to King's College, London, which in those days offered Anglican ordination training at an of-campus site. Its Theology Department reflected the fashions of the time and forcefully pressed liberal theology on all its students. This had little effect on Urquhart who had a streak of solitariness within him that was expressed by self-disciplined spirituality. He would spent many hours in meditation and often 'there would be periods of silent adoration when I was conscious of God's presence'.[1]

Shortly before ordination Urquhart came to a point of crisis. He was painfully shy and afraid to open his mouth in public meetings. He knew that, once ordained, he would have to stand up before congregations many times. He went his room and found himself speaking in other tongues, though without being able to put a name on the experience. Later he shut himself in the chapel and continued praying in this way. This was 1963. He had never met a Pentecostal and hardly met an evangelical. Speaking with other tongues gave him confidence to go through with ordination. A year later he married.

During his curacy he began to grow dissatisfied and frustrated by his inability to help the faithful people who regularly attended the Sunday services. This frustration grew more intense when he visited those who were ill. He formed a prayer group that, instead of reeling off a set list of names, wrestled with the promises of Scripture in preparation for individual ministry to those who needed help.

After 3½ years he was moved to be priest-in-charge at St Thomass, Letchworth. He stayed there from 1966 to 1970 and during this time his

---

[1] C. Urquhart, *When the Spirit Comes*, (London, Hodder and Stoughton, 1974).

own eyes were healed, a fact confirmed by a medical consultant. These were the days when the music scene was divided between mods (who wore stylish suits, rode lambretta scooters and liked The Beatles) and rockers (who wore leather jackets, rode motorbikes and liked Elvis). He spent time with these young people and his car in the car park became a counselling room.[2] They began to come to church although he was aware they came because he had invited them and not because they knew Christ. He still found preaching a challenge. So he shut himself away and fell on his face before God asking for help. He decided to trust the Lord for his Sunday sermons. In the morning he preached an ordered sermon telling people about the importance of the communion service. In the evening he made no preparation and found himself preaching spontaneously and was fascinated by the effect. He almost watched himself preaching. The evening service became packed with people. When he asked one of the church wardens why this was, he was told that this was because of the sermons. They were different from the others. He decided always to preach this way and has done so ever since however large the meeting he has to address. He would find himself saying things he later discovered in the Scriptures. So he learned a form of prophetic preaching.

Then, though only age 29, he was appointed vicar of a new and unpromising church on a housing estate in Luton. This was a large parish with three chaplaincies and two curates. He spent two weeks in prayer and preparatory reading for this ministry during which time God gave him a revelation that he was a son of God. Watchman Nee's book, *The Normal Christian Life*, made a contribution but it was the revelation of filial closeness to God which made all the difference: it gave Urquhart confidence and overwhelming joy.[3] Over the next six weeks a revival started. Each day Urquhart was praying 'what do I do?' He asked the curates to select people whom he could teach in a small group. Meeting in his home for the first night he spoke to them for two hours solidly. The group wanted him to carry on longer and came back the following week. They were asked to list the sins in their lives and then he prayed through the lists with each person individually. Immediately he had done this the love of God swept over them. A second home group was assembled and the two curates asked to join it, and then a third. Soon people in the parish began to be healed and healing prayer groups were formed. In the first 15 months everybody who was prayed for was healed and everyone came through the intensive teaching course was filled with the Holy Spirit.[4] The rudiments of community living took shape, encouraged by prophetic utterances given during times of prayer:

---

[2] Interview with Colin Urquhart, 25 March, 2004.
[3] Interview with Colin Urquhart, 25 March, 2004.
[4] Interview with Colin Urquhart, 25 March, 2004.

You are to commit your lives to me – to be led by my Holy Spirit. You are to promise obedience to the leading of My Spirit within the Community…you are to show the quality of love I require of my children to Christians of other churches.[5] (taken from Urquhart, 1974: 103, 104)

In 1971 Urquhart attended the Fountain Trust conference in Guildford and became aware of the breadth of the charismatic movement and its style of worship. He returned home and abandoned the Prayer Book's regular Evensong service and began unstructured evenings of praise. People came from over the world to see what was happening. He wrote the paperback *When the Spirit Comes* that told the story of his ministry at St Hugh's between 1970 and 1974 and charted the breakthroughs into authentic warm relationships and the periods of repentance following the death, despite extensive prayer for his recovery, of a much loved church warden.[6]

ii. A Developing Ministry

Despite the success of the ministry at St Hugh's and the thriving congregational life that was being built up, Urquhart felt that he should move on. This was a challenge to his faith since, if he resigned his living within the Anglican Church, he would have no salary to support his young family and nowhere to live. He was convinced that God had told him 'I have other sheep, not of this fold. To them I'm calling you'.[7] He went to see his Bishop, Robert Runcie, who later became Archbishop of Canterbury, and discussed the painful decision. Runcie was understanding and so, at the beginning of 1976 on a cold and wintry day, Urquhart began a new chapter in his life. The Fountain Trust had offered a house in Surrey where he and his family could live and from which the ministry could be launched. It began with a conference for clergy at Ashburnham Place, Sussex. Urquhart spoke about the need for individual repentance before the reception of divine revelation and, equally, the need for repentance once revelation had been received; this was the road to individual and congregational renewal.

The lessons of faith were rapidly learnt as a new car and finance were provided and Urquhart felt that God was calling him to encourage local churches to become what they should be: meaningful expressions of the body of Christ. Unlike many other ministers Urquhart concentrated on the fine grain of personal moral behaviour. Negative and critical attitudes had to be dealt with so that communal renewal could fully flower. This ministry rapidly lead to a series of overseas engagements. Urquhart went to Canada

---

[5] Urquhart, *When the Spirit*, (1974), pp.103, 104

[6] Urquhart, *When the Spirit*, (1974).

[7] Many of the details of this paragraph and ones that follow are taken from C. Urquhart *Faith for the Future*, (London, Hodder and Stoughton, 1982).

and then to New Zealand where he taught on submission, authority and leadership. From there he visited Ohio and then went to Toronto as the guest speaker at the Anglican Diocesan Renewal Conference. After the first busy year of itinerant ministry he learned of the deteriorating situation at St Hugh's and realised that 'corporate commitment to one another... was beginning to diminish'[8] and that 'the anointing of the Holy Spirit upon the corporate life of any fellowship depends upon corporate obedience'.[9]

He travelled to South Africa and spoke at large renewal seminars presided over by the Archbishop of Cape Town, Bill Burnett, and at Port Elizabeth, which was still in the grip of the apartheid regime, and on his return felt it right to ask George and Hazel Hoerder to join him and help with administration. Bit by bit a new Christian community was being put together. Later Urquhart travelled to Australia for a series of large and dramatic meetings at one of which he heard a black Pentecostal preacher who appeared to minister with great power so that people fell over in the Spirit. In response to this Urquhart began to teach on faith, especially in prayer. This emphasis in ministry led to a defence of miracles for communicating the gospel of the kingdom of God. The kingdom became a new theme within his preaching. He spoke of the demonstration of God's power inside and outside the church. In 1978 he visited 33 different centres in United Kingdom and, soon after this, David and Jane Brown joined his team and they began to pray together for a large house where the ministry might be based. By a series of intricate and miraculous interlocking events he came to be offered a large 28 acre property, The Hyde, in Sussex. There was enough space here for a community to be properly established. There were individual houses on the estate as well as the main home. Within a short time weekly meetings at The Hyde began and soon attracted a congregation of 150 for which David Brown became the pastor.

iii. The Bethany Fellowship

To define the legal basis for the ministry a trust named the Bethany Fellowship was established in 1979 and covered the work in Britain and overseas.[10] Bethany was a place where the friends of Jesus lived and where Lazarus was raised from the dead and both friendship and miracles were the heart of what Urquhart stood for. The trust embraced the growing community at The Hyde as well as Urquhart's travelling ministry, which was now called Kingdom Faith.

Urquhart went to Switzerland and France, accompanied by David Brown, and began to work from time to time with the evangelist Don

---

[8] Urquhart, *Faith for the Future,* (1982), p.47.

[9] Urquhart, *Faith for the Future,* (1982), p.48).

[10] In 2004 the trust had an income of over £3m per year.

Double. The meetings where Urquhart spoke began to be so large that it was difficult for him to pray for people individually and so he learned to exercise the charisma of a 'word of knowledge'. All this was built upon lengthy periods of personal and collective prayer. The thematic thread of kingdom authority – healing signs and wonders - was coupled with the desire for mutuality and openness in personal relations. Members of the community at The Hyde gave each other the right to confront and correct each other on matters of personal morality and spirituality.

Although he preached widely among Anglicans in Britain and overseas, Urquhart was radical enough to see the value of house churches,

> I, along with others involved in church renewal, had often urged people to remain in their churches as witnesses to others, to share of the new life and vision God had given them, to love and serve... now I sensed, again with many others, that God's prophetic word was changing. Had churches missed the opportunity that God had given them? If they persisted in their traditional ways, could they really be surprised if God bypassed them in what he wanted to do in the nation [the UK]... I had a growing conviction that God wanted to meet powerfully with this nation... did he have to wait until the majority of denominational congregations were alive with the power of the kingdom... were the new house churches God's answer to the dilemma?[11]

Urquhart answered that the new house churches were part of the answer in the same way that 'faithful denominational congregations' were part of the answer. Urquhart was never so embedded within his own denominational affiliation as to regard the house churches as schismatic. He recognised that there were lazy denominations that, despite periods of renewal, subsided into complacency. This was never an option for Urquhart. On one occasion when he was preparing for a mission in Birmingham with his crusade team, he had expected that they would go home for a weekend with their families before the ministry was to begin but he felt the Lord was telling him that they had to spend the weekend in prayer. When he told everybody this, nobody objected. The whole team was repentant and crying to God. They worshipped on Saturday and then on Sunday morning and then in the evening and the holiness and glory of God was revealed to them.[12] All through that summer they prayed for two hours a day. Each day people at missions in Grimsby, Southport, Blackpool, South Wales and Blackpool were converted and filled with the Spirit. One evening while ministering in mid-Glamorgan, Urquhart had a vision of Jesus: 'his face was gaunt, his eyes sunken; his expression one of total grief' and Urquhart desperately

---

[11] Urquhart, *Faith for the Future,* (1982), p.146.
[12] Interview with Colin Urquhart, 25 March, 2004.

pleaded with Christ to revive Wales.[13] Shortly afterwards at a gathering in South Wales there was open confession of sin that awakened long-lost memories of the 1904 revival. Throughout this phase Urquhart became aware that endless renewal services would not affect the life of the nation. At the beginning of the 1980s he felt he should concentrate on short five-day missions with an evangelistic emphasis rather than go preaching for a night or two in many different locations. With help from his team he began to formulate a teaching programme that was intended to feed believers and prepare them for mission. The Kingdom Faith Teaching Course was made up of audio cassettes and study guides and when it was advertised in 1980 over 600 groups immediately enrolled. Meanwhile international ministry in Switzerland, France and other parts of the world continued.

iv. Roffey Place

For three years they ran two conferences a month for pastors at The Hyde in Sussex. Then in 1983 Roffey Place was bought and opened to students a year later as the premises of Kingdom Faith Revival College. In 1989 the entire ministry was practically relaunched. There had been a dozen people on the ministry team but Kingdom Faith itself had grown to nearly 100 full-time staff because, in addition to Roffey place, three other bases had opened in different parts of England. In 1992 Urquhart cut down his travelling ministry and planted a new church less than 2 miles from Roffey Place. The purpose was to create a group of revival churches in different parts of Britain of which this would be the first. So the National Revival Centre, once a factory, was renovated and leased in the summer of 1994 to house the new congregation. In 2002 the building was purchased.

This strategy was designed to make an impact on Britain through revived communities. In this respect, Urquhart had a unique vision. Rather than seeing the congregation through the eyes of conventional charismatic ecclesiology (with structures and spiritual gifts), he wanted an entire Christian community living daily in a revived state. In a sense he was harking back to the original experience of St Hugh's in Luton. He wanted to create a church where members of the community loved and supported each other in a more demonstrable way than was normative in Western Christianity. He did not advocate communal living of the kind that pooled material resources or absorbed the natural features of the family, but he wanted a palpable harmony and unity.

Inaugurated with three weeks of evangelistic 'kingdom' meetings the congregation grew to 230 people and, shortly after this, climbed to 1,000. Meanwhile the College comprised a core of 35 students. The College and the congregation reinforce each other and, on a termly basis, *everybody*

---

[13] Urquhart, *Faith for the Future*, (1982), p.196.

comes together, both from the revival congregation and all the students and staff in the College to stand as a combined community before God. This joint functioning of a church drawn from people living in the locality and the College that attracts students from all over the world is an almost unique configuration. The teaching and ministerial functions of the church can be discharged in various ways and it is easy for members of the congregation to benefit from College and for students at the College to benefit from the congregation. Among the most vibrant of the results of this arrangement are those reflected in a ministry to young people that has produced modern, energetic, unashamed music and drama-based youth evangelism that is easily compatible with the fashions and speech rhythms of today's Britain. A ministry to women has the same upbeat and contemporary feel and is a far cry from the sober and demur sisterhoods of the past.

By 2005 the College had over 100 students doing one, two or three-year courses and a media ministry had been added for producing weekly television broadcasts via satellite on the God Channel as well as a daily radio programme on Premier Radio in the London area. Internet streaming of the Sunday morning service at the church is available through the Kingdom Faith website and other Kingdom Faith churches have now been added so that, within the United Kingdom, there are 60 churches in a relational network and at least three times that number overseas. The network is not governmental but rather intended to encourage both parties, the apostolic teams from Kingdom Faith and the participating churches, to pray regularly for one another, to speak well of one another and to bring church members to one of the two annual Kingdom Faith conferences. Both parties know what is expected of the other and this creates the opportunity for cost/benefit analysis and, unusually in networks, creates a relatively open door policy allowing aspiring churches to apply to join if they wish. Equally, individuals can join.

v. Reflection

Colin Urquhart's personal pilgrimage has taken him a long way. He began as an Anglican vicar attuned to prayer and, bit by bit without pain and recrimination, has moved out of the established church into a fully independent ministry. His pathway has been guided by personal and collective prayer and he has avoided coming under the influence of charismatic fashions or the controlling influences of high-profile ministries in the United States. He began as a preacher of renewal, working at first within the Anglican sector in Britain and overseas, but over time became a force within the house church tradition. Consequently his ministry is more varied than that of many other preachers. Although he would now be identified as an apostle, this is a relatively new classification because he functioned as a healing evangelist with teaching gifts in the 1980s.

Wherever he might be placed on the theological spectrum, he has retained ecumenical perspectives also. He ministers across the denominational divides and is welcome in many contexts. The Revival Church in Sussex belongs to a local consortium of churches drawn from other traditions – Catholic, Baptist, Anglican – implying that Urquhart has no difficulty in working with denominational ecclesiologies: his concern is with the revelation of Christ, and it is notable that most of his writings include reference to spiritual experiences.[14] There is, in his written output, reference to the glory, majesty and mercy of God that, while it is consonant with Scripture, is not simply a matter of exposition, and is not usually found within the writings of other apostolic figures.

This reference to spiritual experience leads to prophetic apprehensions. He listens hard to what he believes to be the voice of God. More than this, his emphasis on personal spirituality and morality goes well beyond that to be found in most apostolic preachers. His appreciation of the impossibility of community life without personal integrity is a characteristic insight. His ministry has been connected with the creation of a Christian community at each stage of the journey. Communities provide a support base to his own itinerant work and generate the resources to allow excursions into the mass media. They are not, however, sectarian in emphasis. For example, they do not incorporate Christian schools to isolate young people at the Revival Church from the rest of society. On the contrary, Kingdom Faith is turned towards the UK and the world. The networked churches are offered help but not government; this means that the bonds tying them together are specifically relational and intended to be expressive of personal commitment rather than of authority and subservience.

---

[14] For instance see chapter 1 of C. Urquhart, *From Mercy to Majesty: moving into revival*, (London, Hodder and Stoughton, 1995).

Chapter 14

Hugh Osgood and Churches in Community (CIC)

i. Hugh Osgood, the Man

Hugh Osgood was born in 1947 into a Salvation Army family.[1] At the age of 11 he left the Salvation Army and joined the Anglicans. After school he went up to Barts (St Bartholomew's Hospital in London) to become an oral surgeon, that is, combining surgery and dentistry. After avoiding the Christian Union in his first year as a student he felt, in the summer of 1965, God was 'on my case'. He read C S Lewis' *Mere Christianity* and found his new vicar to be passionately evangelical. After joining the Christian Union in his second year Osgood felt 'God wants me in full-time ministry'. He approached the Church Pastoral Aid Society (CPAS) about Anglican ordination but was told to continue his secular degree. He did so and, after six years of training, thought that he had no choice but to practice his profession. He passed through a series of preliminary jobs and then discovered there was an opening for a missionary dentist in Zambia. This turned out to be funded by the Brethren. Eventually he signed up and was accepted with the African Evangelical Fellowship and was ready to travel out in 1971 but, in 1972, President Kaunda cut aid and he was unable to go. Having taken to heart the motto, 'don't do anything overseas you have not done at home' he saw the need of acquiring church-planting skills and ended up in London helping with a small church in Forest Hill that was linked with George North's ministry. He was still linked with North when he planted a church in Bromley in 1974.

North was a proto-apostolic figure and one who inspired many of the early leaders of the later apostolic networks. North established his reputation at an independent congregation in Bradford where he was pastor from 1952 to 1965. In 1965 he moved to Liverpool and after 1968 he pursued a full-time itinerant ministry with considerable success. Sociologically speaking, North's congregations failed to develop a communitarian outlook because they over emphasised personal holiness. They were characteristically small in numbers and inward-looking. Even so North was recognised as having apostolic gifting that the younger restorationist preachers appreciated. He was, albeit in a minimal form, their

---

[1] Information and most of the historical judgements in this section are taken from an interview with Hugh Osgood in South Bromley, 4 July, 2006.

model for an apostle: itinerant, persuasive, radical, biblical and charismatic in both the popular and the theological senses of the word.

North's example was an inspiration to the restorationists – and obviously Osgood was among them - who saw possibilities in the setting up of the first networks, even if they did not use that terminology then.[2] North appeared to be founding his own denomination though, again, this would not have been how he viewed it. As well as the work at Forest Hill and Bromley there were also emerging house churches elsewhere in south London. Ian Wilkie was in Lee and Terry Watson was in Eltham. Peter Parris, guided by North, moved up to take on the problematic Bradford congregation. It was there that Parris met Bryn Jones and, after the two of them had brought the Bradford congregation to a new level by joining it with two other congregations, Parris and Jones responded to calls from the south in 1974/75 by saying, 'we feel that God is giving us a pattern we can transfer'. Arthur Wallis was asked to preach at an inauguration meeting for what looked like the first strands of a restorationist network in south London. At the same time Ray Lowe at Biggin Hill Baptist Church began to link with Terry Virgo.

ii. A Developing Ministry

While all this was going on Osgood gave up dentistry incrementally, dropping down to four days a week and then to three. In 1976/1977 he was pastoring the North-linked Bromley Fellowship and sent a request to North asking for help over a discipline problem in the church. North replied, 'do what you think is right and I will support you in whatever you do'. This was typical of North's style. He was 'hands-off' and unwilling to impose himself upon those who might have been his followers. This was the time when there was pressure on the restorationists to submit themselves to the 'covering' of the shepherding movement (see chapter 15). Osgood was pressed to look for covering but he resisted it because he appreciated North's open approach. More widely, shepherding pressures polarised clusters of churches so that it was at about this point that the two demarcations of restorationism identified by Andrew Walker, R1 and R2, became visible.

Meanwhile Osgood continued to work with the Universities and Colleges Christian Fellowship (UCCF) by holding university missions and ministering to students. He did not wish to be identified with evangelicals to the exclusion of restorationists or, conversely, with restorationists against evangelicals. UCCF was sceptical about restorationists and Osgood became a bridge while sensing the demands of each. Matters were further complicated because distaste for shepherding doctrines was driving North

---

[2] A. Walker, *Restoring,* (1998), p.44.

to become more exclusive. On one occasion North was asked, 'who do you submit to?' to which he replied, 'I submit to you, brother', implying that Christianity functioned through mutual submission rather than through the building of a chain of command to a distant apostolic boss. In the early days of restorationism when about 80 leaders came together, North asked the young men to pray for him while refusing to become their official leader. As a consequence many left him and began to link up with R1.

By now Osgood felt that he needed to step away from the George North set-up. He recalls triggering an exchange of correspondence in 1983,

> 'look, I am just finding it really painful. I appreciate everything you have put into my life'. And he [North] wrote a letter back that was a little bit disappointing where he talked about 'marching to the beat of a different drum'...but that's not how I saw it... a lot of other people were trying to marshal us all to go down a different route altogether.[3]

Having come through this Osgood was able to say,

> So I was in this very interesting position. I had negotiated my way through; basically to keep a foot within the George North camp but still had good relationships with people who are now in New Frontiers; a good relationships with Roger [Forster], obviously, doing the university stuff together.... and stepping back a little bit from the George North thing I just felt that it was getting too exclusive... but if you start excluding the exclusives you are also becoming exclusive so I did try to keep all of my links.[4]

In 1983 Luis Palau held his Mission to London and in the south east he began with a mission at Blackheath. Hugh's wife, Marion, worked with Faith Forster and they were both very involved with Hugh saying, 'it seemed as if all my previous experience proved really useful in the whole area of organising the counselling and follow-up...I did a lot of the organisation for that, working very closely with Ichthus which had just passed the 400 people mark for its Sunday morning meetings'.[5] When Palau completed the London Mission in 1984 at Loftus Road, the Queens Park Rangers football ground, Osgood sat on the designation committee and, through this, got to know many people who came from Caribbean pentecostal churches.[6] Philip Mohabir had recently set up the West Indian Evangelical Alliance and was an encouragement to Hugh as he went on to set up South East London Link building on the relationships that had been

---

[3] Interview with Hugh Osgood, 4 July, 2006.

[4] Interview with Hugh Osgood, 4 July, 2006.

[5] By this date Ichthus would have numbered over 400 for its Sunday meetings.

[6] More details are given in H. J. Osgood, 'African neo-Pentecostal Churches and British Evangelicalism 1985-2005: Balancing Principles and Practicalities', (SOAS, London University, unpublished PhD Dissertation), 2006.

forged during the Luis Palau meetings. Clive Calver had wanted to go further and establish a London-wide Evangelical Alliance. There were various people on board for this but only the South East London Link was possible at the time. Having run the south east link from 1985, Osgood was approached in 1988 by Billy Graham to contribute to 'Mission 89'. He accepted this and found himself organising counselling and follow-up. He did all this while he was still leading the Bromley church; the dentistry had by now shrunk to about half a day a week. He was also working with Operation Mobilisation in Bromley (the team pastor to George Verwer's team) and he was chair of the Bromley Evangelical Fellowship while also finding time to put energy into Operation Mobilisation's teams in Pakistan. As a way of rationalising and funding this welter of activity, Spinnaker Trust was set up to cover his inter-church and missions work.[7]

In 1988 the Spinnaker trustees met together and told Osgood they thought it was time for him to step down from the Bromley church. Osgood called his Council of Reference together and prayed with them and received feedback. They felt that it was not the time to hand over his local church leadership. So he gave the Trust away instead and carried out his wider ministry through the local church base. The base rapidly doubled after he was approached by the elders of Bromley Christian Centre (which was an Assemblies of God - classically pentecostal - congregation). They decided to join together his independent church (Bromley North Free Church) and the Bromley Christian Centre. The previous pastor, George Forester, had already fought an outbreak of the cancer that later killed him. The officers agreed to this plan and, when the two churches were combined, there were on paper a membership of 197 people in each of them. One congregation was older, managerial and more conservative and the other was full of young professionals and more radical. Amazingly, the congregations mixed well. However, there were bigger strains within the eldership and eventually the two churches split up again. Osgood admits to his own struggles in saying, 'the thing I came unstuck on was that I could not really function in a church where the young people were expected to be in a separate entity from the congregation as a whole'.

So he left to start out afresh but 'planting out Cornerstone Christian Centre did not turn out as cleanly as I had expected... it was not a re-forming of the church I took in'. He turned out to have that British rarity, an independent pentecostal church. It began with 140 people. In 1989 when Osgood was trying to get the African and Caribbean churches involved in the Billy Graham mission, Philip Mohabir challenged him, 'if you want these churches to be involved in your agenda, you had better be involved with theirs'. Huge numbers of African Christians started to come to the UK

---

[7] Now a schools' charity: see <http://www.spinnakertrust.org.uk/> (accessed 2 June, 2006).

in the late 1980s and early 1990s and many of them wanted to plant churches and the question they were asking everybody was, 'where are the independent pentecostal churches?' Someone pointed them in Osgood's direction and so in 1993 he co-hosted a conference, Faith for London, at the Wembley Conference Centre. About 500 people came onto the mailing list and a Ministers' Fellowship was started in the same year.

'From the outset we want to respect what you are doing in your community' was Osgood's position. This led to culturally-relevant churches not looking for any particular style or praxis. 'I felt very strongly that the values we needed were values of compassion, integrity and cooperation' so, in 1997, Churches in Communities (CiC) was set up as a member-led organisation.[8] Small churches were suspicious of intrusion from secular bodies like the Charity Commission because they thought the spiritual side of their work would be affected. Yet independent churches wanted their voice heard. Free Church denominations needed a means of interface. So Osgood and others worked on a structure acceptable to UK charity law and they now have a small Council elected by members at the annual meeting. Churches can become members as can ministers or ministries. Usually when the church becomes a member, the minister becomes a ministerial member as well. The Council handles accreditation. There are about 70 ministers and churches combined in the UK and, because they have accrediting powers, are allowed to ordain prison chaplains and gain the other benefits of a recognised ministry list. Churches are not accepted into CiC without a willingness to submit a copy of annual audited accounts, subscription to a standard evangelical statement of faith and a willingness to 'accept counsel and discipline'. Members receive guidelines for codes of practice for staff, policies acceptable to Child Protection Agencies and help in establishing financial accountability and standards of bookkeeping expected by the Inland Revenue and the Charity Commission.

There is also an overseas dimension to CiC. Following two conferences in Nigeria and visits to Pakistan, international membership started. Younger ministers there want to work cooperatively but without domination, a model they find lacking within denominational structures. In the UK, ministers often see the need for accountability sooner than their churches – until a crisis arises, when the advantages of the network become apparent. CiC has not really projected itself as being a corporate voice for anyone: the African and Caribbean Evangelical Alliance can do this while CiC negotiates pastorally to solve problems as they arise on the ground. In the UK, too, when a network breaks up, as sometimes happens, it often fragments into mini-networks like the new T-Net or RiverNet, and these then can, if their members wish, work alongside CiC and make use of its services.

---

[8] <http://www.cicinternational.org/CiC.htm> (accessed 10 July, 2006).

iii. Reflection

CiC is distinct from other networks in that it has been assembled from independent churches rather than having been primarily planted by the founding apostle. This gives the network a different feel from other apostolic networks though, using a broad definition of apostleship that includes reorganisation within its ambit, CiC is genuinely apostolic. It has been brought into being by Hugh Osgood and it offers a balance between autonomy and regulation that is recognisably similar to the looser conventional apostolic networks. The difference lies with the obvious service given by the network to its members, the use of voting to choose a council, and the power of individual ministers and ministries over their own congregational jurisdictions. CiC assembles autonomous groups for the benefits that a network can offer, and is only beginning to function as an entity that is greater than the sum of its parts. Nevertheless it illustrates a variant in the network form, and an important one, because it services cross-cultural or migratory people. It makes a bridge between African culture and British culture, especially in terms of charity law and professional standards, while encouraging its members in the direction of compassion and integrity. It resists the one-style-fits-all mentality and glories in diversity to the extent that it encourages young African ministers to see the advantages of styles they might otherwise have regarded as beyond the pale.

Oddly enough the structure chosen by CiC is not dissimilar from the early structure chosen by Assemblies of God in 1924. In both instances, pre-existing congregations came together using a Presbyterian form of leadership, that is, a style of leadership in which representatives of constituent churches were formed into an executive body that dealt with accreditation, mission and other tasks either too great for local church or too small for its minister to become expert in. Where CiC differs from the early Assemblies of God is in the matter of doctrine. CiC does not concern itself with doctrinal minutiae but rather with acculturation to British church norms and with the facilitation of maturing churches and ministries.

Part III

Crossflows

Chapter 15

The Cell Movement

i. Introduction

Having followed the stories of the 12 main networks in Britain in the previous section of this book, the next section turns to events and movements that cut across all the networks. So we leave each particular network's history and turn to the branches and varieties of the cell movement, a movement that has its roots in the shepherding movement of the 1970s. Cell churches, or cells inside churches, or churches with cells, were to be found in the late 1980s and in the 1990s. Naturally argument over the relative benefits of congregational groups and home groups occurred. Then, having examined cells, we look at the Toronto blessing, an extraordinary series of phenomena connected with 'laughing in the Spirit' that were prevalent in most of the networks in the 1990s. Finally we turn to an account of the social and economic conditions, as well as the technological changes, that occurred in the 30 or more years that have elapsed since the networks were founded. We look at the rising tide that lifted the apostolic boats.

ii. Beginnings of Cells

The origin of the modern cell church is impossible to trace. Proponents of cell church trace it back to the New Testament and, in various forms, through 2000 years of church history. The 20th century concept of the cell church is first mentioned, at least in publication, in the late 1950s or early 1960s.[1] What makes analysis difficult is that meetings by Christians in their homes predate this development. There had been cottage prayer meetings among revival-seeking nonconformists well before this and, as is well documented, W. J. Seymour the pastor of the Azusa Street revival, held prayer meetings in North Bonnie Brae Street in Los Angeles in 1906 before he moved to the livery stable where the revival occurred.[2]

The historical evidence that prayer meetings in the home and Bible studies on private premises occurred throughout the nexus of holiness and

---

[1] S. S. Day, I. Harris, B. Elliott, B. Larson, R. Enquist, H. C. Lukens, (eds) *Creating Christian Cells*, (New York, Faith at Work, c. late 1950s, early 1960s).
[2] C. M. Robeck jr, *The Azusa Street Mission and Revival*, (Nashville, TN, Nelson Reference and Electronic, 2006), p.5.

revival meetings is unquestionable.[3] There were even healing homes set up by early or proto-Pentecostals as well as missionary rest homes where conferences might be held. None of these meetings is strictly speaking a cell gathering. The cell church principle takes the vehicle of the home group and, by theological reconstruction, narrows its functions.

ii. From Korea to Latin America

The first modern large-scale use of cell churches appears to have been made by Yonggi Cho in the early 1960s. He tells his story in *Successful Home Cell Groups*.[4] He had been converted from Buddhism and decided to build the largest church in Korea. Starting in 1961 with a church of 600 members he worked tirelessly until, by 1964, his congregation had risen to 2,400 members, a target that was behind his self-imposed schedule. Working with an American missionary, John Hurston, he pressed forward with a physically demanding programme until he collapsed and was taken to hospital with heart palpitations and exhaustion. While in hospital he had time to pray and re-read the bible until he saw a completely new pattern for the church. The ministries set in the church were designed to equip lay people so that lay people could carry out a ministry. The meetings of the early church took place within the home. In the early chapters of the Book of Acts all the Christians could not possibly have met in the Jerusalem temple precincts but must have been forced to distribute themselves in houses, and it was this pattern that grabbed Cho's attention.

He went to his deacons and proposed in re-construction of the inner workings of his congregation so that he would not have to carry the ministerial load alone. He explained to them how home groups were to work but they declined to take part in the ministry he was offering them. It was then, after praying with his future mother-in-law Choi Jashil, that he called into service the women in the church, made them deaconesses, and gave them authority to convene home meetings where they could teach, visit, pray, encourage believers, provide fellowship and collect offerings. After initial turbulence – some of the meetings were undisciplined, some of the women had little grasp of Christian doctrine – the situation stabilised and the church grew rapidly.

The home groups Cho established were organised geographically. Metropolitan Seoul is divided into 13 large districts and a senior district

---

[3] It is unnecessary to give detailed evidence on this point because, in Victorian England and in post-bellum America, religion was soaked into the life of the home and, whenever new movements began (e.g. in the Clapham Sect or reforming movements in Methodism), they frequently, and for very practical reasons to do with cost and size, began in private houses.

[4] Paul Y. Cho, *Successful Home Groups*, (Plainfield, N.J.; Logos International, 1981).

pastor is assigned to each. Each large district is subdivided into sub-districts, of which there are 309.[5] Each sub-district is divided into sections with sectional leaders of whom there are 4,374. Each section is divided into about five cell groups and each cell group contains between five and 10 families. When it gets larger than this, it is subdivided. Each cell group is led by a leader who appoints an assistant leader who then becomes a leader of the new group. The home cell groups meet once a week in each member's home by turns and work through the bible thematically each year using seven themes, meaning that the whole bible study course takes seven years to complete. At cell meetings there is prayer for new members or for others to receive the Holy Spirit, healing and for personal problems. On Sundays the cell groups attend the large combined services at which Cho or his representative preaches.

Cho instituted home cell groups to lighten his own load. During the time when he was ill and studying the Bible he had to overcome his natural Korean reservation about giving leadership to women but he also understood how Moses, at a time of crisis, took the advice of Jethro his father-in-law and delegated judicial functions to appointed officials. Cho's cell church structure is sometimes called the Jethro type since it is essentially derived from a delegation of pastoral function to others who operate using the home as a miniature church building. Cho understood the home groups to provide support for new converts and to be a method of evangelism.[6] Although there was teaching within the home groups, he did not see them as being linked with a strong emphasis on discipleship. Nor were they established to rein in unstable and floating Christians. Neither did Cho set up his home groups for eschatological reasons even though, had there been an invasion from Communist North Korea during the Cold War, his cellular church structure would have had a better chance of surviving than one comprising congregational activities alone.

Cho's illness lasted for 10 years until 1974. His church burgeoned during that time and he understood himself to be emerging from the process of spiritual brokenness whereby personal pride was being demolished. He did receive recognition early on, though, and was appointed general superintendent of all the Assemblies of God churches in Seoul and then served on the advisory committee to the World Pentecostal Conference which was held in Rio de Janeiro (1967) and in Seoul (1973). It is likely that the success Cho achieved was rapidly assimilated by the Latin Americans who became the next national group to major on cell church

---

[5] Young-Hoon Lee, 'The life and ministry of David Yonggi Cho and the Yoido Full Gospel Church', in W. Ma, W. W. Menzies and H-S. Bae (eds), *David Yonggi Cho: a close look at his theology and ministry*, (Goonpo/Baguio City, APTS Press/Hansei University Press, 2004).

[6] The story is told from a personal perspective in Cho, *Successful Home Groups* (1981).

principles. Nevertheless Ralph Neighbour in 1969 formed a non-traditional church in Houston, Texas, where unchurched friends were made to feel at home in cell groups.[7] Neighbour subsequently developed an entire philosophy around cell churches and advanced them as the answer to Christian needs in every culture. Neighbour was certainly not as successful as Cho in building a large cellular church. In the 1970s he became increasingly knowledgeable about cell structure as he visited Singapore and other countries where cell churches were beginning to take root. His own denomination asked him to test the cellular pattern in 80 traditional churches but this failed.[8] His own ministry was eventually opposed by his denomination in 1982 and the cell church that he had built up in Houston floundered in the absence of his leadership. None of this shook Neighbour's belief in cell churches and he continued to propagate them as the means by which growth could take place and personal needs could be met. In the end the Programme Based Design or PBD church that uses a traditional congregational format is seen by Neighbour as a 'virus' that will 'infect the church worldwide... before it finally succeeds in decimating the structures it infects'.[9] According to Neighbour, megachurches and other large group forms of meeting are merely 'holding tanks' for members and they ignore the cry of the non-Christian majority. Cell and only cell is the way of the future.

Juan Carlos Ortiz spoke at a conference in United States in the autumn of 1973 and was heard by Don Basham, Bob Mumford and Derek Prince who later invited him to Fort Lauderdale in October that year. It is not clear if the conference at which Basham, Mumford and Prince heard Ortiz was at Montreat, North Carolina. The sermons delivered at that conference later became *Call to Discipleship* which was published in English in 1975. The book deals with Ortiz's life in Buenos Aires, Argentina, and his struggle to grow a large church. Through good organisation his church doubled in size from about 200 to 600 in two years but, through the revelation that he felt God gave him, he came to see that Christians were called to maturity which meant, in the terms he used, that Christians should be able to do most of the things that pastors customarily do. They should be able to evangelise, to feed themselves spiritually, to be doctrinally mature and understand their lives against the eternal purposes of God. 'In this way the entire church is composed of ministers. The ministers are not a special breed of sheep coming from the seminary'.[10]

---

[7] R. W. Neighbour Jr, *Where Do We Go From Here? A guidebook for the cell group church*, (Houston, TX, Touch Publications, 1990), p.84.

[8] Neighbour, *Where Do We Go From Here?* (1990), p.87.

[9] Neighbour, *Where Do We Go From Here?* (1990), p.39.

[10] J. C. Ortiz (with Jamie Buckingham), *Call to Discipleship*, (Plainfield, N.J.; Logos International, 1975), p.18.

Ortiz set up cell groups within his church. The cells met in the home, in a park, in a restaurant, at a beach and had their services at any time convenient to them. The cells were specifically chosen to create disciples, to make people live in a biblical way with biblical values. In this system, every disciple has responsibilities over two types of cells, one cell 'where he formed the lives of new converts, and another cell where he took the most advanced of those new converts and taught them how to be leaders, knowing that cell will soon be divided and the most advanced disciples [would be] put over additional cells'.[11] Each disciple 'attended two cell meetings in addition to the cell where he received for himself'.[12] So each disciple attended three cell meetings a week. On the fourth night all disciples met together and, if they were married, with their families. Most of the cell meetings lasted between four and six hours so one night a week was laid aside for rest and, on Sundays, the main service started late in the day to allow people to recuperate.

To Ortiz the cell was a miniature church. Within the cell there was voluntary redistribution of wealth and within the cell no one was given any religious title to avoid creating false pride. Disciples learnt the importance of submission and a broken spirit though the cell leader had to be careful not to use cell members to achieve his own aspirations.[13] The meetings themselves had five elements: devotion, discussion, programming, mobilisation, and multiplication. These elements were not present simultaneously in every meeting but were part of the ongoing life of the cell. Devotions entailed praise, worship and confession. Discussion involved chewing over the biblical text until it was part of the disciple's lifestyle.

iii. The Shepherding Movement

The story of the shepherding movement is expertly told by S. David Moore who charts the coming together of the five initially independent ministries of Ern Baxter, Derek Prince, Charles Simpson, Don Basham and Bob Mumford.[14] In the southern United States the group first collaborated in 1970 in relation to the magazine, *New Wine*, that later came to carry their teachings across the world. The charismatic movement had taken place

---

[11] Ortiz , *Call to Discipleship*, (1975), p.101.

[12] Ortiz , *Call to Discipleship*, (1975), p.101.

[13] J. C. Ortiz, *Disciple*, (London, Lakeland, 1975b), p.145. There is overlap between *Call to Discipleship* and *Disciple*. The latter is clearer about the corporate life of the church achieved by cells through 'mashed potato love', the blending of individuals into a single whole.

[14] S. David Moore, *The Shepherding Movement: controversy and charismatic ecclesiology*, (London, T&T Clark International, 2003).

throughout the 1960s against a backdrop of change and disorder in public life, particularly in North America, over the opposition to the war in Vietnam and the growing counterculture of drug use, hippie lifestyles, civil rights and feminist and gay critique. According to Moore's analysis the shepherding movement can be seen as a response to growing individualism and the directionless flow of the charismatic movement:

> This concept of shepherding was a logical next step in implementing the ecclesiologically orientated principles of authority and submission... their already developing concept of discipleship and house church dovetailed nicely with the shepherding emphasis. Discipleship emphasised the need for mentoring by a more mature leader, and house groups provided the venue[15]

As early as 1973 Bob Mumford had said 'I believe right now that the Lord himself by the Holy Spirit is presently dividing the whole body into cells. The move of God in cell groups is about 10 years old'.[16] Mumford's declaration indicates that he, and presumably the other shepherding leaders, saw the cell movement as a biblical answer to the disorder in church. The cell movement which, in Yonggi Cho's hands, had been largely intended for urban evangelisation now became a tool for precise discipleship.

Derek Prince, the shepherding movement's most outstanding teacher, thought that ideally each city should have a single church made up not from historically distinct denominations but from groups of cells from which leaders emerged. These leaders would join together to form the church government of the city.[17] Others like Bob Mumford were far more insistent upon the need for every Christian to have an individual shepherd to whom he or she should submit.[18] Without the authority/submission axis the cell concept might have remained largely uncontroversial but, by exposing young Christians to powerful teaching on the necessity for complete submission and by doing this without clarifying the limits of pastoral authority, there were bound to be casualties and abuses. In reality, authority and submission could exist without the cell concept or power discourse - and in some cases did - but the burgeoning of cells increased the need for leaders and so multiplied the potential for pastoral error.

In 1975 the five shepherding teachers were challenged. The challenge came from a prominent figure on the charismatic scene, a man who founded Christian Broadcasting Network (CBN) and was a Yale-trained lawyer, Pat Robertson. Robertson, in a face-to-face meeting with the Five argued that

---

[15] Moore, *The Shepherding Movement*, (2003), p.56.
[16] Moore, *The Shepherding Movement*, (2003), p.56.
[17] Derek Prince, 'The Local Church: God's view vs man's view', *New Wine*, (May, 1973), pp.14-18.
[18] Moore, *The Shepherding Movement*, (2003), p.55.

'the cell group approach was divisive and exclusive'.[19] To this Derek Prince replied that Robertson's charges were 'a gross caricature of my teaching' and that the central question was about who had the authority to teach. To this question Prince argued that authority should be vested in a 'group of proven leaders with established ministries and fruit who submitted to one another without deception'.[20] When asked 'to whom is Pat answerable?' there appeared to be no ready answer. From that point on the shepherding movement began to slow down, and several years later the Fort Lauderdale Five disbanded their association. Even so, cells of one kind or another continued and Charles Simpson one of the Five, who had moved his ministry to Mobile, Alabama, pressed forward so that by 1981 his Gulf Coast Covenant Church of 1,200 members was divided into three congregations all containing some cells, and Simpson himself inaugurated a kind of apostolic network.

The connection between the shepherding movement in Fort Lauderdale and apostolic networks in Britain was direct and personal. Not only did Ern Baxter preach to congregations within the apostolic networks in Britain but also apostolic figures from Britain like John Noble went over to meet with the American leaders.[21] In the end, no formal links were established and the British networks never at any stage came under the jurisdiction of any one of the five shepherding figures. Although the British leaders did not submit or even collaborate with the Americans (though Prince was British by birth), shepherding ideas and practices *were* influential. The shepherding leaders published often in *New Wine* magazine whose bi-monthly circulation in the late 1970s was more than 60,000.[22] Copies of the magazine certainly found their way to Basingstoke where Barney Coombs was based. It is no surprise to find that in 1979 Ron Trudinger, one of the leaders within the Basingstoke community church, published *Cells for Life*, to promote the cell church concept.[23] Trudinger's book refers both to Yonggi Cho and the idea of a city church made up of cells that Prince had advocated.[24]

[19] Moore, *The Shepherding Movement*, (2003), p.102.

[20] Moore, *The Shepherding Movement*, (2003), p102.

[21] A. Walker, *Restoring the Kingdom* (4th edn), (Guildford, Eagle, 1998), pp.97, 99.

[22] Moore, *The Shepherding Movement*, (2003), p.54.

[23] The book was printed in 1979 by the Olive Tree Press which was a business off-shoot of the Basingstoke Community Church and later reprinted by Kingsway in 1983.

[24] R. Trudinger, *Cells for Life*, (1983), p.43 for the reference to Cho and p.23 for the reference to the city church made of cells.

iv. Variations on a Theme

Although criticism of the shepherding movement may have pushed cells
down the agenda in the western church, they did not disappear from it. Cell
churches continued to function in Latin America, in Asia and in some parts
of North America. The cell philosophy was popularised by other writers
than Ralph Neighbour. Laurence Singlehurst of YWAM, Bill Beckham,
and later the Anglicans, Michael Green, Howard Astin and Moses Tay,
wrote in favour of cells.[25] Some writers gave practical examples of the
advantages of the introduction of cells (Astin) and others traced cells back
down through church history (Beckham) to put the whole movement into
context, even claiming that cells were the key to revival and growth at
every stage in the last 2000 years.[26]

In the Spring of 1996, when cell churches had been flourishing for
several years in Singapore, Australia, parts of Africa and New Zealand
YWAM hosted a Cell Church Conference in Britain to press the case. They
revived Neighbour's argument that Programme Based Churches had failed
and almost all departments within such churches were ripe for
reorganisation into cells. The counter argument that the mobility and
individuality of British society militated against cell churches was
recognised by Moynagh writing on emergent churches and Murray
surveying the post-Christendom landscape. Both of them relativise cell
church concepts and simply see them as one church style among many on
offer.[27]

Within the cell church movement though, especially within the macho
culture of Latin America, it was absolutising rather than relativising that
was the order of the day. Significant innovations and renewed claims for
cells had taken place at the start of the 1990s. In 1986 Cé sar Castellanos
from Bogotá , Columbia, after a visit to Seoul, launched a new version of
the cell movement by adapting the system introduced by Cho. In 1991 the
concept was further adapted to become the G12 system. It operated with
home cells of only 12 people and G12 originally stood for 'Groups of 12';
from 1998 cells were homogeneous groups for men, women, couples,
young professionals, adolescents or children. Each person in the cell was
discipled so as eventually to become a leader of his or her own cell. People

---

[25] Support is also found in: C. K. Hadaway, S. A .Wright, and F. M. DuBose, *Home Cell
Groups and House Churches*, (Nashville, Tenn, Broadman Press, 1987), and D. Finnel,
Life in His Body: a simple guide to active cell life, (Houston, TX, Touch Outreach
Ministries, 1995), the latter connected with Neighbour's perpetuation of the theme.
[26] See Michael Green (ed), *Church without Walls: a global examination of cell church*,
(Carlisle, Paternoster, 2002), which contains chapters by Beckham, Green and Tay. See
also H. Astin, *Body & Cell*, (Crowborough, Monarch, 1998).
[27] Michael Moynagh, *emergingchurch.intro*, (Oxford, Monarch, 2004); Stuart Murray,
Church after Christendom, (Carlisle, Paternoster, 2004).

therefore attended two cell meetings, one where they received ministry from their original cell leader and the other where they themselves were the leader seeking to build up a group of 12 people who then went on to become new leaders. Relationships within the G12 system were permanent so that the person who was your original cell leader remained your cell leader and you, in turn, remained the leader of those who were in your first group of 12. Full development was attained when each of the 12 people in your first cell were themselves leaders of 12 cells. Within a short period of time 'G' in G12 came to stand for 'government' as a seemingly endless line of cells and leaders could track their descent all the way back to Castellanos' original 12 disciples.

In Castellanos' words,

> if I trained 12 people, reproducing in them the character of Christ in me, and each of them did the same with another 12 - the continuation of the process, with every group of 12 transferring what they receive, would lead to unprecedented growth in the church.[28]

Growth certainly followed. By 1991 there were 70 effective cells in Bogotá and by 1999 this had grown to 20,000 cells with 45,000 people who met regularly at celebrations. Currently each cell has between six and 25 people but the idea that everyone has a dual role, one as the leader and the other as a disciple, continues. Cells inculcate a 'ladder of success' of four steps whereby new converts are won for Christ, consolidated in a cell, discipled in a cell and then finally sent out to plant a new cell. Each of the four steps is clearly demarcated and requires sessions of intensive training that take place in larger gatherings outside the home.

The system has attracted criticisms for its exclusivity, its insistence on the number 12, its pyramid structure, its apparent incompatibility with New Testament models of the church, its doctrine of miracles and authority, its franchising tendencies whereby any departure from the system is deemed to be unacceptable, and its willingness to put too much trust in leaders whose philosophy of ministry is formulated on hierarchical Old Testament concepts.[29] Whether these criticisms are fair and valid is difficult to assess though, as we shall see, Kensington Temple/London City Church's broken relationship with G12 argues that tensions appear in a British context.[30]

The complexities and variations of cell church styles are laid out by Comiskey whose 1997 doctoral thesis was completed at Fuller Theological

---

[28] From 'Successful leadership through Groups of 12' on <http://www.reachouttrust.org/articles/relatedsubjects/g12.htm> (accessed 12 April, 2006).

[29] See <http://www.reachouttrust.org/articles/relatedsubjects/g12.htm> (accessed 12 April, 2006).

[30] See <http://www.cellexplosion.com/?p=why_principle_of_12 for Dye's comments on G12> (accessed 12 April, 2006).

Seminary and is available online.[31] Comiskey, using his own extensive fieldwork, offers a descriptive/analytic but noncritical account of the cell church theme in five Latin American countries. As we have seen, at least some of British apostolic networks were aware of cell churches from the 1970s onwards but a determined introduction of the cells to Britain was probably delayed by the expectation that the system would be alien to British culture and, possibly, inapplicable outside areas of high population density. Among the earlier Pentecostals going back to the 1930s there was reticence over home prayer meetings because of the possibly that such meetings could easily break away from the main congregation.[32] Pastors of large congregations needed to be assured that, if they introduced cells, the cell group leaders would not become independent and set up rival congregations nearby. This is why the cell system includes forces driving the church out into the community and, in the opposite direction, forces drawing the church back into a strong unity. The outward force of evangelism must be counterbalanced by the inward force of strong relational ties to the primary leader.

As Cho had seen in the 1960s, the ministry gifts of apostles, prophets, pastors, evangelists and teachers outlined in Ephesians 4 culminated in a common purpose of preparing God's people for works of service. The cell was the place where each Christian might render service and the cell removed from large congregations the spectator mentality that arose when famous preachers, having occupied a pulpit for an hour, flew to their next appointment and left the congregation like a theatre audience awaiting the next captivating speaker. The cell turned church members into workers and it relieved pastors of large congregations from myriad minor calls on their time. Church numbers with problems went not to the senior pastor but to the cell group leader.

In 1999 Kensington Temple/London City Church's Spanish-speaking members adopted the G12 system. They soon grew from 40 to 2,000 members, and by 2003 there were near to 4,000. Colin Dye saw what was happening and took a team of leaders to Colombia to Castellanos' church in 2000. He reported the team came back from Bogotá full of joy and ready for the public launch of Kensington Temple's own G12 vision'. This vision began to be implemented in September 2001 and Castellanos preached at KT in 2002, 2003 and 2004. Every three months leaders from Bogotá came over to London to provide further impetus. By 2004 Castellanos was comparing the 'language' of the cell movement with the universal language before the building of the Tower of Babel: if everyone united in the cell movement nothing would be impossible for the universal church.

---

[31] <http://www.cellchurchsolutions.com/articles/dissertation/index.html> (accessed 2 June, 2006).
[32] According to interviews I carried out with veteran pastors in the 1980s.

At some point after 2004 Colin Dye of Kensington Temple/London City Church broke with the G12 system. He did not abandon cells as the fundamental building block of church life but the G12 variant became unacceptable. Many of the Spanish-speaking members of his congregation remained with G12 and he lost them to Castellanos. Dye who had headed up the G12 within the United Kingdom bowed out and Ken Gott, an Assemblies of God pastor in Sunderland, took over the British leadership and ran his church strictly according to G12 principles.[33] Dye meanwhile devised a variant of the cell system that continued to use 'the ladder of success' marked out by encounter weekends, although different hallmarks of a cell were specified from those set out by Castellanos. For Dye the hallmarks are worship, nurture, fellowship, training and outreach and everything is Christ-centred. Everyone is personally mentored and discipled into leadership and the model Dye espouses is relational rather than supervisory.[34] 'The cell begins from two or three people meeting together in the presence of Christ'.[35]

New Frontiers International introduced cells in the 1990s after after consultation with Bill Beckham. They invited Beckham to teach and preach in the main Brighton congregation and then took his advice about ensuring that their own values were built into the cell system. In this way they constructed a cell format that was entirely compatible with their own existing ethos and, though they used features from several cell models, the whole process was relatively pain free. New converts were put through 'equipping tracks' prepared by church leaders to be trained for works of service.[36] Virgo recognised strengths and weaknesses within cell church principles and certainly did not translate his entire conception of church into the language of cells. When he wrote *Does the Future have a Church?* in 2003, it was an exposition of Ephesians that ignored the properties of cell life and cell function.[37] For Virgo the canonical Scriptures continued to provide the driver for everything that New Frontiers International did. As a matter of record, though, when he introduced cells he found they created a fresh emphasis upon evangelism and prevented evangelistic events becoming top-down transitory special efforts initiated by congregational leaders.

Salt and Light were probably the first British network to utilise cells, as Ron Trudinger's book mentioned earlier would indicate. The current situation is that the network neither encourages nor discourages them. In Steve Thomas's words,

---

[33] <http://mci12.org.uk/mci/> (accessed 12 April, 2006).

[34] <http://www.cellexplosion.com/?p=why_principle_of_12> (accessed 12 April, 2006).

[35] Interview with Colin Dye, 16 January, 2004.

[36] Terry Virgo, *No Well Worn Paths,* (Eastbourne, Kingsway, 2001), p.259.

[37] Published in Eastbourne by Kingsway Communications.

Cell churches: there is no uniformity across the network. Our posture is to encourage what local churches feel they should be doing. A number of churches did go down that road though most have settled back to seeing that you need both - big and small meetings. A number are cell churches. A number have espoused G12 but the jury is still out. Cell churches have brought evangelistic zeal. One area of Oxford only has cells. The end result of this is growth but it is not clear whether growth is caused by cell, by being purpose-driven or by simply being an ordinary church.[38]

His comments are pragmatic rather than ideological and set against the criterion of church growth. He realises that growth may well be multi-factorial and only attributed to cell structures by reductionist analysis. Pragmatism is characteristic of the most durable apostolic networks. They allow variability within their churches so that they can learn from the experience of a range of situations. Stuart Bell of Ground Level takes a similar view and is much happier to think of his congregation as 'a church with cells' rather than a 'cell church' and, where cells are used, they are planted in specialist contexts like those found on university campuses.[39]

Statistics in chapter 20 will show the prevalence of cell churches. The G12 cell church model, turns out not to be present in Cornerstone, Covenant Ministries, the Jesus Fellowship, Kingdom Faith, Salt and Light or Lifelink. All networks, however, have some churches with cells.

---

[38] Interview with Steve Thomas, 12 January, 2006.
[39] Interview with Stuart Bell, 5 December, 2003.

Chapter 16

The Toronto Blessing

i. Introduction

The Toronto blessing reached Britain in April-May 1994.[1] Anyone walking into a congregation where the blessing was in evidence would have seen a variety of things happening. There might have been large number of Christians sitting in their chairs almost helpless with laughter; there might have been Christians lying in the aisles or at the front of an auditorium in sleep-like calm; there might have been preachers standing on a platform juddering and staggering as they tried to prevent themselves falling over or crying out; there might have been sounds of grunting, shouting, even barking, coming from those who were present; and, by the end of the occasion when the Toronto blessing had been fully poured out, the majority of people present would have been rendered helpless and the normal discipline of congregational activity would have come to an exhausted halt. Those meetings anticipating an outpouring of the blessing would almost certainly have moved the seating aside to leave a large open area where ministry might take place. In some centres where the blessing was observable, a rudimentary pattern to the meeting might be followed. There might be worship with many songs at the beginning, preaching that might itself have incorporated Toronto-style phenomena and which led to an appeal for people to come forward to be ministered to by a team of previously authorised people. The team would systematically gather round individuals, pray, often wait for the individual to fall down or laugh, and then move on to the next person. Those who had fallen down or who had laughed reported a deep relaxation, a feeling of being in the loving presence of God that swept away their cares and worries and left them confident of God's mercy.

ii. Historical Threads

An early biblical account of Saul, the first king of Israel, tells of how on one occasion the Spirit of God came upon him and he stripped off all his clothes and lay naked all night and prophesied (1 Samuel 19:24). In an

---

[1] David Hilborn (ed) *'Toronto' in Perspective: papers on the new charismatic wave of the mid 1990s*, (Carlisle, Acute [an imprint of Paternoster], 2001), p.154.

article on worship written in 1969 Millard[2] speaks of bodily prostration in worship as being indicated by the Psalms and adds:

> It is interesting that there have been visitations of the Holy Spirit where bodily prostrations have taken place. Early Pentecostal believers speak of being 'slain under the power of God', meaning physical prostration. Less reverent allusions to this phenomenon brought about the nickname 'holy rollers'. The same phenomenon occurred nonetheless among early Presbyterians and Methodists in this country [United States]. Charles G. Finney described meetings in which the Spirit descended in such power that the congregation was prostrated on the floor. On one such meeting Finney wrote, 'if I had had a sword in each hand, I could not have cut them down as fast as they fell. Nearly the whole congregation were either on their knees or prostrate...'[3]

Finney spoke of the behaviour of people in revival meetings and Jonathan Edwards, the scholarly and philosophical congregational preacher had seen these and similar events in his own Northampton revivals of 1735 and 1740-42, pondered on the nature of religious emotions as well as 'the distinguishing marks of a work of the Spirit of God' (the title of one of his books). The Wesleys and Whitfield had seen similar emotional exhibitions as men and women became convinced of their sinfulness before God in the agony of stricken consciences during meetings where the Gospel had been preached with power. So there were at least the beginnings of a theology for distinguishing between emotional *reactions to* the Holy Spirit and *manifestations of* the Holy Spirit. In the first case fallible human responses might legitimately issue in forms shaped by cultural circumstances but in the second case there was the stronger claim that the outward physical behaviour of a human being, however odd, was a demonstration of the invisible presence of the Holy Spirit.

Classical Pentecostals were not unduly disturbed by emotional or exhibitionist behaviour within their meetings. True, as time went on and as they became more socially conformist and more respectable, they disliked outward shows of emotion during Sunday worship but, in principle, pentecostal pastors were by no means fazed by spontaneous behaviour. In North America, and to some extent in Europe, pentecostal pastors came to align themselves with evangelicals and evangelicals, fighting against liberals, aligned themselves with rationalistic defences of the doctrines of the Reformation. In the 1940s the North American pentecostal denominations put themselves under the umbrella of the National

---

[2] A. D. Millard, 'The Holy Spirit and Worship', *Paraclete*, 3, 4, (1969), pp.14-19.
[3] Quoted from, James G. Lawson, *Deeper Experiences of Famous Christians*, (Anderson, Ind., Warner Press, 1911), pp.255, 256.

Association of Evangelicals[4] and denominational discipline was increasingly applied to ensure that pentecostals behaved themselves to the point when they became largely indistinguishable from evangelicals except in the privacy of a moment when they might speak in other tongues.

Outside denominational structures and restrictions ex-pentecostals chaffed at the betrayal, as they saw it, of their heritage; the Latter Rain movement which was sparked off in Canada in 1948[5] reasserted not only the power and indispensability of spiritual gifts but also the necessity for apostolic and prophetic ministry. From this matrix arose many of the popular healing evangelists who largely operated outside denominational boundaries but who were able to do so as radio and TV broadcasting opened up large audience to them and generated a river of financial support. Among the Latter Rain preachers were William Branham and his proté gé , Paul Cain.[6]

The healing evangelists helped to shape North American religious culture. Their broadcasts entered thousands of homes and they became religious celebrities. More than this, their religious style became normative. If Oral Roberts prayed his way down a healing line of infirm people, then the local pastor followed suit. If T. L. Osborn taught that healing was in the atonement, then who was the local pastor to disagree? If healing evangelists, with local clergy sitting on the platform behind them, demonstrated healings before television viewers, then it was easy to believe that charismatic gifts of healing were only given to certain high-profile personalities and not freely distributed within local congregations. Equally it was easy to believe that there was a big gap between the gifting, power and authenticity of the healing evangelists and the run-of-the-mill pastor in the back of beyond. And if the healing evangelists authenticated falling down or 'being slain in the Spirit' by implying that such visible behaviour confirmed their own God-given powers, the local pastor might well want to see similar results in his own congregation if only to boost his status in the eyes of the faithful. The probability that healing evangelists, as a percentage of those for whom they prayed, saw as many people healed as the local pastor or that the dramatic collapse of people in front of television cameras would be disruptive if the same thing happened in the local church, was simply overlooked. The healing evangelists prayed for different people in different locations as they travelled round the country but the local pastor looked after the same people week after week. Once the local pastor had

---

[4] The National Association of Evangelicals was founded in 1942 and became known for its attacks on liberalism. The Assemblies of God in the United States was a founding member and Thomas Zimmerman was the first Pentecostal to be elected as its president.

[5] See George Hawtin's letter in W. K. Kay and A. E. Dyer (eds), *A Reader in Pentecostal and Charismatic Studies*, (London, SCM, 2004), p.19.

[6] Hilborn, *Toronto*, (2001), p.19.

seen dramatic demonstrations in his own congregation, hard questions followed.[7] Were the people who had fallen down actually healed or did they get up with the same illnesses as they had come to church with? Were the people who had fallen down better and more effective Christians for their falling down experience? As we shall see, the Toronto blessing offered to answer these questions.

Among the healing evangelists was Kathryn Kuhlman (1906-76), unusual not only because she was a woman but for the methods that she adopted. Her views are given in her bestseller *I Believe in Miracles* where by implication she criticises other healing evangelists for their emphasis upon faith:

> Too often I had seen pathetically sick people dragging their tired, weakened bodies home from a healing service, having been told that they were not healed simply because of their own lack of faith. My heart ached for these people, as I knew how they struggled, day after day, trying desperately to obtain *more* faith, taking out that which they had, and trying to analyze it, in a hopeless effort to discover its deficiency which was presumably keeping them from the healing power of God.[8]

The result of her contemporary healers' theology was that sick people now, in addition to their physical problems, also had to carry the burden of being labelled as people without true faith. Kuhlman emphasised the role of the Holy Spirit in bringing healing and she would often pray for those who were ill without asking them forward to the front of a large meeting where they might be made a spectacle of. Using her spiritual discernment she would say quite specific things like, 'there is a man on the upper balcony who has had two operations for gall stones. God is going to heal you this evening'. Such information would inspire faith in the man with the gall stones and so, as he sat in his seat, she would say, 'the Holy Spirit is healing you now'. Some people who were identified in this way might then fall down. But her emphasis was on the untamed power of the Holy Spirit rather than upon her gifting as an evangelist or the faith of the sick person. Although flamboyant in dress and speech, Kuhlman's sensitivity to her congregations as well as her determination not to locate the source of healing within anything to do with her own physical being, set a new context for public demonstrations of charismata. Among those who attended Kathryn Kuhlman's meetings was John Arnott who, with his wife Carol, later became the pastors of Toronto Airport Vineyard.

From 1974 onwards Benny Hinn was also influenced by Kuhlman. He was a healing evangelist like her and he developed his own theology of 'the

---

anointing'.[9] The anointing was conceived as the heavy invisible presence of the Holy Spirit – even the *shekinah* glory of God – resting upon the chosen minister. The anointing could be felt, imparted by touch, and carried around by the evangelist. It was a theology that was able to support the concept of an elite group of ministers and it bypassed much Pauline teaching in the New Testament epistles about the shared nature of charismatic gifts within the congregation. The anointing became a source of protection for the evangelist ('touch not the Lord's anointed' – Ps 105.15) as well as an explanation for the dramatic behaviour of those came into immediate contact with the evangelist. The anointing localised God's power and was seen as deriving from an experience analogous to Jesus's when he was baptised in the River Jordan while the Spirit, like a dove, visibly descended upon him. In public meetings the anointing would be like a force field bringing the transcendent activity of God into the material realm.[10]

Independent of Kuhlman, Arnott and Hinn, Rodney Howard-Browne, a South African preacher brought up in a pentecostal home, experienced uncontrollable sobbing and laughing after a prayer meeting in 1979. Howard-Browne's subsequent theological formation took place at Rhema Bible Training Centre in Johannesburg where he learned to practice Word of Faith teaching. This included positive confession: Christians should speak out or confess God's future blessings of health in prosperity upon themselves in the same way as God had created the worlds from nothing by his words alone. Also, independent of Kuhlman, Arnott, Hinn and Howard-Browne, John Wimber began his ministry in California in the late 1960s and gradually became a leading figure within pentecostal and charismatic circles.[11]

Wimber's personality was characterised by honesty and good humour – 'I am just a fat man trying to get to heaven'.[12] There appeared to be no sense in which he talked up his own anointing or celebrity. He believed that the power of God ought to accompany evangelism but, in this, he was little different from classical pentecostals or charismatics. Where he did stand apart, however, was in his willingness to take literally the 'power work' of the Holy Spirit in evangelism.[13] Although he arrived at his conclusions and

---

[9] Benny Hinn, *The Anointing*, (Milton Keynes, Word UK Ltd, 1997).

[10] Ken Gott, quoted in Hilborn, *Toronto,* (2001), p137, spoke of running to the stage where Benny Hinn was ministering 'I can only describe it as like through a force field about one metre high'.

[11] The *Los Angeles Times* for instance wrote an article about him as early as 1972.

[12] <http://www.deepcallstodeep.sonafide.com/index.php/2004/05/27/john-wimber-a-leader-to-know> (accessed 22 December, 2005).

[13] Wimber's intellectual and spiritual pilgrimage took him through a job as a church growth consultant and studies at Fuller where he imbibed G. E. Ladd's teaching on the kingdom of God and missiological and anthropological discourses about radical

his praxis by a different route, there were overlaps with Kuhlman. He would invite the Holy Spirit by simple prayer to take over a meeting where he had been preaching and, when this happened, everything broke loose. People would fall down, cry, be healed, worship and receive revelation. Wimber appeared to be the facilitator of all this and would sometimes, while it was all going on, slip out of the meeting for a walk or hamburger.[14] There was no self-aggrandisement in Wimber's ministry and it was this, as well as the amazing results, that so endeared him to numerous people. Beginning in the early 1970s Wimber began to build up his Anaheim congregation to about 5,000 people so that, by the early 1980s, he had become the leader of a new wave of the Holy Spirit. All this was consolidated by Peter Wagner, then of Fuller Seminary, who became an academic mentor for Wimber and invited him to teach a course on Signs and Wonders that rapidly became the most popular course Fuller had ever mounted. Wagner's analysis of Wimber as the exemplification of the Third Wave added historical significance and perspective to what was happening. In this scheme the First Wave was the pentecostal outpouring at the beginning of the 20th century. The Second Wave was the charismatic movement in the 1960s and the Third Wave of the 1980s was a new intensification of the divine plan that would transcend human organisational structures and lead to the coming kingdom of God. By 1984 Wimber was travelling internationally though his first trip to Britain had been made in 1981.

iii. Interpretive Pressure

In the criss-crossing of events within the 1980s the people and themes within this narrative begin to interact with each other. Paul Cain went to see Wimber at the end of 1988 to warn him to give greater priority to holiness within the Vineyard movement. Cain brought with him the background influences of the Latter Rain movement. This is Hilborn's interpretation and is probably correct.[15] Although the Latter Rain movement began by reasserting older pentecostal theologies, it later developed an eschatology all of its own. By identifying the new apostles as 'manifest sons of God' whose task would be to restore the church, it rapidly generated hyper-real expectations of its proponents and their central place within the unfolding drama of the end times and, in doing so, moved outside the normal

---

pentecostal-style churches growing in the developing world. After his death, his widow told the story (see next footnote).

14 C. Wimber, *John Wimber*, (1999), p.163. It is also true that after John Wimber had his first heart attack in 1986 he suffered from progressively painful angina (p.177). He may have been relaxed, but he was also ill.

[15] Hilborn, *Toronto*, (2001), p.140.

parameters of biblical doctrine.[16] Cain's own view about end time events, like much of his ministry, does not depend upon systematic teaching. Instead it tends to be fragmentary and enigmatic, and there is no evidence that Latter Rain beliefs were transmitted directly through Cain to Wimber. Nevertheless Cain made an impact on Wimber.

Several participants tell the story of these extraordinary events.[17] The meeting between the two men was engineered by Jack Deere, a onetime professor at Dallas Theological Seminary, who had been fired from his position because of his conversion to Third Wave beliefs.[18] Deere had asked Cain for a sign by which he could persuade Wimber to meet together. Cain replied, 'the day I arrive there will be an earthquake in your area'. When Deere asked whether the earthquake would be a big one, he replied, 'no, but there will be a big earthquake in the world on the day I leave'.[19] So Wimber reluctantly welcomed Cain to his home in Anaheim on 5th of December 1988. Cain, in prophetic mode, told Wimber to 'discipline and raise up a people of purity and holiness' and that Wimber's role 'would be significantly altered – more authoritative (not authoritarian) and directive'.[20] He also told Wimber that, if he issued this call for holiness, Wimber's son Sean would be delivered 'from rebellion and drug addiction'.[21] The earthquake on 3rd of December 1988 occurred at 3.38 am, the day that Cain had reached California. Cain left on the morning of December 7th when the Soviet-Armenian earthquake occurred at 10.51 p.m. (Pacific Standard Time).[22]

In August 1989 Cain prophesied 'revival will find its starting point sometime in October [of 1990] when the Lord will just start moving

---

[16] M. R. Taylor, 'Endtime Sonship from 1940-1985', (University of London, unpublished MPhil. Dissertation, 2004).

[17] The rich information from this and the next paragraph is gratefully taken from J. P. Gouverneur, 'The Third Wave: a case study of romantic narratives within late twentieth century charismatic evangelicalism', (University of Sheffield, unpublished PhD Dissertation, 2004).

[18] Jack Deere, 'The Prophet', in D. Pytches (ed), *John Wimber: his influence and legacy*, (Guildford, Eagle, 1998).

[19] J. Wimber, 'Introducing prophetic ministry', in J Wimber (ed), *Equipping the Saints*, UK edition, Vineyard Ministries International, (1990).

[20] Wimber, 'Introducing prophetic ministry', (1990), p.4,5

[21] Deere, 'The Prophet', (1998), p.111.

[22] Wimber, 'Introducing prophetic ministry', (1990), p.5. The two earthquakes were understood to point to a local prophetic emphasis within the Third Wave and then to 'a shaking internationally'. This international shaking would be 'the last ingathering of souls' leading to the second coming of Jesus Christ according to Mike Bickle, *Growing in the Prophetic*, (Lake Mary, Creation House, 1996), p.40.

through London and through England'.[23] In June 1990 Sean Wimber came back to the family home and returned to the faith. Wimber saw this as a patterning event symbolic of the global revival.[24] 'As more prodigals return', Wimber said, 'pockets of revival spread throughout the house of God'.[25] In obedience to these prophecies, Wimber moved with his family to England and organised a series of regional conferences entitled 'Holiness unto the Lord' throughout the United Kingdom, the largest being at the London Docklands Arena, and this was followed by a series of Revival Fire conferences in United States with the main one in Anaheim, California, in January 1991.

The predicted revival failed to materialise. Wimber initially attempted to account for this by explaining that revival was to come in stages, but this was unconvincing. In January 1991 at the Revival Fire conference Wimber had to face intense criticism. He then asked the question, 'did revival come in October?' and with evident disappointment he answered it himself, 'no, it has not come in England at this time'.[26] And he went on to state that, rather than revival, America would experience the judgement of God in the First Gulf War because of the nation's rejection of the Lord.[27] When the First Gulf War ended rapidly and without any setbacks for the Americans, the role of prophets, which had been a matter of dispute in the Vineyard since the early 1990s, boiled over at a Vineyard Board meeting at Snoqualmie Falls, Washington, in May 1991. Wimber fell out with Cain and later with the entire prophetic movement: 'I don't believe there are such things as prophets today'.[28] It appears that Cain had attempted to rationalise the failure of his prophecy by reference to the interdenominational activities that Wimber fostered. Cain had told Wimber to stop his ministry to the Anglican Church and to come out and be separate but Wimber had replied, 'that's an old Pentecostal thing and I want you to know that I'm called to the camp that you're trying to get me out of'.[29] Carol Wimber's perspective on her husband puts it differently. 'He never rejected the prophetic. He attempted to correct some of the doctrine of the

[23] John Mumford speaking at the St Andrew's Chorleywood Clergy Conference, 7 March, 1990.

[24] Deere, 'The Prophet', (1998), p.111.

[25] John Wimber, 'Revival fire', in J Wimber (ed), *Equipping the Saints*, (UK edition, Vineyard Ministries International, 1991), p.21

[26] Wimber speaking at the Revival Fire conference, recorded at the Anaheim Conference Centre, Anaheim, California, 28 January, 1991.

[27] Wimber speaking at the Revival Fire conference, recorded at the Anaheim Conference Centre, Anaheim, California, 28 January, 1991.

[28] John Wimber, 'The Essence of Discipleship', recorded at Holy Trinity Brompton Focus Week, Summer, 1995.

[29] Wimber, *The Essence*, (1995).

prophetic people... he loved and welcomed the whole spectrum of the gifts of the Spirit'.[30]

The impact of Paul Cain and the Kansas City Prophets did not fade easily. There was a strong and widespread desire for revival and predictions of its imminence, particularly in the light of the approach of the end of the millennium, could not be gainsaid. When in the mid-1990s the Toronto blessing began to appear in United States and then in Britain and all over the world, it was only natural for interpreters of the times to assume that what they were seeing might be the beginnings of the worldwide revival for which they had prayed so much and waited so long. Looked at this way, the Toronto blessing was silhouetted against a natural interpretive horizon. The blessing was nothing less than the start of the great transforming revivification of the church that would ultimately reach out to every stratum of secular society. In Gerald Coates' view, one of the results of the Toronto blessing was to lead to many Christians finding their way into the arts and the media.[31]

A second view could be found in other arguments for interpreting the Toronto blessing as indicative of revival, even if this revival was not fitted into an eschatological scheme. Mark Stibbe argued that the Toronto blessing had many of the characteristics of revival, and he did this by comparing accounts of the early church in the Book of Acts and accounts of the Welsh revival and deducing 18 criteria. For example the Toronto blessing results in continuous and exuberant praise in which Jesus is exalted and all this follows intensive prayer. The criteria that the blessing did not fulfil are those concerning 'large numbers of converts' and 'beneficial effects in the wider community'. More speculatively and more originally, Stibbe proposed that 'God always operates in a guise which is appropriate to the culture concerned' and that late 20th century culture was addictive and experiential with the result that God chose to speak to the church through a form of blessing that was profoundly and overwhelmingly experiential while, at the same time, attracting numerous repetitions.[32] So the Toronto blessing is the beginning of a revival that is culturally adapted, one that can compete with the false ecstasies induced by recreational drugs.[33]

Stibbe's analysis has been questioned by an alternative cultural analysis which, for instance, argues that emotional renewal is simply an indication

---

[30] C. Wimber, *John Wimber*, (1999), p.181.

[31] Interview with Gerald Coates, 4 February, 2004.

[32] Mark Stibbe, *Times of Refreshing*, (London, Marshall Pickering, 1995), quotes from pages 64 and 71.

[33] David Pawson, 'A mixed blessing', in D. Hilborn (ed) *'Toronto' in Perspective: papers on the new charismatic wave of the mid 1990s*, (Carlisle, Acute [an imprint of Paternoster], 2001), pp.75-87, takes a similar line.

of the triumph of secularisation. Secularisation has destroyed the power of religious symbols and the plausibility of religious discourse with the result that traditional religious language has been evacuated of meaning. All that is left is a form of communication that is essentially expressive and poetic, 'a metalanguage that, by definition, avoids direct confrontation with the language of modernity'.[34] In short, the Toronto blessing does not indicate spiritual renewal but intellectual exhaustion.

Beneath these competing interpretations of the Toronto blessing lie more basic points: we cannot properly discuss in merely *sociological* terms why the Toronto blessing occurred. Nor are we obliged to choose between these two possibilities – that the Toronto blessing is 'really' a non-intellectual reaction to secularity or that it is 'really' a divine visitation adapted to late 20th century culture – since it may validly be both at the same time. What matters for understanding the development of apostolic networks is what the participants in the Toronto blessing understood about the events in which they were caught up. Here they were open to countercurrents of *theological* opinion. Hilborn's edited collection of statements demonstrates the seriousness with which theological and denominational bodies addressed themselves to the issue. But at the risk of simplification, most were cautious about condemning what was taking place without wanting to commend it unreservedly. Individuals attacked or defended what was happening with less restraint than denominational bodies but, in many respects, the debate looked similar to an earlier debate about the validity of spiritual gifts. Critics of spiritual gifts tended also to be critics of the Toronto blessing; pentecostals who had refined and clarified their ideas of spiritual gifts over many years, tended to be more cautious of non-biblical phenomena; and charismatics who had rolled back the boundaries of traditional charismatic and ecclesiological interpretation in 1970s, tended to be the most favourable of all.

Looked at in this way it is not surprising that a third position parallel to that of Stibbe was developed by Patrick Dixon.[35] Dixon was associated with Gerald Coates and Pioneer and, as a result, his view fed in to the analysis of at least one apostolic leader directly. Here the argument is psychological rather than sociological. Dixon argued that the Toronto blessing may be understood as 'an altered state of consciousness' like that which is produced by so-called 'triggers', whether these are through body

---

[34] L. Pietersen, *The Mark of the Spirit?* (Carlisle, Paternoster, 1998), p.29. Pietersen is quoting from D. Hervieu-Léger, Present-Day emotional renewals: the end of secularization or the end of religion?' in William H. Swatos, Jr (ed), *A Future for Religion: new paradigms for social analysis*, (London, Sage, 1993), pp.129-48.

[35] P. Dixon, 'An altered Christian consciousness', in D. Hilborn (ed) *'Toronto' in Perspective: Papers on the New Charismatic Wave of the Mid-1990s*, (Carlisle, Acute [an imprint of Paternoster], 2001), pp.88-98.

chemistry, sensory stimulation, sensory deprivation, fasting, meditation, liturgy or by other means. Such states of consciousness have an integrating effect on the mind and are psychologically and spiritually beneficial. The net result of this analysis is that the Toronto blessing should be welcomed and normalised within the range of behaviours and practices that marked churches belonging to apostolic networks.

Equally telling is a fourth interpretation of the Toronto blessing that made use of a sociological understanding of church history. Margaret Poloma was one of the few people to carry out any empirical research on recipients of the blessing. Poloma believes, on the basis of previous sociological analysis, that revivalist movements tend to be cyclical.[36] They begin in a blaze of glory and settle down into a humdrum routinisation of charismata. Only a new blaze of glory will break churches free from that routine and enable them to recapture the meaning behind the doctrines that first inspired them. For Poloma, pentecostal churches that had begun with bright hopes at the beginning of the 20th century were, by the end of the century, showing signs of tiredness, of bureaucracy, of decline, and only a completely fresh wave of the Spirit could overturn the now entrenched and Spirit-quenching mind-set that threatened the features that made pentecostalism distinctive. The Toronto blessing was a divine visitation sent to renew and, if necessary, reconfigure the pentecostal churches since some of the churches would accept it and others would reject it and, as a consequence of the tidal wave of the Spirit, the ecclesiastical landscape would subsequently be completely rearranged.

Poloma could buttress her argument by reference to the empirically observable benefits of the Toronto blessing. To the critics who argued that it was merely an emotional excrescence, Poloma was able to show that people who had been affected by the blessing were able to report long-term benefits of a kind that even its opponents could applaud. These benefits included a greater sensitivity to other people, greater compassion and a sense of wholeness and well-being. Poloma's first report on Toronto came out in 1996 and at least one other publication followed in 1998.[37] Her favourable assessment of the blessing came at a time when the controversy associated with it was dying down and when it was clear to most commentators that no large-scale, world-changing revival appeared likely in the 1990s. What she did, however, was to colour post-blessing analysis.

For those who had pastoral responsibility for large numbers of people and who had to make an assessment at the time when the blessing was in

---

[36] Margaret Poloma, *The Assemblies of God at the Crossroads: charisma and institutional dilemmas*, (Knoxville: University of Tennessee Press, 1989).

[37] M. Poloma, *The Toronto Report*, (Bradford-on-Avon, Terra Nova Publications, 1996); M. Poloma, 'Inspecting the fruit of the 'Toronto Blessing': a sociological perspective', *Pneuma*, 20, 1, (1998) pp.43-70.

full flow, urgent practical wisdom had to be applied. The response of New
Frontiers International to the blessing is instructive not only because NFI
was fully involved in Toronto but also because it has come through the
phenomena without damage or disillusionment. Terry Virgo had seen the
effects of the blessing in the United States before it reached the UK. He
recalled how a man who was planning to leave the church had given a
testimony saying that, on the previous Sunday morning, the Holy Spirit had
fallen on him and he had dropped to the ground and was now sorry for his
previous attitude. Similarly, a respected schoolteacher had been
overwhelmed by the Spirit on the previous Sunday and had 'received …
fresh commission to give herself to witness and intercession'.[38] Returning
to England and meeting with elders in his church, several fell to the floor
and some began to prophesy. Later at a meeting with NFI leaders from
other parts of the world, a similar outpouring of the Spirit occurred
resulting in prophetic utterances. Comparable scenes occurred during the
following Sunday morning congregation in Brighton. Speaking at
Stoneleigh in 1994 to 14,000 people, Virgo gave an account of the
breakthrough of God's presence as described in Acts 10. He pointed out
that many strange phenomena are associated with the Jerusalem church's
sudden acceptance of converted Gentiles. There was a dream, a trance,
angelic visitations, and an interruption by the Holy Spirit of Peter's sermon
in the house of Cornelius before the sermon finished. By analogy, we
should not be surprised at the unusual acts of God when great changes are
afoot.

David Holden, also speaking from a senior position within NFI, looked
back and evaluated Toronto from the vantage point of a decade.[39] 'No, it
wasn't a distraction … It was essential and fuelled what was already
happening. It kicked us off. I think it got hold of what we were and moved
us forward.' These metaphors illustrate the energy the blessing brought to
existing church efforts. On the other hand, 'it didn't really build something'
but this is 'because we were already building something quite solid...' More
than this, the blessing incited a strong teaching ministry, 'actually when I
look back at that time I taught *more* on the Holy Spirit and *more* on the
gifts and *more* on phenomena and *more* on what this is all about. 'This is
for the nations'. I taught more on this than at any other time'. Equally, the
blessing impacted charismatic and pentecostal churches in need of re-
ignition. 'Toronto lit the fire of churches where the fire was going out... If
being charismatic meant using an overhead projector and singing
charismatic songs, then Toronto really challenged that. There were a whole
load of people who thought that "maybe I'm not so spiritual as I thought or
as I was"'.

---

[38] Terry Virgo, *No Well Worn Paths,* (Eastbourne, Kingsway, 2001), p.234.
[39] Interview with Dave Holden, 27 April, 2004.

Outside this, the blessing caused different church groups who were affected by it to come together.

Another big thing that it definitely did: it brought new church people in their different streams and networks, it broke those barriers down. So we made friendships or rediscovered friendships... and more than this I personally suddenly found myself preaching at celebrations all over the country. Prior to 1994 I wasn't doing any of that at all. I found myself in Anglican churches and Brethren assemblies and all kinds of strange places. So there is no doubt that between 1994 and 1997 huge barriers came down.[40]

Other preachers came into NFI and spoke to them, 'It works both ways: we were running meetings that David Pytches[41] came to and John Arnott was coming in' and so 'it really opened up lots of things...with people that we'd known for years but had been so busy getting on with our own thing – suddenly we were reunited again. There were a lot more gatherings and coming together'.

Specifically, Holden pointed to evangelistic benefits as a result of the blessing,

I think you can look back at good tangible fruit that you can still see today. It made people more open to the things of the Spirit. I think it propelled us in terms of the Holy Spirit's support for evangelism. Never once did it distract from our evangelism or church planting...we had 1000 people turning up at Sidcup night after night. It was an amazing time.

Despite this, 'you could never maintain that level of activity unless you only saw it as something for Christians that they could revel in. And I think we always saw it as something beyond that. Someone described it when you are on the beach and a wave comes up, it often leaves lots of things there and then goes back down again. And ... actually it is what is left behind that was important'. The wave could not keep reaching higher and higher on the beach. In any case, 'that was only for a season and we [NFI] must move on'.

In the second part of the 1990s, the Toronto blessing began to disappear and, as it did so, a new reason for hope appeared in the distance. The end of the second Christian millennium inspired expectation of new divine intervention. It is hard to pin down this expectation, and there were certainly voices that warned against any excessive attachment to the importance of dates (after all, how accurate was the calendar's dating of the birth of Christ?) and Thompson is right in identifying elements of

---

[40] Interview with Dave Holden, 27 April, 2004.
[41] Former Bishop of Chile and a charismatic Anglican.

millennialism.[42] There were those who expected the millennium bug to strike down the computers of the West forcing civilisation into meltdown and others, taking quite the opposite view, entertained unrealistically high material hopes for the future.[43] Such hopes were not confined to Christians because the forces of global capitalism conspired to ensure that the stock markets of the West peaked in the year 2000. From July 1997 onwards Gerald Coates organised meetings at Emmanuel Centre, Marsham Street, at the heart of London, calling the church to prayer for the revival that had failed to come 10 years previously. In January 1998 the American Dale Gentry, exercising a prophetic ministry, described that year as one of 'breakout' whereby the 'seeds of revival' would be sown through the UK.[44] Yet, as had been the case after Paul Cain's prophecy, there was no evidence that it was true.

Holden commented,

> You know what it's like in the Christian world, you suddenly hit something in every continent and everywhere you go is all suddenly about the latest thing. Again we felt we had to teach into this... keeping a steady hand on the tiller, I think you have to do that lest there is great disappointment, and I think there was, I think some people became very disillusioned and expected Toronto to lead to revival which it didn't do.

But, he concluded philosophically, 'the way we handle the going back down is just as important as the way we handle it when it came'. In the end 'there's a job to be done' and the church must do what it is called to do regardless of exceptional events.

---

[42] D. Thompson, *The End of Time: Faith and Fear in the Shadow of the Millennium*, (Vermont, University Press of New England, 1999).

[43] I received unsolicited emails taking both positions.

[44] <http://www.wild-fire.co.uk/seeds.html> (accessed 3 January, 2006). See also <http://www.dalegentry.com/> (accessed 4 January, 2006).

Chapter 17

Forty Years at a Glance

i. Introduction

This chapter takes the focus away from individual networks and steps back to look at features and events that impinged in one way and another on all the networks. We now return fleetingly to the 1970s and consider the background that contributed to the success of the apostolic networks. It was fortuitous for the networks that they began their journey at a time when the graph of material prosperity was starting to take an upward turn. Material prosperity and deregulation of the labour market, however, also had other consequences, especially in respect of commonwealth immigration, broadcasting, digital media and ministerial training, all of which were conducive to innovative Christianity. Equally, the large inter-denominational conferences of Spring Harvest, the Alpha course and New Wine were also favourable to apostolic networks, either by offering them a platform for their ministry or by giving them a tool for church planting and evangelism.[1]

ii. Background

The emergence of the apostolic networks in the period after 1970 did not take place in a social or cultural vacuum. There were rolling changes to British society in the decades that followed, changes that made it easier for the networks to grow. Britain in 1970 was a very different place from Britain in 2006. Before 1970 it would not be an exaggeration to say that left-wing discourse commanded attention in intellectual and political circles. For most young people who thought about politics in the 1960s, the answers to Britain's problems were to be found within the canon of socialist literature.[2] Trade unionism was supported by historically high

---

[1] Terry Virgo's book *Men of Destiny* was revised and updated as *The Tide is Turning* (2006) and published and distributed by New Wine. Alpha was used as a church planting tool in New Frontiers. Most of the key leaders of apostolic networks spoke at one time or other at Spring Harvest.

[2] This was my experience as a student in the 1960s. The Conservative Research Department chaired by R. A. Butler produced the *Industrial Charter* (1947) but this only confirmed the Conservatives' willingness to continue the welfare state while not surrendering their willingness 'to reclaim a prominent role for individual initiative and

numbers of trade unionists, and governments in the 1960s and early 1970s found themselves constantly at variance with the demands of trade union officials. Wilson's government had attempted to solve the problem by ill-fated curbing legislation in 1969.[3] Edward Heath, Conservative prime minister, was said to have lost the 1974 general election fought on the slogan 'who governs Britain?' when he challenged the pay demands of coal miners.[4]

In the early 1970s there were no cable televisions in Britain, no mobile phones, no desktop or laptop computers, there were no extended drinking hours in pubs and clubs and the housing market was relatively quiescent. Council houses had not been sold off to owners thereby creating a fresh cohort of property holders who might after a short period move upmarket and push up property prices. Sandbrook's magisterial account of the 1960s argues that, contrary to received opinion, the decade was one where the underlying life of most people remained much it had been since the 1950s. The notion of the 'swinging 60s' was the invention of journalists, musicians and young intellectuals for whom the era of the 60s did, indeed, swing. For the majority of the country in Scarborough or Southampton, Walsall and Winchester, life continued very much as it had before without any sense of cultural earthquake or moral revolution. The change was to come later.

By 2006 the housing market had boomed and busted and boomed again. Trade Union power had been severely curbed by legislation brought in by Mrs Thatcher after a year-long miners' strike 1984-5. A combination of anti-unionism and an attack on bureaucratic restrictive practices had produced a buoyant if ruthless labour market that created numerous jobs in service industries as well as any number of new small businesses. The eventual removal of the scourge of Irish terrorism was left to Thatcher's successors. In any event Marwick is clear that,

> For the majority, prosperity did increase throughout the 1980s, real household disposable income per head rising on average by 3 per cent per year between 1981 and 1987... for the rich, Britain was a better place to

---

private enterprise' (R. A. Butler, *The Art of the Possible*, (Harmondsworth, Penguin, 1971), p.149). Douglas Hurd worked in the Conservative Research Department and describes the 1960s in a section entitled 'backroom politics'. It was not the engine room of ideas nor did its deliberations reach the general public.

[3] D. Sandbrook, *White Heat*, (London, Little, Brown Group, 2006), p.670f. Barbara Castle's *In Place of Strife* White Paper was Wilson's instrument.

[4] D. Hurd, *An End to Promises*, (London, Collins, 1979); E Heath, *The Course of My Life*, (London, Hodder & Stoughton, 1998). See also R. Hattersley, *Fifty Years On*, (London, Little, Brown, 1997), p.221.

be than at any time since 1939. Everyone in full-time employment did fairly well.[5]

And the Office for National Statistics in 2002 noted,

In 1972, just over half (52%) of households had access to at least one car or van. This proportion had increased to 71% by 1995, and in 2002 almost three quarters (73%) of all households had access to a car. The proportion of households with one car has remained relatively constant during this time, and was 45% in 2002. However, the proportion of households with two or more cars or vans has increased substantially. In 1972, 8% of households had two cars and 1% had three or more cars. By 1995 22% had two cars and 4% had three or more. These figures have remained relatively constant since then (22% and 5% respectively in 2002).[6]

The mobility and prosperity of British society in the 1980s did not come without a cost, although this cost may have been due to factors lying beneath the radar of social analysts in the immediate post-war period. Amongst children born since 1970, over 20% experienced the dissolution of their parents' marriage by the time they are aged 16.[7] Even though the 1960s may have remained much as they had been in the 1950s, there were the beginnings of the breakdown of long-established working class communities. This led to measurable changes in the years that followed. Unskilled male unemployment rose, together with the incidence of depression.[8] Between 1996 and 2002 sexually transmitted diseases rose sharply. Syphilis increased from 123 cases to 1,193 and gonorrhoea from 12,140 to 24,953 or 106%.[9] Drug-taking also rose to the extent that the police practically gave up the fight against marijuana and the government reclassified possession as a lesser offence to reduce the amount of police time being taken on its detection and prosecution. Ecstasy tablets which were sold largely to teenage clubbers tended to be treated more as a health risk than an indication of criminal activity. Nevertheless, the prison

---

[5] A. Marwick, *British Society Since 1945*, (Harmondsworth, Penguin, 1996, (3rd edn), p.367.

[6] <http://www.statistics.gov.uk/cci/nugget.asp?id=822> (accessed 31 August, 2006).

[7] K. Kiernan, 'Family changes: issues and implications', in M E Morgan (ed), *The Fragmenting Family: does it matter?*, (London, IEA, 1998), p.56.

[8] W. K. Kay and L. J. Francis, 'Suicidal Ideation among Young People in the UK: churchgoing as an inhibitory influence?' *Religion, Mental Health and Culture* 9, 2, (2006), pp.127-140.

[9] Health Protection Agency, (2004); see <http://www.hpa.org.uk/> (accessed 22 August, 2006).

population rose steadily (up 3,000 in 2003)[10] to the extent that the prison building programme of the government was unable to keep pace with offences, and overcrowding became endemic.

Despite the under funding of universities, enrolments rose roughly in line with the eventual government targets to provide higher education for 50% of school leavers.[11] So far as apostolic networks are concerned, the burgeoning of education created a mobile and well-qualified population of young people prepared to leave their homes in search of work.[12] It also created young people looking for well-paid jobs to enable them to pay back the student loans that were the cost of their undergraduate education. Increased numbers of young people at university also had the effect of making for a technically literate society, one that was at ease with electronic communication. The apostolic networks surfed on the waves of social change letting the forces of youth culture and material prosperity flow into the churches. Youth culture led to a vibrant music scene that was picked up by Christian songwriters. Prosperity and home owning created the conditions for generous giving that supported the ministries and projects of the new churches. Meanwhile the casualties of the new economy – men and women caught in negative equity, young people who had experimented with drugs, had abortions, been victims of crime – also, in some cases, found their way into the new churches. There was a consonance between young people leading experience-rich lives carried along by alcohol, drugs, meditative techniques and those who found within the pentecostal and charismatic movement a new and meaning-giving experience in Christ. Equally for the postmodern young person for whom absolute truth had been banished by the intellectual argumentation of the sophisticated textual philosophies of Europe, there was one unexpected outcome: ideological absolutism – whether feminist, Marxist or racist – had been deconstructed and Christianity, which offered a personal relationship with Christ through the Spirit, did not seem so unbelievable after all. Christian Unions were often the largest clubs or societies on university campuses.[13]

---

[10] <http://www.hmprisonservice.gov.uk> (accessed 22 August, 2006), see 'publications and documents'.

[11] Dearing Report, formally known as *National Committee of Inquiry into Higher Education*, was published in 1997 and endorsed the expansion of higher education funded by tuition fees.

[12] There were over 100 students in the New Frontiers congregation at Brighton (Anne Dyer's interview with Terry Virgo, 25 August, 2005).

[13] Phone conversation with UCCF (12 September, 2006).

iii. Immigration

Immigration did not have a direct effect on the growth of apostolic networks although it did have an effect upon the growth of black churches that shared some of the characteristics of the networks. Immigration to Britain was a political *cause célèbre* throughout the post-war period, and this ensured that border controls opened or closed according to fluctuating public opinion and the political complexion of the government. The first immigrants to Britain after 1945 came on the *SS Empire Windrush* in 1948. Almost 500 Caribbean migrants arrived in this iconic moment and thereafter until 1961 the black and Asian population grew to about 337,000.[14] The majority of these West Indians were of Christian origin and, on arrival, they began to look for churches where they might be welcome. Finding themselves rebuffed or only coldly admitted, they began to set up their own churches. The Church of God had planted five congregations with about 150 members in all in the Birmingham area by October 1957.[15] In the years that followed these numbers multiplied till they embraced about 20,000 people, but they did not have a great impact outside their own community because their concerns were often related to social issues that the majority of pentecostals and charismatics ignored or felt no need to address. This was the transfer of an existing denomination formed out of the American holiness substratum and with it came a conventional, if unique, denominational structure that could not be viewed as a network.

In the years that followed, other waves of immigration arrived, particularly from Africa. In 1971 the African population of Britain stood at about 75,000 but by 2001 this had risen to around 500,000.[16] Nigerians did not need visas till 1988 and in the period during which apostolic networks were coming into existence significant numbers of black Africans were moving over to England, usually to the London area. Most of these came for work or study and some of those who came for both reasons found themselves wanting to start new congregations. Hugh Osgood traces what happened next through five phases of neo-Pentecostal church-planting.[17] In the first phase which began in the 1970s a few long-term African residents called their fellow nationals together for prayer or bible study. In the second phase begun in the mid-1980s, neo-pentecostal churches in Africa sent men to establish branch churches in Britain. The churches largely replicated the

---

[14] D. Sandbrook, *Never Had It So Good*, (London, Little, Brown, 2005), p.296.

[15] Details are given in Kay, 2000, pp.31-36.

[16] D. Coleman, 'The Demographic Consequences of Immigration to the UK', in H. Disney (ed.) *Work in Progress: Migration, Integration and the European Labour Market*, (London, Institute for the Study of Civil Society, 2003), pp.9 -40.

[17] H. J. Osgood, 'African neo-Pentecostal Churches and British Evangelicalism 1985-2005: Balancing Principles and Practicalities', (unpublished PhD Dissertation, SOAS, London University, 2006), chapter 3.

African organisational features of the home country. In the third phase that occurred in the late 1980s and early 1990s a small number of African church leaders who had been sent by denominational churches decided to leave the churches that had sent them and plant new and fresh churches independent of the parent body. In the fourth phase that also took place in the late 1980s and early 1990s a small number of British bible colleges capitalised on the easy availability of student visas, took students in and, when the students left the colleges, African churches with an admixture of British culture were the result. In the final phase that occurred from the mid-1990s onwards, new African churches were set up independent of existing denominational organisations by entrepreneurial church-planters.

Matthew Ashimilowo

The patterns of immigration and church planting within the African community in London had an effect on the size of Kensington Temple. At the beginning of the period it was one of the best-known London churches. Wynne Lewis and Colin Dye both preached in west Africa and so Africans coming to London gravitated to the church that had a connection with their home congregation. Gradually, as expatriate African churches were formed – and these were churches that enjoyed African leadership, African music and often African theological emphases – the old white-led churches seemed less adequate. As we have already seen, African Christians were much more likely to be interested in prosperity and business success than in the minutiae of eschatological doctrine (see chapter 10). Similarly, African Christians were interested in the problems of transition from an African continent with its rich extended family ties to the loneliness and anonymity of densely populated cheap London housing. After a short stay within Kensington Temple, the pull of specifically African congregations became overwhelmingly strong and Matthew Ashimilowo, who started the Kingsway International Christian Centre (KICC) in September 1992, was one of the beneficiaries of this trend.

In 1984 Matthew Ashimilowo (b 1951) was sent to Britain by the International Church of the Foursquare Gospel.[18] This denomination in America had been founded as far back as 1922 by Aimee Semple McPherson. In 1993, 'under the irresistible direction of the Holy Spirit' Ashimilowo resigned his pastorate and branched out on his own with a church of 300 adults in rented accommodation in Holloway, north London.[19] The congregation quickly grew until it reached a thousand people in four services each Sunday. Free of his denominational ties

---

[18] Ashimilowo was converted to Christ while serving in the Nigerian army. He was trained at the Four Square Seminar in Lagos and then took his first pastorate there.
[19] Quotation from briefing notes by Paul Cunningham sent by KICC.

Ashimilowo was able to make decisions rapidly and personalise his leadership style. He found Premier Radio, which broadcast to Christians within the orbit of the M25 motorway, a highly effective platform for his ministry though the benefit to him was equalled by the benefit to the radio station itself. The audience figures increased. Ashimilowo also worked with the leaders' quarterly meeting that followed from Billy Graham's Mission 89 and then, from 1993, he played a key role in Morris Cerullo's Mission to London. Mission to London, unlike the Billy Graham crusade, was specifically pentecostal in its emphasis and majored on miraculous healing, even to the extent of attracting severe criticism from disabled groups in Britain.[20]

Cerullo had spoken at Earl's Court in the summer of 1992 and, from the outset, was strongly supported by London's African churches as well as Caribbean denominations.[21] By supporting Cerullo, Ashimilowo was risking the diminution of attendance at his own Gathering of Champions. When Cerullo handed over the leadership of Mission to London in 1996, he passed it to Colin Dye of Kensington Temple. Ashimilowo attended Mission to London for a number of years and preached at Dye's invitation but by 1998 'Cerullo preferred to preach to Ashimilowo's Gathering of Champions rather than at the event he had founded'.[22] After this, Mission to London stalled and the August 2000 event did not take place, a cancellation that benefited the newly renamed International Gathering of Champions (IGOC). In 2006 IGOC was expected to attract 160,000 visitors drawn from more than 30 nations over eight days.[23]

By 2006, Kingsway International Christian Centre, projecting a positive classically pentecostal message supported by a vibrant choir, had become the largest congregation in London (with more than 30 nationalities in attendance) with a building that was reputed to be the largest indoor auditorium in the country. It had spread out across the UK and formed districts in Luton and Birmingham as well as London. It divided its congregations into chapels (which were smaller) and branches (which were larger, and sometimes made use of older traditional church buildings). There were three branches in London and one in Luton and Birmingham and there were some 20 chapels, mainly in the London area but some stretching as far as Milton Keynes. Overseas KICC could point to churches in Ghana and Nigeria. Television broadcasts on the God Channel, Trinity Broadcast Network, and in Africa, the Caribbean and United States were

---

[20] Cf. T. Shakespeare, and K. Gillespie-Sells, and D. Davies, *The Sexual Politics of Disability: untold desires*, (London, Cassell, 1996), chapter 7.

[21] Osgood, 'African neo-Pentecostal churches', (2006), chapter 3.

[22] Osgood, 'African neo-Pentecostal churches', (2006), chapter 3.

[23] <http://www.premier.org.uk/engine.cfm?i=751> (accessed 23 August, 2006).

also in play and a video and audio library was available through the website.

iv. Premier Radio

In 1990 a group of Christians applied for broadcasting permission. It was one among 40 applications for a medium wave licence. It was rejected. Some years later a second application was made and Premier Radio began broadcasting in June 1995 as the first Christian terrestrial radio station in the UK.[24] The station is owned by the registered charity Christian Media Trust which funds the broadcast production. After the initial start-up problems, Premier Radio found itself in financial difficulty and the entire £2,000,000 of initial capital was exhausted and borrowings were growing by £100,000 per month. The audience reach was below 1%, having been over 2% at launch. As a result the trustees initiated a complete change of the management and the year 1996 was a financial struggle for survival. Among the rebalancing measures taken by the trustees were a revision of programming distinctives and the dropping of secular music and features for an exclusive concentration on Christianity. Audience figures picked up with results that donations also increased and the station now receives just under 50% of its revenue from giving and the rest in advertising and profit from the associated three magazine titles, *Christianity+Renewal* being the most well known.[25] There is a synergy between the magazines and radio output, especially as journalists and broadcasters share the same open plan offices.

The station serves community life through a telephone helpline that receives about 200 calls a day and its output is directed to all parts of the traditional church from African Caribbean/Pentecostal to Russian Orthodox with all the bible-based churches in between. As the broadcast schedules have become better known, denominational barriers have become almost undetectable.

The station's output functions 24 hours a day and every day of the week and offers news, bible study, music discussion and, indeed, all the elements of a church service: a sermon, music, notices. It enables the church to talk to itself and to reflect upon its activities. Speech content runs to about 40% of the total output with the rest being music across the full spectrum of the Christian heritage from modern gospel through to Bach. The website carries back numbers of programs and discussion for streaming and the current resilience of the station reflects the resilience of London church attendance. According to Peter Brierley's figures, in 1979 10.1% of Londoners attended church but, by 1998, this figure had dropped to 8.6%. However this lower

---

[24] Interview with David Heron and Peter Kerridge, 13 January, 2004.

[25] <http://www.christianitymagazine.co.uk/index.cfm> (accessed 24 August, 2006).

figure was actually the highest of any region in England despite having been the lowest in 1979. Consequently it is arguable that churchgoing in London is different from any other part of England. London church attendance declined by 5% against a countrywide decline of 22% and in 1998 Sunday churchgoing in Greater London accounted for approximately one sixth of the total churchgoing in England, a proportion that may well rise by 2011. As many as 24% of all church attendance in Greater London is from the African Caribbean community while other ethnic minorities account for a further 12%. This demographic pattern of church attendance is reflected in Premier's music and preaching output. The website carries notices of the International Gathering of Champions and streamable TV of Ashimilowo's preaching.

Editorially the station seeks to be neutral although its mandate is to take 'the whole of the gospel, from the whole of the church to the whole of London'.[26] Since its inception, Premier's audience has grown though David Heron and Peter Kerridge admit 'legislation has not helped us'.[27] The audience of Premier is greater than the readership of the whole Christian press (for example the *Baptist Times*, the *Church of England Newspaper*, the *Church Times*, the *Methodist Recorder* and so on) combined. When one considers that the Labour Party only has 201,374 members,[28] while the mainstream church has many times that number of members, it is astonishing how tight a rein on Christian broadcasting the regulator holds and how high is the annual licence fee charged to every broadcasting group. It is ironical that, after the corruption charges over donations or loans to political parties in exchange for honours, there has been discussion of the funding of political parties out of taxation while Christian broadcasting has struggled to make itself heard.[29]

v. Digital Media

The Apple Mark 2 home computer was released in 1977 and the first IBM personal computer was marketed in 1981. In 1985 the first version of the Windows operating system appeared and then, in 1990, Windows 3 was launched, a much more user-friendly version that helped make computing

---

[26] Premier Radio, An Application for the existing local AM licence for the greater London area on behalf of London Christian Radio Limited, (2002), p.44. Many of the figures in the previous paragraphs are also taken from this source.

[27] Interview with David Heron and Peter Kerridge, 13 January, 2004.

[28] See <http://en.wikipedia.org/wiki/Labour_Party_(UK)> (accessed 24 August, 2006). quoting figures filed with the Electoral Commission on 31 December, 2004.

[29] <http://news.bbc.co.uk/1/hi/uk_politics/4812822.stm> (accessed 24 August, 2006). <http://www.taxpayersalliance.com/opinion/individual_opinion.php?opinion_id=35> (accessed 24 August, 2006).

accessible to the non-technical.[30] The new personal computers made it possible for individuals to create musical, verbal or pictorial content from their own desktops in digital form. The digital form is crucial because it implies that the material created on a computer screen could be translated into a mathematical language that could be shared between computers almost regardless of other design or operating features. Digital media includes compact discs, digital video, digital television, video games, interactive media and all this naturally includes sound and music as well as pictures.

By the mid-1990s the PC-Windows era had reached a plateau, and there it remained until the concept of a World Wide Web made its debut and was rolled out. The first website was created in 1991 and, by 1996, internet users had risen from 600,000 a few years before to 40 million. The rest, as they say, is history.[31]

The arrival of personal computing and the World Wide Web were welcomed by apostolic networks. The networks had, by then, been up and running in Britain for about 20 years but the web provided an immediate method by which groups could be linked together, churches could be advertised, conferences could be notified and connectivity intensified. All the British apostolic networks offer a home page that draws together profiles of their leaders, links to churches within the network, gives shopping options for people who want to buy music or teaching materials and usually provides a brief history. The World Wide Web makes it possible for a relatively small group to project itself internationally at a remarkably low cost. When this facility is taken alongside the enormous versatility of personal computers in the realm of print and musical output, an apostolic network can disseminate itself far more effectively than was the case when it began.

Even so, the apostolic networks were founded at a point in time when cassette and video were becoming accessible to British consumers. Audio cassettes allowed for the circulation of important teaching materials while video cassettes, the first of which was sold in 1971 by Sony, coincided nicely with the launch of the networks.[32] Although the Dales and Downs Bible Weeks would almost certainly have been a success without recording apparatus, the availability of cheap and efficient recording machines enabled preachers and teachers to multiply the impact of their message with new rapidity. To see a preacher on a video cassette projected onto one's television at home somehow gave him, or her, an added authority and panache. Being on television, especially in an era with few TV channels,

---

[30] T. L. Friedman, *The World is Flat*, (Harmondsworth, Penguin, 2006), pp.54-55.

[31] Friedman, *The World is Flat*, (2006), p.61.

[32] <http://inventors.about.com/library/inventors/blvideo.htm> (accessed 31 August, 2006).

was becoming an indication of celebrity and importance so that the video cassette enabled the preachers of the 1970s to gain a status they would not otherwise have had.

Internet access multiplied over the years so that, by 2006, 57% of households in United Kingdom benefited from this form of communication, and the figure rose to 66% in the southeast of England.[33] Internet access brought with it email communication, a method of moving text and pictures around at infinitesimal cost, that was quickly taken up by the middle-aged. Over a third of those around 45 years of age in the UK were emailers by 2000.[34] It is not surprising that some social commentators noted that there would be a division between the information-rich and information-poor.[35] To receive video or audio material in the early days of the networks was to move in the desirable direction of becoming information-rich.

There is one additional benefit the internet conferred upon those with access to it. The flow of communication could establish electronic communities whether by chat rooms or noticeboards on internet sites. Such communities could function alongside or within the networks. Vineyard, for instance, makes use of its own private web site replete with materials that are only accessible to its members. The result of this process is to create social capital, an exact parallel of financial capital. The man or woman rich in social capital has many friends and acquaintances upon whom he or she can call for help in a variety of situations. Such a man and woman has the opportunity to sell goods, to meet like-minded people, to receive support by prayer or finance and who is therefore advantaged in comparison with the isolated individual without an emotional or personal support system. The networks were, without realising it, generators of social capital that met a thousand needs among men and women stumbling among the debris of fragmented families or industrial alienation.[36]

vi. Ministerial Training

The impact of the charismatic and pentecostal churches was felt within the field of ministerial training. The extent of this impact was assessed by a 2004 survey of all 105 theological colleges listed in the 1999 *UK Christian*

---

[33] <http://www.statistics.gov.uk/cci/nugget.asp?id=8> (accessed 31 August, 2006).

[34] Source: Omnibus Survey, Office for National Statistics, <http://www.statistics.gov.uk/statbase/Product.asp?vlnk=5672> (accessed 31 August, 2006).

[35] <http://news.bbc.co.uk/1/hi/special_report/1999/10/99/information_rich_information_poor/466651.stm> (accessed 31 August, 2006).

[36] Discussed convincingly and at length by, R. D. Putnam, *Bowling Alone*, (London, Simon & Schuster, 2000).

Handbook.[37]   Using a simple multiple-choice technique, a questionnaire collected information about the size, denominational affiliation, date of founding, main purposes and curriculum of the colleges and then, on a five-point scale, asked respondents to evaluate the influence of the Pentecostal and charismatic.

The results show that just under a third of colleges were denominationally independent and therefore effectively inter-denominational and that of the rest 14.3% were Anglican, 8.9% Baptist, 7.1% Roman Catholic and 7.1% Pentecostal. Over half of these colleges had been founded after 1924 and 25% after 1972. The earliest was founded in 1410. Ministerial training was the main priority of these colleges (79%) though this was often combined with a pursuit of academic theology – for example over a third of colleges emphasised the teaching of New Testament Greek.

Pentecostal and charismatic influence was greatest in the areas of music and worship (32% of colleges) but was also strongly marked in the teaching of Acts (29%) ecclesiology (25%), church history (14%) and in teaching about divine healing (17%). Library acquisitions were impacted in 20% of colleges. Student prayer groups were influenced in 25% of colleges and preaching styles in 18%. In 15% women's ministry showed Pentecostal and charismatic influences. Perhaps most influential, in the long run, may be the influence on the balance in the roles of clergy and laity in 24% of colleges and church planting in 20% of colleges .

When the figures are examined in relation to geographical distribution and denominational affiliations, it was clear that Presbyterian institutions in Northern Ireland and Scotland and high church Anglicans have been least receptive to Pentecostal and charismatic trends. Interdenominational colleges, wherever they are, in nearly every case were influenced to some degree, even if only to report that they distanced themselves from the new theology and practices.

Another way of probing these findings is to look at the impact of the Pentecostal and charismatic movements on specifically denominational colleges, excluding those that belong to pentecostal denominations. Here we find that just over a fifth (22%) say their view of the roles of clergy and laity has been touched by pentecostal and charismatic practices and 26% say the same of their worship. A tenth (11%) report an influence on their attitude to church planting. These figures indicate how norms relating to the *style* of church life have permanently changed: lay involvement, free flowing worship and active church planting are now implicit in many parts of the denominational spectrum.

---

[37] The grant was funded by the British Academy (SG 34643). A total of 56 respondents / colleges replied. Anne Dyer and I carried out the work.

Worship is the area where the pentecostal charismatic movement has had most impact. Even strict liturgical traditions have been loosened up by new songs, dances, banners and prayers. Yet the influence upon the intellectual core of ministerial training as found in ecclesiology and church history is significant, and it seems likely that a discussion of divine healing in 17% of colleges would hardly have occurred without an awareness of Pentecostal and charismatic teaching on the operation of the Holy Spirit. What this means is that there was a gradual shift towards charismatic experience and worship in the main training institutions and therefore among many younger ministers. This helped prepare the ground for apostolic networks and made it easier for ministers in other denominations to accept them and, in some cases, to transfer allegiance to them.

vii. Spring Harvest

The impact of apostolic networks was felt by, and often transmitted through, Spring Harvest. It happened like this. Clive Calver, as the youthful director of British Youth for Christ, and Peter Meadows of *Buzz* magazine decided to gather Christian young people together. They launched Spring Harvest festival in 1979. The festival was a success, but its numbers skyrocketed shortly afterwards.

In 1983 Calver was appointed as General Secretary of the Evangelical Alliance. The Alliance dated back to the Victorian era and stood as an umbrella organisation for many evangelical churches and causes. After vigorous early beginnings, it had fallen into decline. Calver, as the youngest secretary in the Alliance's 137 year history, was just the man to revive it. One of the first things he did was to instigate a recruitment drive. This was highly successful so that, whereas in the early 1980s, there were less than a thousand individual Alliance members, that figure had reached an astonishing 56,000 by the mid-1990s. Correspondingly, the number of churches in membership grew from under a thousand to almost 3,000 in the same period. This rapid growth of the Evangelical Alliance was stimulated by a synergistic relationship with Spring Harvest. In 1984 alone, after the Alliance received high-profile exposure at Spring Harvest, membership increased by almost 50%.

Calver, coming from a Brethren background, was converted through the ministry of Roger Forster, a key leader within the apostolic networks and who himself later became Vice-President of the Alliance. After a period of activism among young Liberals and community work in east London, Calver studied in London Bible College and led evangelistic youth teams for several years. In 1975 he became director of British Youth for Christ and, with Peter Meadows, was instrumental in launching Spring Harvest as a youth event four years later. At the time of his appointment to the General Secretaryship of the Alliance, Calver was a program director for Billy

Graham's Mission England. But, to the surprise of those who knew him, Calver delved into the Alliance's founding impetus and came to understand its historical role as society for collective evangelical action: it was essentially a non-denominational body that could bring the different tribes of evangelicalism together.[38]

Evangelicalism, though conceptually a single force, was divided into two streams and models that jostled with each other. There were certainly reformed evangelicals, some of whom held fast to Karl Barth, but who, in any case, displayed a tenacious Calvinistic conservatism in matters of theology and practice. Keswick, somewhat to the left of the reformed wing, combined holiness and conversionist elements whereas the Inter-Varsity Fellowship (IVF)/ Universities and Colleges Christian Fellowship (UCCF) ran across a wider set of evangelical declarations of faith. The revisions of the various defining documents since 1846 are far too complicated to be summarised here partly because there were so many different areas that might need adjustment or defence – should one refer in statements of faith to 'the death of Christ' or, more broadly, to 'the work of Christ'? Should one affirm 'virgin birth' rather than 'virginal conception'? Should one employ righteousness/justification terminology regarding the work of Christ and thereby diminish emphasis upon penal substitution? These and many other finely calibrated verbal formulations were re-tuned by different groups over the years but, following the 1977 National Evangelical Anglican Congress at Nottingham, more inclined to focus on social and justice issues. Then by the early 1980s, the UCCF was facing a rising tide of biblical illiteracy among students who were disinclined to be doctrinally discriminating.[39] If evangelicalism were to remain coherent as a movement, it needed leaders who could distinguish between essentials and non-essentials and who could put aside disagreements in the interests of effective campaigning.

Added to this was the obvious surging strength of charismatic Christianity that moved doctrinal preoccupations away from the great themes of the Protestant Reformation to matters associated with Christian initiation, eschatology or spiritual gifts. Charismatics who had not invested deeply in the intellectual debates of evangelicalism found that 'power for service' in the Holy Spirit consumed their time and attention. They were barely concerned with debates within evangelicalism and wanted to see

---

[38] Ian Randall and David Hilborn, *One Body in Christ: the history and significance of the Evangelical Alliance*, (Carlisle, Paternoster 2001), provides details about Calver's career and the start of Spring Harvest from which much of this section is taken, p.284ff. See also C. Calver, and R. Warner, *Together We Stand*, (London, Hodder and Stoughton, 1996), p.128f.

[39] Rob Warner, 'Fissured Resurgence - Developments in English Pan-Evangelicalism 1966-2001,' (Unpublished PhD thesis, King's College, London, 2006).

above all else the practical success of Christianity in the market place of ideas and the rhythms of popular culture. Indeed, Rob Warner suggests that engaged evangelicals who had taken on board the imperatives of the Lausanne Covenant of 1974 were shortly afterwards overtaken by entrepreneurial evangelicals of whom Clive Calver was one. Such evangelicals, even if they remained in their old denominations, were at home with the values of house churches and apostolic networks. Spring Harvest provided a window where apostolic ideas and house church music could be displayed to the wider church. 'One could say that Baptist and Anglican leaders at Spring Harvest were taught by new church leaders and benefited from their style and faith'.[40] In short, Spring Harvest became an interface between apostolic networks and the rest of evangelicalism.

By 1988 Spring Harvest attendance topped 50,000 and by 1993 over 70,000 attended its four locations, including one in Scotland. Thereafter its numbers fell back slightly because it is not always easy to fill the weeks that fall outside the Easter holidays; the camp facilities are highly attractive to families with young and energetic children (Ishmael's children's work has been important) but not so exciting for older couples or singles. Over the years the format has hardly changed: there is teaching in the morning, afternoon seminars and an evening celebration. Every year there is a theme and the strapline is 'equipping the church for action'. The pre-selected theme is the basic core of what happens in each year but the gatherings do pick up on what is going on today as well as on the wider flows and topics within the church – for instance, cell philosophy or all-age worship or Christian art. In one year, there was a focus on the Siberian Seven (imprisoned pentecostals in the Soviet Union), in another there was discussion of the theology of the 'just war' and in another scrutiny of the proposed Broadcasting Bill laid before Parliament. The Evangelical Alliance offers a basis of faith, although the wider Lausanne Covenant is perhaps the closest thing to the heartbeat of the whole operation. Even so, there is a missional theology at work as well. At one point Louis Palau's evangelistic meetings ran in parallel to the first week. Equally, there is a charismatic dimension. The Big Top is generally not a place where gifts are expressed but, in the years when John Wimber and Reinhard Bonnke spoke, there was public prayer with the laying on of hands for those who were ill.

We could say that originally Spring Harvest capitalised upon the momentum that had been created by the charismatic movement and the Fountain Trust, especially bearing in mind that the Fountain Trust stopped operating in 1980. People who had been involved in the Fountain Trust switched across to Spring Harvest. If one were to trace the line of Spring

---

[40] Interview with Spring Harvest leaders: Peter Broadbent, Steve Chalke, Ian Coffey, Ruth Dearnley, Alan Johnson, Gerald Kelly, Jeff Lucas and Rachel Orrell, 26 January, 2005. Other comments in this section are also taken from this interview.

Harvest's theology, then one might say that, whereas Calver wanted personal renewal, the next generation of leaders was concerned with social justice. In this connection it is arguable that the Marches for Jesus fitted the priorities of Spring Harvest well.

Nearly all the apostolic network leaders have at one time or other been involved with Spring Harvest except for Bryn Jones. Colin Dye spoke there, as did Gerald Coates, Roger Forster and Terry Virgo. Yet, Spring Harvest has deliberately remained in the mainstream, a middle ground between the New Churches which were identified with radicalism and denominational charismatics who were not. The pentecostals tended to stay away for one reason or another and Spring Harvest allowed various trends to co-exist but were careful not to allow the overall balance to be upset. For example, the controversies about demons and the prosperity Gospel were kept in perspective. It is also a place where charismatic gifts might be exercised or experimented with and this experimentation could occur safely and outside classical pentecostal settings. By 2006 45% of attenders at Spring Harvest were Anglican and 25% were Baptist and about 50% of people in any one year might be attending for the first time.

In the early days contentious issues were raised in seminars: there was a series on baptism and on the Second Coming of Christ but more recently contentious issues have only been raised if they fit in with the immediate preoccupations of the church. In short, Spring Harvest is about partnerships and respect. It sees itself as being concerned about the renewal of churches and congregations rather than a forum for individual renewal. It has also benefited from the versatile musical talents of Graham Kendrick and Noel Richards. Non-renewed churches have come and been renewed and then gone back to their parishes or districts and brought others along. They have come for some years and then, after a while, may stopped attending because they have received what Spring Harvest has to give them. In this way Spring Harvest has fulfilled its mandate to equip the wider body of the church. In this way, too, the ideas circulating within apostolic networks have been dispersed and assimilated.

viii. New Wine

Although Spring Harvest is an interface between apostolic networks and charismatic denominational churches, it is by no means the only significant agency in the field. Another starts with the life of Bishop David Pytches. Pytches had gone out to Chile as a missionary and been impressed by Latin American Pentecostal churches. He wanted to see Anglicans copy the Pentecostal example and let the overflowing life of the Spirit result in the planting of new churches although, at that time, he did not know how to integrate spiritual gifts into church life. During the 1980s Pytches became impressed by the ministry of John Wimber and he invited Wimber to speak to his own congregation. At the end of one of his visits to St. Andrews, Chorleywood, where Pytches was the minister, Wimber handed over £3000 and explained, 'this is seed money. Don't give it away; invest it in conferences so that it makes a return'.[41] At roughly the same time as each other, David Pytches and John Mumford, who afterwards came to lead Vineyard in the UK and was at that time curate at St Michaels, Chester Square, learnt to lead clergy in regular gatherings for prayer and ministry. This was the pattern Pytches adopted in what was to become the New Wine network.

Training days on the gifts of the Spirit and 10-day leaders' retreats led to larger and larger conferences. In 1987 and 1988 conferences were organised at Swanwick in Derbyshire and, on each occasion, gathered leaders 'wanted to know how St. Andrews was handling renewal, worship and the gifts of the Spirit'. Personal renewal in terms of spiritual experience and prayer had been kindled ten years earlier by Michael Harper's ministry and the pioneering work of the Fountain Trust but renewal at parish level was lacking. This was the mission that New Wine came to see as its own. In 1989, as many as 3,500 leaders and church members met at the Royal Bath and West Showground in Somerset. The week of Bible teaching and worship became part of the way New Wine now operates. Undergirding this is John Wimber's theology of the kingdom – now and not yet – and this is related to healing since healing may take place now or may not yet be seen. After 1996, when David Pytches stepped back, a leadership team was set up and annual meetings of New Wine grew to about 11,000 people. New Wine's youth work developed its own identity and this culminated in the launch of separate Soul Survivor conferences after 1994. At about the same time a Scottish conference, Clan Gathering, was rejuvenated through affiliation and now attracts about 2,500 people.

In 1997 a second full week of teaching was organised and about 11,000 people attended each.[42] New Wine's mission to church leaders was expressed in 1998 by the formation of a network.[43] By 2002 the growth had gone beyond multiple conferences of different lengths in different locations. There were 600 church leaders affiliated to New Wine in the UK

---

[41] See <http://www.new-wine.org/resources/Sowing%20Seeds.htm> (accessed 29 August, 2006), article in New Wine magazine by Fiona Campbell, from which other elements of this section have been taken.

[42] Interview with John Coles, 17 July, 2004.

[43] The cost of being a member is around £30 pa but every month there is a teaching CD, and being on the mailing list means that all the events are noted as well as getting John Coles' news which ties one into the national and international network of 900 leaders. Interview with Laura McWilliams by Anne Dyer, 10 April, 2005.

but its vision had moved far afield.[44] In addition to its work in Scotland, Ireland and Wales it was involved in more than 20 countries including New Zealand, Finland, Sweden, Holland, Norway, Estonia and the United States. A sister work in East Anglia called Living Water has also started up so that, when the two New Wine weeks, Soul Survivor, Living Water and Clan Gathering are added together probably 50,000 people or more are involved. By 2006 New Wine Networks in the UK had about 750 church leaders as members, 100 Anglican ordinands, and the summer conferences draw from over a 1000 different churches.[45] To gain a true appreciation of the scope of the renewed element within the Church of England all these people and churches needed to be added to the Anglican contingent within Spring Harvest. The charismatic movement of the 1960s within the Church of England did not die with the Fountain Trust but rather flows through strong new networks.

In 2001, David and Mary Pytches passed the oversight of New Wine onto John Coles, then vicar of St Barnabas, North Finchley.[46] He works full-time for New Wine and is able to encourage and coordinate the burgeoning activities of members. The network comprises some 45 mini-networks that meet as often as the groups desire but usually between six and eight weeks apart. Charismatic Anglican bishops are part of what is going on and contribute to the smaller local subsets of New Wine churches as well as to the larger summer conferences. To understand New Wine it must be placed alongside other reform movements within the Church of England although its ministry is wider than this. The issue of the day is the ordination of practising homosexuals and New Wine supports the traditional Anglican view concerning the expression of human sexuality. Yet, in other matters New Wine is more radical. The traditional evangelical position demands orthodox belief first, and then asks for traditional Christian behaviour and, only then, considers that the new convert is able properly to belong to the Christian community. New Wine takes the view that it is right to bless people first and then let them come and belong to the church and find out what is going on and then, gradually, to come to believe and behave. In this way the New Wine parishes are open to all comers in the conventionally broad Anglican manner. New Wine congregations are not exclusivist but work with and in Anglican parishes that are transitioning through spiritual renewal into a broadly based and socially aware Christian ministry. It is true that incumbents who have oversubscribed church schools in their parishes may encourage new parents to attend church and so fulfil the criteria for their child's admission but, in

---

[44] <http://www.new-wine.org/resources/Sowing%20Seeds.htm> (accessed 29 August, 2006).

[45] Interview with John Coles, 17 July, 2004; and email (1 September, 2006).

[46] Interview with John Coles, 17 July, 2004.

other respects, New Wine wants to see its members actively 'doing works for the kingdom of God'.[47]

Although New Wine is not an apostolic network in the same way as the others, it shares features with them. The appointment of Anglican clergy to their parishes is complicated because each parish is situated within a diocese, and each diocese is governed by a bishop. Yet for historical reasons parishes do not all stand in the same relation to their bishop. The result is that, although most appointments within a diocese are at the disposition of the bishop, not all are. The running of a network within the Anglican Church must negotiate local bishops, some of whom, understandably, are unhappy that appointments to parishes within their jurisdictions may be made by prioritising local arrangements. Even so, New Wine now has a recognisable nation-wide profile and can function largely independently of any liberal policies that an unsympathetic bishop might bring into play. The consequences are these: in terms of organisation, New Wine is distinct from the new apostolic networks but in terms of theological purpose, there is considerable overlap.

ix. The Alpha Course

Alpha advertises itself as a course for everyone, especially those wanting to investigate Christianity or who are new Christians, newcomers to the church or who want to brush up on the basics.[48] It has been astonishingly successful in Britain and internationally. Based at Holy Trinity, Brompton, one of the London Anglican mega churches, the course had been completed by over one million people across the world by 1995 and a further 2m or 3m by 2002. By 2004 there were said to be some 28,000 courses running world-wide in more than 140 countries.[49]

The program, which has been advertised as 'a 10 week practical introduction to Christianity' can be traced back to 1969 with the publication of *Questions of Life* that served as a four-week introduction to Christianity and was run at Holy Trinity, Brompton. In 1977, Charles Marnham, one of the staff at the church, devised the course so as to present the principles of the Christian faith in a relaxed and informal setting. To start with, Alpha was intended to educate new converts and only later was it evangelistically broadened and aimed at friends and colleagues of church members. In 1981 John Irvine took control of the programme and extended it to 10 weeks and

---

[47] <http://www.new-wine.org/about_us/> (accessed 30 August, 2006).

[48] <http://alpha.org/welcome/whositfor/index.htm> (accessed 30 August, 2006).

[49] S. J. Hunt, 'Alpha and the gay issue: a lesson in homophobia?' *Journal of Beliefs and Values*, 26.3, (2005), pp.261-271, and S. J. Hunt, 'The Alpha Programme: some tentative observations on the state of the art evangelism in the UK', *Journal of Contemporary Religion*, 18.1, (2003), pp.77-93.

added a weekend retreat on the person and work of the Holy Spirit. By 1985, although the course was running exclusively at Holy Trinity, Brompton, it was beginning to attract in excess of a hundred people. In 1990 Nicky Gumbel took over. He developed the course to make it longer and more informal and, using feedback from questionnaire responses from those who had completed the course, he further refined the content and presentation, especially when other churches began to use the materials. Gumbel also takes a leading part in the video talk which is the central presentation at each weekly Alpha meeting. His performance is polished, humorous, friendly, anecdotal and easy to understand. It was under Gumbel's directions that the number of people taking the course rose exponentially.

The runaway success of Alpha took place in the 1990s and helped to make charismatic Christianity normative in Britain; in 1998 10,500 churches were using the course in the UK.[50] Alpha presumes not only a personal encounter with Christ but also an experience of the Holy Spirit that may lead to the exercise of spiritual gifts. Critics of Alpha have complained that its presentation of Christianity is too narrow and fails to do justice both to alternative interpretations of the atonement as well as to large sections of church history.[51] Such criticisms are almost drowned out by the voices of its numerous defenders and participants. So far as apostolic networks were concerned, Alpha was an ideal complement to their own discipleship or church planting programmes. Alpha could be used with small or large groups, in the settings of a private home or a rented hall, and the discussion generated by the presentational materials could be owned and customised by course leaders. The Holy Spirit weekend of ministry within the course ideally suited the experiential dimension of apostolic networks while the meal together easily fitted in with their existing church style. Moreover, although there were critics of Alpha, there were also imitators who constructed courses that were more to their own liking.[52] This imitation of Alpha only serves to demonstrate precisely what a cutting edge tool it is. Alpha led the way in late 20th century and early 21st century evangelism and apostolic networks found its presumptions and methods entirely to their liking. It may even be said that both Alpha and the apostolic networks grew out of the common root of the charismatic movement of the 1960s and are fruit of the same branch of the Spirit.

---

[50] S. J. Hunt, 'The Alpha Course and its Critics: an overview of the debates', *PentecoStudies*, 4, (2003), 1-22.

[51] Hunt, 'The Alpha Course and its Critics', (2003).

[52] E.g. John Finney, An interview with John Finney concerning the Emmaus course, <http://www.chpublishing.co.uk/feature.asp?id=2389830> (accessed 30 August, 2006).

x. Reflection

None of the factors and changes described here automatically lead to church growth or to the formation of networks. After all, other churches lived through the same social and economic conditions and did not grow. What drove the apostolic networks was a theology of apostolicity, but the material conditions of British culture were undoubtedly helpful and speeded up what would, without technological innovation and financial buoyancy, have been a much more laboured and slower process.

London comes out of this analysis as being quite different from the rest of the country both in respect of churchgoing patterns and in respect of prosperity, broadcasting and immigration. London, in any case, dominated political events in Britain and, because of the abundance of journalists and broadcasters within the London area, also dominated intellectual discourse on the great matters of the day. London almost invariably ran with a more liberal or progressive agenda than the rest of the country in relation to sexual mores, drug-taking, curriculum development in schools and, when the BBC spoke, listeners were often given the impression that London values were held in every town and village of the country: they were not. It is no surprise that networks innovative in the arts and worship (like Pioneer) were situated in the London area while those outside London could appear more staid.

What the appearance of New Wine indicates is that there were other methods of forming networks than those used by the free church apostles. It is arguable that David Pytches and, later, John Coles function in an apostolic capacity and that their gathering of the New Wine network, despite the restrictions of canon law and Anglican tradition, shows that networks will form despite institutional and organisational obstacles. Given that theology appears to be the formative force of apostolic networks, it is to this we now turn.

Part IV

The Qualitative Analysis

Chapter 18

Apostolic Networks: Theology

Introduction

Apostolic networks are new and unusual structures within the body of the 20th century church. This chapter deals first with the theological definition of an apostle as understood by those who founded apostolic networks in Britain. It continues with a discussion of the characteristic features of networks and distinguishes between different types of networks.

i. Apostles

The pentecostal outpouring at the beginning of the 20th century argued on both experiential and theological grounds that the Holy Spirit was restoring charismata to the church after a lapse of many centuries. The essence of Pentecostalism was and is the presumption that the work of the Holy Spirit within the life of the individual and of a Christian congregation is the same today as it was at the very beginning of the era of the church. The claim is made that the Holy Spirit, as part of the eternal Trinity, has not changed and that those manifestations of the Spirit that were current within the time of the first apostles should also be expected today. This argument for the rediscovery of charismatic gifts by virtue of the work of the Holy Spirit was applied by many pentecostals to other aspects of the church including the definition of Christian ministry itself. In a nutshell, if charismatic gifts were restored, then so also apostles, prophets, evangelists, pastors and teachers were restored. The logic of Restoration is an all-or-nothing logic. Restorationists cannot argue for the partial renewal of the work of the Holy Spirit but must, to be consistent, argue for everything that the Spirit gives and inspires. Since pentecostals argued that ministerial function flows from the gift of the Spirit, it follows that the New Testament pattern of ministry is being restored along with charismatic gifts.[1]

At the start of the 20th century, the Apostolic Church certainly made these connections and enshrined them within their written constitution. As early as 1913, for instance, in a report of the August conference a Pastor Reade gave an address on, 'The Foundation Chapters of the Church' and argued that,

---

[1] W. K. Kay, *Pentecostals in Britain*, (Carlisle, Paternoster, 2000).

the seal of an Apostle was that he was a founder of churches. Are there any today? I do believe so. I do believe that our dear brother, Pastor Hutchinson, should have that title as a founder of churches. That is his seal, I do believe that God is restoring his church, and is restoring these primitive gifts. The restored church is to be built upon Apostles (original capitalisation).[2]

When the Apostolic Church agreed its constitution in around 1916, it defined its terms stating that 'apostle means one of the gifts of Christ in the Ascension ministries and is the first office in church government'. Among the powers of the apostle were the responsibility to clarify doctrinal matters and to call, ordain and locate ministers.[3]

Although the Apostolic Church was relatively small in Britain, it was strongest in South Wales (where Bryn Jones was born) and its teachings were known by informed ministers within the two other indigenous classical Pentecostal groups in Britain, Elim and Assemblies of God. Donald Gee referred to the Apostolic Church within his early history, *The Pentecostal Movement*, published in 1941 and explained not only why other Pentecostal denominations rejected the praxis of the Apostolic Church – because prophetic utterances were used governmentally – but also recalled how the Apostolic Church took part in Unity Conferences with other Pentecostals in 1939 and 1940, thereby largely healing the breach between them. Consequently the distinctive governmental doctrine of the Apostolic Church regarding 20th century apostles and prophets was, if not accepted by other Pentecostals, at least open for discussion. In any event there were undoubtedly non-Apostolics who could see that is was illogical to believe firmly in pastors, teachers and evangelists without a corresponding belief in apostles and prophets. Where the non-Apostolics drew the line, however, was over the role of prophets: whatever prophets should do in contemporary congregations, they should not make their inspired utterances the basis for church order.[4]

When Arthur Wallis began to convene conferences on the nature of the church after 1957, he argued for the testing of tradition against the 'clear, unequivocal teaching of a word of God'.[5] Inevitably he began to broach the idea of contemporary apostles. Admittedly, these early conferences were more concerned with the notion of self-governing congregations ruled by elders appointed by the Holy Spirit but he prepared the ground for the more

---

[2] G. Weeks, *Chapter Thirty Two – part of: a history of the Apostolic Church 1900-2000*, (Barnsley, Gordon Weeks, 2003).

[3] These quotations are taken from the constitution of the Apostolic Church reprinted in 1987. The constitution was originally written in Welsh and has been modified only very slightly since then, first in 1937 and then in 1961.

[4] Personal conversations.

[5] J. Wallis, *Arthur Wallis, A Radical Christian*, (1991), p.128.

precise and prolonged exposition that was to follow. Throughout the 1960s when the charismatic movement was in full swing, talk of apostles was limited. I have not been able to discover any reference to the subject in *Renewal* magazine but, at the beginning of the 1970s, the subject was again in circulation. John Noble published *First Apostles Last Apostles* as a sequel to his explosive text *Forgive us our Denominations.*[6]

The structure of the argument of *First Apostles Last Apostles* became familiar to restorationists. Noble gave an account of the history of the church starting with the high noon of first century and then lamenting the gradual loss of authority and power. He asserted that Christ had created 'a delicate structure to support the body and allow growth... a united people who... would obey and serve Him faithfully in showing His love to a dying world. The structure has not been altered'.[7] Quite soon apostleship was lost. In the early years after the first apostles died, the wrong people stepped in. Elders or bishops took over the place originally filled by the first apostles and a central organisation emerged making way for a Pope: 'hundreds of years of darkness followed'. Christ himself was the original apostle and he called The Twelve but, after Pentecost, the apostles of the Holy Spirit were sent out, and there were many more than 12 of these. The replacement of Judas by Matthias was certainly not a mistake and the writing of the Scriptures cannot be attributed only to apostles since at least some of the gospels, Mark and Luke, were not written by apostolic hands. One of the mistakes of Catholicism is to invest authority in one man; the non-episcopal non-conformist Protestants make the opposite mistake of giving every individual the right to rule the church. God's intention was that there should be a plurality of leadership in mutual submission and that local elders will come into a relationship of trust with apostolic and prophetic ministry. 'The special work of the apostle and prophet is one of foundation laying' in contrast to the mistaken work of men who have tried to pile up converts 'on doctrines and creeds instead of friendship and revelation'. Though the apostle is a foundation for the local church, apostles make Christ 'the foundation of all that they build'. Additionally the apostle is like a father and has the power to appoint elders by choosing people from within the body of the fellowships to whom he relates.

John Noble's booklets and the themes of *Fulness* magazine were resoundingly echoed by *Restoration* magazine. The first volume began in March/April 1975 and, by September/October 1975, an entire issue was devoted to apostles and prophets today. David Tomlinson began his article by declaring 'apostles are alive and well!' Apostles and prophets take

---

[6] Andrew Walker in *Restoring the Kingdom* (4th edn), (Guildford, Eagle, 1998), places the date of *Forgive us our Denominations* as 1971 and Noble states that *First Apostles Last Apostles* was written nearly three years later.

[7] The booklet is without page numbers.

Christians off the 'charismatic roundabout' and build them together into churches. The apostle turns the vision of the prophet into reality and brings a new congregation to birth. The contemporary situation is not as simple as it was in the days of the early church because fragmented and disjointed remnants lie around in the form of Christian groups here and there. These need to be renewed and rebuilt in the way that Nehemiah rebuilt the walls of Jerusalem from the surrounding rubble. If apostles are really to make progress then they will do so by 'committed relationship' rather than by preaching specially wonderful sermons. The apostle is concerned to assemble the family of God and make it fit together into a church by taking individuals, households, local bodies and other units and placing them in a functional relationship. In so doing the apostle must exercise a God-given authority. Despite concern with the theology of the kingdom, discipling, revival, spiritual warfare and leadership from 1976 onwards, it was the theme of apostleship to which *Restoration* returned in the early 1980s. Arthur Wallis, Bryn Jones, Terry Virgo and David Tomlinson wrote on the subject in November/December 1981 and, in 1988, an edited selection of articles were republished in book form as *Apostles Today* to present the fullest elaboration of the case.[8]

Wallis argued that apostles bring revelation and direction into living situations where God was building and that apostles are the 'experiential foundation' for each redeemed community. Tomlinson made it clear that apostles are church planters or builders who need a field to work in. This means that the authority of an apostle in one church does not necessarily transfer to another church and, in any case, the apostle is not licensed to dominate congregations because it is by a relationship between congregation and apostle that fruitfulness is guaranteed. While churches may tithe their income to their apostle (as was the case with Cornerstone), the apostle is accountable to his own team or to peer relationships with other apostles. As to the test of apostleship, signs and wonders are not essential and apostolic authority is best compared to parental authority in that it continues indefinitely over congregations planted by the apostle. There might be women on the apostolic team and 'no reason forbids a woman from apostleship' (p 35) (though other restorationists did not accept this). Virgo drew a distinction between great 'preaching centres' produced by teachers and genuine churches produced by apostles. It was the 'master builder' (1 Corinthians 3:10) quality that marked out an apostle and meant that the apostle was not simply a managing director. This implied that apostles should appoint elders and be able and willing to travel and have the capacity to bring objectivity to the appraisal of any congregation's present condition while, through relationships with these congregations, being able

---

[8] Edited by David Matthew and published by Harvestime.

to bring a sense of unity to the work of God at large. So can we manage without apostles today? Not if we wish to see a mature church.

Bryn Jones pointed out that physical buildings are erected in an ordered sequence of phases and asserted that the same principle applies to the spiritual building of the church. The apostle is the first builder on site as well as the architect of the completed structure. The apostle described in 1 Corinthians 12:28 is not first in status but the first in 'a functioning order for accomplishing the task' of making a properly constructed congregation.[9] The apostle's own ministry springs out of a deep encounter with Jesus Christ and divine purpose and authority are generated by the anointing of the Holy Spirit rather than by mere technique. The apostolic anointing is given for the apostolic task, and the task includes reference to the overall programme of a congregation or group of congregations. All this ensures a supernatural dimension to the ministry of the apostle. Yet, against or competing with this, is the underlying notion that the apostle's work is rational because it follows a biblical blueprint for church life.

Although the London-based leaders like Gerald Coates and John Noble believed in apostleship, there was a much more developed theology lying behind the northern group centred on Bryn Jones. As early as issue 24 of *Fulness* (in about 1980) Noble and Coates were suggesting that, 'we have to re-evaluate and overhaul our idea of the apostolic ministry and how it should operate in the light of so many believers already existing all over the country. We must learn to build community without becoming sectarian'.[10] This re-evaluation of the apostolic role to enable it to fit in more easily with traditional denominational structures would not have been music to the ears of Bryn Jones and, because he wanted to adhere to the scriptural model as faithfully as he could, would not have been acceptable to Terry Virgo either. In the end, one of the differences between the northern and southern groups, between what Andrew Walker called R1 and what he called R2, lay in the conceptualisation of the apostolic role. Terry Virgo's view did not change and, when he wrote *Does the Future Have a Church?* in 2003, he continued to believe that 'the apostles were foundational, absolutely no question... if we consign apostles and apostolic ministry exclusively to the early church, we are left without one of the key factors in world mission'.[11]

Equally, emphasis on apostles was to be found in the teaching of Barney Coombs.[12] Like the others, Coombs dealt first with the arguments against contemporary apostleship before teaching how he saw apostles operating

---

[9] Bryn Jones, 'Wise men of action', in D. Matthew (ed), *Apostles Today*, (Bradford, Harvestime, 1988), p.46.

[10] *Fulness*, 24, p.11.

[11] T. Virgo, *Does the Future have a Church?* (Eastbourne, Kingsway, 2003), pp.120, 123.

[12] B. Coombs, *Apostles Today: Christ's love gift to the church*, (Tonbridge, Sovereign World, 1996).

today. He believed the apostle is a master builder who builds relationally, pastorally, supernaturally and on a strong foundation of grace. Apostles are a gift from Jesus designed to help local elders build governmentally, prophetically and in a balanced way. His original contribution lay in his notion of the spiritual fatherhood of the apostle and the spiritual sonship of many of his team. The motif of spiritual family genes running through Coombs's ministry led him to invest the mentoring and caring role of the apostle with great importance. Relationships were intended to be personal and permanent rather than professional and transient. Yet the apostle might offer a review of any local church, a kind of check-up, intended to uncover imbalance and bad practice so local elders could correct their community. In this way, the apostle's ministry was not confined to church planting or building but had entrance to extant congregations whose leaders wanted to invite apostolic input.

In summary, the British restorationists believed apostles:

- are being raised up by God today;
- are church planters and/or master builders;
- act foundationally though Christ himself is the foundation of all an apostle builds;
- are not necessarily wonderful preachers but have the ability to fit human relationships together so that congregations flourish spiritually;
- carry particular authority, though this is expressed in and through personal relationships rather than by virtue of rank;
- have the right to appoint elders;
- travel and acquire experience enabling them to detect the strengths and weaknesses of congregations;
- may work with prophets and often in teams.

ii. Networks

Given scholarly debate over the dating, authorship and provenance of New Testament documents, there is academic disagreement over the organisational shape of the early Church. For those involved within apostolic networks in Britain, however, the canon of the New Testament was accepted without question. Deductions might be made from the Book of Acts or the epistles without complicated assumptions over the chronological development of church order. The picture drawn by evangelicals generally and those involved in apostolic networks in particular looked like this: apostles divided the territory of the ancient world up so that some apostles (for instance Peter) went to Jewish communities and others (for instance Paul) went to Gentile communities. The result of this division was that separate networks of churches were founded although, because the Jerusalem Church had, in the early years, an eminence and authority lacking elsewhere, all networks ultimately met up at the Jerusalem congregation and, possibly, under the leadership of this congregation in the person of James. Early apostles, like Paul and Barnabas travelling out from Antioch, planted fresh congregations on entirely new territory and, once these congregations had been established, ordained elders there so that the congregations became self-sustaining and self-governing to a large extent even if, when the apostles returned, they expected to be able to make any changes to the congregations that were needed as a result of failures by the elders they had previously installed. Even so the churches were practically autonomous as a consequence of the relatively slow and uncertain communications within the Roman Empire. The emperor and his commanders might be able to dispatch hasty commands but no one else had imperial couriers at their disposal. Local church leaders, under the authority of the Holy Spirit, had to do their best to solve local problems.

Once congregations had been established like those on Cyprus or in Asia Minor, they functioned as freestanding units and, if the apostle was unable to visit them, they received his letters which were read out (probably during meetings to break bread on the Lord's Day i.e. Sunday) and later shared with any other congregations in the vicinity (Colossians 4:16). As a result, the original networks were flat in the sense that there were no intermediary administrators or functionaries between the elders of one of the new congregations and the apostle or apostles who had founded the congregation. Not only was the structure flat but the structure might, of its own initiative, expand sideways by planting congregations in nearby towns or villages or in other parts of the town where it had been established. The local elders, despite their unique relationship with their founding apostle, were also able to invite other ministry from reputable sources so that, for instance, Apollos might travel to Corinth or, even, Peter himself, when passing through to Rome, might pay a visit. In this respect the network founded by one apostle was not exclusive but was open to other recognised preachers, particularly where letters of recommendation were available (2 Corinthians 3:1). Although the Jerusalem Church was important to the first years of the expansion of Christianity, as the years passed, other churches at major urban centres (especially Rome) appeared to replace it and, after AD 70 when Jerusalem was besieged and the temple burnt, the Jerusalem Church was scattered and could no longer provide the venue for important inter-network gatherings. It was, after all, at the Council of Jerusalem in Acts 15 that decisions were taken about the correlation between Jewish Christians in Peter's network and Gentile Christians in Paul's network in an attempt to ensure doctrinal and lifestyle harmony across the entire body of Christ.

The British networks began at roughly the same time. Almost all of them began in the 1970s and, though some of them formally registered as charities in the 1980s, the initial groundwork had in every case occurred several years before this. The beginnings of the networks were also similar. There were two basic patterns, which might be combined. In the first pattern a large individual congregation was established, often by joining two or more congregations and sometimes by transforming a non-charismatic congregation into a charismatic congregation. Once the large congregation had been created, resources were released for activities outside the city where the congregation was situated. In the second pattern an itinerant ministry took in numerous small groups and knitted them together into a single entity (as in the case of Ichthus). The two patterns were combined if the large congregation released the minister into an itinerant lifestyle that allowed him to connect the new, and usually smaller, groups with his own large base. New Frontiers, Salt and Light, New Covenant, Pioneer, Cornerstone, Kensington Temple and Ground Level all made use of large initial congregations from which to launch their networks. Colin Urquhart of Kingdom Faith began in a different way by setting up a residential training centre after a period of travelling ministry and then planting a new congregation near the residential centre. Terry Virgo of New Frontiers managed to fit in a travelling ministry in the southern part of England with the creation of a large central congregation in Brighton. Bryn Jones was also able to combine both the establishment of a large congregation and itinerancy.

Once the large congregation had been established, the senior minister needed to leave it in charge of other people and so he created relational links between himself and his deputies. The setting up of a large congregation along restorationist lines provided the senior minister, who came to be seen as the apostle, with a wealth of practical experience about congregational transformation and charismatic practice. The large congregation gave the apostolic figure credibility while also supplying a template of the steps needed for turning the standard congregation into a restorationist congregation. The key issue for the apostolic network concerned the relationship between the apostolic figure and the leaders of local congregations, and this key was exactly analogous to the relationship between New Testament apostles and the elders of newly formed congregations. The flat structure of the New Testament could be replicated by a flat structure in Britain so long as the apostle had time to travel to the various congregations making up his network. In the early stages the networks grew entirely by the accumulation of congregations and house groups around the apostolic ministry: it was a matter of invitation, often a cry for help from groups that had become detached from their denominational moorings during the turbulence of the charismatic movement.

In the early days the networks were simple and the pristine vision of restorationists precluded the setting up of committees and bureaucratic procedures for the administration of new congregations. Everything was relational. Elders formed a relationship with the apostle and, particularly if they had recently escaped from the clutches of denominational bureaucracy, they were glad to jettison the mindset that magnified the rule of canon or constitutional law. Once buildings had been removed from denominational control, elders were delighted to find an apostolic figure who would provide encouragement and vision – something that denominational officials almost uniformly failed to do.

There was a sense in which the networks looked at denominational structures and decided to do the opposite. While many of the Free Church denominations made use of voting systems to ratify decisions, apostolic networks threw this democratic paraphernalia out of the window. Apostles themselves had never been recognised by voting systems and understood the weaknesses implicit in such procedures. As Terry Virgo pointed out, one-person-one-vote systems gave the most immature member of the annual general meeting of the church the same voting power as the pastor.[13]

As the apostolic network grew, adjustments were made to its simple structure. The flat ideal was retained. Once the network had reached about 40 churches, it was impossible for the apostle to visit them all while retaining a proper ministry within the flagship church to which he belonged. Given that there were something like 30 or 40 Sundays when the apostle might be away from his own church and given that there were about 30 or 40 midweek meetings when the apostle might preach to members of his network, once a network totalled more than, say, 50 congregations, there were logistical difficulties in getting round to everyone. It was not practical to preach in a different church every Sunday and it was an inefficient use of the apostle's time to speak to small groups of leaders within a home. If the congregations were separated by distances of more than about an hour, it was unreasonable to ask people to travel to a central point for a meeting either on Sunday or during the normal working week. The apostle had to find fresh methods of bringing elders and other leaders together for teaching, direction and encouragement: the annual meeting of the network was the answer. The Bible Weeks during the summer were effective because they could offer different types of ministry to different people. Leaders could attend seminars, ordinary congregational members could receive ministry on family life or practical Christian living and, in addition, there could be special events for children and young people. Even so, the apostle could not be expected to carry the ministry of an entire Bible Week and it was here that the network opened its heart to the ministry of other apostolic figures.

---

[13] Terry Virgo, *No Well Worn Paths,* (Eastbourne, Kingsway, 2001).

Actually, New Frontiers instituted days of prayer and fasting for their UK leaders three times a year as well as an annual conference for all leaders. Ground Level and Kensington Temple also offered meetings for their leaders outside the annual cycle. Ground Level's pattern was the most complicated in that it offered a mixture of monthly meetings for leaders, a short residential gathering of leaders and the big summer event. Kensington Temple, which could draw upon the London transport system, could offer Saturday events and quickly pull everyone into a central point. There was no pre-determined plan behind all this and the networks were able to adjust their pattern of meetings continually to cope with growth or with unexpected trends like the Toronto blessing. The relatively small size of the networks gave them a wide choice of venues at the beginning – big denominational groups needed large conference settings of which there were not many in the country – and the short history of the networks prevented the emergence of a traditionalist cadre complaining of change. Unburdened by years of tradition, networks could rapidly adapt. Nevertheless the more successful of them did value continuity and Ground Level built up the size of its summer camp, Grapevine, over 25 years.

The apostle was the principal ministry of the network and yet, as the New Testament showed, apostles did not function as solo ministers. Paul travelled in an entourage with a changing circle of assistants whom he could send to deal with specific tasks for which he did not have time or opportunity. Titus was sent to appoint elders in Crete and Timothy was involved with Corinth. The planting of churches might also involve a collection of ministries with the apostle playing a coordinating role. Paul appears to have been in northern Greece with both Silas and Luke. This implied that the apostle was part of the team providing a fully rounded ministry to the young churches. This had a double advantage: members of the team could learn first-hand and on-the-job from the apostle and the apostle could advance on a broader front leaving members of the team behind or sending some ahead of him as he worked systematically through a defined geographical area. The team extended the ministry of the apostle and widened the ministerial centre of the network. It was no longer focused on one individual but, like local church leadership, expressed through plurality.

Even with an apostolic team the network remained a flat organisation. True, members of the apostolic team were not quite afforded equal status with the apostle himself but, even so, they did not function as intermediaries between the apostle and the churches. Rather, the members of the apostolic team represented the apostle and offered a complementary ministry. This still left the question about entrance to the network. At one point during the shepherding controversy Bob Mumford insisted that shepherds were the door to the church but this theology was quickly discarded.[14] While British apostles never claimed to be the entrance to the network, the network might still be summarised as comprising those 'in relationship with' so-and-so, whoever the apostle was. This was an inevitable consequence of refusing to bind members of the network to credal statements or quasi-legal formulae.

Decision-making in apostolic networks was never entirely within the hands of the apostle. The apostle did not sit on the top of the pyramid issuing orders; as restorationists were quick to declare 'we left pyramids behind in Egypt'. The leadership of the apostle over a group of churches grew out of the collective leadership that the apostle had established within the flagship church. This, at least, was the best way of doing things. There might be networks that were less consultative in their mode of decision-making and others that had veered between more autocratic and more consultative modes. Within New Frontiers, the apostolic team functioned rather like a collection of elders at a local church. Relationships were informal and easy. It was more like the government of the cabinet than the government of the king, and the apostle was the first among equals. There might be prophetic utterances or visionary declarations during the days of prayer and fasting and these would be tape-recorded, collected up and then weighed later by the apostolic team as they tried to find the mind of God (1 Corinthians 14:29-31). Such decision-making benefited from collective wisdom and was open to new directions and ideas arising from charismatic gifts emanating from all the gathered leaders who were not part of the apostolic team. As the apostle became older and more venerable, it became more difficult for younger ministers to disagree with him but, where the apostle maintained good relationships with co-ministers over many years, there was no danger of splendid isolation and the failure associated with being out of touch.

So decision-making within the networks was at two levels. At the lower-level elders oversaw their congregations and made local decisions. At the upper level, the apostolic team provided direction, resources, training and advice. This meant that the local churches could be left to run themselves while, at the upper level, the apostolic team was normally employed in launching big new projects. New Frontiers began to emphasise a concern for the poor. Kingdom Faith became interested in Christian broadcasting. Ground Level took on support of missions projects overseas. These decisions concerned all the churches acting collectively and contributing resources and were therefore the natural domain of the apostolic team.

By way of contrast it is important to appreciate what apostolic networks do not countenance. They are neither Episcopal nor Presbyterian. They are not Episcopal in the sense that the apostle is not elevated to a position above all other ministers by virtue of an ecclesiastical promotion

---

[14] Moore, *The Shepherding Movement*, (2003), p.74.

mechanism. If the apostle carries more weight than others within the network, this is because the apostle is seen to be specially gifted. The gifting of a person determines their eventual weight within the network, and gifting is both natural and charismatic. Gifting can be recognised and can not be argued against. There is no avenue open for the ungifted minister to rise to the position of apostle whereas, in the case of an Episcopal form of government, it is arguable that ecclesiastical promotion is less well protected from common or garden ambition. Equally the networks are not Presbyterian in their structure in the sense that they do not assemble a collection of ministers into a governing presbytery that has power over local church elders. It is virtually an article of faith that there is no voting within apostolic networks. Gifting and function determine ministry and, since ministry includes preaching, everyone has an opportunity to evaluate an important aspect of the ministerial capacity of others.

The 'recognition' of a ministry is not made by any set procedure utilising a committee poring over a carefully prepared CV. Recognition is more subtle than this and evidence of the genuineness of ministry is in the flesh and blood of the congregations where people have worked (2 Corinthians 3:2). Good ministers, like good football managers, will produce good results. Consequently a man or woman cannot simply claim to have a particular ministry because it will rapidly become apparent when such a claim is false.

The decision-making functions within a network are related to the structure of the network itself. In addition to being a flat structure, the network may be more or less richly interconnected. It would be possible to imagine a network where all the individual congregations were related directly to the apostle but not to each other. This would be a network that might grow by the addition of congregations introduced by the apostle but could not grow by the addition of congregations planted out by other congregations. In practice, the congregations within a network are related to each other in a variety of ways as well as to the apostle. Wherever summer events or annual meetings are held, leaders within the congregations comprising the network can meet together and they often form friendships and learn to collaborate. Yet, even if there are interconnections between the leaders of congregations within the networks, it is still likely to be true that the apostle will know the largest number of people within the network since he is the one who will travel most widely. In this way, the apostle, even apart from the matter of gifting, has the best claim to being the most informed about the needs of the whole network.

Many networks see individual congregations as made up of sets of relationships and it would make little sense for leaders of these congregations to be blind to the possibility of establishing connections with nearby congregations. In the large networks, congregations come together in clusters and often find that resources of personnel and money can be distributed from larger churches to smaller ones. This means that networks grow by filling in the gaps between the big congregation in their cluster and the rest. At the same time networks may link with other networks to form networks of networks. This is particularly the case when a network in one country joins with a network in another. Salt and Light functions in England and in Canada and, although there is interchange between the two countries, there is a sense in which the networks in each place are distinct. Conversely if a network breaks up, it may collapse into mini-networks as in the case of Cornerstone which eventually lost its 'apostolic hubs' overseas. Where the network stretches over large distances, personal relationships have to be maintained by travel and, where travel is impossible, networks find themselves only able to operate in limited geographical areas. There is a New Frontiers cluster of churches in India but it is confined to a small part of the country.

If networks are to be successful in church planting they must be open and outgoing. New Frontiers will invite (or not exclude) members of other churches to their days of prayer and fasting or to their leaders' conferences. This may lead congregations to like what they see and to ask to join. Yet there are networks where joining is more complicated. For instance, Kingdom Faith allows individuals to join the network. Kensington Temple, because it is within Elim, plants congregations that automatically relate both to it *and* to the denomination. This means that congregations planted by Kensington Temple are pastored by men who take credentials with Elim and who are therefore entitled to detach themselves from Kensington Temple to move elsewhere within the denomination, a situation that benefits the denomination but not necessarily the KT network.

iii. Types of Network

Although the networks are similar in the centrality they give to the role of the apostle, there are detectable differences between them. These differences are often more a matter of style and ethos rather than being profoundly theological or structural. There are five factors that influence the feel of the network:

Leaders' Genders

Two of the networks, Ichthus and Pioneer, allow female leadership. Ichthus has made the most explicit statement about female apostles and, for many years, has seen its founding apostle, Roger Forster, as operating in tandem with his wife, Faith, who is equally apostolic. Since apostolic ministry is identified by function, and if this function is carried out by women, there is no reason to deny that women may be apostles.[15] Such is the fluidity of a functional definition of apostles that a man or woman may be an apostle for a period of time and then, because of life changes, withdraw from apostolic ministry. Other networks, like New Frontiers, Salt and Light and the Jesus Fellowship specifically exclude women from governmental roles. They believe that biblical injunctions forbid female governance. This means that women are allowed to do almost everything else within these three networks – they can preach, baptise, lead worship, preside over the celebration of communion – but they cannot carry ultimate responsibility either for an individual congregation or at the apostolic level. It is important to see what women are permitted to do within such networks as well as what they are not permitted to do. Because the role of minister is not equivalent to the role of the priest within Roman Catholic or Anglo-Catholic settings, women within male-led apostolic networks enjoy opportunities for ministry that are well beyond those found within Catholic and Anglo-Catholic settings. It would be a mistake to think of male-led apostolic networks as being repressive environments for women even if postfeminist critical theory struggles against their underlying value system.[16]

Although it is hard to put one's finger on the precise differences between male-led and mixed gender-led networks, the impression given to me is that the male-led networks are more task-orientated, more focused on goals and expansionist plans and less inclined to classify themselves as responsive banks of resource for the whole church. Both the three male-led networks have managed to sustain their growth over three decades and have maintained relationships between their senior leaders without notable friction, indeed with continuing warmth. The male-led networks speak of themselves as 'families' and conceive of the nuclear family with the father in a leading position of responsibility as the fundamental building block of church, and therefore network, life. The empirical evidence presented in chapters 21-23 amplifies these impressions.

Exclusivity of Membership

Networks vary in their 'purity' in the sense that some of them contain leaders with dual or triple membership and others are almost entirely made up of leaders with single membership. The nature of some networks is to allow churches or individuals to become members while, at the same time,

---

[15] <http://www.ichthus.org.uk/Default.aspx> (accessed 6 October, 2005); see the shop section on teaching about apostles.

[16] See for instance, K. J. Aune, 'Postfeminist Evangelicals: the construction of gender in the New Frontiers International churches', (unpublished PhD Dissertation, King's College, London, 2004).

retaining membership in their denominations or with other networks. Exclusivity of membership may be a weakness and a strength. Bryn Jones was exclusive in his demands. Other networks have been happier to include congregations that retain denominational links. New Frontiers has congregations that retain a Baptist connection and Kingdom Faith incorporates Baptist, Roman Catholic and Anglican congregations.

Again, empirical analysis will help to clarify the extent of multiple memberships. Where congregations or individual ministers hold multiple membership, there are several reasons why this may be so. The impression given is that London congregations, especially those for African immigrants, find it beneficial to join as many networks as possible so as to gain the maximum support system. Others may have a valuable building that is locked into a denomination by its trust deed but who do not find the denomination compatible with their own philosophy of ministry. Yet others may be governed by elders unable to reach agreement about whether to leave or join specific networks and so end up as members of more than one.

Governmental Expectations

Kingdom Faith is not a governmental network. It offers a covenant or contractual relationship with its members but does not seek to control their lives. Other networks are more controlling, more governmental, more directive. Yet, because of local church autonomy, the government of each of the network is not and cannot be mechanically enforced. Networks have given thought to the balance between apostolic leadership and congregational independence. Vineyard stresses the core values that hold congregations together. If congregations or their leaders do not want the values of the Association, then they are free to leave. So the Vineyard uses Wimber's sociological notion of a 'centred set' to allow variation in non-core values. A 'bounded set', by contrast, would not allow variation of belief and practice and would ensure everything was tightly drawn round a common centre.

In the Jesus Fellowship, governmental expectations are all bound up with common ownership of property and businesses. Even so, gradations of life-style commitment within the Fellowship give choice to members over their degree of autonomy. In any of the networks where there is an element of communal life, for instance within their colleges and campuses, an element of authority is bound to be found, but this does not necessarily stretch out to the congregations in one way or another linked to the centre. Government is most likely to be visible when local elders find themselves in disagreement with their apostle. Here there are examples of confrontational stand-offs (as in the case of Bryn Jones's desire to impose his choice on a community church in London),[17] but these are rare. If friction and disagreement were the norm, the network would never survive. Usually, the apostle or his delegate has the tact and authority necessary to persuade elders to do as they are asked and, in instances where disagreements might arise, as in the adoption of cell principles, apostles are often pragmatic. Bryn Jones, the apostolic figure most prone to expect elders to follow his lead, noted that congregations varied according to local giftings and this was the evidence that contradicted accusations that he imposed uniformity by authoritarian means.[18]

Where network members have a dual membership, governmental expectations are bound to be diluted. The network positions itself as a supporting agency – for instance Kensington Temple might let its name be used by new churches wishing to open business accounts – and the only expectation it might place on participating churches might be attendance at meetings where the apostle preaches or is available for consultation.[19] Dual membership is bound to cause diary clashes and may also lead to theological tension. Some of these difficulties are met by contractual delimitations even if the contract is never actually confined to a signed paper.

Attempts to arrange the networks along a spectrum from hands-on to hands-off government seem to have been most appropriate to the shepherding era of the mid-1970s and are less easy to apply in the current post-modern climate.[20] This is especially so in the light of current lowered thresholds between network and surrounding society - that is, there are no visible features that would distinguish members' lifestyles from the rest of society.

Sectarian and Non-sectarian Orientations

The openness of networks to inter-denominational gatherings is most easily measured by reference to Spring Harvest which gathers many streams of charismatic worship together within its conferences. Spring Harvest is overtly interdenominational and by providing different tracks within its schedule of meetings, can accommodate worshippers with a range of preferences. Such is the size of Spring Harvest (over 50,000 per year) that it employs a full-time staff all year round and manages to fill two sites for a

---

[17] Interview with David Tomlinson, 4 May, 2005.

[18] *Restoration*, (May/June, 1989), p.39.

[19] Interview with Marlon Nartey, 10 December, 2003.

[20] N. Wright, 'The nature and variety of restorationism and the 'House Church' movement', in S, Hunt, M, Hamilton and T, Walter (eds) *Charismatic Christianity: sociological perspectives*, (Basingstoke, Macmillan, 1997), pp.60-76.

fortnight.[21] Networks like Ichthus and Ground Level approve of Spring Harvest. Networks like Kingdom Faith, which runs its own bible week, New Frontiers and Kensington Temple are less likely to approve. It is reasonable to deduce that Ichthus and Ground Level are less sectarian in their orientation and Kingdom Faith, New Frontiers and Kensington Temple are more sectarian but such a conclusion needs to be treated with caution since Kingdom Faith may well only have reservations about Spring Harvest because the big meeting is in competition with its own summer event. This said, the more open mentality of Ichthus and Ground Level probably *does* reflect the theology of its founding apostle while the less open approach of Kingdom Faith, New Frontiers and Kensington Temple may reflect the confidence these networks have in their own home-grown enterprises. In essence those networks that are doing well see no need to open themselves to potentially messy collaboration while those networks that are doing less well welcome the impetus given by large Christian events. So, surface sectarianism is driven by practicalities rather than theology.

Another way of looking at this is through the predominant prior religious membership of leaders. For instance, 32% of Ground Level leaders originated within the Church of England as did 50% of Ichthus leaders. On the other hand 50% of Pioneer leaders came from a Baptist background as did 23% of Salt and Light leaders. So it would be reasonable to argue that the more inclusive Anglican attitude is partially retained by the more open leaders and the more exclusive Baptist attitude is retained by the others. This is by no means a scientific test but merely a suggestive finding, and one that will be more fully discussed in chapter 23.

Geographical Extent

The networks vary in their geographical distribution. Salt and Light established a base of inter-linked congregations in Basingstoke and another base of inter-linked congregations in the Oxford area. To these two main bases in the UK they added other congregations in major locations. On top of this, the Canadian congregations form a separate set. Ichthus and Kensington Temple are localised in south and north-west London respectively, though both have connections with other churches some distance away as well as within other countries. Neither has configured itself like Salt and Light with shared eldership across the inter-linked congregations. New Frontiers expanded from the south of England up towards the north of England and into Scotland and Ireland and then, from the United Kingdom base, out to Europe and other parts of the world.

---

[21] Interview with Spring Harvest leaders, 26 January, 2005. See also <http://www.springharvest.org/mainevent.html> (accessed 20 May, 2006).

Cornerstone (c.net) was located around Southampton. The Jesus Fellowship continues to hold a base in Bugbrooke. Covenant Ministries International was centred first in Bradford and later in Nettle Hill. Pioneer has remained strongest in the south of England and the London area. The first challenge to the network is to overcome its parochial horizons and to expand strategically and systematically. If the network succeeds in going beyond its local base, it becomes national and then international. If the development is less well directed, the local base will be added to by groups of congregations that appear to be scattered haphazardly. Where this happens the local base continues to dominate the group. If, on the other hand, the network manages to spread out of from its original parish into a national distribution, then the network begins to match the demographics of Britain and to take on a genuinely national complexion.

iv. Conclusion

The apostolic networks that came into being in the 1970s had first to establish their doctrine of apostleship which, with a large measure of consensus, they did. There were variations of opinion about the need for apostles to plant churches as a sign of apostleship but, apart from this, there was agreement about the right of a trans-local ministry to offer direction to local congregations and appoint elders. Once the role of the apostle was accepted, the next step was to map the biblical account of the extension of the early church onto the contemporary world. The Acts of the Apostles became a source of inspiration and information showing how the apostles travelled from place to place evangelising and establishing new congregations while the Pauline epistles, especially Corinthians, where Paul defended and explained his own apostolic role, provided insight into the mindset of the master builder.

Once the restorationist paradigm for reading off contemporary ecclesiastical practice from the canonical account of the first century is accepted, everything falls into place. Subsequent doctrinal and institutional development of the church in the Constantinian and post-Constantinian era can be consigned to the scrapheap. What matters is the authoritative account of the supple, powerful and simple structures of the early church and their transferability to the present era. That there were differences between Pauline and Petrine churches within the first century does not matter. Rather it strengthens the view that there may be differences between apostolic networks today. Similarly, just as there were attempts to harmonise Jewish and Gentile expressions of the church that had been planted by different apostles, so, also, there were good grounds (through round table discussions or smaller meetings) for trying to find minimal common denominators among the networks, as the Council of Jerusalem attempted to do in Acts 15. This said, contemporary apostolic networks live in the world shaped by 20 centuries of Christianity and the profound friction between denominational and apostolic values is difficult to parallel in the pages of the New Testament. Rather, apostolic networks look like reforming movements within church history and they fight hard to avoid suffering the same fate as most of these. As we shall see in chapter 20, the theological life of apostolic networks is interestingly poised in balance with their sociological life. Before this, we look at the role of apostolic networks in mission: in this evangelistic context the well-adapted nature of their self-propagating structures is most evident.

Chapter 19

Apostolic Networks: Mission

Around 1990, Paul Cain gave a prophecy to a New Frontiers leaders'
meeting in Brighton. He said,

> This is a matter of a sovereign work of apostolic character and nature and
> chemistry and the Lord is going to use it to change the expression of
> Christianity all over the world. And that's the word I came to bring. The
> Lord will use you here in a sovereign way to change the expression of
> Christianity throughout the world.[1]

The prophetic announcement given by Cain indicated that New Frontiers
International (NFI) was to make ground-breaking changes to the expression
of Christianity and, consequently and among other things, to the way
mission is carried out. To understand this fully and to assess whether the
announcement is credible, it is necessary to look back on Protestant
missionary enterprises to see historically how they have operated. The
focus of this chapter is largely upon the structures through which mission is
actuated rather than the theology driving it though, as we shall see,
theology *is* of crucial importance in the conduct of mission within apostolic
networks.

i. Typology of Missionary Societies

Klaus Fiedler (1994) devised a typology of Protestant missionary
movements and arranged them on a timeline. Like many others he regards
*An Enquiry into the Obligation of Christians to Use Means for the
Conversion of the Heathen* written by William Carey in 1792 to be crucial.[2]
The first group within his typology comprises denominational missionary
societies (like the Baptist Missionary Society of 1793) that were organised
independently of any individual congregation but were strongly related to
the denomination as a whole. Missionary societies were usually organised
as voluntary associations 'in which every member other than the
missionaries – to whom the principle of voluntary association did not apply

---

[1] Terry Virgo, *No Well Worn Paths,* (Eastbourne, Kingsway, 2001), p.192.
[2] K. Fiedler, *The Story of Faith Missions*, (Oxford, Regnum, 1994). Carey is recognised
by K. S. Latourette, *A History of the Expansion of Christianity*, (Grand Rapids,
Zondervan, 1976); D. L. Edwards, *Christianity: the first two thousand years*, (London,
Cassell, 1997).

because they were employed by the mission – had a say' (page 20). These denominational missionary societies reflected the internal structures and ecclesiologies of the denominations with which they were connected. Missionaries were supported by financial contributions donated by church members and certified and regulated by denominational officials who, by virtue of geography, were disconnected from the fieldwork of the missionary.

The second group are inter-denominational missionary societies. The first of these was the London Missionary Society of 1795 and it followed a similar pattern apart from the greater range of congregations offering financial support. Within such missionary societies a board was convened for the control of missionary activity in ways similar to those utilised by denominational missions. Regular communication to and from the field enabled the board to feel that it had an appreciation of the progress and problems confronting individual missionaries; boards responded by giving written instructions and sending or withholding money. The Basel Mission founded in 1815 functioned in this way and regularly sent out men and women to Africa where, in the early years, most of them died. In one gruesome statistic, there were for several years more deaths among missionaries than converts. As the mission boards became more adept at their work, language training, cultural preparation, biblical teaching, financial systems and the provision of visas and other documents, became part of their role. Missionaries, in both denominational and inter-denominational missions, often confined themselves to mission stations or secure compounds where they lived in relative safety and with the ability to go out to preach, offer medical help, supervise the building of schools and run local congregations.[3] Inter-denominational missionary societies were obliged to ensure that no doctrinal controversy among the missionaries themselves blighted the work and it was common, in such circumstances, for policies on water baptism to be settled in advance. In most cases believers' baptism was not welcomed and the default position of paedobaptism was propagated.[4]

As ecumenical and liberal movements took place within the churches of Europe and North America, denominational and inter-denominational missionary societies converged and differences between them became blurred.[5] In both instances the missionary was the agent of the board. It seems incredible to 21st century commentators that, for example, the Basel Mission should send out wave after wave of young men and women to work in appalling conditions where their life expectancy was low, where

---

[3] According to Fiedler the strategy might be to set up a chain of mission stations across hostile terrain each fifty hours of travelling time from the next, pp.73-74.

[4] Fiedler, *The Story of Faith Missions*, (1994), p.21.

[5] Fiedler, *The Story of Faith Missions*, (1994), p.21.

they had little control over what they did and where they could be disciplined by the withholding of finance if they disagreed with the board's decisions. In many instances those who were sent out, however, were tenant farmers or in other ways obligated to their social superiors who sat on the board. 'People like us have always told people like you what to do' was the attitude of the board and an attitude accepted by the missionaries.[6] Denominational missionaries appeared to fare little better even though, in theory, those who sat on the board, were fellow members of the same denomination. Had the missionaries functioned as ministers within their own country, they would never have accepted the interfering directives that they had to put up with on the field.

In 1865 Hudson Taylor founded the China Inland Mission (CIM) and established it along faith lines; that is to say, CIM missionaries received no salary beyond that which they received through centralised distribution after communal prayer. The missionaries were not employees of the mission or subject to the board but were members of the mission and, more than this, their calling to China took pre-eminence over cultural norms within the country of their origin. CIM Missionaries were expected to identify with the Chinese people, to dress like them, to eat their food, to learn their language and, when strategic decisions had to be made, these were made on the field by other missionaries within the same society and not handed down from distant boards in the countries where money was collected. Faith missions were the third group in the typology.

It should be emphasised that this discussion is not intended to diminish the heroic and sacrificial efforts of many missionaries in the 19th century.[7] Nor is it intended to be an exhaustive classification system. Mission societies changed over the course of time and could diversify their activities so that they became less close to their originating type. For instance, although faith-based missions were intensely evangelical, they could also engage in charitable works like the building of schools and hospitals (as was the case with the CEM founded by W F P Burton in 1919[8]). Equally faith missions might also be inter-denominational in their composition – as was the CIM – while inter-denominational missionary societies might emphasise to their missionaries that funds could not be guaranteed and that, as a consequence, personal faith for provision was required. The

---

[6] Jon Miller's answer at EPTA 2005 to a question posed during a visit to the Basel Mission.

[7] Protestant missions in Africa trebled between 1886 and 1895. Many died young (N. Ferguson, *Empire: How Britain Made the Modern World*, (Harmondsworth, Penguin, 2004), pp.158, 160).

[8] Though the earliest form of association dates to 1915. Burton himself was an apostle by any definition of the word and the Congo Evangelistic Mission he founded showed many of the characteristics of an apostolic network.

Pentecostal Missionary Union (PMU) made this kind of stipulation: its missionaries were not guaranteed an income even though the PMU council in Britain did attempt to raise money inter-denominationally and to control the activity of its missionaries from afar.[9] During the 19th century and within the first part of the 20th century many missionary societies were founded so that, for instance, Fiedler needs nine pages to enumerate them all, particularly since the sending countries were situated throughout the world (pp 92-101). Between 1918 and 1940 19 new missionary societies were founded solely for the evangelisation of central Africa.

ii. Denominations and Networks

Alongside this typology of missions, can be placed a typology to include denominations and apostolic networks. As the next chapter shows more fully, denominations have been sociologically defined by reference to their doctrine (especially along the exclusive/inclusive dimension) and to their attitude to the world (especially contrasting those that are pro-world and those that are anti-world). Parallel or implicit within this distinction, is the contrast between denominations that recognise the equal rights of other denominations to exist and sects which are opposed to all other groups that differ from their own.[10] This sociological classification between sect, denomination and church has encouraged recent complex variants but, for the purpose of this discussion, it is the structure that is important. Structure cuts across many of the other defining features of sects and churches. Traditional religious structure, as we shall see, contrast with such structures as are put in place by apostolic networks.

Regardless of theological doctrines, churches and denominations usually balance the free action of the congregation against overarching governmental arrangements. The Catholic Church is the most obviously controlling of all churches. Ecclesiastical personnel are ranked in an order between deacon at the bottom and Pope at the top, and each bishop has power over the religious outlets within his diocese. There may, it is true, be religious orders like the Jesuits that function outside the diocesan system

---

[9] It is also true that Cecil Polhill's *Practical Points Concerning Missionary Work* did distinguish between mission stations and church planting. It also warned against becoming occupied with education, medicine and philanthropy.

[10] See Martin Weber, *The Protestant Ethic and the Spirit of Capitalism*, (London: Unwin University Books, 1930); Brian R. Wilson, 'A typology of sects in a dramatic and comparative perspective' in *Archives de Sociologie de Religion*, vol. 16, (1963), pp.4,9-63; Peter L. Berger, *The Sacred Canopy*, (New York: Random House, 1967); William Sims Bainbridge, *The Sociology of Religious Movements*, (London: Routledge, 1997); Duncan MacLaren, *Mission Implausible: restoring credibility to the church*, (Carlisle: Paternoster, 2004).

but in essence the ranking system within the Catholic Church is unwavering and vests supreme authority in the Pope who speaking *ex cathedra* is infallible. Other denominational systems are less authoritarian. Anglicans have a House of Clergy, a House of Laity as well as a House of Bishops and by voting each house contributes to synodical decisions binding on everyone.[11] This means that the laity and the clergy have an opportunity to voice their opinions independently of and, if they wish, in opposition to the voice of the bishops.[12] Nevertheless it is clear that there is a ranking system within Anglicanism. The same is true within other Protestant groups. The essence of the ranking system is that power is vested within the individual so that, just as all colonels outrank all corporals, so all bishops outrank all deacons.

Within the Presbyterian systems, ministers are all equal with each other but power is vested in bodies to which ministers may be elected and to which all have an equal chance of being elected. Each congregation may have its own presbytery and then, above this, may be a regional presbytery or an executive presbytery. It is not that the individuals who sit on the executive presbytery outrank ministers on presbyteries lower down the system but that one presbytery, defined by constitution, does outrank another. The voting system expresses the reality of the equality of the ministers within their denomination. The constitution, because it is also agreed by voting, ensures that where denominational authority is exercised, consent is implied.

Denominational missionary societies set up within this structure operate by electing members to a presbytery or collective group (which may be called a Missions Council or Missions Board) and this has power over the special category of ministers within the denomination that are designated missionaries. In this sense the missionaries are directly subject to a higher authority within their denomination. Additionally missionaries are not able to be both on the home board or council and, at the same time, to be on the field; distance precludes this. Consequently missionaries are always excluded from and subservient to their governing body and, since they must communicate with it individually and directly, are rarely able to act collectively to make their opinions count.

The point is that missionaries are answerable to their boards within denominational settings. In the case of inter-denominational missionary societies, the board also wields power since it collects the finance from contributing churches. In practice, it is difficult to discern a greater degree of missionary autonomy within inter-denominational missions than is the

---

[11] See <http://www.cofe.anglican.org/about/gensynod/> (accessed 26 June, 2006).

[12] Proportionately, of course, the House of Bishops is more powerful than the House of Laity since the relatively small number of bishops can cancel out the vote of the much large number of laity that its house represents.

case in denominational missions. In short, it is arguable that many missionary societies of the 19th and early 20th centuries derived their ethos from the social and theological presumptions of the denominations of their day. These denominations were largely authoritarian in outlook, and their hierarchies ran in precise parallel with the social stratification of the age.[13] Only faith missions, where authority is vested in a collection of missionaries on the field, really give missionaries the degree of control over their own lives and strategy that many of them might wish. Only faith missions escaped the worst results of class-based governance. In case this is thought to be an oversatement, consider the following quotation from an Anglican bishop in the 1840s describing the separation between leaders and followers in the Church Missionary Society,

> it has been the custom to think of missionaries as an inferior set of men, sent out, paid and governed by a superior set of men formed into the committee in London. Of course then you must have examiners and secretaries and an office to see that the inferior men are not too inferior; and you must have a set of cheap colleges in which the inferior men may get an inferior education and you must provide an inferior sort of ordination which will not enable them to compete in England with the superior men.[14]

In almost every case the work of missionaries is typically determined by someone other than themselves. It is true, and was especially true when global communications were slower and more fragile than they are today, that missionaries in practice enjoyed a measure of autonomy whatever their mission boards might dictate. Nevertheless the missionary was obliged to carry out tasks assigned to him or her by the board, and the tasks did not necessarily, or even usually, involve the planting of churches. Missionaries were teachers, evangelists, carers, supporters and administrators within indigenous churches but the planting of churches was rare partly because this capacity required rare gifting but also because church planting was uncommon within the Christian culture from which the missionary had

---

[13] Thousands of young men were sent, apparently uncomplaining, to their deaths in the trenches of the 1914-18 war. This was an age of duty and deference. C.f . 'God's call must be obeyed, whatever the cost. Were not his old school friends gladly giving their life's blood in Flanders at that very moment for an earthly king?' in Harold Womersley's account of the life of W. F. P. Burton (Harold Womersley, *Wm. F. P. Burton: Congo Pioneer*, [Eastbourne, Victory Press, 1979] p.52). Or consider, 'Archbishop Temple's concern expressed in a letter in 1943, that an authoritarian organization of religion was always bound to find itself drawn to authoritarian politics' (C. Patten, *Not Quite the diplomat*, (Harmondsworth, Penguin, 2006, pp.48, 49) for another parallel between religious and political organisation.

[14] Quoted by John Miller, *Missionary Zeal and Institutional Control*, (Grand Rapids, Mich, Eerdmans, 2003), p.37.

come. For example, for many years the Baptists in Britain planted no new churches and so it is hardly surprising that their missionaries overseas were also deficient in this respect.

Apostolic networks were established in the 1970s in Britain. They defined themselves by avoiding the obvious hallmarks of denominations and emphasised that their own method of 'doing church' was relational rather than hierarchical or official. Where denominations set up hierarchical systems, apostolic networks ensured that their own structures were as flat as possible. Where denominational systems achieved decision-making through voting, apostolic networks eschewed all forms of balloting. Where denominational systems appointed committees, apostolic networks prioritised spiritual and ministry gifts. Essential to the structure and functioning of apostolic networks was the role of the apostle himself (in almost every case this was a male). The apostle was viewed as someone with a God-given capacity to plant and design congregations. He was, in Paul's words, a 'master builder' (1 Corinthians 3:10) and specifically modelled on the apostolic pattern found within the Book of Acts and in the Pauline epistles. The apostle was concerned primarily and specifically with the creation of new congregations and, once a congregation had been planted, it was the apostle who had the authority to appoint elders.[15] Apostolic networks are consequently made up of a series of autonomous congregations governed by elders over whom there is an apostolic figure who normally works within a complementary team of ministers. The connection between the autonomous congregations and the apostle is relational: it is not legal or encased in denominational tradition. The apostle does not own the building used by the congregation nor does he have the right to impose his will upon the congregation's elders even though, in practice, the elders, since they have been appointed by the apostle, are likely to value his advice.

Although the apostolic network carries echoes of an episcopal system of government (since the apostle is analogous to the bishop) there are huge practical differences between the two forms of operation. Whereas within an episcopal system the bishop outranks all those within his diocese and, by virtue of ecclesiastical law or constitutional precept, has power over the congregations and ministers under his charge, the apostle has a lighter touch. Moreover, and importantly, the apostle is not put in place by a voting system or by government appointment but is a truly charismatic leader

---

[15] See Stuart Mayho, '"Do not be hasty in the laying on of hands" (1 Timothy 5:22): The Role, Recognition and Release of Leadership in the New Testament and Their Relationship to Recruitment in the Church Today', (University of Wales, Bangor, unpublished MTh Dissertation, 2006, section 5.8.).

whose authority stems from his gifting and ministry.[16] The congregations ask the apostle if he will take them under his wing and, since the apostle has a record of planting churches or of re-structuring older ones, it is apparent that the apostle possesses the gifts that define his calling. Or, to put this in another way, denominational bishops are appointed to fill empty spaces within an ecclesiastical structure, and the man appointed in this way may or may not be suitable for the task. Apostles draw a network around them and are only able to do so because of their obvious gifts.

When apostolic networks begin to work overseas, it is the apostles who begin to plant churches in new locations, or to facilitate this planting, and to appoint elders in new fields. This is where the contrast is most sharp. With traditional missionary work, the missionary is sent to function within a new field while the bishop or denominational officials stay at home. In the apostolic network, it is the apostle who goes overseas and facilitates the work and who then calls upon the resources of the network at home to support the church overseas. So missionary work in apostolic networks is typically performed by apostolic figures who, to use conventional terminology, are the most senior people within their grouping. This immediately changes the dynamics of the entire process. Mission is driven from the top of the church and not placed on the shoulders of sacrificial foot soldiers at the bottom. Additionally the apostle is a travelling figure who may stay a short while overseas ministering to elders and congregations and who, on his return home, has the influence to send out other people within the network for short-term purposes. The apostle is not, like the missionary, sent overseas where he may be forgotten but comes and goes as he sees fit. The apostle, unlike the missionary, can set up training in the home country or determine what social or medical needs could best be deployed overseas.

The great strength of the apostle in networks in respect of church planting is that it is apostles who have planted or facilitated new churches within their own cultures who venture overseas to carry out the same function there. Equally important is the determination of apostolic networks, and of New Frontiers International in particular, to confine their work within the parameters of local churches. There is, as a result, no missionary parachurch organisation separate from the local church with its own financial responsibilities and authority structure. On the contrary parachurch organisations – and missionary societies must be seen in this light – are deemed to be outside the New Testament pattern and therefore undesirable.

---

[16] Senior positions, including Archbishops, within the Church of England are appointed by the Prime Minister though, obviously, he takes advice from the church. But for many Anglicans this arrangement expresses the church's undesirable subservience to the state.

iii. Examples and Reflections

All the major apostolic networks within Britain have overseas work. New Frontiers International, as the largest network, best exemplifies the strengths of the new form of organisation but Salt and Light, Ground Level and c.net in its heyday would do almost equally well. The early contact with overseas churches was through the travelling ministry of the founding apostle, Terry Virgo, and can be traced directly to his preaching itineraries in India, in South Africa and in North America and in other parts of the world. The decision-making systems within New Frontiers International are, as we have already said, specifically charismatic. About three times a year the leaders within local churches in Britain are called together for two days of prayer and fasting and, at these events, prophetic utterances and visions are manifested. The prophecies are recorded and subsequently evaluated by the apostolic team but they function to provide not only a huge stream of creative impulses but also to motivate the assembled leaders. There is no debate at these gatherings where a vote for a proposition may be passed by the 51% to 49%. Rather the leaders who gather come to pray and, once charismatic utterances are given, the content of these utterances may be woven into intercessory prayer. In this way leaders leave the meetings motivated to carry out prophetic direction even if the transformation of prophetic utterance into policy rests with the apostolic team using whatever methods seem fit to it.

New Frontiers International grew rapidly in the 1980s and early 1990s but, as the overseas work became more important, prophetic insight provided a vision showing how the balance between the work at home and work overseas needed to be re-adjusted. There was no point in concentrating entirely upon overseas work to the detriment of work at home. Equally the work at home did not exist simply as a self-contained Christian enterprise. It existed within wealthy Britain for the sake of poorer countries. So church planting was initiated in Britain in the consciousness that successful new congregations would help resource mission overseas.

There is, in this way, a seamless connection between what is taking place at home and what is taking place overseas. In both locations there is church planting and the justification for this is that the New Testament pattern knows no other way to establish the gospel in any geographical area. Congregations are the forum for the development of spiritual and ministry gifts and there is no human culture that negates this principle. The dynamics of congregational growth at home can be the same as the dynamics of congregational growth overseas.

Although faith is fundamental to everything that is carried out by NFI, Salt and Light, Ground Level and the other networks, the faith principle is not elevated to the basis of life as it was in the faith missions. This means that resources are moved around the network to meet the needs of the poorer parts of it without a danger that men and women working overseas will find themselves impoverished or insensitively controlled by a supervisory body. Indeed it is arguable that the benefits of the faith missions (the devolution of decisions to the field, an incarnational theology encouraging missionaries to identify with the local culture and freedom to operate with a range of church configurations) are also to be found within the overseas work of New Frontiers. Certainly there is a devolution of decision-making to the overseas location, especially when fresh apostles emerge within the network, as happened in the case of NFI where one of the apostolic team in Britain (Simon Pettit) went overseas to lead the work in South Africa. Equally, particularly because elders are appointed from indigenous congregations, there is an implied incarnational theology that permits local churches to organise themselves as they wish though, clearly, the style of worship and ministry will tend to follow what has been tried and tested in Britain.

iv. Theology and Practice

The theology that drives apostolic networks flows out of a restorationist matrix. Because of the outpouring of the Holy Spirit at the beginning of the 20th century, charismatic gifts are being restored to the church. For the same reasons apostolic and ministry gifts (Ephesians 4:11) have also been restored. Apostolic gifts are historically therefore an expression of restorationist theology and are not the product of power struggles within denominational hierarchies. Moreover apostolic gifts are seen as intended to produce congregations. In this they contrast with various types of mission, particularly faith missions, where the driving motivation was concerned with the salvation of the lost. The missionary society in the 19th century might be seen as a mechanism designed to rescue men and women from hell. This is not to denigrate these missions since their motivation needed to be powerful to move them out of the comfort of civilised Europe into the more primitive conditions to which they went. But the point of the contrast is to show that whereas missionary societies were concerned with evangelistic activities that *might* lead to the formation of congregations, apostolic activities are *primarily* set on building congregations. Both kinds of mission may superficially appear to generate the same result but, in reality, there are enormous differences between them. An apostolically founded congregation is far more rounded than a congregation founded by a missionary evangelist.[17] In practice, networks produce congregations that are themselves apostolic: the churches are not only restorationist in

---

[17] Comment to me by Arnold Bell of New Frontiers International that, after many years of observation, I take to be correct.

orientation in terms of ministries and charismatic gifts but also are inspired to produce indigenous apostles who will further extend the network.

Equally there are differences between the old-style missionary societies and apostolic networks in relation to exit strategies. The exit strategy of the old-style missionary society concerns the gradual withdrawal of the missionary from control over the entire operation to an advisory or supportive role and then complete departure. Apostolic networks have no exit strategy because congregations are connected with the apostle and remain connected whether the apostle is in one country or another. In this respect apostolic networks deal with their congregations in exactly the same way regardless of the country where the congregation is situated. There is no need for the apostolic network to devise a transitional exit strategy. The network appoints elders and the elders run the congregation with the supervisory help of the apostolic team. In an era of global communications apostolic networks are feasible in a way that would have been impossible a hundred years ago. Electronic communications as well as rapidity of travel allow apostolic visits to occur at regular intervals and, in some networks, conferences of apostolic teams rotate annually.[18] This means that the network of churches within an overseas country will receive the benefit of an enormous input of apostolic team ministry in the year that it is their turn to host the conference.[19] In other years the overseas leaders will have the benefit of travelling elsewhere and of seeing how congregations related to the same apostle function within cultures different from their own.

It is arguable that the theology of apostolic networks is more closely based on the bible than the theology of missionary societies. Missionary societies base themselves on the Great Commission of Matthew 28 and take the words of Christ given to the original disciples as a binding on all Christians. Normal exegetical methods would presume that the best way to understand the Great Commission would be to see how it functioned within the life of the early church, particularly within the Book of Acts. Here it is evident that the commission was carried out by apostles and the paradigmatic example of this is to be found in Acts 13 where Paul and Barnabas are sent out by the church at Antioch. Paul and Barnabas are the first missionaries. Yet, as Acts 14.14 indicates, Paul and Barnabas are 'apostles' and, as the first missionary journey is examined, it is evident that the work of these two men led to the founding of congregations. In this respect the example of Paul and Barnabas, the work that they did, the relatively short duration of their missionary trip, the charismatic gifts with which they were endowed, the guidance of the Holy Spirit both in initiating the journey and on the way, are very different from what is typical among

---

[18]   For instance in Salt and Light, another British-based network (see <http://www.saltlight.org/)> (accessed 22 August, 2006).

[19] Salt and Light uses this pattern.

missionaries in the 19th and early 20th centuries. Seen in this light apostolic networks conform much more closely to the Acts pattern than does the work of missionary societies. Terry Virgo puts it this way:

> The word 'missionary' obscures rather than clarifies, since it does not honour Biblical definitions and categories. A modern missionary may be an agricultural worker, a nurse, a schoolteacher, a Bible translator, or a literature distributor (all very worthwhile and wonderful ministries). Some missionaries may in reality be evangelists or apostles. But the term is vague and unhelpful, since it has come to indicate anyone who works overseas. Historically, some have established 'mission stations' rather than churches.[20]
>
> [without apostles] local churches were seen as static and built on Scripture, while isolated individuals could leave those churches and become 'missionaries'. In contrast, our burning passion is to see apostolic churches focused on world mission together.[21]

It may be that the days of the missionary society are, in any case and for other reasons, already numbered. This is because charity law in western countries (e.g. Britain) places the control of assets within the hands of trustees who cannot themselves be beneficiaries of the trust they are administering. This means that missionary societies based in England must be run by trustees, which prevents the delegation of power to a missionary body on the field. Thus missionary societies that currently delegate decision-making to the field may find themselves having to withdraw these governmental rights. This will complicate future missionary work and, in addition, as a consequence of anti-terrorist and money laundering regulations, missionary societies may find themselves much more closely scrutinised in respect of the transfer of funds. It would appear that apostolic networks, because they move personnel rather than money around, are better placed to avoid the destruction of their overseas work than missionary societies.

v. Conclusion

It is too early to say whether apostolic networks will change the face of Christianity as Paul Cain predicted but there is evidence that they may change the face of missions. As yet, the impact of apostolic networks, particularly British ones, on traditional mission fields is relatively small though, given the numbers of people involved and the amount of time that

---

[20] <http://www.newfrontiers.xtn.org/magazine/vol2issue4/article_index.php?id=147> (accessed 28 June, 2006).

[21] <http://www.newfrontiers.xtn.org/magazine/vol2issue4/article_index.php?id=147> (accessed 28 June, 2006).

has elapsed since apostolic networks were founded, impressive. Although this chapter has focused on New Frontiers International, there are other apostolic networks springing up from the non-western world. These also may have an impact upon emerging states and even upon traditionally Muslim nations. It is too early to make a judgment. What does seem evident from this analysis is threefold: apostolic networks have the capacity to function as missionary organisations; they fit the post-modern, globalised, non-hierarchical world well; and, in doing so, they have both theological and practical advantages over old-style missionary societies, even the faith-based societies that delegated decision-making to the field.

Chapter 20

Apostolic Networks: Sociology

'I wanted a web not a wheel', Hugh Osgood

Apostolic networks are unusual structures within the body of the church. This chapter examines apostolic networks from a sociological perspective.

i. Sociology of Religion: Categories and Themes

Ernst Troeltsch (1865-1923), a German Protestant theologian and scholar, tried to reconcile historical relativism with his belief in permanent and universal ethical values. In doing so he explored the characteristics of *sects* and *churches*. He described the sect and distinguished it from the church.[1] He depicted the sect as a small group, composed in the main of the poor who, having renounced worldliness, went in search of direct personal religion. In his own words:

> the essence of the sect does not consist merely in a one-sided emphasis upon certain vital elements of the Church-type, but it is itself a direct continuation of the idea of the Gospel. Only within it is there a full recognition of the value of radical individualism and of the idea of love; it is the sect alone which instinctively builds up its ideal of fellowship from this point of view, and this is the very reason why it attains such a strong subjective and inward unity, instead of merely external membership in an institution. For the same reason the sect also maintains the original radicalism of the Christian ideal and its hostility towards the world, and it retains the fundamental demand for personal service.[2]

Regarding the church,

---

[1] The word sect is used by Calvin in the *Institutes of the Christian Religion*, IV, 13, 14. Troeltsch's church/sect distinction appears to have been first made by F. D. Maurice in 1842. See M. J. Thompson, 'An Illustrated Theology of Churches and 'Sects': with the churches of New Frontiers International', (University of Kent at Canterbury, unpublished PhD Dissertation, 1996), p.46. Troeltsch also described cults, but they are not relevant to this discussion.

[2] Extract from *The Social Teaching of the Christian Church* and taken from Robin Gill (ed) *Theology and Sociology: a reader*, (London, Geoffrey Chapman, 1987), pp.67-8.

...The Church does not represent a mere deterioration of the Gospel, however much that may appear to be the case when we contrast its hierarchical organization and its sacramental system with the teaching of Jesus. For wherever the Gospel is conceived as primarily a free gift, as pure grace, and wherever it is offered to us in the picture which faith creates of Christ as a Divine institution, wherever the inner freedom of the Spirit, contrasted with all human effort and organization, is felt to be the spirit of Jesus, and wherever His splendid indifference towards secular matters is felt, in the sense of a spiritual and inner independence... there the institution of the Church may be regarded as a natural continuation and transformation of the Gospel. At the same time, with its unlimited universalism, it still contains the fundamental impulse of the evangelic message.[3]

These ideas were refined but not altered by the next phase of sociology. The most widely used system of classification begins with Max Weber's book, *The Protestant Ethic and the Spirit of Capitalism*, where he elaborated on the distinction between a *church* and a *sect*.[4] The church is 'a sort of trust foundation for supernatural ends, an institution including both the just and the unjust' (p 144) which, nevertheless, claims a universal validity and mission. A sect, on the other hand, is 'a believer's church' that is necessarily exclusive in its membership and frequently hostile to the outside world.[5]

Both Troeltsch and Weber (1864-1920) begin their analysis in the contours of history. They draw their data from the historical events while watching the slow transformation of western civilisation. Their analysis, especially Weber's, takes in the context of religion as well as its forms. Weber saw religion as retreating before rationalism. He understood rational explanations of the universe and the embodiment of rationalism within science and bureaucracy as having the power to chase religion away from the central place it had occupied during the mediaeval period. As rationalism advances, mystery retreats. As rationalism advances, religion retreats. There are fewer opportunities for religion to explain or control the puzzle of human existence. Though, subtle thinker that he was, Weber understood religion as providing the values that drove forward the development of civilisation. In the post-Reformation period religious values sanctified everyday work and released usury from sinfulness. Once daily work was seen as a vocation and surplus money could be banked and lent

---

[3] Extract from Troeltsch, *The Social Teaching of the Christian Church* in Gill, *Theology and Sociology: a reader*, (London, Geoffrey Chapman, 1987), pp.67, 68.

[4] M. Weber, *The Protestant Ethic and the Spirit of Capitalism*, (London, Unwin University Books, 1930).

[5] See also W. S. Bainbridge, *The Sociology of Religious Movements*, (London, Routledge, 1997), pp.38f.

out on interest, conditions were in place for the rise of capitalism. The Reformation produced men and women who understood their vocation through secular employment and Calvin, in lifting the ban on usury, exercised a religious judgement against an earlier interdiction. There was thus an interaction between religious concepts and social reality and, in the other direction, between rationalistic social reality and religion.

Weber's analysis made way for an understanding of secularisation, the process whereby religion is stripped of its social importance, intellectually weakened, institutionally eroded and, eventually, pushed out of the public sphere into the private consciousness of disempowered individuals. As the process proceeds, Protestantism which holds sway in parts of Europe and North America, becomes so liberalised that it is secularised from within. The church-sect dichotomy helps to explain what is happening since, in the sect, religious individuals gather together for mutual support against the onrushing tide of secularisation whereas, in the church, with its broad accessibility to the state, secularity becomes impossible to resist and the church ceases to be a generator of value and becomes instead only the harmless performer of rites of passage and other ceremonial functions.

Sects, by this analysis, are advantageous to the development of religion since they preserve vital religious truths until the tide of secularisation turns. This is especially so since, over time, sects (and some would see apostolic networks in this way) may evolve out of their sectarianism into something more closely resembling the church – but this is to jump ahead of the story.

The debate over secularisation became central to the sociology of religion in the period after 1945. By most indices religion, which in this case means Christianity, was beginning to decline in the 1930s in most European countries and, although there was spirited argument over the causes of this and the interpretation of the statistics on which the secularisation case was based, many churches felt cold winds blowing.[6] In the post-war period the local country vicar found his status within the community was declining; religion became more of a source of comedy than comfort in satirical television; church attendance dropped; Sunday schools melted away; candidates for ordination became fewer; religious solemnisations of marriage declined, as did religious funerals; religious education in schools clung on by its fingernails by changing from the study of Christianity to religious studies.[7] Even so, surveys of the levels of religious belief in Britain and most of Europe showed that, despite

---

[6] See for instance, G. Davie, *Religion in Britain since 1945*, (Oxford, Blackwell, 1994); S. Bruce, *Religion in Modern Britain*, (Oxford, OUP, 1995); C.G. Brown, *The Death of Christian Britain*, (London, Routledge, 2001).

[7] W. K. Kay, 'Society, Christian beliefs and practices: the large scale', in W. K. Kay and L. J. Francis (eds.) *Religion in Education (3)*, (Leominster, Gracewing, 2000), pp.7-38.

widespread non-attendance at church, faith in God continued at unexpectedly high levels.[8] Such faith was undoubtedly bolstered by the arrival of immigrants to Europe, most of whom brought with them religious beliefs of one kind or another. The largest number of migrants were Islamic and, after the oil crisis of 1974, Islam became more strident and its adherents more willing to assert their religious visibility in the face of a religiously indifferent host community. At the same time new religious movements found the soil of Europe hospitable. The net result of this was that, although belief in God among young people in Britain was declining and, in the 1990s reached, perhaps, 35%, the population as a whole could muster a figure over 70%.[9] Meanwhile, the hard-line agents of atheism or secularism could probably only count on about 15% of the total population and, surprisingly, even unbelieving young people, especially young women, felt that a religious wedding ceremony was more desirable than the secular equivalent.

As sociologists struggled to explain the complex changes taking place within Britain and within the Western world as a whole, the secularisation debate polarised. On the one hand there were those who argued that secularisation could not be a function of modernity, of the advance of scientific rationalism, because, despite the weakening of religion within Europe, there was no comparable weakening within the United States. Since Europe and the United States were open to the same rationalistic forces, it made no sense to attribute the differences of religious belief and practice to the cultural feature common to them both. If secularisation is to be understood, it must be understood by reference to *differences* between European and American life.[10]

The most likely explanatory factor was in the difference between the United States and Europe in terms of established, monopolistic churches.[11] Within Europe, the Anglican Church in Britain or the Catholic Church in France or the Lutheran church in Scandinavian countries, was tied to the functions of the state and had, historically, been part of the culture of the ruling elite. Indeed in a country like Belgium, Catholicism was seen as a component of national identity. In the United States, by contrast, there had never been a national or established church – the Constitution specifically forbade such a thing. Consequently religion in the United States had always

---

[8] W. K. Kay, 'Belief in God in Great Britain 1945-1996: moving the scenery behind classroom RE', *British Journal of Religious Education* 20, 1, (1997), pp.28-41.

[9] See L. J. Francis, and W. K. Kay, *Teenage Religion and Values*, (Leominster, Gracewing, 1995).

[10] Steve Bruce tended to argue the case for secularisation and David Martin and Peter Berger to argue the case against.

[11] D. Martin, *A General Theory of Secularisation*, (London, Harper Collins, 1979).

been part of a free market and denominations and churches within this market had competed against each other for customers, for members.

On the other hand were those who argued that secularisation was taking place and, although it was less obvious in the States, it was still inexorably occurring. All forms of religion were giving way before the spectacular advances in science and technology and, though the retreat might be disguised by the influx of religious immigrants to the wealthy West, it was only a matter of time before religious belief withered. Even the apparent vitality of religion within fundamentalistic congregations was an admission that the end of religion was in sight since fundamentalism was a reaction against modernity.[12] Fundamentalism was merely a throw-back, a dinosaur walking in a climate that would eventually destroy it.

The point of the debate is that, if sociological theory is correct, we are in a position to predict the likely course of religious life in Britain. For the time being it is sufficient to note that, if the current religious situation is conceived of in terms of pro- or anti-secularisation, apostolic networks, which have grown over the last 30 years, may be understood as fundamentalistic fortresses that will eventually succumb to the spirit of the age. Yet, prediction is clouded by sociological disagreement over how current religious data ought to be understood. It is not simply a matter of secularisation being challenged by occasional religious revival but of the nature of religion itself.

If religion is understood as a response to human existential anxiety, to the fear of death and to the vicissitudes of existence, then religion will *always* be a part of the human condition. If, by contrast, religion is understood only in institutional terms as the powerful agency that legitimates the social order, then its existence will be dependent upon the state. And if the state looks for legitimation within an ideological framework that denounces religion, religion will be attacked. Communist Russia and Maoist China were governed by fearsome secret police and cultural pressure derived from a Communist view of history. Religion had no role to play – although Stalin manipulated the Orthodox Church to generate patriotism in the darkest days of a 1939-45 war – and was consigned to the past. Sociological understanding of religion that concentrates upon its outward institutional appearance, its machinery for generating doctrine, its patterns of worship, its sanctions and its rituals, sees only the upper part of the iceberg. Yet, to materialistic sociologists like Durkheim, that was all that there was. Social facts created social reality and individual psychology can offer next to nothing. If, against this institutional interpretation of religion, religious belief is seen as being a rooted in, and responding to, our contingent existence, then there will always be religion. Beneath the water, invisible to the naked eye, is the mass of hopes, fears,

---

[12] A. Giddens, 'Reith Lectures', broadcast on BBC Radio 4 in May 1999.

aspirations and emotional entanglements that comprise our humanity. It is from this that religion arises.

'Rational choice theory' was designed to meet just such an interpretation of religion.[13] The theory argues that human beings make rational choices in the marketplace of religion in the same way that they make rational choices in the marketplace of consumer goods. Each choice is determined by a cost/benefit analysis. We look at the cost and work out whether it will outweigh the promised benefit. In religious terms costs might include the giving up of leisure time or money and the dropping of old friends or an old lifestyle for the benefit of salvation, security, new friends, purpose and holy joy. The theory proposes that church-type groups tend only to ask a relatively low cost of the individual but offer a correspondingly low benefit: occasional Sunday attendance might or might not lead to eternal life. Sect-type groups demand a higher cost but deliver a higher benefit: attendance at religious meetings and unswerving trust in Christ definitely leads to eternal life as well as to a happier life in the here and now.

The theory presumes that there is an almost fixed quota of religious need within the population at any one time and that this religious need, the need for certainty and salvation, is met by whatever is on offer in the religious market. So rational choice theory works best where multiple religious options are available. It works well in the United States and, indeed, it is arguable that religious needs are stimulated by the competitive religious market: people come to feel that they have religious needs even when they do not. In much the same way people buy consumer goods their parents would never have dreamt of buying simply because of the stimulus produced by advertising. The theory is in direct conflict with the secularisation thesis since it is based upon what are taken to be unalterable aspects of human existence.

ii. Sociology of Religion: Reflection and Expansion

Weber's account of religion had taken note of the developmental path followed by religious movements. At first a charismatic leader appeared, drawing supporters and followers into a coherent band. While the charismatic leader lived, the band followed him (it usually was a man) and received both revelatory teaching and personal inspiration. The charismatic authority of the leader was derived from the gifts that he had and the gifts were charismatic, God-given, not natural endowments nor the consequence of an established position. When the leader died, the religious group underwent metamorphosis. Charismatic leadership gave way to bureaucratic leadership so that within a century or less the religion, if it survived, was no longer the radical vibrant force that it had once been but

---

[13] L.A. Young (ed), *Rational Choice Theory and Religion*, (London, Routledge, 1997).

was now weighed down with bureaucratic procedures and cumbersome decision-making processes. The place of the charismatic leader became an office that might be filled by an entirely un-charismatic individual.[14] Miracles were replaced by rituals and the religion, though accumulating wealth and power, now often found ways to turn the radical teachings of its founder upside down. In short, the charismatic sect allowed its charismata to be routinised, its claim to unique truth to be softened and its moral rigour to be relaxed and, in so doing, it became a church.

The pair of categories, sect and church, has undergone refinement at the hands of subsequent writers. Yinger expanded the church category into two, the *universal church*, which has an international claim and appeal that transcends social and political boundaries, and the *ecclesia*, which is more limited in its scope and tends only to offer a social integration with the governing social class of a particular society, though, in theory, it may be open to all and sundry.[15] At the other end of the scale the sect is divided into the *institutionalised sect*, which has had time to set up bureaucracy and other organisational support systems, and the *sect*, which is still socially unformed, though theologically it is exclusive and uncompromising in its claims. Between the ecclesia and the institutionalised sect is the *denomination*. The denomination is like a church in many respects except that it accepts the legitimacy of other similar religious groups. Whereas the church considers itself to offer the only way of salvation, even if this offer is tempered by less than stringent entry requirements, the denomination by definition recognises that other organised groups of Christians offer an equally valid path to God. The diagram below illustrates the situation:

Sect		**Denomination**	**Church**	
Sect	Institutionalised sect		Ecclesia	Universal church

Bryan Wilson, in a discussion of the typology of sects, sees their defining criterion as their 'response to the world'.[16] Any attempt to define them by reference to ideology and doctrine, he believes, is flawed by the inability of such attempts to cope with Christian and non-Christian sects in the same classificatory system. For this reason he enlarged the sect category by distinguishing between seven sect types: the conversionist, revolutionary, introversionist, manipulationist, thaumaturgical, reformist and utopian.

---

[14] C.f. D. L. Edwards, *Christianity: the first two thousand years*, (London, Cassell, 1997), p.52, 'in many ways bishops continued the work of the apostles to be met in the New Testament'.

[15] J. M. Yinger, *Religion, Society and the Individual*, (New York, Macmillan, 1957).

[16] B.R. Wilson, 'A typology of sects in a dramatic and comparative perspective', *Archives de Sociologie de Religion*, vol.16, (1963), pp.4,9-63.

Taken with the two church types, this expansion of the possible sect categories has given sociologists a comprehensive and flexible system for classifying most kinds of religious groups and orientations. But, although this theoretical work is valuable for coping with the many historical possibilities, it remains true that, in discussions of the contemporary religious situation in Britain, the three main categories - church, denomination and sect[17] - are the most useful.

In this scheme there is a convergence over time towards the centre. Sects tend to become more accommodating to the world and less exclusive in their beliefs and so to become denominations. The same is true of churches, which come to recognise their own relative position vis-àvis other churches.

It needs to be stressed, again, that the purpose of this sociological analysis is to understand apostolic networks and to predict their future course. The assumption of the model is that, if apostolic networks are sects, they will eventually become like denominations. Yet, against this scenario, it is also reasonable to argue that the networks represent a *new kind of sociological animal*. How can it be fitted into the classificatory scheme?

Sect	Denomination	Church	
Conversionist [usually evangelical] Revolutionary Introversionist [inward facing] Manipulationist Thaumaturgical [healing] Reformist Utopian		Ecclesia	Universal church

Before attempting to do so two other avenues must be explored. The first concerns the more general work on religion of Peter Berger and David Martin. The second concerns sophisticated attempts to describe the networks sociologically.

Peter Berger argued that the key role of religion is to order the world meaningfully.[18] Religion offers a protective canopy of transcendent legitimacy, meaning and order to the precarious constructions that society calls reality; the social order is tied to religion. 'The historically crucial part of religion in the process of legitimation is explicable in terms of the unique capacity of religion to locate human phenomena within a cosmic frame of

---

[17] The 'institutionalised sect' is left out of this diagram. It does not add much.

[18] P. L. Berger, *The Sacred Canopy*, (New York, Random House, 1967).

reference'[19] or, in different words, 'religion is the audacious attempt to conceive of the entire universe as being humanly significant'.[20] Religion provides order by drawing on a distinction between the sacred and profane and also by opposing itself to the category of chaos. 'The sacred cosmos emerges out of chaos and continues to confront the latter as its terrible contrary'.[21]

The *plausibility structures* created by religion operate sometimes across the whole world and sometimes across whole societies or some sections of society. The Amish believer within the community is living within a protected environment, and the same would apply for the Muslim within Saudi Arabia: there is no alternative world view on offer and, until the present age of globalisation, countries could remain more or less hermetically sealed from each other. However the worlds that are constructed are always threatened by the forces of chaos and the inevitable fact of death. The plausibility structures that support a set of religious beliefs are challengeable and nowhere more so than in a pluralist society where these structures are constantly jarring against each other. If there is a loss of religious belief, it may be attributable to pluralism rather than to rationalism and modernity. But, by the same token, if a religious movement can build plausibility structures that counter pluralism, then religious belief can flourish.[22] This is perhaps another way of saying that religious groups need firm boundaries between themselves and society and strong assertive teaching, something that apostolic networks are well capable of providing.

David Martin who, as a sociologist, has written extensively about Pentecostalism recognises the rhetorical and adversarial nature of sociological discourse. The sociologist, in his view, makes a case as a lawyer makes a case before a court, using the terms and style of the discipline but, unwittingly or inevitably, hiding a great number of value judgements within the discourse.[23] The terms 'left' and 'right' or 'liberal' and 'fundamentalist' are bound up with the paradigms of progress and secularisation that stem from the enlightenment. The result of this is that the language intended to describe religious events may 'cripple our understanding'.[24] Massed religious rallies may be implicitly compared with the demagoguery of fascist dictators and religious conservatism may be translated into fundamentalism, a catch-all term of condemnation that describes an enormous range of phenomena, some good and some bad.

---

[19] Berger, *The Sacred Canopy,* (1967), p.35.

[20] Berger, *The Sacred Canopy,* (1967), p.28.

[21] Berger, *The Sacred Canopy,* (1967), p.26.

[22] See also D. MacLaren, *Mission Implausible: restoring credibility to the church,* (Carlisle, Paternoster, 2004).

[23] David Martin, *Forbidden Revolutions,* (London, SPCK, 1996), p.3.

[24] Martin, *Forbidden Revolutions,* (1996), p.5.

Instead of seeing spiritual movements as having the ability to 'break-up the hegemony of ideological power' to create an 'autonomous space for the egalitarian exercise of spiritual gifts' religious phenomena are damned in crypto-Marxist language for belonging to an earlier epoch.[25]

Reflecting more broadly on sociological theory, Martin muses on the master narratives that could be constructed by sociologists of different kinds – Catholic, Pentecostal, evangelical and, indeed, of narratives that do not simply point in one fixed direction but are made up of waves of expansion and recession. The territorial faith of Eastern Orthodoxy contrasts with 'portable faiths based on movement and transit'.[26] The eventual position of religion in any part of the world may depend on its contribution to national survival: where it props up a hated regime, the regime, when it falls, takes religion with it; where it opposes a hated regime, the regime's fall redounds to the glory of the religion. Sociological theory is a cousin of political theory and the two are needed for any proper prediction. Sociological theory, though, has so far failed to foresee the shape of major socio-cultural movements with the result that any predictions about smaller religious structures and constructions must remain speculative. What we can say by looking at the past is that many religious denominations do *not* have sectarian origins – which makes the argument that sects move to a central position difficult to sustain - and that some sects are similar to monastic orders and exist as a church-within-a-church, which also upsets the notion of convergence.

iii. Sociological Theory Applied to Apostolic Networks

Mike Thompson's doctoral dissertation examined the appropriateness of the sect, church, denomination categories in relation to New Frontiers International.[27] What he says in relation to New Frontiers is largely applicable to other apostolic networks in Britain as well. He takes issue with Wilson's dismissal of theological criteria in the definition of sect. Wilson wished to expand the notion of sect to apply across a wide range of religions and could not find a single theological criterion that would work properly. As we have seen, he used the criterion of 'response to the world' to show that sects tended to be in opposition to their local culture and to set themselves up as countercultural havens. Thomson argued that, in respect of Christian groups, theological criteria should be retained. This is because there are sects that are doctrinally quite different from churches and

---

[25] Martin, *Forbidden Revolutions*, (1996), p.6.

[26] David Martin,'Secularisation and the future of Christianity', *Journal of Contemporary Religion*, 20, 2, (2005), pp.145-160.

[27] M. J. Thompson, 'An Illustrated Theology of Churches and "Sects"', (University of Kent at Canterbury, unpublished PhD Dissertation, 1996).

denominations, and which could never denominationalise. He had in mind such groups as the Jehovah's Witnesses or Christadelphians.

He proposed dividing sects into S1, which were Trinitarian, and S9, which were not.[28] Having divided sects into two groups he also divided denominations into two groups on an exclusive/inclusive basis (D1 and D2), and the same with churches (C1 and C2).[29] He argued that exclusivism is a mark of the early church and that, without exclusivism, the early church would never have survived and that later, during long periods of church history, theological exclusivism surfaced, often in periods prior to reformation.[30] Denominations could also be divided along the same lines.

In broad terms he ended up with a fourfold categorisation:

	Trinitarian	**Non-Trinitarian**
Exclusive	S1, C1, D1	S9
Inclusive	C2, D2	

Once he had established the categorisation, there was still difficulty in placing New Frontiers in the right place. If churches, sects and denominations could all be more or less exclusive, the difference between them was harder to pin down.[31] He argued that New Frontiers showed evidences of being a church because it was gathered round the person of Christ rather than a 'notion' (to use F D Maurice's word[32]) and because it was not exclusive in many of its attitudes. It worked within the Evangelical Alliance. Yet, it did have a formalised entry procedure in terms of the training of new church members and, in this, fitted one of Wilson's denominational criteria.

Part of the complexity of the analysis stems from the sophistication of the networks when they were set up. They did not want to repeat the mistakes of church history. I wrote to Arthur Wallis in the mid-1970s suggesting to him that he was present at the birth of a new restorationist denomination. He politely replied by saying that he and the others who worked with him had no intention whatever of being involved in the

---

[28] Thompson does not have S2, S3, S4, S5, S6, S7 and S8. He wants to make as big a distinction in the terminology between Trinitarian S1 groups a non-Trinitarian S9 groups as possible.

[29] Exclusivism/inclusivism is clearly compatible to Wilson's 'opposed to the world/accepting of the world'.

[30] Thompson, 'An Illustrated Theology', (1996), p.100.

[31] Especially if 'world-rejecting new religious movements are the ones which most closely resemble the epistemologically authoritarian sect'; see A. Aldridge, *Religion in the Contemporary World*, (Cambridge, Polity Press, 2000), p.51.

[32] Thompson, 'An Illustrated theology', (1996), p122 quoting F. D. Maurice, *The Kingdom of Christ*, (London, J. M. Dent & Co, 1842), p.58.

founding of a denomination. We may have both been right because, over the years, although many of the functions of a denomination appeared to accrue to restorationist groups, that first bright intention *was* maintained. Of course, as this discussion has noted, it is all a matter of theory and definition. If denominations are defined as having distinctive doctrines, distinctive criteria for verifying their membership and their ministerial list, distinctive communication publications and conferences, distinctive life-style emphases, and, importantly, are willing to accept the equal validity of other types of distinctiveness, it is arguable that apostolic networks are indeed denominations. If, on the other hand, denominations are defined by their democratic decision-making processes, by their bureaucracies and by their hierarchical tendencies, then apostolic networks are not denominations.

Although apostolic networks were formed by men who had studied the ups and downs of church history, their driving intention was to model themselves on the New Testament. They saw decision-making as crucial to the progress of the church and they took for granted the pentecostal and charismatic estimation of the role of the Holy Spirit and charismatic gifts. Or, to put this another way, they built upon the legacy of the pentecostal and charismatic movements so that it would be difficult to imagine apostolic networks that were not firmly rooted within pentecostal and charismatic experience. That was their starting point, which is why the early proponents of restorationism included ex-pentecostals like Bryn Jones.

Stephen Briers also turned his attention to an analysis of restoration, though he concentrated upon one particular community near Cambridge that related to Bryn Jones.[33] He accepted that even social scientists have found difficulty in drawing a sharp dividing line between churches and sects but he took the church in general to be a wider body that 'embraces and undergirds the whole of society' which, in the case of a pluralistic society, is made problematic because 'church-state relations become increasingly attenuated'.[34] Organisationally, though, the church is fully integrated with the infrastructure of society. Members of sects may also be fully integrated within the full range of social institutions but 'the crucial distinguishing feature of the sect is that it is *ideologically* enclosed'.[35] The Cambridge Community Church does not fit neatly within either category since the boundary with society is 'deliberately negated on the grounds that the kingdom of God "doesn't have a frontier"'.[36] The Community Church

---

[33] S. J. Briers, 'Negotiating with Babylon: responses to modernity within a restorationist community', (University of Cambridge, unpublished PhD Dissertation, 1993).

[34] Briers, 'Negotiating', (1993), p.ii.

[35] Briers, 'Negotiating', (1993), p.iii, original italics.

[36] Briers, 'Negotiating', (1993), p.iii.

provides a spiritual legitimation for contemporary western culture and the assumption is that the restored church will grow in size and influence until church and society become fully integrated. There is no rejection of society here but rather an aspiration to assimilate it. Members of the Community Church are not cut off from society and are not required to make any ascetic renunciation comparable to monastic vows. Quite the contrary. Yet, and it is an important 'yet', restorationists are sectarian in that they 'rail vociferously against traditional churches from which they have broken away'.[37] For these reasons they have been accused of exclusivism and elitism by the traditional churches.

Briers examines the way that restorationist congregations interact with the secular world. His case is that these congregations help their members to achieve goals within secular society and that this is a part of their potency. The restorationist congregation is a 'therapeutic community' that facilitates the 'management of the self' and provides 'a powerful antidote to the potential alienation implicit in a scientific world-view'.[38] In terms of the church/sect and divide, the restorationist emphasis is harder to categorise. It has been criticised from within the Christian community for its 'worldliness' since its aims were, apparently, intended to help its members take over aspects of ordinary human society in the name of the government of God. 'As one ex-member, claimed: "the apostles were not really apostles; they were business managers..."'.[39] Briers concludes that Jones's utopian vision of a harmonisation of church and society is unrealisable and that it is far more sensible to become assimilated within a 'nascent and evangelical super-culture which preserves the outlook, liturgical mannerisms and general 'tone' of restorationism but without the latter movement's narrow emphasis on orthodox dogma or New Testament structures'.[40]

Whatever Briers says about the individual Cambridge Community Church, his analysis is overstated in respect of other parts of restorationism. There was triumphalist rhetoric within the early phases of restorationist hymnology and preaching but there was also a clear appreciation of the vast injustices facing the world.[41] Bryn Jones was never under any illusion that he, or his congregations within Britain, could bring apartheid down or assuage the poverty of Africa. To suggest that restorationists thought they were going to conquer the world in a generation is hyperbolic but, this said,

---

[37] Briers, 'Negotiating', (1993), p.iv.

[38] Briers, 'Negotiating', (1993), p.150.

[39] Briers, 'Negotiating', (1993), p.222.

[40] Briers, 'Negotiating', (1993), p.222.

[41] A. E. Dyer, 'Some theological trends reflected in the songs used by the British charismatic churches of 1970s-early 2000s', *Journal of the European Pentecostal Theological Association*, 26.1, (2006), 36-48.

restorationist did, because of their acceptance of divine empowerment and elements of the prosperity Gospel, expect to succeed within business and commercial life. In this respect it is clear that the unworldliness of evangelical and pentecostal churches within the 1950s was being replaced by a more confident and aggressive form of Christianity. The old unworldliness was justified in the name of holiness, but it also stemmed from simple fearfulness. It was introversionist in Wilson's terms whereas the new restorationism was reformist.

We are now in a position to summarise sociological theory as it might relate to apostolic networks. The original designations of sect, denomination and church (leaving 'cult' out of this because the term only confuses an already complicated picture) is based upon elements within the history of Christianity and different emphases within the Gospels. The church aspires to be co-terminus with society and to match its infrastructure while claiming that all the members within the society, unless they opt out, belong inside its fold. Because of its social scope, churches may make few, if any, demands on their members even if there are public rites of admission like baptism. Sects stand in contrast to churches in that they are voluntary associations that appeal to a small number of members seeking high spiritual ideals and following rigorous moral precepts. In between the two extremities are denominations which may begin as sects or, alternatively may come from churches but, in any case, are a kind of harmonious mid-point between the two other types. Whereas the sect is exclusive in its doctrinal position and whereas the church is more liberal in its doctrinal position, the denomination recognises the relativity of its truth in relation to other denominations. Yet, the classic system needs to be extended by positing both more and less exclusive churches and by subdividing sects into various types. More than this, if sects are not to be determined by doctrinal considerations, they must be determined by social considerations and these usually involve 'attitude to the outside world'. The sect is set against the outside world whereas the church is not.

Even when all this is said and done, the application of sociological theory to apostolic networks is still problematic. There is no unambiguous match. In some respects networks may appear like sects but, in other respects, they appear like churches, especially if churches have more or less exclusive expressions. We may argue that there is a greater contrast between life inside the apostolic network and life outside the network as compared with life inside the denomination and life outside denomination. Yet, even this attempted distinction fails to capture the essence of the networks. We can modify their theory by adding exclusive/inclusive attributes to each of the three main categories and, as Thompson has suggested, by adding theological criteria as well. This produces a model that is not only sociologically driven but also theologically nuanced and it allows apostolic networks to be grouped closely with conservative churches and conservative denominations along lines that are derived from Trinitarian orthodoxy. Although this is helpful, it fails to demonstrate essential differences between apostolic networks and other religious groupings.

For these reasons, Andrew Walker's analysis of restorationism made use of his own terminology, that of R1 and R2. R1 is more exclusive, more bounded and more structured than R2 which is more amorphous and affiliative.[42] In other words, Walker recognised early on that it was almost impossible to classify aspects of restorationism within the normal categories of sociological description. His decision was a wise one. He created his own terminology. In what follows, a further theoretical development will be attempted and the distinctive features of restorationism as expressed through apostolic networks will be explored through their *structural* features.

iv. Structural Features of Networks

Weber's original sociological theory recognised a distinction between charismatic authority and bureaucratic authority. Bureaucratic authority functions to maintain the religious organisation set up by the charismatic leader. The bureaucracy is not an expression of the religious life of the movement but a kind of machine that administrates it. As Wilson showed in a study of Elim churches, bureaucracy comes to deal with the ownership of property, the collection of money, the balance of constitutional power and the running of annual events.[43] It does not deal with the growth of the religious movement or its interface with the general public. It is behind-the-scenes, collecting and counting, maintaining continuity and, in the first generation, serving the charismatic leader by building his platform, advertising his meetings, arranging his travel and protecting him from untoward distractions. When the charismatic leader dies or retires, the bureaucracy tries to maintain the religious organisation without his impetus. Inevitably, it fails. The bureaucracy then becomes an end itself and, as religious life dies out, the religious organisation at first appears unaltered but it is, in reality, only a shell left behind by the power that once lived there.

The role of the bureaucracy need not, of course, lead to religious decline. There is, in all successful religious movements, a balance between bureaucracy and religious life and, for the most part, steps are taken to ensure that the first charismatic leader is replaced by someone whose religious priorities and gifts ensure the survival of the movement. Nevertheless, it is often the bureaucracy that helps to transform sects and

---

[42] A. Walker, *Restoring the Kingdom* (4th edn), (Guildford, Eagle, 1998), pp.41-42.
[43] B. R. Wilson, *Sects and Society*, (London, Heinemann, 1961).

churches into denominations. It is, after all, bureaucracies that are a common feature of religious movements and one bureaucracy is very much like another. They are hierarchical, rational, ordered, procedurally orientated, financially competent, painstaking, slow, and often unimaginative and committee-led. The radically novel thing about apostolic networks is that, from the first, they set their faces against bureaucracy.

Apostolic networks grew up in the very beginnings of a post-modern era. The relationship between a religious organisation and other organisations prevalent within society is parallel. In highly stratified hierarchical societies one expects to find highly stratified hierarchical religious organisations. Where there is an absolute ruler, a king by divine right, there is a Pope with unassailable religious authority. Absolutism in society is twinned with absolutism in religion. Where there is an open, democratic and accountable government, one expects to find an open, democratic and accountable religious organisation. Admittedly, social and religious organisations may be unsynchronised and a religious organisation may be more hierarchical than its social context, as occurs in the United States where the Catholic Church continues to be more authoritarian than the democratic culture in which it finds itself. Yet, in general, there is a consonance between social and religious organisations.

Apostolic networks grew up just at the point when social deference was in decline. Those born in 1945 in Britain were not required to carry out national service in the Armed Forces. The period of the 1960s saw not only a liberalisation of legislation but a relaxation of social and moral norms.[44] The old were treated with less respect, styles of dress were relaxed, comprehensive schools were introduced, class distinctions diminished, families began to break up and social mobility increased. The networks were formed as travel and communications soared and in an era of relative prosperity.[45] Nearly every home had a telephone and nearly every minister enjoyed a car. Motorways began to cover the country. Apostolic networks came into being at a point when social organisation was itself undergoing change. Not only were the great heavy industries of the past laying off workers but the new service industries of finance, insurance and commerce were beginning to take off. The office and the factory were less able to dictate the pattern of life and, more than ever, the rhythms and expectations of the urban majority drowned out the ancient rural cycles that had shaped the lives of those born in the first part of the century.

It is true that the original apostolic networks in the New Testament grew up in a world that was widely diverging from the 20th century. Yet, as studies of the first urban Christians have shown, there were within Roman

---

[44] D. Sandbrook, *Never Had It So Good*, (London, Little, Brown, 2005).

[45] A. Marwick, *British Society Since 1945* (3rd edn), (Harmondsworth, Penguin 1996).

culture the ties and bonds for making networks.[46] Families were extended and larger. Households comprised servants and slaves as well as family members and, within the commercial world, trade guilds formed an instant set of contacts and acquaintances. Paul could travel from one city to another and find himself at home among leather-workers. Priscilla and Aquilla, expelled from Rome, could move to Corinth and find a Jewish community that would welcome them. This combination between extended family, ethnic identity and trade guilds provided the social nexus that could be re-knotted into apostolic networks.

With regard to the last part of the 20th century, so pervasive has the network become that one informed commentator has written three volumes on *The Rise of the Network Society*.[47] In analysing business, 'the main shift can be characterised as the shift from vertical bureaucracies to the horizontal corporation'.[48] The horizontal corporation seems to be characterised by seven main trends: it is organised around process rather than task; it has a flat hierarchy; team management; it measures performance by customer satisfaction; its rewards are based on team performance; it maximises contacts with suppliers and customers; and it offers training and re-training to employees at all levels. These trends echo several features of apostolic networks. The organisation is flat, it is based around processes, it certainly embraces teams and it is happy to encourage training to everyone involved from the oldest to the youngest.

Further analysis shows that the old large vertical business corporations went through a crisis (echoing the crisis of the old denominations and churches in the religious sphere) and that, in their place, a variety of models and organisational arrangements were set up but all based on the network principle. Moreover, the crisis experienced by the isometric vertical corporations with their rigid hierarchies quickly threw up an *array* of networks, not simply one network that served as a one-size-fits-all replacement.

If the network society is indeed the society of the future then there will be changes not only to employment, to the flow of capital and investment, and to the dissemination of information but also to the social structures accompanying these other technological changes. The network itself is a set of interconnected nodes, where the node is a point of intersection. In an economic network the point of intersection may be banks or stockmarkets and, in a service network, the nodes may be connections between client and provider or between operatives within the provider's corporation. The point

---

[46] W. A. Meeks, *The First Urban Christians: the Social World of the Apostle Paul*, (Yale, Yale University Press, 1984).

[47] M. Castells, *The Rise of the Network Society* (vol.1), 2nd Edn, (Oxford, Blackwell, 2000).

[48] Castells, *The Rise of the Network Society*, (2000), p.176.

of the network is that it is an open structure, able to expand without limits and able to integrate new nodes as long as they are able to communicate with other nodes in the network.

> A network-based social structure is a highly dynamic, open system, susceptible to innovating without threatening its balance. Networks are appropriate instruments... for work, workers and firms based on flexibility and adaptability; for a culture of endless deconstruction and reconstruction; for a polity geared towards instant processing of new values and public moods; and for a social organisation aiming at the supersession of space and the annihilation of time.[49]

In short, apostolic networks may be precisely the right kind of religious organisation to map onto a society that is itself composed of networks of many kinds. Though the networks may have arisen out of a study of the New Testament, it is arguable – and members of networks would argue – that their arrival on the religious scene is not merely fortuitous but also providential.

The study of networks in relation to religion indicates that kinship networks were crucial to the life of Welsh chapels. The kinship network of interlocking extended families made the chapel central to Wales in the 19th century.[50] In the 20th century social networks may also be important, according to empirical evidence taken from modern Britain, in the decline or renewal of religious belief within urban areas. Those growing up in Britain may well do so without any link either to a local church or with others who attended church with the result that the only way 'that a non-church attender will be influenced by the beliefs of organised religion is through some kind of network connection'.[51] The picture here is of young people growing up with networks of friends (which may have replaced kinship networks in rural societies in the 19th century) that are entirely irreligious. Only if church-attending people belong to secular social networks is there any hope that church attendance might arrive on the personal horizon of these floating young urban populations.

A more thorough exploration of the characteristics of networks reveals surprising information about how they work.[52] If networks are drawn out in social clusters it is possible to model likely forms of social interaction. One can imagine six social clusters that are highly integrated internally but

---

[49] Castells, *The Rise of the Network Society*, (2000), p.502.

[50] P. Chambers, 'Social networks and religious identity: an historical example from Wales', in G. Davie, P. Heelas and L. Woodhead (eds), *Predicting Religion: critical, secular and alternative futures*, (Aldershot, Ashgate, 2003).

[51] R. Hirst, 'Social networks and personal beliefs: an example from modern Britain', in Davie, Heelas and Woodhead (eds), *Predicting Religion*, (2003), p.90.

[52] See the illuminating chapter on this in: P. Ball, *Critical Mass*, (London, Arrow Books, 2004).

which do not relate between one cluster and the next. The so-called 'caveman world' imagines all the people living in the same cave know each other very well but do not know people in adjoining caves. Even if one person in each cave knows people who live in the adjacent caves, the path length needed to connect everybody together is characteristically long. If, however, path lengths are randomised then we create the 'small world' phenomenon. The small world phenomenon is the one that occurs when we discover that chance acquaintances have a friend in common. The classic small world experiment was carried out by Stanley Milgram in the 1960s. Milgram sent packages to 196 people on the west coast of the United States with a request that they forward them to someone they did not know living on the east coast. He provided no addresses but simply the name and the profession of the intended recipient. The 196 people had to forward the package to someone whom they thought might be in a better position than themselves to reach the intended target. At each stage the people forwarding the package were asked to include the same kind of details about themselves as had been provided about the target person. When the packages arrived, it was possible to reconstruct the route that they had taken. Milgram discovered that, on average, just six separate journeys were needed before the packages found their way to the right person. The implication was that anyone in the United States could be linked with any one else in the United States through five acquaintances and this led to the notion that everybody in the world is separated from everybody else in the world only by 'six degrees of separation'.

By mathematical modelling that looks at the path length between the various nodes in a network and the average distance necessary to connect one node with another, it is possible to work out what happens when connections between the nodes are gradually made more and more random while retaining a high degree of clustering, that is, where clustering is defined as the number of connections between the nodes divided by the total number of possible connections. In high clustering almost every node (person) is fully connected to all the people he or she could be connected to; in low clustering there are some richly connected people and some isolated people. What the mathematical model shows is that the 'small world' phenomenon occurs when clustering is high and paths lengths are averagely low; this is because the relatively small number of *random* links between one cluster and the next make it possible to discover surprising common friendships.[53]

In a network system this means that we might think of a team of leaders over a congregation that were themselves a highly connected cluster. This cluster, because some members of the team knew members of other teams

---

[53] For instance see D. J. Watts, and S. H. Strogatz, 'Collective dynamics of 'small-world' networks', *Nature*, 393, (1998), 440-442.

some distance away, would result in a sense of 'small world' within the network as a whole. For instance, imagine a team of five church leaders in Sussex. All these people would know each other well and meet together frequently. Imagine one member of the team knew church leaders in Glasgow and another knew church leaders in Manchester. Immediately there would be a sense in which *all* the Sussex team leaders would have access to Glasgow by their link person and access to the Manchester people by their link person but, equally, the Glasgow and Manchester groups would have their long-range links and so quite quickly it will be possible to establish, when all the leaders were together, a sense of the greater unity despite the fact that the main part of each person's time was spent within his or her small own team cluster in his or her own location.

v. Conclusion

There is no obvious fit between apostolic networks and the big categories of sociological analysis. Apostolic networks display inclusive and exclusive features which make them difficult to classify as sects; equally, they cannot be said to line themselves up against the world in a typically sectarian manner. Apostolic networks do not favour bureaucracy which makes them difficult to classify as denominations; it is bureaucracy that holds together the invisible strands of denominational culture. Apostolic networks do not claim their membership is coexistent with the wider membership of society; they are hardly large enough to be identified as national churches. Lastly, apostolic networks do not easily fit into the general theme of secularisation since they demonstrate precisely the reverse characteristics.

If apostolic networks do not fit into ordinary sociological categories, it becomes difficult to use these categories and the theories that deploy them to predict the networks' futures. The historical narratives given in earlier chapters show how dependent networks are upon their apostolic figure. Where the figure is effective, and continues to be effective, the network grows and maintains its momentum. Sociologically and theologically what is distinctive about the networks is their concentration upon the ministry of the apostle. If there is something that the networks are epistemologically exclusive about, it is this. Nevertheless, this chapter suggests that one of the more profitable ways to look at apostolic networks is in respect of their structures since the structures express the essence of their being. The network structure springs out of a theology, a theology of ministry gifts, of fellowship and of New Testament ecclesiology. The structure is the vehicle by which apostolic ministry is expressed and the apostolic team, with its balance of gifts, its mobility, its changing membership, its focus on relationship and training, is a distillation of the entire theological ethos.

Part V

The Quantitative Analysis

Chapter 21

The Quantitative Investigation

This chapter introduces a step change. So far the analysis has used historical information and interviews to construct a narrative of the events which led to the founding and growth of the apostolic networks. Having written about the historical trajectory of the networks, they were open to theological and sociological analysis. Even so, none of this allows the voices of many of those involved in apostolic networks to be properly heard. Through the interviews that I carried out, the voice of the apostolic leaders themselves is registered but a different method is needed to allow leaders of congregations and other members of the networks to be accounted for. The only way to do this is by questionnaire since it would be impossible to interview them all.

Information collected by questionnaire has lots of advantages to it. Exactly the same question is presented in exactly the same way to numerous people and they can answer this question privately, honestly and, in most cases, anonymously. Modern computerised handling of data allows large numbers of responses to be rapidly accessed so that, for example, it is quickly possible to see the average age of ministers within one network or to make complex statistical comparisons between networks. The perspectives of different groups of people can be checked and compared and then reflected on theoretically and theologically.

i. The Research Programme

I grew up aware of the charismatic movement of the 1960s. I had begun to see changes take place within the Anglican and Baptist Churches and had attended interdenominational events that promised a renewal of the entire Christian landscape within Britain. As the charismatic movement developed, and behind the scenes and often hidden from ordinary congregational view, there were clearly discussions and, even, battles going on. By the start of the 1970s various congregations came into existence that were loosely organised under apparently disconnected travelling preachers. These loosely organised churches began to assume a definite identity, particularly after the Dales Bible weeks began in 1976. Quite quickly these travelling preachers came to be recognised as, or at least referred to as, 'apostles' and the clusters of churches with which they were associated came to be seen as 'the new churches'.

I had written about the formation of pentecostal denominations in Britain and had told the story of their history from their beginnings in the early part of the 20th century.[1] I wanted to find out whether pentecostal churches were in good heart and what was actually going on within their congregations. To this end I sent out questionnaires in the late 1990s to all ministers within the four pentecostal denominations within Britain, the Assemblies of God, Elim, the Apostolic Church and the Church of God. This was a time-consuming task but was made possible by the presence of denominational handbooks that provided the addresses of all the ministers. Ministers, like everyone else, are not keen on filling in questionnaires but, with some persuasion and encouragement, about 50% of them did so and I ended up with a database of 930 ministers who told me what they thought about a whole variety of beliefs as well as about the conditions of their lives. They told me what they were paid, where they were trained, how old they were, whether they were married or not, whether they owned their houses, what they believed about the Bible, Jesus, the Holy Spirit, healing, evangelism, spiritual gifts, and many other things and, by putting together information from these questionnaires with the story of these churches, it was possible to construct a detailed survey of these denominations.

Having mapped out the pentecostal terrain, I wanted to do a similar job with the apostolic networks. I wanted to see how they compared with pentecostal churches in terms of their beliefs, their lives and practices but also in terms of the dynamics of the congregations. Would they use charismatic gifts in the same way and did they grow in the same way? Were there any differences in belief between pentecostal ministers and ministers in apostolic networks? These questions were important because, in many respects, the apostolic networks had taken over the 'cutting edge' that had previously been the assumed prerogative of pentecostal churches. The pentecostal churches had set the trends but, in the 1970s and the 1980s, the churches within apostolic networks began to do that. How was it that churches within apostolic networks were able to grow, attract and retain young people? Was it something to do with their beliefs and practices or was there some other explanation?

After securing funding from the Arts and Humanities Research Council (as it was then called in September 2003), I was keen to collect information from the leaders in apostolic networks and had assumed that it would be relatively easy to elicit information by questionnaire from these leaders that could be analysed in much the same way as the pentecostal data had been analysed. Many of the questions on the two questionnaires were deliberately identical to allow comparison to be made. There were, it is true, a number of specific questions added to tap into the essential life of the networks but this did not alter the thrust of the enquiry. Quite early on,

---

[1] W. K. Kay, *Pentecostals in Britain,* (Carlisle, Paternoster, 2000).

it became apparent that the networks were not going to respond in the same way as the pentecostal denominations. There were three difficulties: first, the apostolic networks were simply not as organised as the denominations. The denominations had established procedures for recognising their ministers, for communicating with them and for recording their names in denominational handbooks. Certain privileges and responsibilities accompanied the granting of credentials. The apostolic networks did not work in this way. Although they recognised their ministers, there was a greater fluidity about the process and a deliberate avoidance of bureaucratic mechanisms, particularly those that might be likely to lead to the production of ministerial handbooks containing sets of denominational rules. Second, there were differences between the pentecostal denominations and apostolic networks with regard to the use of the word 'leader'. The leader of the pentecostal congregations is invariably the minister of the congregation. There may be reference to house group leaders but the house group leaders are not in any sense equated with the full-time minister. In apostolic networks, the situation was rather different since the word 'leader' was much more widely applied and, particularly in young congregations, leaders might be people who held full-time secular posts but who, only as the congregation grew, gave up the secular employment to become what would in the denominations have been recognised as full-time ministers. So, when one asked the question: how many leaders are in this network, the answer was not parallel to the kind of answer that would have been given had one asked, in a pentecostal denomination, how many leaders are there in this denomination? Third, leaders of apostolic networks might find themselves members of more than one network which meant that there was far greater flexibility within and among the networks than was the case among pentecostal denominations. It would be rare, if not impossible, for a minister to be a member of two denominations at the same time.

In any event, contacting ministers or leaders of apostolic networks proved to be more complicated than I had anticipated. And then there was a difficulty with working out how the statistics should be interpreted. Taking figures from the *Religious Trends no 3*, there are 2,094 New Churches in the UK with 2,385 leaders but, closer inspection of these figures, revealed a more complicated and less solid picture.[2] Emailed correspondence both with Peter Brierley and with church leaders suggest that these figures are either overestimated or else include churches that stand outside the apostolic sphere and are therefore not relevant to this project.[3] There are

---

[2] P. Brierley (ed), *Religious Trends no 3*, (London, Christian Research, 2001).
[3] Some 5,520 churches resulted from a Google search for 'community church' based on the web site <http://www.findachurch.co.uk/> (accessed 28 January, 2005). Since the term is used outside the networks, it was no use in finding which ones to contact. An

various websites available by which fuller information can be gathered but these also do not give an accurate or complete pictures.[4] A more detailed analysis indicates that there are some 12 relevant networks in England and Wales with 647 congregations.[5]

In alphabetical order these are:

C.net
Ground Level
Ichthus
Jesus Fellowship[6]
Kensington Temple
Kingdom Faith,
Lifelink
New Frontiers International
Together[7]
Pioneer/ Spirit Connect
Salt and Light
Vineyard.

This list is not exhaustive since there are other groups that share features with networks even if they do not function in quite the same way. Kingsway International Christian Centre is the largest of these and its network of chapels are organised in districts headed by District Superintendents in London, Birmingham and Luton.[8] Churches in Communities International is another network that describes itself as 'a world-wide voluntary association of independent churches and ministries that offers a system of mutual accountability and accreditation', which implies a lower profile for the apostolic figure.[9] New Wine is a similar network, though it is larger and has a strong Anglican constituency.[10] Nevertheless the 12 networks from which data has been collected, apart from Vineyard, all originated in the UK in the 1970s and 1980s and all

email from Peter Brierley 19 March, 2004 points out that the figures presented in the relevant table in *Religious Trends 3* are 'estimates'.
[4]   E.g.   Evangelical   Alliance's   Website   <http://www.ea.org.uk>, <http://www.upmystreet.com> and <http://www.churchesuk.co.uk> <http://www.findachurch. co.uk/>
[5] Here I count Pioneer and Spirit Connect as one network even though they have distinguishable histories.
[6] Also called Multiply Network
[7] They were once part of Covenant Ministries International.
[8] <http://www.kicc.org.uk/network.asp> (accessed 2 June, 2006).
[9] <http://www.cicinternational.org/CiC.htm> (accessed 2 June, 2006).
[10] <http://www.new-wine.org/> (accessed 2 June, 2006).

represent the concept of apostolic ministry as it came to be understood by restorationists.

Once the main groups had been identified, the main administrative officers of each network were asked for their permission to write to their churches' leaders with a questionnaire. While not all were willing to send their address list, Ichthus, Ground Level and c.net kindly volunteered to send questionnaires out in their own general mailings. Table 1 indicates distribution and response. The overall response rate was 35.7%.

Table 1: Distribution and completion of questionnaires

Network	Sent	Online completion	Postal returns	Response rate %
C.net	50		16	32
Ground Level	77		29	38
Ichthus	45	1	13	31
Jesus Fellowship[11]	53		11	21
Kensington Temple	54		10	19
Kingdom Faith	13	2	9	84
Lifelink	6		3	50
New Frontiers	200	71	82	76
Together	12		3	25
Spirit Connect /Pioneer	12	10	8	100
Salt and Light	50	1	21	44
Vineyard	75		26	35
Total	647	85	231	48.8

The 18 page questionnaire was made up of 8 sections. The first asked questions about age, gender, training, church size, annual rates of births, baptism, deaths, marriages, church structure, growth, decline and congregational charismata. The second section dealt with the frequency of ministerial charismatic and evangelistic activities. A third section gave 150 statements on doctrinal issues and offered respondents five options from agree strongly to disagree strongly on each issue; these varied from Christology to ecclesiology, from cell church to belief in 'apostolic ministry'. A fourth section presented items related to mysticism, a fifth

---

[11] Also called the Jesus Army and Multiply Network

comprised the Eysenck Personality Questionnaire,[12] a sixth dealt with burn-out, a seventh with ministry priorities and an eighth comprised the Francis Personality Type Sorter.[13]

As a way of adding to the information elicited from the networks, a second questionnaire was constructed using online facilities. A questionnaire was constructed that could be completed using a web link embedded in a circular email. After pilot testing, it was obvious that the original postal questionnaire was too long to put online and so a shortened version was used and this produced a further 87 responses. One of the questions in the online questionnaire asked whether the respondent had completed a paper-based version and two respondents replied in the affirmative. These were eliminated from the online set. The online database could not be merged with the postal database because the two sets of questions were not identical in every way even though some of the questions were the same. As a result, analysis of frequencies will, where questions are the same, make use of both datasets and present the findings in one table. Other forms of analysis will be confined largely to the longer postal questionnaire.

As can be seen from table 1, the online questionnaire increased the response rate from Spirit Connect/Pioneer considerably. The extra responses from New Frontiers International were welcome but did not change the overall picture. New Frontiers were the most numerous respondents in both postal and online modes and the weight of replies from their leaders show them to be about four times larger than any other network. Responses from both questionnaires were coded and analysed using SPSS 12.0.

ii. Analysing the Results

The first results of the analysis of the material collected by questionnaire are presented here in a series of paragraphs. In almost every case the paragraphs reflect information given in the postal questionnaire but where a subset of this information is given or where information is given by combining online and postal data, this is indicated at the head of the paragraph. The text is written in such a way that it should still make sense to those unfamiliar with the statistical tests. Analysis of variance is a way of looking at differences between groups and crosstabulation is a way of relating two variables to each other. Significance is assessed by the normal

---

[12] L. J. Francis, L. B. Brown, and R. Philipchalk, 'The development of an abbreviated form of the Revised Eysenck Personality Questionnaire (EPQR-A): its use among students in England, Canada, the USA and Australia.' *Personality and Individual Differences*, 13, (1992), pp.443-449.

[13] Devised by Leslie J Francis but not included in the analysis presented in this book.

conventions, that is, by departures from random patterns at a level more frequently than 5 times in 100, which is expressed as p < .05.

The presentation is methodical and looks first for significant differences between the networks and then at the frequencies of relevant variables. It begins with a look at the leaders and moves on to look at the networks.

Age

Table 2 shows the ages of the congregational leaders in the networks. The youngest average age of leaders is with the Vineyard and the oldest with Ichthus and the Jesus Fellowship. An overall average age of 47 compares well with the average ages of ministers within Pentecostal denominations whose ministers average about 50 whereas the average age of the Church of England clergy in 1994 was 52 and the modal age of Roman Catholic parochial clergy in England and Wales is in the decade 55 to 64 years of age.[14] What is most striking about these figures is the age of the youngest leaders. Is clear that New Frontiers are prepared to entrust congregations to relatively young men (age 25) and eight of the networks accept leaders in their thirties.

Table 2: Average ages of congregational leaders by network

	N	Mean years	Minimum years	Maximum years
C.net	15	50	30	68
Together	2	48	43	54
Ground Level	21	49	34	69
Ichthus	10	52	35	72
Jesus Fellowship	10	53	40	59
Kingdom Faith	5	48	39	64
New Frontiers	58	44	25	64
Pioneer	7	51	37	65
Salt and Light	19	49	31	64
Vineyard	19	42	32	56
KT	6	51	30	63
Lifelink	3	44	43	46
Total	175	47	25	72

---

[14] Kay, *Pentecostals,* (2000), p193, 194, 207

At the other end of the scale are leaders who have gone on well beyond normal retirement age, in one case to 72 (Ichthus). The differences between average ages of ministers in the networks is significant.[15]

Even the addition of online data and of other leaders does not alter these findings. The average age of all leaders is still 47 and the relative position of networks in respect of average age remains the same.

Gender

The combined sample (online and postal) was mainly composed of men with 27 (8.5%) women. Of these women only one was in sole charge of a congregation but this was a congregation of less than 25 people. Five women functioned as senior ministers, though only 2 were paid, and seven functioned as part of a team. Altogether 9 women were paid for their ministry and, in the online set, all those who were in leadership were either married or widowed. The average age of women leaders was 50 years of age, a little older than the generality of leaders. There did not seem to be any particular role earmarked for women: leadership of women was carried out by some men, as was music ministry and children's ministry while 10 of the women regularly preached outside their home congregations.

Religious Background

There were no significant differences between networks in respect of denominational origins, childhood commitment to Christianity or the suddenness of conversion. The most frequently cited denominational origin was with the Church of England (36.6%) and, behind this, came the Baptists with 15.9%. After this were Methodists (12.3%) with a scattering of Assemblies of God, Brethren, Elim, Presbyterian, Roman Catholic, 'other' and 'none'. Kingdom Faith contributed the largest proportion from the Church of England (71.4%) with Ichthus contributing 50% and the Vineyard 42.3%. Pioneer had the largest proportion from the Baptists with 50%. The network that recruited most widely across the spectrum was New Frontiers which had people whose religious denominational roots lay everywhere apart from within the Salvation Army. Vineyard was the next most widely recruiting network and it also attracted the largest group of ex-Roman Catholics.

The figures indicate how long and varied are religious pilgrimages in modern Britain. They also indicate that the networks do not recruit from exclusively pentecostal backgrounds which, in terms of theological experience, are their closest neighbours. Equally they indicate that people can make a journey from the Brethren, which tend to be explicitly anti-

---

[15] $F = 2.3$, p.$< .011$

charismatic, to apostolic networks which tend to be explicitly pro-charismatic.

Just under half of these ministers (45%) had made Christian commitments in childhood which implies that just over half only became Christians in adolescence or adult life. Just under half (47%) had had sudden conversions which implies an evangelical conversion. Other evidence suggests that sudden conversions are associated with evangelistic preaching and therefore with church growth.[16]

As might be expected from the fact that nearly half of the network leaders made a Christian commitment in childhood, about half (54%) had a mother who attended church nearly every week and just under half (47%) had a father who attended church nearly every week. So about half of these leaders came from churchgoing homes and it is no surprise that those who go to apostolic network churches are aware of the importance of creating an environment and a ministry that is supportive of Christian families and children. Of course, at the other end of the scale about a third of these leaders (37%) had fathers who never attended church and a quarter (26%) had mothers who never attended. The highest proportion of non-attending parents, whether fathers or mothers, is drawn from the Jesus Fellowship, a finding that reflects the driving evangelism of that network. There is also, as is well-known, a relationship between class and church attendance in the sense that church attending families tend to be more middle-class.[17] This means that the leaders who came from church attending homes are likely also to have come from middle-class homes, a finding that can be linked with the professional ethos to be found in many network churches.

Training

About a fifth (19%) of these leaders had undertaken distance learning in theology and there was no significant difference among the networks in the proportions of people who had taken this training route. The variety of places used for training was enormous and altogether about 28 places were mentioned. Full-time residential training had been undertaken by 27% of leaders and a further 12% had undertaken part-time residential training. When these figures are added up and assuming that those who undertook distance learning courses do not overlap with those who took residential training either part- or full-time, about 58% of leaders have received some form of training or another. Putting this the other way around, about 40% of

---

[16] W. K. Kay, 'Childhood, personality and vocation', in L. J. Francis and Y. J. Katz (eds), *Joining and Leaving Religion: research perspectives*, (Leominster, Gracewing, 2000), pp.215-231.
[17] S. Bruce, *Religion in Modern Britain*, (Oxford, OUP, 1995), table 2.9.

these leaders have received no training apart from that which has been church-based or practical.

Healing and Miracles

There are no significant differences between the networks in relation to the number of leaders who have been 'healed as a result of prayer' or who have witnessed a miracle. This is because both events are widespread. As many as 57% of these leaders have been healed physically as a result of prayer, 3% have been healed mentally and a further 22% have been healed mentally and physically which means that in total 82% have been healed in one way or another. Only 11.5% have *not* been healed as a result of prayer. In terms of miracles 81% have a 'witnessed a miracle'.[18] The point of the figures is that these leaders have an experiential base from which to draw when they speak with others. Their own first-hand familiarity with healing is one that many would want to acknowledge. Similarly, these leaders have no doubt about the miracles that they have witnessed.

Baptism in the Spirit

As many as 97% of senior or sole leaders believe they are 'baptised in the Spirit', and this figure only drops to 95% when all leaders are included. A small number of leaders would not use the term but none would deny the experience. In this respect, leaders of apostolic churches are very similar to pentecostal leaders in their acceptance of a theology of a crisis experience of the Holy Spirit. Baptism, by its very nature, cannot be a slow and gradual process but must be sudden.

Type of Ministry

Table 3 shows the distribution of ministry types. The most common type is pastoral and, after this, is teaching. This is what might be expected for ministries that look after a congregation. Between them, pastoral and teaching ministry amounts to nearly two thirds of the total ministerial emphasis of all kinds of leaders. The second row provides the figures for sole or senior leaders and it is immediately apparent that these leaders are less pastorally orientated than the generality of ministers and that they are more inclined to be evangelistic, prophetic or apostolic. The comparison between the two rows tells us about the way the ministry within apostolic networks is viewed. Apostles, prophets and evangelists are more likely to be senior ministers whereas pastors are more junior. And what would surprise those outside the apostolic churches is the sheer number of

---

[18] Quotations in this paragraph are taken from the questionnaire filled in by respondents.

apostolic ministries that are recognised. Apostles are not rare specimens seen once in a lifetime but rather part of the working life of the church.

Table 3 Ministry type (%)

Ministry is mainly...	All Leaders (n = 225)	Sole or Senior leaders (n = 110)
Apostolic	13.8	16.4
Prophetic	9.3	11.8
Pastoral	37.8	31.8
Evangelistic	6.2	8.2
Teaching	25.8	24.5
Other	7.1	7.3

There is no significant difference between the ministry categories in respect of age or the number of baptisms they administer. There *is* a difference in respect of how often they preach away from their local congregations.[19] As might be expected, mainly apostolic ministries preach away from home more than pastoral and teaching ministries. Connected with this, apostolic ministry is significantly responsible for more congregations than pastoral or teaching ministry.[20] Equally, apostolic ministries are exercised by those who have longer ministerial experience.[21] This implies that people may grow into apostolic ministry after a period of a pastoral or teaching ministry.

There is no statistically significant difference between networks in respect of the distribution of ministry types nor, surprisingly, given that networks vary in the extent to which they accept the ministry of women, is there any significant difference in respect of the distribution of ministry types by gender. There are proportionately nearly as many women whose ministry is 'mainly apostolic', 'mainly prophetic' and so on as men, and the same goes for the other categories. Whatever differences there are, are not sufficient to register statistical significance.

Bible Reading, Prayer and Prophecy

Three quarters of all leaders (76%) speak in tongues 'nearly every day' and over four fifths (86%) read their Bibles 'nearly every day'. There is no significant difference in the frequency of bible reading between the networks but some difference in the frequency with which leaders speak in tongues.[22]

---

[19] $F = 3.91$, $p < .002$

[20] $F = 3.39$, $p < .006$

[21] $F = 3.76$, $p < .003$

[22] $F = 2.02$, $p < .027$

There are significant differences between networks in respect of the frequency with which leaders prophesy.[23] For instance leaders in Kingdom Faith, New Frontiers, Salt and Light and Vineyard are all significantly more likely to prophesy than Kensington Temple leaders. Overall just under half (47%) of leaders will prophesy 'at least once a month' and nearly a fifth (18%) will prophesy 'at least once a week'. About a third (31%) of leaders will prophesy 'occasionally'. This means that over 90% of these leaders will prophesy in the regular course of their ministries and, for some, it will be an essential part of what they do.

Payment of Congregational Leaders

Payment of congregational leaders varied from network to network. Whereas 7% of c.net leaders were unpaid, the figure rose to 100% for the Jesus Fellowship. In detail the percentage of unpaid congregational leaders is: Kensington Temple (33%), Vineyard (32%), Ichthus (30%), Pioneer (29%), Salt and Light (26%), Ground Level (24%), Lifelink (15%), Kingdom Faith (11%), New Frontiers (5%), Together (0%).

The figures may be interpreted to show the financial strength of the networks since one would expect congregational leaders to receive a salary if they are to devote themselves full-time to this demanding work. The most financially organised of the networks are able to subsidise the payment of congregational leaders whereas, if financial ties are loose, cash flows from one part of the network to another are restricted. New Frontiers is evidently in a position to pay well over 90% of its congregational leaders. The Jesus Fellowship falls into a different category from all the others because of its policy on communal living and the sharing of possessions.

Pensions and Finance

Respondents were also asked about financial contributions to their networks and their own pension schemes. The data were analysed only in respect of those ministers who were paid for their ministry. In both cases there were significant differences between networks.[24] The vast majority of ministers (82%) made no financial contributions to their networks but 12% did so and a further 3.4% made minimal contributions. Ministers in Together and Kensington Temple were more likely than others to make financial contributions to their networks.

What these figures demonstrate is that the networks are not fundamentally tied together by financial arrangements. There is no sense in

---

[23] $F = 3.88$, p $<.000$

[24] For financial contributions to the network $F = 4.83$, p $< .000$; for pensions, $F= 2.68$, p $< .005$.

which the networks operate as pyramid systems with money passing up the ranks to the top. The theological claim of networks that they function relationally is borne out by these findings. Such financial flows as do occur are directed by church leaders of essentially autonomous congregations and the giving that takes place is voluntary.

Only 64% of ministers contributed to pension schemes. The Jesus Fellowship was excluded from this analysis because its ministers are not paid but, in any case, 91% of its ministers had no pension scheme. For the other networks Pioneer (83%), Vineyard (63%), Ichthus (56%), Kingdom Faith (50%) and Lifelink (50%) had no pension schemes. Or, to put this another way, New Frontiers (81%), Kensington Temple (67%)[25] c.net (57%), Together (57%), Salt and Light (56%) were the networks most likely to have ministers who made contributions to pension schemes.

It is difficult know how to interpret these figures. In the case of some networks, ministers may be encouraged to make their own pension provision and may simply have failed to do so. This may be for theological reasons because they believe that 'the Lord will provide' or for practical reasons because their salaries are too low to allow them to do so. If paid ministers are unable to afford contributions to a pension scheme, this suggests that the financial strength of the network needs to be buttressed. Where, for instance, a majority of ministers within the network have no pension scheme, questions need to be asked about why this is so.

Baptisms per Year

Congregational leaders varied considerably the number of people they baptised annually. The average numbers are as follows: c.net was five (with a maximum of 20), Ground Level was five (with a maximum of 28), Ichthus was three (with a maximum of 11), Jesus Fellowship was eight (with a maximum of 50), Kingdom Faith was seven (with a maximum of 16), Lifelink was one (with a maximum of two), New Frontiers was four (with a maximum of 24), Together was seven (with a maximum of 10), Pioneer was four (with a maximum of 10), Salt and Light was four (with a maximum of 15), Kensington Temple 10 (with a maximum of 35) and Vineyard was five (with a maximum of 30).

The maximum numbers reveal evangelistic success. The Jesus Fellowship is known for its vigorous evangelism within inner-city areas, Kensington Temple is located within the densely populated urban environment of northern London while Vineyard has the advantage of young ministers and a reputation for young congregations.

---

[25] However ministers who are part of Elim - which would be the case with congregations connected with KT - would participate in the Elim pension scheme.

Strictly speaking congregational numbers will grow if baptisms exceed funerals. When statistical tests were carried out the only significant mismatches occurred in: c.net, Ground Level, Kingdom Faith, New Frontiers and Vineyard and, in each case, baptisms significantly exceeded funerals. In all the other networks the difference between baptisms and funerals was not statistically significant. For the five networks with a surplus of baptisms over funerals, there is evident growth within the constituent congregations.

Weddings and Funerals

Weddings and funerals are indicators of the vitality or age of congregations. All the congregational leaders of the networks apart from Lifelink marry one or two couples per year with a maximum for c.net of six marriages; statistically there was no difference between the networks on this. Funerals in several networks are more numerous than weddings – a serious pointer to congregational erosion if maintained, and there are significant statistical differences between them.[26] For instance within c.net, Together, Ground Level, Ichthus, Pioneer, Salt and Light and Kensington Temple, congregational leaders on average conduct more funerals than weddings (although, of course, each marriage involves a couple whereas a funeral does not). The largest number of funerals is carried out by c.net (maximum of 12), Together (maximum of 26) and Salt and Light (maximum of 20).

Multiple Network Membership

Networks varied in the extent to which congregational leaders belonged to more than one network. For instance, whereas 80% of Kensington Temple leaders belonged to a second network, this figure dropped to zero for Together, Kingdom Faith and Lifelink. The actual figures for multiple membership for congregational leaders are: Kensington Temple (80%). c.net (50%), Ichthus (42%), Vineyard (32%), Jesus Fellowship (29%), Salt and Light (29%), Ground Level (24%), Pioneer (17%), New Frontiers (11%), and Kingdom Faith, Together and Lifelink all zero.

The figures may be interpreted to demonstrate the way networks operate. A network with no multiple membership is going to be tighter and more exclusive though, probably, smaller. A network with multiple membership over 50% is going to be less able to forge a collective identity and find difficulty in assembling all its congregational leaders at distinctive events. It is also in danger of losing congregations if it takes a particularly tough line on contentious issues. Kensington Temple is in a different category

---

[26] $F = 3.9, p < .000$

from the other networks because it is already a member of Elim with the result that the default position of its associated churches is to come under the Elim banner.

Congregational Size and Multi-congregational Responsibility

Two thirds (63.2%) of apostolic network congregations are made up of a hundred adults or fewer on a Sunday morning. At the other end of the scale 5.1% of congregations comprise 350 adults or more. The distribution curve shows two humps, one at the 25-49 level and another at the 350+ level. This means that, though just over 20% of apostolic congregations contain less than 50 adults, there is a disproportionate number of very large congregations as well. There is evidence of powerhouse megachurches within the apostolic grouping.

When the figures are looked at by network, it is possible to see where the megachurches are in this sample. Kingdom Faith has one, New Frontiers have two, Salt and Light have one, Vineyard has one and Kensington Temple has one.

There were 53 ministers (all male apart from one woman with Pioneer) in the sample who had responsibility for more than one congregation and they were asked to estimate the total number of people for whom they had responsibility. The largest number of people for whom any individual minister had responsibility was 2000 and there were nine men responsible for more than 1000. New Frontiers had the largest number of ministers responsible for more than one congregation (15) but were also nine people with Ground Level, six with the Jesus Fellowship, three with Kingdom Faith, two with Pioneer, five Salt and Light and five with Vineyard.

The apostolic concept includes the notion of translocal ministry and the figures illustrate that significant numbers of ministers, about a fifth of the total sample, have this type of responsibility. Where it differs from the multiple parish or multiple benefice system found within the Anglican, Methodist or Roman Catholic churches is that the ministers within apostolic networks responsible for more than one congregation will expect those congregations each to have their own leaders in place. With the multiple parish system found elsewhere, the full-time minister finds him or herself in *sole* charge of several congregations with a consequent dilution of effectiveness.

Cells and Housegroups

When senior leaders were asked whether their congregations were cell churches, figures show that Kensington Temple is most likely to reply that it has adopted the G12 style. In total only 3.6% of these respondents have opted for G12. The most common response by senior leaders is that they have a 'church with cells not a cell church' (48.2%) and the next most common reply (34.5%) is that they do not adopt the cell principle. Apart from Kensington Temple which has espoused the cell principle, all the other networks are pragmatic. None of the congregations with over 300 adults used G12 though there were five congregations with fewer than 50 adults that did; this implies that G12 is seen as a growth strategy by small congregations rather than the route by which large congregations have reached their present size.

House groups were popular among charismatic churches in the 1980s until they were challenged by the cell group philosophy. The figures show that 53% of respondents say that their congregations use house groups 'as opposed to cell groups'. House groups are popular with Together, Ichthus, Kingdom Faith, Salt and Light, and Vineyard, more than 80% each of whose respondents say that their congregations use them. No statistical link could be found between congregational size and the use of house groups. There were congregations of more than 350 that used house groups and congregations of less than 25 that did not. Again, the issue appeared to be pragmatic.

Where congregations did use house groups, there was the expected statistically significant connection between congregational size and the number of house groups deployed.[27] Roughly speaking, house groups accommodate 10 people so that a congregation of 300 might have 30 house groups while a congregation of 50 might have four or five.

Growth and Decline

Respondents were asked about the annual numerical growth of their congregations. Half of congregational leaders reported growth in some of their congregations up to 10% and in some of their other congregations growth of over 11% per year – with one exception: Pioneer reported no growth beyond 10%. The network whose growth caught the eye was Vineyard, 82% of whose senior congregational leaders reported growth of 11% or more. The comparable percentage of senior congregational leaders for New Frontiers was 40.5%. There was no statistically connection between network and growth, however.

When attempts were made to discover any relationship between numerical growth and congregational size, none could be found. Growth appeared to be independent of the original starting size of the congregation. The importance of this finding is that there is a natural presumption that it is easier to hit high growth rates in smaller congregations because the addition of just one family to a small church translates into a high percentage.

---

[27] Chi square = 734, p < .000

As a way of checking the numerical health of networks, congregational leaders were also asked about numerical decline. The majority (64%) reported no numerical decline though 26.5% reported decline in the range between 1% and 5%, and 8.2% reported decline in the range between 6% and 10%. Only one congregation reported decline more drastic than this. There was no statistical relationship between the decline of congregations and their starting size: it was not the case that small congregations were more vulnerable to decline than larger ones. Nor was there a statistical relationship between the presence or absence of home groups or cell groups and numerical decline. Cells are not a winning formula guaranteeing growth.

Putting these figures together we can say that about two thirds of apostolic network congregations appear to be growing and about a third are either static or have suffered decline. Those that are growing appear to be growing well since just about half them are increasing at more than 11% per year. Overall, about a third of the churches within the networks are growing dramatically and another third are growing steadily.

Spiritual Gifts

Respondents were asked about the percentage of their congregations exercising charismatic gifts. There was no statistical difference between the networks in this regard. Over half (54%) of respondents replied that more than 30% of their congregations exercise spiritual gifts. A somewhat lower number (16%) reported that between 21-30% exercise spiritual gifts and a similar number (16.5%) reported that a relatively lower number, between 11-20%, exercise spiritual gifts. The essence of these findings is that apostolic congregations are highly charismatic. Interestingly, there was a statistically significant association between the exercise of charismatic gifts and congregational size. Congregations within the range 25-74 adults were more likely to see large proportions exercising these gifts. This is not surprising given the practical difficulty of exercising vocal charismatic gifts within large settings. In a small congregation, an individual can be heard in a room or small hall but, in a large setting, this is impossible without amplification.

There was no statistical relationship between the percentage of congregational members exercising spiritual gifts and numerical growth nor was there a relationship with decline, apart from at one level. The congregations that showed no decline were more likely to exercise spiritual gifts.[28] This implies that spiritual gifts are associated with lively congregations and, where there is congregational life, congregations will not shrink.

---

[28] Chi square 76.3, p < .01

When the percentage of the congregation exercising spiritual gifts was crosstabulated with the frequency with which leaders prophesied, there was a statistically significant association.[29] This implies that the example of ministers is sufficient to prompt or model charismatic behaviour within the congregation. Where the minister never prophesies or only occasionally prophesies, a lower proportion of the congregation act in a similar way. Where the minister or ministers prophesy at least monthly, this also has an impact on the congregation. All this implies that life within apostolic churches is such that ministerial charismatic behaviour stimulates congregational charismatic behaviour.

iii. Conclusion

The networks are more alike than they are different. In most cases they are led by relatively young men (younger than those leading denominational congregations) who would claim an experience of baptism in the Holy Spirit and who lead congregations where charismatic gifts are frequently manifested, and manifested by a good percentage of the congregation. There are significant numbers of men and women claiming apostolic and prophetic ministry and these ministerial claims are evidently accepted by the congregations to which they belong. Apostolic and prophetic ministry is integrated into the milieu of apostolic networks and is not an afterthought or extra luxury. The importance of the relationship between charismatic gifts in apostolic congregations and the growth of these congregations is a focus of the next chapter.

---

[29] Chi square 60.8, $p < .047$. The statistical association held good (though only one-tailed) when it involved senior or sole leaders alone. In practice, all leaders set an example that congregational members can follow, which is why it is appropriate not to limit the set of leaders reported on.

Chapter 22

Church Growth and Charismata

This chapter begins by examining the dynamics of church growth in apostolic networks. In particular it analyses the drivers of congregational growth and, in finding these to be connected with charismatic gifts, it concludes by explaining how the leaders of apostolic congregations understand these gifts.

i. The Dynamics of Growth

Margaret Poloma researched pentecostal churches in the United States and found that there was a connection between the charismatic experience of pentecostal congregations and church growth.[1] Her theoretically-grounded thesis was that charismatic activity stimulates evangelism and other forms of outreach as well as exemplifying life within a congregation. Charismatically-active congregations grow, and the point of her analysis was that Pentecostal congregations that subside from a high point of charismatic activity into respectable formality are likely to suffer numerical decline. I carried out a similar study of British pentecostal congregations and found that the dynamics of growth were similar.[2] Where there was charismatic activity in the congregation, the congregation grew. The question now is: will a similar dynamic be found among apostolic congregations?

Ministerial Charismatic Activity

The measurement of charismatic experience was made using a scale that was composed of six items. The six items in the scale were based upon answers to the questions 'how often in the past three months *you* have...' (original italics) given a public utterance in tongues, interpreted tongues, prophesied, danced in the Spirit, given a word of wisdom/knowledge, and felt led by God to perform a specific action. To each of these items ministers could reply: none, 1 to 6, 7 to 12, 13 to 18 or 19+. The items were tested for scale properties by computing the alpha coefficient. This was .747, a satisfactory indication of the scale's reliability and slightly higher than that recorded by Poloma in her equivalent measure of charismatic

---

[1] M. M. Poloma, *Assemblies of God at the Crossroads*, (Knoxville, TN, University of Tennessee Press, 1989).

[2] W. K. Kay, *Pentecostals in Britain,* (Carlisle, Paternoster, 2000).

experience within American Assemblies of God congregations. The six items of the scale were different by one item from the items used to measure charismatic experience among British pentecostals.[3]

The scale of charismatic experience covers a variety of charismatic indicators which cohere well into a measuring instrument. Although individual items are worth reporting on, results from a scale are more robust. Analysis of variance showed that there were differences between the networks in relation to charismatic experience.[4] Comparison between the networks shows that Kingdom Faith registered the highest level of charismatic experiences and that this was significantly higher than c.net, Ground Level, Ichthus, Jesus Fellowship, New Frontiers, Pioneer and Kensington Temple. Apart from this there were no significant differences between the networks in the frequency of charismatic experience – in short, if Kingdom Faith had not been so exceptionally high there would have been no significant differences between the networks.

Computations were then carried out to discover the relationship between charismatic activity and congregational growth using the scales described in the previous chapter. Again, analysis of variance revealed a clear relationship such that higher levels of charismatic activity were associated with higher levels of growth.[5] In order to verify this finding, stepwise multiple regression was carried out to remove any network effects before examining the effects of charismatic experience on growth. The analysis showed that, while network had no significant effect upon growth, when charismatic experience was added to the equation, there was an immediate significance. In other words, variations in growth can be accounted for by charismatic experience alone and need not be attributed to any variations that might have been caused by other features of the networks.

Ministerial Evangelism

A similar procedure was adopted for the construction of a ministerial evangelism scale. The items were again based upon responses to the question 'how often in the past three months *you* have...' (original italics). And the items were: talked with friends or neighbours about your church, invited a new person to an activity at your church, invited a backslider to

---

[3] The item concerning 'singing in tongues' was replaced by the item concerning 'being led by God to perform a particular action'. The reliability of the scale was somewhat lower using the original item referring to singing in other tongues. Presumably this is a practice that is rarer in apostolic congregations than in classical pentecostal congregations with the result that this item does not function with the same effectiveness among apostolic networks.

[4] $F = 3.90, p < .000$

[5] $F = 2.69, p < .001$

return to your church, offered to drive a new person to your church, invited children of new people to children's meetings, and prayed for the salvation of specific people. In each case again respondents could reply: none, 1-6, 7-12, 13-18, 19+. The six items were the same as those used among pentecostal ministers apart from one possibly important variation. Among pentecostal ministers the item 'talked with friends or neighbours about Christ' was used but, when this was put into the scale using the present dataset, the alpha coefficient became low. The item was dropped and this then gave an alpha coefficient of .763.

The difference between the two scales is small and both are concerned with evangelism but, whereas pentecostal ministers appear to be willing to talk to friends or neighbours directly about Christ, apostolic network leaders are more inclined to talk to friends and neighbours about the church and then to invite people to attend. This may be simply a tactical variation.

There were no significant differences in the ministerial evangelism across networks. This implies that ministers are equally likely to invite a new person to church, to offer to drive a new person to church, and so on. We should not see the differential growth of apostolic networks in terms of the differential evangelistic drive of their ministers.

ii. The Dynamics of Congregational Growth

To explore the relationship between ministerial evangelism and congregational growth, a simple model can be envisaged. We can envisage that ministerial evangelism will lead to congregational growth. This will occur either directly or by means of the example set to congregational members who will themselves follow suite and begin to evangelise the people they know. Given that these are charismatic congregations, it is worth speculating on the impact of ministerial evangelism on the percentage of the congregation that exercises spiritual gifts.

Analysis of variance was used to explore the relationship between ministerial evangelism and congregational growth and there was indeed a clear and significant statistical effect.[6] The more active the minister was in terms of personal evangelism, the larger the congregation grew. When the relationship between ministerial evangelism and the percentage of the congregation exercising spiritual gifts was explored, there was no significant statistical relationship. The model is confirmed in the sense that the evangelistic work carried out by the minister is effective and does bear fruit in terms of a growing congregation but it does not produce a charismatic congregation. See Model 1

---

[6] $F = 1.79$, $p < .026$

Model 1

Ministerial evangelism	(associated with)	Congregational growth
Ministerial evangelism	(not associated with)	Congregational charismata

A second model is necessary to envisage the charismaticisation of the congregation. We may assume that charismatically active ministers generate congregations with a high percentage of people who exercise spiritual gifts. Again, when analysis of variance was run, the predicted relationship was found.[7] Ministers who are themselves charismatically active will produce congregations in which large percentages of the congregation exercise spiritual gifts. But what of church growth? Here we find that there *is* a relationship between the charismatic activity of the minister and the congregation's growth.[8] The implication here is that, whereas ministerial evangelism produces congregational growth, ministerial charismatic activity produces both congregational growth and the presence of spiritual gifts within the congregation.

Model 2

Ministerial charismatic activity	(associated with)	Congregational charismata
Ministerial charismatic activity	(associated with)	Congregational growth

The second model is illuminating but it may not tell the whole story. This is because there is a clear statistical relationship between ministerial evangelism and ministerial charismatic activity. The ministers who are most evangelistic are also the ministers who are most charismatically active, and vice versa. Thus ministers who are charismatically active may produce growing congregations by virtue of the evangelism that they also carry within their ministerial profile, and not solely by virtue of the profusion of their charismata.

A further statistical test is necessary to discover what is happening. In this, congregational growth was related to three variables simultaneously: ministerial charismatic activity, congregational charismata, and ministerial evangelism. Multiple regression showed that congregational growth was related to the first two variables significantly but that the third variable was

---

[7] $F = 1.95, p < .016$
[8] $F = 2.69, p < .001$

eclipsed by the other two.[9] In other words, it was significant on its own but, when the other two variables were taken into account, the variance associated with ministerial evangelism lost its significance. What this implies is that ministerial charismatic activity and congregational charismata lead to congregational growth and that ministerial evangelism is not a factor in congregational growth when all these things are taken together. In many ways, this finding is intuitively obvious. The entire weight of church growth cannot be placed upon the evangelistic efforts of the minister or ministers and must be diffused to the congregation at large, particularly when the congregation becomes a substantial size. The dynamics of church growth illustrated by these associations do not deny the value of ministerial evangelistic activity but they do place it within a larger context. It seems that ministerial evangelistic activity is important in relatively small congregations but that, as the congregation grows, ministerial evangelistic activity takes second place to the charismatic life of the congregation and it is this that sustains and presses growth forward once the congregation has reached a reasonable size.[10] Model 3 illustrates the idea.

Model 3

Ministerial charismatic activity	(associated with)	Congregational growth
Congregational charismata	(associated with)	Congregational growth
Ministerial evangelism	(not associated with)	Congregational growth

The analysis of the relationship between ministerial gifts, congregational charismatic activity and congregational growth throws light on the way congregations in apostolic networks function. Congregational charismatic gifts involve the congregation and empower large sections of the congregation to minister. The impact of congregational charismatic gifts is to ensure that congregations are participatory, full of people who have stopped being spectators and are now active within the entire ministerial effort of the church. Where people have become ministers, they shoulder

---

[9] For the ANOVA model $F = 14.30$, $p < .000$; t for proportion of members exercising spiritual gifts 2.34, $p < .02$; t for ministerial charismatic activity 3.48, $p < .001$; t for ministerial evangelism 1.84, $p < NS$.

[10] This is because in separate computations the relationship between ministerial evangelistic activity and growth was not found in congregations over 150 people but was found consistently in congregations below 50.

responsibility and feel confidence in the capacity of their congregation to help newcomers. We can see this process as one that spreads the load of ministry out from the full-time clergy to the core of the congregation. And it does so in the context of relationships within and beyond the congregation to produce a lifestyle that is conducive to friendship-based evangelism. By looking at charismatic gifts in this way we can move the focus of sociological and theological discussion away from arid arguments about secularisation and cessationism to a clear-eyed study of how these congregations actually work.

iii. Charismatic Emphases

Restorationism in essence argues that the power and pattern of the early church can be restored to the contemporary church. Along with a belief in charismatic gifts is the belief in 21st century apostles. The two are intimately linked because apostles may be recognised, among other things, by their exercise of charismatic gifts.

Among the most prevalent charismatic gifts are those relating to healing. In many meetings within apostolic congregations, there will be opportunities to receive prayer for healing. There is usually little restriction on who may pray for those who are ill, especially when such praying occurs in mid-week housegroups. Similarly, Christians in these congregations will speak in tongues in the normal course private prayer or during collective worship.

Apostles

When respondents' beliefs were examined on the defining issue of apostles, more than two thirds (66.1%) believe that 'apostolic networks are more important than denominational structures', a huge proportion (84.5%) believe that 'apostolic leadership is vital to the 21st-century' and an even larger number (88.8%) accept the statement 'I believe in the authority of apostles today'. Nearly all respondents (95%) were able to say 'I believe in the ministry of apostles'.[11] The sample, then, clearly coheres around the notion of apostolic ministry. Even so, there are differences between the networks with regard to their belief in the importance of apostles.[12] The

---

[11] In each case respondents agree or agree strongly with the statement.

[12] Comparisons between networks were made by an analysis of variance that covered them all and it is these F ratios and p values that are footnoted. Post-hoc Bonferroni tests that compared each network individually with all the others were used where overall differences had been found and in the paragraphs that follow I have reported on these individual differences when they occur. I have not, however, given the significance levels on each separate occasion.

main difference concerns the comparison between Vineyard and other networks. Vineyard is much less likely than the others to insist on the importance of apostolic ministry today. Kingdom Faith, New Frontiers and Together were significantly more likely to accept the importance of apostles than Vineyard, Kensington Temple and Lifelink. In particular New Frontiers were significantly more likely to accept the importance of apostolic networks than c.net, Ichthus, Salt and Light, Vineyard, Kensington Temple and Lifelink. In relation to the item 'I believe in the authority of apostles today' Vineyard was more reticent than the others and c.net, Ichthus, Jesus Fellowship, Kingdom Faith, New Frontiers and Salt and Light all significantly differ from it, though it must be said that even Vineyard respondents were more positive than negative about the authority of apostles. It is just that the other networks were *very* positive. Similarly with the item 'apostolic leadership is vital for the 21st century' Vineyard were also reticent and were significantly different in their assessment from Ground Level, Jesus Fellowship, Kingdom Faith, New Frontiers and Salt and Light though, again, on average Vineyard was still more positive than negative about the concept.

The contrast between Vineyard and the other networks rests upon the conceptual differences between them. Vineyard understands itself to utilise an episcopal form of government modified by congregational autonomy, and it has an interdenominational history going back to the ministry of John Wimber. The other networks see themselves as specifically apostolic and lack an interdenominational past.

Healing

There is substantial agreement about the role of healing in the church today. Leaders in apostolic networks believe that the church should be involved in healing as part of its regular ministry. Yet there are distinctions between the networks in five specific areas.

The teaching popularised by the American TV evangelists is that healing is a matter of faith and that, if the faith exercised is great enough, then all illness of any kind will be removed.[13] The usual position here is that it is the responsibility of the person who is ill to exercise faith for their own healing. This position was examined by the item 'divine healing will always occur if a person's faith is great enough'. There is a dramatic and significant statistical difference between nearly all the networks and Kingdom Faith. Members of Kingdom Faith believe that healing will occur infallibly if sufficient faith is shown. The other networks do not take this

---

[13] E.g. T. L. Osborn, *Healing the Sick*, (Oklahoma City, OK, T. L. Osborn Evangelistic Associates, 1992).

position and, in fact, specifically reject it. Presumably Kingdom Faith reflects Colin Urquhart's early ministry as a healing evangelist.

The traditional Pentecostal theological basis for healing has been found within the atonement of Christ. Christ died for our illnesses as well as our sins according to an exposition of Isaiah 53 (e.g. verses 4 and 5 'surely he took up our infirmities and carried our sorrows... by his wounds we are healed'). As a result healing is available to Christians, and some preachers would argue that this healing is a 'right' rather than given at the gracious but by no means inevitable disposition of God.[14] All networks basically agree that healing is in the atonement though New Frontiers is least likely to be dogmatic on the matter and Kingdom Faith most likely to be dogmatic.

Healing of the memories has been popularised in connection with the removal of long-term problems.[15] Belief in this kind of healing may belong within a counselling context or may be related to the gradual improvement, through sanctification, in the inner life of those who have been converted from a difficult and damaging background. There are statistical differences between the networks. Kensington Temple rejects healing of the memories and this contrasts statistically and significantly with Ichthus and Vineyard, both of which accept this form of healing. The Jesus Fellowship, which evangelises in tough inner-city areas also holds to healing of the memories, though the contrast here is not statistically significant.

Prayer for those who are ill has, within pentecostal settings and in the early days, been seen as the prerogative of every Christian though, with the professionalisation of clergy, this notion has slipped away from time to time only to be periodically restored. John Wimber's ministry underscored the capacity of the entire body of Christ, every Christian, to be involved in prayer empowered by the Holy Spirit. There are significant differences between the networks. Vineyard, not surprisingly, takes the view that all Christians may pray for the sick and they are joined in this view by New Frontiers and Kingdom Faith and, in this, they differ significantly from Kensington Temple which appears to confine prayer to a limited elite of Christians. This restriction puts healing evangelists or those who regularly pray for the sick on a pedestal and diminishes the priesthood of all believers.

A corollary of the theological position that God will heal people if their faith is great enough is that 'it is a sin not to ask for prayer if one is ill'. Here all the networks basically disagree with the item apart from Kingdom Faith. Kingdom Faith in keeping with its emphasis on healing tends to regard the omission of a request for prayer as sinful, though it is important

---

[14] For a critical examination, see A. Perriman, (ed) *Faith: Health and Prosperity*, (Carlisle, Paternoster, 2003).

[15] R.C. Stapleton, *The Experience of Inner Healing*, (New York, Thomas Nelson, 1977).

not to misread the figures. This tendency is slight and not pronounced though the distinction between Kingdom Faith and c.net and New Frontiers is statistically significant.

Tongues

Speaking with tongues, or glossolalia, was the hallmark of pentecostal experience at the beginning of the 20th century.[16] Pentecostals saw speaking with other tongues as indicative of the experience of the baptism with the Holy Spirit. After early debate and examination of Scripture, a large number of classical Pentecostals agreed that speaking with other tongues was the 'initial evidence' of the baptism with the Holy Spirit and they embedded this belief within their statements of faith. The charismatic movement of the 1960s initially entertained this position but, gradually, a broad position was accepted with the result that most charismatics, while believing that the baptism with the Holy Spirit is a Christian experience subsequent to conversion, denied that any particular charismatic gift is associated with the initial experience of Spirit baptism.[17]

Leaders within apostolic networks show themselves to be in step with general charismatic opinion. Only 16.9% believe that 'speaking with tongues is necessary as initial evidence for baptism in the Spirit', the Pentecostal position, while all the rest either reject this position or are uncertain. Conversely, 89.8% agree with the proposition that 'baptism in the Holy Spirit can occur without speaking with tongues'. On the other hand 95.8% say, 'I believe there is a distinct Christian experience that might be called "the baptism in the Spirit"' and 87% believe that 'the baptism in the Holy Spirit is evidenced by "signs following"'. These figures show that these leaders not only believe in a distinct post-conversion experience but that this experience is marked by signs although they are unwilling to restrict the signs to glossolalia alone. Baptism in the Spirit remains central to the theology of these leaders and cannot be written off as a nominal or symbolic event. For these reasons the apostolic networks have affinities with classical pentecostals that go beyond common lines of historical development.

The vast majority (94%) of these leaders believe that speaking with tongues is a form of private prayer and nearly 98% believe that speaking in tongues is an edifying experience and, in this, they are echoing the words of St Paul in 1 Corinthians 14 'anyone who speaks in a tongue does not speak

---

[16] E. L. Blumhofer, *The Assemblies of God: A Chapter in the Story of American Pentecostalism*, 2 vols., (Springfield, Gospel Publishing House, 1989).

[17] S. Tugwell, *Did You Receive the Spirit?*, (London, DLT, 1971). The presumption that tongues and the baptism in the Holy Spirit runs through. M. Harper, *As at the Beginning*, (London, Hodder and Stoughton, 1965).

to men but to God... he who speaks in a tongue edifies himself'. For these reasons only a tiny minority (1.3%) think that tongues is 'an uncontrollable experience'; these leaders (74.1%) are much more likely to think of tongues as a 'holy experience'. While a majority (58.7%) believe that tongues are real languages, many others (46.3%) believe tongues are unreal prayer languages. Tongues, therefore, according to 98.3% have a practical use and churches benefit from them according to 84.7% of these leaders. One of these uses is within the realm of spiritual warfare, a position endorsed by 94%.

There are a few differences between networks but not many. There is a significant spread of views about whether tongues is a holy experience and an equal spread over the issue of whether tongues are real languages.[18] Kingdom Faith is most likely to think that tongues are a holy experience and Lifelink are least likely to think this. Kingdom Faith and Together are most likely to take the view that tongues are real languages whereas Salt and Light and Lifelink are least likely to take this view. There also significant differences over whether tongues should be encouraged in congregations with Pioneer and Kingdom Faith encouraging this and Kensington Temple being the only network that is likely to discourage their use. These differences are substantive as well as statistically significant since they indicate how welcome lay participation within congregational meetings might be. Where tongues are present in congregational worship, the whole congregation will tend to wait for an interpretation of the utterance and, in this way, to remove control of the gathering from the hands of the full-time minister. We might interpret encouragement of congregational tongues as encouragement to lay participation. There are also significant differences in the matter of spiritual warfare. Kensington Temple typically takes a view of tongues as being unhelpful within spiritual warfare and nearly all the other networks take the opposite point of view. To them speaking with tongues functions as a means of changing the spiritual climate or praying against forces opposing the church.

Prophecy and Interpretation of Tongues

Prophecy within charismatic and Pentecostal churches is unpremeditated utterance that the speaker feels is inspired directly by the Holy Spirit.[19] Although there are differences of opinion about the way that prophecy should be exercised within Pentecostal and charismatic congregations, the typical scenario is this: during an open time of prayer, praise and worship,

---

[18] $F = 1.899$, $p < .041$ and $F = 2.104$, $p < .021$ respectively.

[19] W. A. Grudem, *The Gift of Prophecy in 1 Corinthians*, (Washington, DC, University Press of America, 1982); W. K. Kay, *Prophecy!* (LifeStream Publications/Mattersey Hall, 1991).

an individual within the congregation will stand up and speak, addressing advice or exhortation to his or her hearers. Prophecy may be given at the front of the meeting through the amplification system and, in these instances, permission from the leader of the meeting may be needed. The prophecy will normally be no more than two or three minutes long and may contain a concatenation of Scripture verses or, in some forms, may describe a 'picture' that the speaker has received. Neither type of prophecy is considered to be infallible or inspired to the same level as Scripture and each should in any case be judged by the leadership who may, on rare occasions, add a corrective rider to what has been heard. Prophecy will cover a number of topics but the effect of a prophetic utterance is to break open the predictable routine of a meeting and infuse fresh and unexpected directions for worship or prayer.

Utterances in tongues will be interpreted (1 Corinthians 14:26) and, although traditionally within Pentecostal churches these utterances were interpreted as exclamations of praise to God, more recently they have been understood as discourse from God to the congregation. An utterance in tongues plus interpretation is therefore almost exactly equivalent to a prophecy when this view of interpretation is held.

There is overwhelming agreement among these leaders (97%) that prophecy brings life to the church and equal disagreement (94.5%) with the notion that prophecy causes disorder. The direction of interpretation is, however, much more balanced. While 51.9% think that interpretation is not directed by God to the congregation, 37.3% disagree. Or, to put another way round 64.9% think that interpretation ought to be in the direction of God while 24.1% think the opposite. About 10% in both cases is uncertain. What these figures show, in any event, is that there will be considerable numbers of interpretations of tongues that will function like prophecies in some networks.

There are significant differences between networks on all these matters although there is general favourability to prophecy as a whole.[20] All networks are in favour of it though Lifelink and Kensington Temple are least likely to think that prophecy brings life. None of the networks thinks that prophecy causes disorder, though there are significant differences between Kensington Temple (which is more likely to think that prophecy causes disorder) and New Frontiers, Vineyard and c.net. Overall this finding, and findings concerning praying for those who are ill, suggest that Kensington Temple holds a tighter rein on its public meetings than other apostolic networks.

---

[20] On prophecy $F = 2.055$, $p < .025$ (brings life) and 3.026 $p < .001$ (causes disorder); on interpretation $F = 5.755$, $p < .000$ (God to congregation) and F 6.679, $p < .000$ (congregation to God).

Prosperity Teaching

Although 'prosperity teaching' is not logically related to doctrine about the Holy Spirit in the contemporary church, there has, since the rise of the TV evangelists, been an historical relationship between belief in miracles and prosperity.[21] If faith in God can lead to healing, faith in God can lead to other material miracles including the provision of finance.

Belief in prosperity as the result of Christian faith is not quite the same as a more modest belief that God will supply the needs of Christians. Prosperity implies abundance; meeting needs implies sufficiency. There is widespread agreement (79.7%) among these leaders that God will meet the needs of Christians though the only significant difference between networks occurred in the contrast between the Jesus Fellowship and New Frontiers. The Jesus Fellowship perhaps because it was more closely in contact with the urban poor is less inclined to take the view that God will supply Christian's needs whereas New Frontiers is confident that God would.

Belief that 'all Christians should experience material prosperity' was largely rejected by the networks. As many as 80.4% rejected the position. Yet 12.8% agreed with it. Analysis of variance demonstrated that there were differences between networks on this matter.[22] In terms of individual comparisons between networks Kingdom Faith was confident in prosperity and differed significantly from c.net, Ground Level, Ichthus, Jesus Fellowship, New Frontiers, Salt and Light, and Vineyard. Equally Kensington Temple also favoured material prosperity and differed significantly from c.net, Ground Level, Ichthus, Jesus Fellowship, New Frontiers and Vineyard. Kingdom Faith and Kensington Temple were the two networks most positive about material prosperity whereas Lifelink, Jesus Fellowship and New Frontiers were the least positive. So high were the levels in favour of material prosperity found among Kingdom Faith that prosperity teaching appears to be an important tenet to its leaders.

The converse position, that 'material poverty is a curse removed by the gospel' showed a roughly mirror image set of figures. Kingdom Faith and Kensington Temple were inclined to agree with this position whereas Lifelink, Jesus Fellowship and New Frontiers were inclined to disagree. Kingdom Faith found itself significantly different from c.net, Ground Level, Jesus Fellowship, New Frontiers, Salt and Light and Vineyard. This is as clear an indication as could be given that Kingdom Faith stands apart from the other networks in relation to its belief in prosperity theology.

Yet none of the networks majored on the view that 'material posterity can be ensured by successful spiritual warfare'. Spiritual warfare is, as far

---

[21] W. K. Kay, 'Prosperity Spirituality', in C. Partridge (ed), *Encyclopedia of New Religions: New Religious Movements, Sects, and Alternative Spiritualities*, (Oxford, Lion, 2004), 91-93.
[22] $F = 8.357$, $p < .000$

as the networks are concerned, not concerned with prosperity or poverty but with other dangers. The networks are rooted in everyday reality in the sense that they understand that poverty does not evaporate through prayer. Rather, poverty is removed as the gospel begins to make its beneficial effects felt on individuals and communities.

So far as the payment of ministers is concerned, there were significant disagreements among the networks.[23] The Jesus Fellowship, whose ministers are unpaid, was least likely to think that ministers are underpaid whereas Pioneer was most likely to think this.

iv. Conclusion

The dynamics of congregational growth within apostolic networks appear to be very similar to the dynamics found within pentecostal churches in Britain and classical pentecostal churches in the United States. In each case charismatic gifts within the congregation are associated with growth and in each case ministerial charismatic activity correlates with congregational charismatic activity. Ministerial evangelism is important but only crucial when congregations are small.

Congregations within apostolic networks share a strong confidence in apostolic leadership and take a positive view of healing, though there are variations between them. The variations suggest that Kingdom Faith is more nearly akin to the position popularised by healing evangelists than the other networks are. All the networks generally agree that healing is to be found in Christ's atonement and some of the networks emphasise healing of the memories as part of the repertoire of healing available. Speaking with tongues is also widely regarded positively though the doctrinal position taken by classical pentecostal churches that indissolubly links speaking with tongues to baptism in the Holy Spirit is rejected. Prosperity teaching is rejected by the majority but accepted by a minority of roughly 13%.

The ethos of the networks is similar though Kingdom Faith appears to show marks deriving from the healing evangelist's ministry of its founder and Kensington Temple is more likely to see full-time clergy as privileged above ordinary congregational members and therefore to be less welcoming of congregational charismata. It is possible to explain the predispositions of Kensington Temple by reference to non-British members of its congregation. There may be cultural preferences among African members of Kensington Temple leading to the acceptance by the leadership team there of a more prominent role for ministers. This may also explain the preference for a prosperity slant since the poverty in Africa is conducive to this form of theology.

---

[23] $F = 2.047$, $p < .025$

And, finally, when the empirical information like this is examined, it is difficult to discern emphases that might be connected with the R1 or R2 categorisations. A fuller consideration of this awaits a final review.

Chapter 23

Non-Charismatic Beliefs

This chapter deals with the beliefs of leaders in apostolic networks over a range of doctrinal and practical matters and concludes by attempting an empirical testing of the R1 and R2 constructs.

i. Jesus

Examination of the survey results showed beliefs about Jesus are almost without exception uniformly orthodox and evangelical. All respondents believe that Jesus is God and nearly all believe that Jesus is fully human (only one person in the entire survey disagreed). All except one believe that Jesus rose again from the dead physically on Easter Day. All respondents without exception believe that 'Jesus died for my sins' and all except one believe that Jesus literally walked on water. All respondents believe that Jesus literally turned water into wine. All respondents believe that all Christians should tell others about Christ, and that Christ was born of a virgin. All except two believe in hell. The only item on which there was a spread of opinion concerned the rule of Christ on earth during the millennium and here about a fifth (19.6%) disagreed with the concept of millennium, almost exactly half (50.2%) were uncertain and the remainder believe in the millennial reign.

ii. Bible

Beliefs about the Bible are equally evangelical and orthodox. Only 2% either disagreed with or were not certain that the 'Bible is the infallible word of God'. This said, nearly a fifth (18.7%) either disagreed with the statement that 'the Bible contains no verbal errors' and just over a fifth (23.2%) were uncertain about this. Thus the majority of respondents believed that the bible contains no verbal errors (though a significant minority is prepared to concede this) while, at the same time, believing the bible to be infallible. This is a nuanced position. Such nuancing is also shown by preferences for bible translation. Conservatism of a kind is also shown in unwillingness to accept the New International Version as the best version of the Bible: under a third (27.5%) selected this option and more than a third (39.7%) disagreed with it. A much larger percentage (90.3%) disagreed with the proposition that the Authorised Version is the best version of the bible. When the networks were compared with each other, there were significant differences between them.[1] Kensington Temple showed a somewhat higher level of support for the Authorised Version than other networks.

iii. Tithing

Nonconformist churches have long depended for their income upon the financial giving of their members. The older nonconformist churches may own land or other equity that produces income but the newer nonconformist churches have no such benefits. They must rely entirely upon what is put into the offering bag. In most new free churches, giving is encouraged and is typically at a higher per capita level than in other kinds of churches.[2] In addition, where churches are supported by giving of this kind, they can increase what they receive through 'gift aid' regulations. These allow churches to claim back the money that was paid in tax on the money that has been given charitably. Nearly all charities within Britain utilise 'gift aid' and the government supports the scheme because large numbers of civic activities can be funded in this way without being a burden to the taxpayer.

Tithing, or giving a tenth of one's income, has a long pedigree dating back into the history of Israel. The priests of Israel were supported in this way and, because there were 12 tribes, giving a 10th of personal income ensured that the priests enjoyed a standard of living similar to that of the rest of the nation. The priests themselves gave their own tithe directly to God through the sacrificial system of the temple. Although tithing is not stipulated within the New Testament, many nonconformist churches argue that, if during the Old Testament period a tenth was given, Christians should give at least this much - even if chapter and verse for this argument are hard to pin down.

Leaders in apostolic networks are strongly in favour of tithing and 71.5% of respondents thought that 'all members should tithe'. A slightly larger number (76.6%) agreed that the tithe belonged to the local church which, presumably, can be interpreted as meaning that the tithe does not belong to the network or to any outside agency but is at the disposal of the local church's leadership.

---

[1] $F = 5.053$, $p < .000$. Comparisons between networks were made by an analysis of variance that covered them all and it is these F ratios and p values that are footnoted. Post-hoc Bonferroni tests that compared each network individually with all the others were used where overall differences had been found and in the paragraphs that follow I have reported on these individual differences when they occur. I have not, however, given the significance levels on each separate occasion.

[2] P. Brierely (ed), 'How Christians use their Money and Why', *Christian Research*, (London, Christian Research, 2006).

Although there are significant differences between networks, these differences occur largely because the Jesus Fellowship is in a different position from the others in that its people do not receive a personal income.[3] All the other networks show support for the principle of tithing; the highest degree of uncertainty (25%) occurs in the case of Pioneer but, even so, more than half its leaders support the principle. There is also a difference between four of the networks (Kingdom Faith, New Frontiers, Vineyard, and Kensington Temple) and Lifelink over the issue of whether the tithe belongs to the local church. Lifelink is less inclined to accept this principle, though it is also less inclined to accept the principle of tithing *per se*.

iv. Church Attendance

In keeping with their clearly articulated doctrines and focused leadership, apostolic networks encourage frequent church attendance. There is strong support for 'all Christians should attend Sunday morning worship' and 'all Christians should attend mid-week meetings' though there are significant differences between the networks.[4] Only three of the networks (Pioneer, Vineyard and the Lifelink) are rather obviously lower than the others in regard to Sunday morning attendance.[5] Sunday evening attendance is only significantly supported by the Jesus Fellowship and Kensington Temple, and even then the frequency of support is hardly overwhelming. Midweek attendance is seen as important by all fellowships though Pioneer and Lifelink are less committed to the practice than all the others.

If there is one surprise from these figures it is that Sunday evening attendance has now become less important for these network churches than midweek attendance and that two of the networks (Pioneer and Lifelink) appear to be moving towards a profile of optional church attendance – a position that accords with the lifestyle of emergent churches.[6]

v. Cells

Commitment to cell structure was tested by the item, 'I believe all churches should have a cell structure'. There was flat disagreement with this and no significant difference between networks. Conversely, 'I believe cell structures are not appropriate for British churches' did significantly

---

[3] $F = 3.538$, $p < .000$; $F = 2.336$, $p < .010$

[4] F varies between 3.039 and 4.338, all significant at .000

[5] Some networks have found young professionals prefer Sunday afternoons to Sunday mornings.

[6] D. A. Carson, *Becoming Conversant with the Emerging Church*, (Grand Rapids, Mich, Zondervan, 2005); M. Moynagh, *emergingchurch.intro*, (Oxford, Monarch, 2004).

differentiate between networks even though all of them on average disagreed with the thought.[7] Regarding the G12 system, this was tested by the statement, 'I believe G12 is vital to the future of the church'; all networks without exception rejected it. When, however, asked to respond to, 'cell groups are the key to church growth', there was a significant spread of views.[8] New Frontiers, Salt and Light and Pioneer all endorsed the connection between cell groups and growth whereas c.net, Kensington Temple and Lifelink did not. There were significant differences between New Frontiers and Kensington Temple.

To check whether the networks appreciated the theological and practical difference between home groups and cell groups they were presented with the item, 'there is no difference between home groups and cell groups'. All of them thought there was a difference except Kingdom Faith. Indeed on this matter there was significant divergence between Kingdom Faith and New Frontiers; Kingdom Faith were uncertain about the difference between home groups and cells whereas New Frontiers' leaders were sure that there was a difference.

All the networks apart from Kensington Temple firmly believe that home or cell groups enhance church life. On this issue there were significant differences between Kensington Temple and Together, c.net, Ground Level, Ichthus, New Frontiers, Pioneer, Salt and Light, Vineyard and Jesus Fellowship. Given the disruptions caused by the G12 system within Kensington Temple it is not surprising that its leaders are unconvinced by the claims of cell philosophy and extend this lack of conviction to all kinds of home groups.

The pragmatic stance of apostolic networks in Britain is implicit within these figures. The networks are not sold on cell structures though they accept that cell principles may work in Britain. They do not like the G12 type of cell group and most of them do not think that cell groups are a key to church growth although there is a spread of opinion here. The networks, apart from Kingdom Faith, see a difference between home groups and cell groups and nearly all of them welcome intimate domestic gatherings alongside the larger congregational meetings held on Sundays.

vi. Ministry of Women

The ministry of women within nonconformist churches has not been subject to the same debate and media attention as is found within the larger Protestant denominations.[9] There has always been variety over the

---

[7] $F = 2.124$, $p < .02$

[8] $F = 2.753$, $p < .002$

[9] L. J. Francis, and M. Robbins, *The Long Diaconate 1987-1994: women deacons and the delayed journey to priesthood*, (Leominster, Gracewing, 1999); H. Harris, and J.

acceptability of the ministry of women within nonconformist churches and groups. The Salvation Army has accepted this ministry from the beginning, as have Methodists while other groups, like the Brethren, have been consistently opposed. The apostolic networks show equal variety. This variety stems from interpretation of the pastoral texts like 1 Timothy 2:12 'I do not permit a woman to teach or to have authority over a man'; some argue that these texts are specific to a first century situation and others that they enshrine enduring doctrine. This means that apostolic networks, even if they reject teaching and authoritative roles, may still welcome the ministry of women in other parts of church life.

Seven separate items tapped into the issues. 'Women should have exactly the same opportunities for ministry as men' was strongly supported in most of the networks. Four of them, however, did not support the proposition: the Jesus Fellowship, New Frontiers, Salt and Light, and Lifelink. In these last four networks there was negativity although, in the case of Salt and Light, neutrality. Yet the item 'women should not serve as church officers' attracted no support. In other words even those networks that rejected the idea that women and men should have the same opportunities for ministry accepted that women *could* function as church officers. Similarly, 'women should not preside at Holy Communion' was rejected by all the networks and not one of them even averaged uncertainty on the issue. In the same way, also, all the networks rejected the item 'women should not speak in church meetings' – the Brethren position – decisively. Neither did any of the networks accept that women were required to wear head coverings in public worship. Nor were any of the networks in favour of the stipulation 'women should not baptise'.

By contrast, all the networks, including those that believe that women should have the same opportunities for ministry as men, believed that 'women should obey their husbands'. There was no significant difference between the networks in their acceptance of this principle. Equally, concern for authority was shown in the response to the item, 'women should not exercise a preaching ministry'. Here the Jesus Fellowship and New Frontiers were significantly different from nearly all the other networks. The Jesus Fellowship and New Frontiers stood against the preaching ministry of women while all the others were unconcerned. An even stronger rejection of the idea that women should be charge of congregations was found in the Jesus Fellowship and New Frontiers though several other networks including Cornerstone, Together and Salt and Light had reservations on this count.

Shaw (eds), *The Call for Women Bishops*, (SPCK, London, 2004); J. Baker, (ed.) *Consecrated Women? A contribution to the women bishops debate*, (Norwich, Canterbury Press, 2004).

vii. Lifestyle

Table 1: Lifestyle items: Leaders' responses

Item	Agree %	Not Certain %	Disagree %
Christians should not drink alcoholic beverages	1.6	3.0	95.4
Christians should not attend the cinema	1.3	2.5	95.8
Christians should not buy or sell on Sundays unless absolutely necessary	20.6	11.8	67.5
Christians should not take part in social dancing	4.2	4.2	91.5
Christians should not smoke	61.6	10.7	27.8
Christians should not gamble	83.8	11.1	5.1
Christians should not engage in sporting activities on Sundays	9.7	15.2	75.1
Christians should not watch TV on Sundays	3.3	6.4	90.3
Christianity is always opposed to the dominant culture in society	39.8	28.1	32.0
I believe Christian rock music helps young people to worship	58.5	31.4	10.1

Pentecostal churches and holiness churches in the first part of the 20th century laid down a rigorous Holiness code for their people.[10] Early pentecostals were determined to avoid anything remotely worldly including the drinking of coca-cola and the eating of chewing gum. Even as late as the 1980s there were pentecostal churches that refused to allow screens into their buildings for overhead projectors that displayed worship songs. 'The silver screen belongs in the world, brother, and not in the church' said one elderly elder.[11] The charismatic movement in the 1960s had no truck with such restrictions or the more widespread evangelical taboos that dated back to the 1930s.[12] The new apostolic networks, having come out of the

---

[10] G. Wacker, *Heaven Below*, (Cambridge, Mass, Harvard University Press, 2001), p.122.

[11] Declared vigorously to me by an elder in Preston in about 1984.

[12] O. R. Barclay, *Evangelicalism in Britain 1935-1995: a personal sketch*, (Leicester, IVP, 1997), p.25.

charismatic movement, were resolutely free. The figures in table 1 show how leaders in apostolic networks overwhelmingly accept the drinking of alcohol, cinema attendance, social dancing and watching television on Sundays. In each case more than 90% of leaders disagree (or disagree strongly) with the interdiction. Yet there are traces of the holiness code in a fifth of leaders (20.6%) who do not like buying or selling on Sundays unless absolutely necessary and the 9.7% who disapprove of sporting activities on Sundays. Similarly, gambling and smoking arouse strong disapproval despite a small minority of liberal dissenters. Surprisingly over a fifth of leaders (27.8%) do not condemn smoking.

There are significant differences between the networks.[13] The Jesus Fellowship emerges as the most rigorous and stands out statistically against most other networks on many of the items. Even so it is important not to misread the trend. Although the Jesus Fellowship is significantly different from c.net, Ground Level, New Frontiers, Pioneer, Salt and Light, and Vineyard on the matter of drinking alcohol, the leaders in the Jesus Fellowship are still more inclined to *dis*agree with the restriction than otherwise. The same is true of cinema attendance and social dancing though, when it comes to smoking, Together, the Jesus Fellowship, Kingdom Faith and Kensington Temple are the most likely to disagree with this practice whereas c.net and Lifelink are most likely to be permissive. Sunday sport attracts disapproval from the Jesus Fellowship while all the other networks accept it, and the differences between the Jesus Fellowship and the other networks are statistically significant (apart from Kensington Temple and Together). Regarding the watching of sport on television on Sunday the Jesus Fellowship stands alone in condemning the activity and is significantly different from every other network.

Christian rock music comes into a category of its own. It is supported by Pioneer and Vineyard but not by Kensington Temple, with the other networks falling in between. The differences are statistically significant and may indicate nothing more than the presence of large numbers of young people in the approving churches. Yet the item may be indicative of general permeability to youth culture and its values in stark contrast to the sect-like holiness codes promoted by early pentecostals. In every case (apart from Kensington Temple) the networks agree that 'Christian rock music helps young people to worship'.

The final item 'Christianity is always opposed to the dominant culture in society' attracts a common response from the networks – there are no significant differences between them. Approximately a third of leaders agrees with the proposition, a third is uncertain and the remaining third disagree. Reaction to the dominant culture is a marker of deeper

---

[13] F numbers vary on these items from 2.085 (over gambling) to 10.458 (watching TV on Sunday) with p values no lower than .022.

motivations: does the network find itself at perpetual loggerheads with the British way of life or is it at ease with Britain and glad to enjoy the many cultural fruits on offer? The full range of responses is present and seems to be connected with the way individual leaders see the world rather than with network policy.

viii. Calvinism

Calvinism, with its doctrines of election and predestination, has a long and honourable history within Protestantism. It is associated with intellectual rigour and, in some forms, with an ability to integrate scientific domains with theological ones.[14] New Frontiers is exceptional, if not unique, in combining Calvinism with charismatic theology. Although the two are perfectly compatible with each other, historically Calvinists (despite the fact that religious revivals among Calvinists are as enthusiastic as any) have tended to be unwelcoming of religious experience, and that includes a recognition that charismatic gifts may function in the contemporary church.

As expected, the networks differed very significantly in respect of the item 'my theology is Calvinistic'.[15] New Frontiers was firmly in favour and Ichthus and c.net were firmly against and, as anticipated, there were significant differences between individual networks so that, for instance, New Frontiers was significantly more positive than c.net, Ichthus, Jesus Fellowship, Pioneer and Vineyard.[16] Kensington Temple was significantly more Calvinistic than c.net. In this way the figures confirmed expectations. In percentage terms less than 10% of New Frontiers' Leaders took a non-Calvinistic view of theology whereas among c.net and Ichthus the proportions were reversed.

ix. Creationism and Governance of the World

The belief that God created the world in six days of 24 hours is associated with fundamentalism. Although it is possible to be fundamentalist and not to be a creationist, the two things go hand-in-hand because the interpretive process brought to the biblical text is similar in both instances. Fundamentalism, like creationism, tends to read the canonical text literally without any metaphorical or symbolic gloss.

There were no significant differences between the networks in respect of creationism nor are there any differences between individual networks. In general the networks were uncertain about what to believe. For instance

---

[14] J. B. Bratt (ed), *Abraham Kuyper: a centennial reader*, (Carlisle, Paternoster, 1998).

[15] $F = 11.764, p < .000$

[16] Roger Forster of Ichthus has written against Calvinism in: R. T. Forster, and V. P. Marston, *God's Strategy in Human History*, (Wheaton, Il, Tyndale House, 1974).

61.5% of Ichthus, 45.5% of the Jesus Fellowship, 50% of Pioneer, 42.9% of Salt and Light, 34.6% of Vineyard and 37% of New Frontiers registered themselves as being 'not certain'. There were proportionately more creationists among Kingdom Faith than any other network but there was also a percentage of non-creationists in that network. In short, the topic does not have the salience that it commands in the United States.

In an attempt to probe the worldview of these leaders, the item 'there is usually a spiritual cause behind material events' was subject to analysis. In the context of leaders of apostolic networks, it is reasonable to assume that three basic positions might be held that: (1) spiritual experiences and material events are unconnected and that each operates within a sovereign and independent sphere (2) material events cause and lie behind spiritual experiences or (3) the converse is true and that spiritual causes lie behind material events. The second position is the classic materialist and reductionist position propagated by the early Marxists.[17] The first position is more agnostic and possibly postmodern. The third position, if it is held, presumes an interventionist and controlling spiritual realm that may or may not be benign; it is a supernaturalist position.

A frequencies count found that nearly half (45.9%) of the sample agreed or agree strongly that spiritual causes lie behind material events, just under a third (32.6%) were uncertain and the remaining fifth (20.1%) disagreed. Consequently the third worldview is the one most likely to be held with any certainty by this group of leaders, even though it was not held by a majority. There were significant differences between networks but *post hoc* tests did not discern any significant differences between particular groups.[18]

As a way of understanding how this worldview is integrated into the theological outlook of these leaders, a scale was constructed using five other items. The items are:

o   I believe Christians are daily in conflict with demons
o   Material prosperity can be ensured by successful spiritual warfare
o   Spiritual warfare is part of my lifestyle
o   Divine healing will always occur if a person's faith is great enough
o   The existence of the European Community is prophesied in the Bible.

These six items formed a scale with an alpha coefficient that was satisfactory and the scale was named Spiritual Control since it implies that the spiritual dimension is able to control the material dimension whether in relation to prosperity, healing, material events or even the larger political picture within the European Community.[19] The networks were significantly

---

[17] E.g. V. I. Lenin, *Materialism and Empirio-criticism*, (Moscow, Foreign Languages Publishing House, 1947).

[18] $F = 1.895$, $p < .04$

[19] Alpha was .618

different in relation to the scale with Lifelink and New Frontiers scoring low and Kingdom Faith, Together, Vineyard and Ichthus scoring high.[20] The means scores are shown in table 2. When multiple comparisons were made, Kingdom Faith was found to be significantly higher than most of the other networks including c.net, Ground Level, New Frontiers, Salt and Light, Kensington Temple and Lifelink.

Table 2: Spiritual Control by Network

	Mean scale score
Lifelink	13.0
New Frontiers	15.9
KT	16.0
Salt and Light	17.1
c.net	17.2
Ground Level	17.1
Pioneer	17.4
Jesus Fellowship	17.5
Ichthus	18.0
Vineyard	18.1
Together	19.7
Kingdom Faith	21.8

To put this interpretation more bluntly we could say that the low scoring networks on the Spiritual Control scale take a position much closer to the ordinary man or woman in the street whereas the high scoring networks live in greater tension with their surrounding culture. High scoring networks are more inclined to discern an invisible hand shaping everything for good or ill whereas low scoring networks are more inclined to look for material or psychological explanations of events. Even so, the tendencies of both groups should not be overplayed. The maximum possible score on the scale is 30 points and, even the high scoring networks do not average more than 22.

x. Orientation to Other Christians

Large numbers of Christians in Britain attend inter-denominational summer events. Greenbelt is geared towards young people not only in music but also in the political, justice and arts topics covered within its seminars.[21]

---

[20] $F = 4.688$, $p < .000$
[21] <http://www.greenbelt.org.uk/?s=9> (accessed 10 July, 2006).

Spring Harvest is the largest of the inter-denominational gatherings and brings families together on several sites in different parts of Britain.[22] It is, in some respects, the heir of the 1980s Bible weeks in the Dales and the Downs though the balance between charismatic and a non-charismatic tracks is usually discernible within the program.

There is a variety of opinions about Greenbelt but none of the networks is opposed. Together and Kensington Temple are neutral while c.net, Ichthus and Pioneer are in favour.[23] In comparisons between networks New Frontiers is significantly more negative than c.net, Ichthus, Pioneer and Vineyard. We can put it another way around by saying that New Frontiers is confident of its own identity and less inclined to merge itself within an inter- denominational setting whereas the other four networks are more inclined to join with other Christians in an event that they do not themselves organise and whose agenda they do not set.

There is equally a variety of opinions about Spring Harvest though the networks are more likely to favour it than Greenbelt.[24] Typically only about 3% of respondents are against Spring Harvest, between a quarter and a half are uncertain and the remainder in favour. The most lukewarm are Kensington Temple, the Jesus Fellowship and New Frontiers and the most hotly in favour are Ichthus, Ground Level and c.net. When individual networks are compared with each other New Frontiers is significantly less favourable to Spring Harvest than Ground Level and Ichthus, and Ichthus is significantly more in favour than Kensington Temple.

It is possible that the position of New Frontiers was formed by its own very successful summer camp at Stoneleigh that attracted large numbers of people in the 1990s by putting forward an engaged restorationist message as well as being open to everyone. Members of Kensington Temple are able to attend the Elim Pentecostal Conference which has the same kind of holiday and teaching atmosphere that Spring Harvest generates. Even so, Ichthus, which is in favour of Spring Harvest and Greenbelt, also runs its own summer event so that the positivity of opinion towards the inter-denominational camps is not merely the product of in-house alternatives.

The item 'inter-denominational gatherings of Christian leaders are more important than denominational structures' registered significantly varied opinion.[25] Pioneer and Ground Level were most inclined to agree with this while the Jesus Fellowship and Kensington Temple were least inclined to agree. Endorsement of this item implies a broad and warm interdenominational attitude and little or no faith in denominational structures. Since apostolic networks major on relationships, an implication

---

[22] <http://www.springharvest.org/index.html> (accessed 10 July, 2006).

[23] $F = 4.556$, $p < .000$

[24] $F = 3.561$, $p < .000$

[25] $F = 3.187$, $p < .000$

of agreement with this item is that denominations would function far better if they stressed relationships more and structures less. The difference between Ground Level, in favour of interdenominational gatherings, and the Jesus Fellowship and New Frontiers were significant.

The item 'apostolic networks are more important than denominational structures' also attracted a mixed response.[26] Whereas Kensington Temple, Vineyard and Lifelink were opposed to the idea, New Frontiers, Kingdom Faith, Ground Level and Together were in favour. There were significant differences between networks on this matter: Kingdom Faith contrasted significantly with Vineyard and Kensington Temple, New Frontiers contrasted significantly with c.net, Ground Level, Ichthus, Salt and Light, Vineyard, Kensington Temple and Lifelink. It is evident that Kingdom Faith and New Frontiers are quite clear that their own networks, and networks like them, are of substantial importance.

The ecumenical movement offers another route to Christian unity than that posited by interdenominational gatherings or by the networking of networks. The item 'I believe the Holy Spirit is at work in the ecumenical movement' attracted a significant range of responses.[27] Kingdom Faith and New Frontiers were most uncertain about the ecumenical movement and Pioneer most positive. None of the networks rejected the idea that the Holy Spirit is at work in the ecumenical movement out of hand but more than half registered uncertainty, which is why there were no significant differences between any of the networks.

The item 'Pentecostal and charismatic churches should cooperate more with each other' attracted a varied response with the Jesus Fellowship and New Frontiers being at one end of the scale and Lifelink at the other.[28] The responses range between a cautious agreement and strong agreement but the variation was not a cause of significant contrasts between individual networks. The item 'Pentecostal and charismatic churches should cooperate more with other Christian denominations' also elicited significantly varied responses with a range between cautious agreement and strong agreement.[29] Again the Jesus Fellowship and New Frontiers were on one end of the scale and Lifelink was on the other. Again there were no significant differences between individual networks. The item 'I support interdenominational prayer groups' received endorsement with a similar pattern to the previous two items.

To find out what was going on behind the nine variables analysed in this section, they were factor analysed and, by this means, grouped into three

---

[26] $F = 10.196, p < .000$
[27] $F = 2.150, p < .018$
[28] $F = 2.0\ 63, p < .024$
[29] $F = 3.186, p < .001$

groups of three.[30] The three groups fell into meaningful scales and two of them showed strong psychometric properties but the third was rather weaker.

The first to scale was named P/C Cooperation.[31] It was made up of the items:

- o Pentecostal and charismatic churches should cooperate
- o Pentecostal and charismatic churches should cooperate with other denominations
- o I support interdenominational prayer groups.

The second scale was named Ecumenism.[32] It was made up of the items:

- o I believe the Holy Spirit is at work in the ecumenical movement
- o I approve of Greenbelt
- o I approve of Spring Harvest.

The third, and weaker scale, was named Core Apostolic.[33] It was made up of the items:

- o Apostolic networks are more important than denominational structures
- o interdenominational gatherings of Christian leaders are more important than denominational structures
- o I think non-Pentecostal and non-charismatic churches will die out

The three scales were then tested in relation to the networks and, in each case, significant differences were found.[34] The P/C Cooperation scale was then tested among the networks separately and two of the networks, New Frontiers and Jesus Fellowship, were significantly less in favour of cooperation than c.net, Ground Level, Ichthus, and Salt and Light. The implication of this finding is that New Frontiers and the Jesus Fellowship are the networks least likely to look for cooperative ventures with Pentecostal and charismatic churches. They feel self-sufficient in many respects.

The Ecumenism scale also showed significant differences among the networks[35] with New Frontiers being significantly less ecumenical than c.net, Ichthus, Vineyard and Pioneer. In fact, Kensington Temple was the least ecumenical of the networks though comparisons with the other

---

[30] Principal Components, rotation by Varimax with Kaiser normalisation.

[31] Alpha was .669

[32] Alpha was .627

[33] Alpha was .352

[34] $F = 5.154$, $p < .000$

[35] $F = 5.171$, $p < .000$

networks were not statistically significant. By contrast those at the top end of the scale, were much more open to broad ecumenical activities.

The Core Apostolic scale again showed statistical differences between the networks.[36] Here the picture was a little different since Kensington Temple and Vineyard had relatively weak commitment to the core apostolic position and both were significantly different from Ground Level, Kingdom Faith and New Frontiers. Kensington Temple was also significantly different from c.net and Pioneer.

Table 3: Mean Core Apostolic, Ecumenism and P/C Cooperation scores by Network

Core Apostolic		Ecumen-ism		P/C Coop-eration	
KT	6.9	KT	9.8	J F'ship	10.5
Lifelink	8.0	NFI	9.8	NFI	11.3
Vineyard	8.2	KF	10.0	Together	12.0
J F'ship	8.5	J F'ship	10.1	Vineyard	12.1
Ichthus	8.9	Together	10.7	KF	12.3
S and L	9.1	Lifelink	10.7	Pioneer	12.4
Together	9.3	GL	11.0	KT	12.4
c.net	9.6	S and L	11.0	GL	12.5
NFI	10.0	Vineyard	11.3	S and L	12.9
GL	10.0	c.net	11.7	c.net	13.0
Pioneer	10.1	Pioneer	12.0	Ichthus	13.3
KF	10.8	Ichthus	12.2	Lifelink	14.5

Table 3 gives the mean scores of the networks on the three scales and this permits a profile of the networks to be drawn. For instance Pioneer is committed to apostolic networks while also being ecumenical. Ichthus is both ecumenical and willing to cooperate with Pentecostal and charismatic churches but is not so strongly committed to apostolic leadership. Kensington Temple is not ecumenical or strong on apostolic leadership but is relatively favourable to Pentecostal and charismatic cooperation. Ground Level is relatively committed to apostolic leadership but also open to ecumenical and Pentecostal/charismatic cooperation. Salt and Light comes in the middle in relation to ecumenical and Pentecostal/charismatic cooperation and its commitment to apostolic leadership is less strong than Pioneer and Kingdom Faith.

In other words the total picture is rather more complex than the R1/R2 categorisation. The original R1 networks would have been Salt and Light, Cornerstone (now c.net), New Frontiers and Covenant Ministries. Covenant ministries has now devolved into Together and Lifelink so that, if the

---

[36] $F = 5.026$, $p < .000$

original categorisations had remained in place, we might expect Salt and Light, c.net, New Frontiers, Lifelink and Together to belong in a set and the old R2 made up primarily of Pioneer and Ichthus to belong in another set. Although there are traces of these distinctions, it is clear that c.net is more ecumenical and cooperative than might be expected from its origins and that Pioneer, though ecumenical, is also strongly in favour of an apostolic leadership. If one were to look for the archetypal R1 network, it would be New Frontiers and for an archetypal R2 network it would be Pioneer with the others having shifted their positions up and down the scales.

xi. Conclusion

Four general conclusions can be drawn. First, the Spiritual Control scale deals with matters that are largely within the capacity of the individual or the church. In psychological terms the 'locus of control' rests within the grasp of the Christian, or the Christian community, rather than outside. This means that Christians, if they engage with sufficient vigour in spiritual warfare or if they have enough faith, can guarantee their own prosperity and health. Since health tends also to involve miracles of healing, the scale implies that there is an integration between the human and the miraculous or between charismata and one's general worldview. Those who score highly on this scale are those who aim to take a firm grip on their own destiny (table 2). These are not passive Christians who wait for events to unfold but these are active Christians who, by spiritual warfare, attempt to take events by the scruff of the neck.

Second, the contrast between R1 and R2 is pointed up by the results in table 3. The original distinction between the two groups was that R1 was exclusive and committed to the restorationist vision, particularly in relation to the sweeping away of the older denominations and the complete transformation of the church and, ultimately, of human society. The R2 position was softer, more moderate, more willing to work alongside other evangelical and charismatic Christians and, within another dimension, to work in the field of arts and self-expression in worship. The R2 concept did not originally include a distinction between ecumenical cooperation and Pentecostal/charismatic cooperation. In many respects Pentecostal/charismatic churches are similar in experience and outlook to restorationist churches whereas the ecumenical movement is an altogether different animal – larger, more cumbersome, more institutionally focused, more driven by joint committees. Table 3 allows a distinction to be made between the ecumenical and Pentecostal/charismatic dimensions of the R2 concept and thereby to provide a more precise method of placing the different networks in relation to each other and to the wider church.

Although the Ecumenism and Pentecostal/charismatic cooperation scales correlate significantly, the relationship is by no means exact.[37] There are networks that are more willing to be ecumenical than they are willing to cooperate with pentecostal and charismatic churches e.g. the Jesus Fellowship and, equally there are networks that are more willing to cooperate with pentecostal and charismatic churches than they are to cooperate with the ecumenical movement e.g. Kensington Temple. Or, to put this another way, for some networks it would be possible to conceive of a pan-pentecostal/charismatic/apostolic movement more easily than a pan-apostolic/ecumenical movement.

Third, there is a sense of freedom within the apostolic networks in terms of lifestyle. There is a surprising unwillingness to condemn smoking among some networks, until now an evangelical taboo, and an equal unwillingness to condemn sport and other activities that 'keep Sunday special'. Alongside this lifestyle freedom is an insistence that it is right for women to 'obey' their husbands. We have what appears to be a paradox: there is freedom within a range of lifestyle choices while maintaining a clear demarcation within the home. So although these networks could not be characterised as authoritarian or restrictive, there is, nevertheless, an underlying discipline within the bonds of relationship by which the networks are held together.

Fourth, the basic beliefs of the networks are roundly and soundly orthodox and evangelical. The networks belong to the Evangelical Alliance and, indeed, did much in the 1980s to help in the resurgence of the Alliance. Some of its key members were members of the Alliance's committees and helped to set its direction.[38] In many respects the apostolic networks are cousins to the evangelical community and share common interests and passions. It is not inconceivable that in the future the evangelical community and the apostolic network community would make common cause on social or political issues they felt to be crucial to the life of Christianity within British society.

---

[37] Spearman's rho is .446, $p < .000$
[38] This was when Clive Calver led the Alliance.

Chapter 24

Retrospect and Prospect

i. Retrospect

Trends and Traditions

There are pages towards the beginning of his chapters on the 1960s where Adrian Hastings, in his masterly account of the English Church, cannot resist displaying his fine sense of irony. At the beginning of the 1960s, when Michael Ramsey was enthroned as the hundredth Archbishop of Canterbury, the Anglican church was in good heart and confident: confirmations and ordinations were at a high point; Anglican theological colleges were busy training clergy for the future and departments of theology within British universities were largely Christian and often Anglican. In this setting Leslie Paul was asked to produce a comprehensive report on *The Deployment and Payment of the Clergy*, the Anglican clergy, and he wrote his text in 1962 or 1963. He predicted the number of Anglican ordinations for the next nine years and, in his expert opinion, the ascending sequence of numbers was, if anything, an under estimate. As Hastings pointed out, Paul was wrong in his predictions for every single year and, as the years passed, his errors became worse. In the end, Paul predicted 831 ordinations for 1971; the actual figure was 393, less than half.

The very year when Paul wrote appears to have been the zenith. Decline set in to the Church of England in the second part of the 1960s though whether John Robinson's best-selling *Honest to God* was a symptom or a cause is less easy to decide.[1] Robinson's book, which popularised the demythologising ideas of leading German theologians, led to sales of nearly a million in three years. The book implied or argued that there could rightly be a divergence between the beliefs of clergy (who held complex, non-literalist and philosophical views) and the beliefs of the laity (who held traditional ideas about God, heaven and hell). There was, apparently, nothing jarring about professional clergy who believed one thing while letting their congregations believe another. Robinson's intentions appear to have been pastoral and by no means destructive of the church that he loved. Nevertheless, the church that he loved was in the throes of change. The ecumenical movement, largely led by professional theologians and liberal

---

[1] J. A. T. Robinson, *Honest to God*, (London, SCM, 1963).

clergy, began with high hopes but failed to 'make much impact on the walls of institutional division'.[2] Even the publication of the New English Bible, though it sold well, proved impenetrable to many ordinary young people.[3]

What did take place in the 1960s, though its impact was not measurable in terms of confirmations or ordinations, was the charismatic movement. Some of its proponents tended to regard it as the true ecumenical movement and the energies and excitements of charismatic gatherings grabbed the attention of parts of the religious press. In deciding how to interpret the 1960s, and later the 1970s, 1980s, 1990s and the first part of the 21st century, there is always a difficulty in picking out what is of enduring significance. There are some public events picked up by the press and broadcasting media and there are other public events that the press and broadcasting media studiously ignore. By and large the secular press ignored the charismatic movement. By and large the academic world also ignored it. The students of religious studies, psychologists of religion or sociologists of religion may have picked up its traces but, in almost every case, they did so in ways that failed to appreciate the extent of the movement and its capacity to change the religious landscape.[4] As a result, even such a perceptive commentator as Hastings, underestimated what he saw.

The Networks and their New Streams

The argument of this book is that the charismatic movement, with all its energies, innovations, activities and dreams, eventuated in the house churches and these, in many cases, rapidly became apostolic networks. The recurrent metaphor here is of energy and excitement that is released to flow in newly constructed channels or branching pathways. This is the metaphor picked up by Terry Virgo who saw charismatic activity as leading to very little of lasting worth without apostolically constructed structures to channel the spirituality that had been released. So, to look back over the 40 years that have elapsed since the charismatic movement really began, is to see the first emergence of a radical theology – not a heavy duty systematic

[2] A. Hastings, *A History of English Christianity*, (London, Collins, 1986), p.540.

[3] The New English Bible replaced the Authorised Version in many classrooms, but proved to be equally incomprehensible to young people, especially the 80% in Secondary Modern schools. See R. A. Goldman, *Religious Thinking from Childhood to Adolescence*, (London, Routledge and Kegan Paul, 1964).

[4] David Martin is a shining exception. His *Forbidden Revolutions,* (London, SCM, 1996) and his *Pentecostalism: the world their parish* (Oxford, Blackwell, 2002) are cases in point. See my summary of the psychology of speaking in tongues W. K. Kay, The mind, behaviour and glossolalia: a psychological perspective, in M. J. Cartledge (ed), *Speaking in Tongues,* (Carlisle, Paternoster, 2006).

theology but a straightforward biblical theology – that, once it was grasped and implemented, led people to make lifestyle choices and decisions about their ultimate Christian commitments. The theology of Arthur Wallis and the theology of Martyn Lloyd-Jones were sufficiently robust, when coupled with the pentecostal theology of spiritual gifts, to produce confident new congregations. The theology could not only interpret, or reinterpret, church history but it could be applied to current debates within the church; it could make sense of religious experience; it could provide guidelines for family life; it could offer themes that could be developed into Christian social action; it could provide a perspective on the relationship between faith exercised within the worshipping congregation and faith exercised in professional and business relationships. Even where apostolic networks, after they had begun to appear in the 1970s, broke up in disarray, there was still sufficient life within the fragments for each new part to begin to grow again. The network founded by Bryn Jones ended up with about six different offshoots, each of which put down roots and began to bear fruit all over again. Grace Davie is right in her account of *Religion in Modern Europe*, to see the transformations of faith as being slow and generational rather than dependent upon single dramatic events, whether positive or negative.[5]

The Networks and the Public

The big public events of the Dales and Downs Bible Weeks brought restorationism to public notice in the 1970s. Before then its following had been small and invisible. The big Bible Weeks made a resounding declaration and established a trend that other groups were later to follow. It is true that the Keswick Bible Weeks had existed for many years but the message preached from its platform was not of interest to charismatics and its meetings were not geared to their style of worship. The Dales Bible Weeks quickly fostered enthusiasm, and such criticism as they attracted tended to be of their theology rather than the concept of a family summer camp. Looking back, it seems that the preaching from the Dales and the Downs was more radical and more triumphalistic than later events justified. The theology lying behind restorationism was broader than one that asked people to return to the primitive church. But this broad restorationist doctrine only appeared gradually through the later preaching and writing of Bryn Jones. The simplest form of restorationism gave charismatics an understanding of how their spiritual gifts might be utilised within newly-formed tradition-free congregations and, at the same time, gave Pentecostals a theology that removed the gloomy remnant mentality from

---

[5] G. Davie, *Religion in Modern Europe: a memory mutates*, (Oxford, Oxford University Press, 2000).

their dispensationalism and gave them a sense that Christians here and now and today could be more than conquerors in Christ. In retrospect, the claims of restorationism look too big and the worship songs about 'taking the land' appear too aggressive. Yet, given that the other extreme of introverted pietism was all too frequently the norm, the swing to extroverted restorationism is understandable.

The Marches for Jesus were, in hindsight, a natural development of triumphalist restorationism. Marches for Jesus, whatever their theology of spiritual warfare, served to bring Christianity out onto the street. They took Christianity out of ancient buildings with stained glass windows and put contemporary young people and their children into the market square or the busy High Street and made onlookers stop and stare. It is here that the media played their part, both giving the Marches the oxygen of publicity and denying it to them. The early Marches attracted news editors but, as the Marches became more frequent and better organised, it became easier for journalists to treat them like press releases – the mere efflorescence of a pressure group that wanted to grab free publicity. Even so, the Marches for Jesus helped Christians not to be ashamed of the gospel and served as a kind of baptism of publicity for those who had been coy about their faith. The theology of the Marches (which was never fully worked out) sometimes claimed that the trumpets, songs and banners of the marchers impressed principalities and powers in the spiritual realm; this was harder to verify.

We could say that restorationism gradually developed a theology of public spaces and public life. Public spaces, whether they were schools that were hired or streets that were marched on or showgrounds to be camped on, could be claimed for Jesus. Putting this in another way, we could say that Christianity could make all spaces sacred spaces and did not have to localise the holiness of God through sacramentalism. Restorationism managed to move the boundaries between the sacred and profane so that what had previously been outside in the profane area, could now be brought within the domain of the sacred. Football on a Sunday or the local pub could, within reason, be accommodated inside restorationist theology. If Jesus was Lord, he was Lord of football and Lord of the pub.

The Networks, the Arts and Education

In the same way the arts which had, during the 20th century, begun to replace religion in the minds of the intelligentsia, might also be invaded and Christianised.[6] It was Virginia Woolf who wrote, on hearing that T. S. Eliot had become a Christian, 'there is something obscene in a living person

---

[6] A theme implicit in the opening chapters of J. Carey, *The Intellectuals and the Masses*, (London, Faber and Faber, 1992), and is elaborated by Hastings (1986), ch 12.

sitting by the fire and believing in God' – her reaction was visceral.[7] This rejection of Christianity in the novels, plays and high art of the mid-20th century was so pervasive that it went virtually unnoticed.[8] Restorationism saw no reason to agree with this and, though it produced no art that captured the public imagination or sold in millions, began to offer young people through skilful music an alternative to the unchallenged culture of their age. Only Pioneer and its associated churches appear to have taken the arts seriously, yet the very fact that they did so is indicative of the scope of restorationist theology.

And if the arts and public spaces could be accommodated within restorationist theology, so too could education. There is a logic, and not simply a sectarian logic, that sees education as belonging within the domain of the kingdom of God. Several of the networks have founded Christian schools, most notably Salt and Light, or have set up their own training programmes for young ministers, most notably KT/LCC. The Christian schools have survived unpromising beginnings and their educational standards, judged by normal secular criteria, are high. Their standards, judged against the purposes for which they were founded – namely to nourish and stimulate the faith of Christian children, are harder to assess and deserve examination in a full-scale research study. Even without this sort of evidence, though, the numbers on school rolls and the good examination results, appear to vindicate bold financial and strategic decisions made in the 1970s.

The Networks and Relationships

Looking back on the apostolic networks over 40 years, there is a striking match between the early rhetoric on relationships and subsequent practice. The emphasis upon relationships in the 1970s entailed a concentration upon interactions between Christians. What restorationists wanted to do away with entirely was the formal, stilted, deferential basis for relationships that allowed Christians to hide behind facades. Real relationships, as far as restorationists were concerned, entailed meeting each other in casual clothes, playing games together, talking about football or children and behaving in one's leisure time like the vast majority of the British population. Real relationships naturally excluded sexual immorality or financial double dealing but, within the parameters of Christian ethics, relationships depended upon the ability to speak honestly, to keep one's word, to forgive other people, to be kind, to be generous and to fulfil responsible family roles. Although to those outside restorationism incessant talk of relationships could seem artificial and laboured, the net result was to

---

[7] Quoted by Hastings, *A History of English Christianity*, (1986), p.236.
[8] V. Cunningham, *British Writers of the Thirties,* (Oxford, OUP, 1989), p.32.

create family-friendly congregations and a more natural environment for Christian men.[9]

These relationships were worked out in many different kinds of meetings. There were home meetings, prayer meetings, cell meetings, men's breakfasts, old people's meetings, youth meetings, mums' and toddlers' meetings, leaders' meetings, regional meetings, conferences, prayer partners, barbecues, seminars, children's outings, and a host of others. Restorationist Christians were always coming together for one reason or another and the life of worship spilled over into social occasions. Grace might be said at the summer barbecue by singing one of the worship songs from Sunday morning. Prayer for someone in pain might occur spontaneously as when a child was stung by a wasp. These relationships naturally enough led to courting and marriage in the case of the young and, in the case of the old, provided an antidote to loneliness and endless hours of meaningless television. It is true that talk of relationships was partially hijacked by the shepherding movement of the 1970s but, by the mid-1980s, it was back on track although, when the cell movement came along, the churches that adopted a strong line on cells bent relationships into a cellular pattern. For the majority of congregations, though, relationships continued to be essential to the functioning of church from top to bottom. Meetings of leaders were dependent for their success upon trust and willingness to take part in untrammelled discussion. It became important to 'hear the heart' of other people – to let them say what they really thought without fear of disapproval. And relationships were crucial to the connection between groups of leaders and their apostle or apostolic team. There needed to be self-discipline on all sides: it had to be possible to say exactly what one thought without in any way descending to personal abuse or insult. The continuance of apostolic networks over 40 years is an indication that such conversations could be held and were held. Indeed, the strength of a relationship might be tested by working out exactly how forcefully one could disagree without jeopardising the bonds of friendship.

Relationships were private and behind-the-scenes. They were not, like the Bible Weeks, part of the public domain. So, in looking back on the past 40 years, relationships hardly show up on the historical record. They are there in the background making things happen and causing churches and networks to stick together. Only in private discussion with apostolic leaders does it become clear that their relationships with their churches and with each other go back a long way and are part of their mental landscape. As family relationships helped form personal identity, so networked relationships helped form Christian identity. In this nexus of invisible

---

[9] Cf. C. L. Craig, L. J. Francis, and M. Robbins, 'Psychological type and sex differences among church leaders in the United Kingdom', *Journal of Beliefs and Values*, 25, 1, (2004), 3-13.

connections there was enormous financial generosity. The churches would have been unable to operate without consistent flows of money. Almost every network could tell stories of generosity to individuals or in the funding of projects. Buildings were bought, overseas aid was given, debts were covered and ministry was paid for. The most obvious examples of financial giving occurred at the big Bible Weeks when appeals for money were successfully made.[10] Such offerings were counted and the totals announced and, to this extent, they fell into the public domain. Yet there was private giving that was unannounced and unrecorded and that was part of the lifestyle of many restorationists. The theology of finance could, it is true, overbalance into demands for money and prosperity preaching of the most blatant and acquisitive kind but, when the balance was right, it led to simple acts of generosity. Without appreciating the culture of giving, it is not possible to understand restorationism.

The Networks and the Globe

There was also mission. Here the principles of relationship and finance lay behind dangerous and sometimes life-changing journeys to distant continents. A full audit of the overseas work of the apostolic networks is impossible to present in detail: Ground Level worked with emerging networks in South Africa, New Frontiers International had connections with India and Africa as well as other parts of the western world; Ichthus made links with the Middle East; Salt and Light worked with churches in Europe as well as Africa; Covenant Ministries International made contact with China; c.net worked in Nepal; and so on. For the most part mission did not at first show up on the public radar. It grew out of relationships of trust and was supported by reliable and regular donations. Looking back on the trajectory of apostolic networks, serious engagement with mission is both the most logical and the most surprising aspect of what has happened. It is logical because it follows from the apprehension that restorationism is a world-wide movement for the benefit of humankind. It was surprising because the first little bible study gatherings in front rooms in English towns seemed so utterly unpromising. In the 1980s, when mission had moved firmly up the agenda, there were issues of strategy to address. The coordination between expansion and church planting in Britain and mission overseas is most pronounced in New Frontiers International. Other networks followed suit bit by bit and, as their capacity to take on significant overseas projects increased, their preaching reflected their changing priorities.

---

[10] As with Dales, Downs, Grapevine and Stoneleigh.

ii. Prospect

Most of the leaders of apostolic networks were born after 1940 and many of them have now reached the point where retirement beckons. Most of them are unlikely to retire at the statutory male age but, within the next 10 years, most of them will be unable to travel as extensively as they once did. Nor will they be able to carry the ministerial load they once carried. This presents them with the problem of transition. Leadership will have to pass from the first to the second or third generation within the apostolic networks. Traditional denominations, even traditional pentecostal denominations, have well oiled machinery for transferring leadership from one generation or one officer to another. The machinery usually involves voting and, in any event, since leadership is often collective, the next-in-line for high office is often in place before the most senior leader leaves his post.[11] Apostolic networks eschew voting. It is the one procedure that they have almost uniformly opposed, and opposed on the grounds that voting nullifies charismatic gifting. Voting presumes a vacancy that must be filled, an office that needs an officeholder. Charismatic gifting is unpredictable and in one phase of existence one type of gifting may be required but, in another, a quite different form of gifting may be needed. Charismatic gifting is initiated by God and not subject to human manipulation – that is the presumption of those within apostolic networks. Consequently the next major challenge facing almost all the networks is to find the right person to fill the shoes of their founding apostle.

In some instances the transition has already occurred. John Wimber found a way to 'anoint' John Mumford, his successor. Barney Coombs found a way to pass on his mantle to Steve Thomas. In both these cases the handing over of authority was publicly enacted so that there could be no mistake about who was chosen. And in both these cases the founding apostle remained in service at an international level and simply handed his authority on country by country. This model of transition has worked well and brought with it fresh dynamism to the networks that could now benefit from the energies of the younger leader. In other networks, the transition is incomplete or unstarted.

So, in prospect, is the issue of the changing of leadership. If a network chooses the wrong leader or breaks up through disagreement, the work of the first generation will be eroded though, as was the case with those networks that have already suffered disruption, not necessarily destroyed. There is no standard operating procedure to explain how transition should occur and numerous solutions to the problem are possible. We can envisage a scenario where some networks stumble at the point of transition and others moved serenely on. New Frontiers International as the largest of the

---

[11] Historically, usually a man.

networks will be watched by the others to see how events unfold. The experience of c.net and Covenant Ministries International suggests that, even when there are transitional difficulties, there is sufficient momentum within the network for many of the values that defined it to be perpetuated.

Andrew Walker's classification of the networks into two categories, R1 and R2, has been tested against empirical data and found to be supportable. The networks are variably open to ecumenical and cooperative influences although their positions upon the axes of collaboration are not always predicable. Some networks appear to be open to the collaboration with evangelicals while other networks show greater interest in collaborating with pentecostal and charismatic groups. Some make a virtue of their openness while others are single-mindedly focused upon the path they feel called upon to follow. Where networks become more diffuse in their values and more diverse in their aims, they are likely to transform themselves into service providers for other Christians and for the communities where they are situated. Where networks are focused on their values, they are likely to move forward to achieve long-term goals, whether of church planting, of missions, of education or of broadcasting. The choice between being wide and porous or being narrow and impervious faces all the networks, but it is the R2 group that is most likely to be susceptible to the ripple effects from British culture. In this connection, the networks that have resisted female leadership are most obviously those that can, if necessary, stand against cultural expectations.

It is impossible to work out what British culture will do over the next 10 or 20 years. It may become more multicultural, more open to global influences, more radically post-modern or, if there are terrorist atrocities, may batten down the hatches and become more nationalistic. It may be that apostolic networks will continue to be seen as trend-setters for the wider body of the church, that is, if the wider body of the church continues to exist in any substantial way.[12] It may be that apostolic networks will encroach upon non-Christian communities and began to gain converts. Alternatively, it may be that, as demographic forces exert themselves, non-Christian communities will gain widespread political leverage within British society and that this will leave the apostolic networks struggling to maintain their success. Non-Christian religious groups are by and large younger than the rest of the population. This means that, as the years pass, these groups become proportionally more numerous.

---

[12] E.g. J. M. Haley, and L. J. Francis, *British Methodism: what circuit ministers really think*, (Peterborough, Epworth Press, 2006). 'Here is a group of men and women who express great emotional loyalty to the Methodist Church but who are also anxious about the future of their Church. The worrying features of these data concern the way in which among the younger generation of ministers loyalty is lower and anxiety is greater' p.251.

We cannot predict whether the Anglican church will remain established or disestablish. If it disestablishes, the best predictor of its likely course is to be found in Wales where disestablishment occurred in 1920. After early setbacks, the Anglican Church rallied and adapted better than the apparently invincible nonconformist churches.[13] Today the situation is different. According to Leslie Francis and his collaborators, the current Anglican church is in danger of fragmenting along already discernible fault lines.[14] One of these fault lines is to be found in the division between those who are positively influenced by the charismatic movement and those who are not. Differences here are found over gay issues.[15] Charismatic Anglicans resist calls for gay ordination and gay marriage much more strongly than noncharismatic Anglicans. Similarly charismatic Anglicans are more inclined to accept lay presidency of communion services, the authority of Scripture and the exclusivity of the creeds.[16] If the large charismatic Anglican congregations of London like Holy Trinity, Brompton, continue to thrive and prosper, they may become more influential than they already are. In the same way that the division between liberals, Anglo-Catholics and evangelicals within the Church of England has begun to shift towards evangelicals, it is possible that this change in the centre of gravity may move whole the Anglican church in a more evangelical and charismatic direction.[17] Such an outcome would be welcomed by the New Wine network, though it is difficult to believe this kind of theological reappraisal would be painless or without acrimony.

In consequence, the prospect for apostolic networks may be tied to the condition of the older and larger denominations. Anglicanism has capitalised upon the charismatic movement much more effectively than Catholicism or Methodism. Consequently the Anglican church, with its range of diverse churchmanship, contains pockets and streams of charismatic activity; the same cannot be said of contemporary British Roman Catholicism. The future growth and success of apostolic networks is connected to the future charismatic life of the Anglican church in Britain in a paradoxical way: if the Anglican church becomes more charismatic and offers many features that are currently offered by apostolic networks, it is possible that the networks will lose members to the Anglican church in the

---

[13] D. D. Morgan, *The Span of the Cross: Christian Religion and Society in Wales 1914-2000*, (Cardiff, University of Wales Press, 1999).

[14] L. J. Francis, M. Robbins, and J. Astley, *Fragmented Faith? Exposing fault-lines in the Church of England*, (Carlisle, Paternoster, 2005).

[15] Francis, Robbins and Astley, *Fragmented*, (2005) pp.126, 133.

[16] Francis, Robbins and Astley, *Fragmented*, (2005), p.136, 120.

[17]<http://www.telegraph.co.uk/news/main.jhtml?xml=/news/2003/08/25/nevang25.xml> (accessed 14 September, 2006) reporting on the Daily Telegraph August 2003. About 35% of Anglicans were evangelicals in 1998 and this figure could rise to 50% by 2010.

same way that the Dales Bible Week lost ground eventually to Spring Harvest. Or, to put this another way, if people can find within Anglicanism everything that apostolic networks offer, they may be happier to attend an Anglican congregation rather than an apostolic network congregation.[18] Thus the success of charismatic Anglicanism may endanger the success of apostolic networks. There must be a tipping point here where, if the Anglican church is mildly charismatic, it will offer support to the apostolic networks but not entice future members away from them but, if the Anglican Church is strongly charismatic, the apostolic networks find themselves eclipsed.

Against the background of these uncertainties, apostolic networks have undoubtedly set a structural example to other Christian groups. We may begin to see other church groups re-invent themselves as networks. Such re-invention has the potential to be highly disruptive as traditionalists and ecclesiastical bureaucrats fight a rearguard action against the claims of apostolic figures within their denominations. Yet, such reinvention *is* possible where churches and ministers are enabled to hold dual affiliation: a minister can be a member of the Baptist Union and also of New Frontiers International. An Anglican congregation can belong to New Wine as well as to its own diocese. In this way the influence of networks may permeate gradually rather than demand sudden coups.

So the religious landscape will change. Instead of being covered with institutional churches that, to the practised eye, reveal the ebbs and flows of church history – the old dissenters from the 17th century, the Methodists of the 18th, the Oxford Movement of the 19th and the Pentecostals of the 20th – new structures may come to into being. Networks may replace institutions and the flexibility and relational emphases of the networks might then be widely felt within the simplified and purposive rhythms of a renewed church life. The warehouses of Vineyard or Salt and Light as well as the converted theatres of Pioneer may come to have more significance than the expensive stone architecture that was historically raised to the glory of God.

The New Testament presents a picture of the latter stages of the early church. John was exiled on Patmos and his Apocalypse begins with an account of the seven churches of Asia.[19] Some of the churches were founded by Paul and others were not – they belonged to different networks. Christ himself is depicted moving among the churches and the message of the Spirit, conveyed by John, is individualised: some are commended, others are warned. So, like the seven churches of Asia, the religious landscape of the future may be dotted by a variety of different church

---

[18] This is not such a fanciful idea in the light of the Church House Publication, *Mission-Shaped Church*, produced under the chairmanship of Graham Cray, Bishop of Maidstone, in 2003.

[19] Revelation, chapters 1-3.

groups, each suffering its own fiery trials and each giving light to an unwelcoming world.

Bibliography

Books, Articles and Dissertations

Armstrong, John, 'John Wimber', *The Standard*, The Baptist General Conference Magazine, (May 1991).

Astin, Howard, *Body & Cell*, (Crowborough: Monarch, 1998).

Aune, Kristin J., 'Postfeminist Evangelicals: the construction of gender in the New Frontiers International churches', (Kings College, London, unpublished PhD Dissertation, 2004).

Bainbridge, William Sims, *The Sociology of Religious Movements*, (London: Routledge, 1997).

Baker, Jonathan E., *Consecrated Women? A contribution to the women bishops debate*, Norwich: Canterbury Press, 2004).

Baker, S and D. Freeman, *The Love of God in the Classroom: the story of the new Christian schools*, (Fearn: Christian Focus, 2005).

Ball, Philip, *Critical Mass*, (London: Arrow Books, 2004).

Barclay, Oliver R., *Evangelicalism in Britain 1935-1995: a personal sketch*, (Leicester: IVP, 1997).

Bell, Stuart, *Rebuilding the Walls*, (Tonbridge: Sovereign World, 2003).

— (2005), Email from Stuart Bell.

Berger, Peter L., *The Sacred Canopy*, (New York: Random House, 1967).

Bickle, Mike, *Growing in the Prophetic*, (Lake Mary: Creation House, 1996).

Bittlinger, Arnold, 'The Function of Charismata in Divine Worship', *Theological Renewal*, 1, (1975), pp.5-10.

Blumhofer, Edith L., *The Assemblies of God: A Chapter in the Story of American Pentecostalism*, 2 vols. (Springfield: Gospel Publishing House, 1989).

Boulton, E. C. W., *George Jeffreys: a ministry of the miraculous*, (London: Elim Publishing House, 1928).

Bratt, James B. ed., *Abraham Kuyper: a centennial reader*, (Carlisle: Paternoster, 1998).

Brierley, Peter ed., 'How Christians Use their Money and Why', (London: Christian Research, 2006).

Briers, Stephen J., 'Negotiating with Babylon: responses to modernity within a restorationist community', (University of Cambridge, unpublished PhD Dissertation, 1993).

Brown, Callum G., *The Death of Christian Britain*, (London: Routledge, 2001).

Bruce, Steve, *Religion in Modern Britain*, (Oxford: OUP, 1995).

Butler, Richard A., *The Art of the Possible*, (Harmondsworth: Penguin, 1971).

Calver, Clive and Rob Warner, *Together We Stand*, (London: Hodder and Stoughton, 1996).

Calvin, John, *Institutes of the Christian Religion, IV, 13, 14.* (Geneva / London: James Clarke & Co. Ltd., 1962 edn.).

Carey, John, *The Intellectuals and the Masses,* (London: Faber and Faber, 1992).

Carson, Donald A., *Becoming Conversant with the Emerging Church,* (Grand Rapids: Zondervan, 2005).

Cartledge, Mark J. ed., *Speaking in Tongues,* (Carlisle: Paternoster, 2004).

Cartwright, Desmond, *The Real Wigglesworth,* (Tonbridge: Sovereign World, 2000).

Castells, Manuel, *The Rise of the Network Society,* (vol.1) 2nd edn., (Oxford: Blackwell, 2000).

Chambers, P., 'Social networks and religious identity: an historical example from Wales', in Grace Davie, Paul Heelas, and Linda Woodhead (eds), *Predicting Religion: critical, secular and alternative futures,* (Aldershot: Ashgate, 2003).

Charman, P. A., 'The Rival Kingdoms of the New Churches empowerment and enfeeblement', (Lancaster University, unpublished PhD Dissertation, 1995).

Cho, Paul Yonggi, *Successful Home Groups,* (Plainfield, NJ: Logos International, 1981).

Coates, Gerald, *What on Earth is this Kingdom?,* (Eastbourne: Kingsway, 1983).

— *An Intelligent Fire,* (Eastbourne: Kingsway, 1991).

Coggins, James R. and P. G. Hiebert (eds), *Wonders and the Word: an examination of issues raised by John Wimber and the Vineyard Movement,* (Winnipeg, MB: Kindred Press, 1989).

Coleman, Dan, 'The Demographic Consequences of Immigration to the UK', in H. Disney, (ed.), *Work in Progress: Migration, Integration and the European Labour Marke,* (London: Institute for the Study of Civil Society, 2003), pp.9-40.

Comiskey, Joel, 'Cell Church Solutions', (Fuller Theological Seminary, unpublished PhD Dissertation, 2006).

Coombs, Barney, *Snakes and Ladders*, (Tonbridge: Sovereign World, 1995).

— Apostles Today: Christ's love gift to the church, (Tonbridge: Sovereign World, 1996).

Cooper, Simon and Mike Farrant, *Fire in our Hearts,* (Northampton: Multiply Publications, 1997).

Cotton, Ian, *The Hallelujah Revolution,* (New York: Time Warner Paperbacks, 1995).

Craig, Charlotte L., Leslie J. Francis, and Mandy Robbins, 'Psychological type and sex differences among church leaders in the United Kingdom', *Journal of Beliefs and Values*, 25, (2004), pp.3-13.

Cunningham, Val, *British Writers of the Thirties,* (Oxford: OUP, 1989).

Davie, Grace, *Religion in Britain since 1945,* (Oxford: Blackwell Publishing, 1994).

— *Genius, Grief and Grace,* (Glasgow: Christian Focus Publications, 2001).

Day, S. S., and I Harris, B. Elliott, B. Larson, R. Enquist, H. C. Lukens, (eds), *Creating Christian Cells,* (New York: Faith at Work, c. 1960).

Deere, Jack, 'The Prophet', in David Pytches (ed.), *John Wimber: his influence and legacy*, (Guildford: Eagle, 1998).

Devenish, David, *Demolishing Strongholds: Effective Strategies for Spiritual Warfare*, (Milton Keynes, UK: Authentic Lifestyle, 2000).

Dixon, Patrick, *The Truth About AIDS*, (Eastbourne: Kingsway, 1994).

— 'An altered Christian consciousness', in D. Hilborn (ed), *'Toronto' in perspective: papers on the new charismatic wave of the mid 1990s* (pp.88-98), (Carlisle: Acute [an imprint of Paternoster] 2001).

— *The Truth about AIDS: and a practical Christian response*, (ACET International Alliance, 2004).

Du Plessis, David with Bob Slosser, *A Man Called Mr Pentecost*, (Plainfield, New Jersey: Logos International, 1977).

Dyer, Anne E., 'Ground Level Research', (unpublished MTh Essay on Empirical Theology, University of Wales, Bangor, 2000).

— 'Some theological trends reflected in the songs used by the British charismatic churches of 1970s-early 2000s', *Journal of the European Pentecostal Theological Association*, 26, (2006.1), pp.36-48.

Edwards, David L., *Christianity: the first two thousand years*, (London: Cassell, 1997).

Evans, Gillian R., A. E. McGrath, and A. D. Galloway, *The Science of Theology* (vol. 1), (Basingstoke: Marshall Morgan & Scott, 1986).

Ferguson, Niall, *Empire: how Britain made the Modern World*, (Harmondsworth: Penguin, 2004).

Fiedler, Klaus, *The Story of Faith Missions*, (Oxford: Regnum, 1994).

Finnel, D., *Life in His Body: a simple guide to active cell life*, (Houston, TX: Touch Outreach Ministries, 1995).

Forster, Roger, T. and V.P. Marston, *God's Strategy in Human History*, (Wheaton, Il: Tyndale House, 1974).

Fox, Stephen, *Grapevine: the story so far*, (Lincoln: Ground Level, 2006).

Francis, Leslie J., L. B. Brown, and R. Philipchalk, 'The development of an abbreviated form of the Revised Eysenck Personality Questionnaire (EPQR-A): its use among students in England, Canada, the USA and Australia', *Personality and Individual Differences*, 13, (1992), pp.443-449.

Francis, Leslie J., Mandy Robbins, and Jeff Astley, *Fragmented Faith? Exposing fault-lines in the Church of England*, (Carlisle: Paternoster, 2005),

Francis, Leslie J. and W. K. Kay, *Teenage Religion and Values*, (Leominster: Gracewing, 1995).

Francis, Leslie J. and Mandy Robbins, *The Long Diaconate 1987-1994: women deacons and the delayed journey to priesthood*, (Leominster: Gracewing, 1999).

Friedman, Thomas L., *The World is Flat*, (London: Allen Lane/ Harmondsworth: Penguin, 2005).

Goldman, Ronald J., *Religious Thinking from Childhood to Adolescence*, (London: Routledge and Kegan Paul, 1964).

Gouvernor, Joseph P., 'The Third Wave: a case study of romantic narratives within late twentieth century charismatic evangelicalism', (University of Sheffield, unpublished PhD Dissertation, 2004).

Graham, Billy, *Just as I Am*, (London: HarperCollins, 1998).

Green, Michael (ed.), *Church without Walls: a global examination of cell church*, (Carlisle: Paternoster, 2002).

Grubb, Norman, *Rees Howells Intercessor,* (Cambridge: Lutterworth, 1952).

Grudem, Wayne A., *The Gift of Prophecy in 1 Corinthians,* (Washington D.C.: University Press of America, 1982).

Gunton, Colin E., S. R. Holmes, and M. A. Rae, (eds), *The Practice of Theology: a reader,* (London: SCM, 2001).

Hadaway, C. K., and S. A. Wright, and F. M. DuBose, *Home Cell Groups and House Churches,* (Nashville, TN.: Broadman Press, 1987).

Haley, J. M. and Leslie J. Francis, *British Methodism: What Circuit Ministers Really Think,* (Peterborough: Epworth Press, 2006)

Harper, Michael, *None Can Guess,* (London: Hodder and Stoughton, 1971).

Harris, H. and J. Shaw (eds), *The Call for Women Bishops,* (London: SPCK, 2004).

Hastings, Adrian, *A History of English Christianity,* (London: Collins, 1986).

Hattersley, Roy , *Fifty Years On,* (London: Little, Brown, 1997).

Hawtin, George, 'George Hawtin's letter', in W. K. Kay and A. E. Dyer (eds) *Pentecostal and Charismatic Studies: A Reader,* (London: SCM, 2004) pp.19-24

Heath, Edward, *The Course of My Life,* (London: Hodder & Stoughton, 1998).

Hervieu-Lé ger, Daniè le 'Present-Day Emotional Renewals: the End of Secularization or the End of Religion?', in J. William and H. Swatos (Eds.), *A Future for Religion: New Paradigms for Social Analysis,* (London: Sage, 1993).

Hewitt, Brian (1995), *Doing a New Thing,* (London: Hodder & Stoughton, 1995).

Hilborn, David, *'Toronto' in Perspective: Papers on the New Charismatic Wave of the mid 1990s,* (Carlisle: Acute [an imprint of Paternoster] 2001).

Hinn, Benny, *The Anointing,* (Milton Keynes: Word UK Ltd., 1997).

Hinton, J., *Renewal: an Emerging Pattern, Graham Pulkingham and others,* (Poole: Celebration Publishing, 1980).

Hirst, R., 'Social networks and personal beliefs: an example from modern Britain', in P. Heelas, L. Woodward and G Davie (eds), *Predicting Religion: critical, secular and alternative futures.* Aldershot: Ashgate, 2003).

Hocken, Peter D., *Streams of Renewal,* (Carlisle: Paternoster, 1998).

Horn, Nico, 'Power and Empowerment in the Political Context of South Africa'. *Journal of the European Pentecostal Theological Association,* 25, (2005) pp.7-24.

Horton, M. S. (ed.), *Power Religion: the selling out of the evangelical church?,* (Chicago, Il.: Moody Press, 1992).

Hunt, Stephen J., 'The Anglican Wimberites', *Pneuma,* 17, (1995), pp.105-118.

— 'The Alpha Course and its Critics: an overview of the debates', *PentecoStudies,* 4, (2003), pp.1-22.

— 'The Alpha Programme: some tentative observations on the state of the art evangelism in the UK', *Journal of Contemporary Religion,* 18, (2003), pp.77-93.

— 'Alpha and the Gay Issue: a Lesson in Homophobia?' *Journal of Beliefs and Values,* 26, (2005), pp.261-271.

Hurd, Douglas, *An End to Promises*, (London: Collins, 1979).

Hywel-Davies, Jack, *The Story of Kensington Temple*, (Eastbourne: Monarch Books, 1998).

Jackson, B., *The Quest for the Radical Middle: a History of the Vineyard*, (Cape Town: Vineyard International Publishing, 1998).

Jenkins, R., *Gladstone*, (Basingstoke: Papermac, 1995).

Jones, Bryn,
— 'Wise men of action', in D. Matthew (ed.), *Apostles Today*, (Bradford: Harvestime, 1988).
— *The Radical Church*, (Shippensburg, PA: Destiny Image Publishers, 1999).

Jones, Brynmor Pierce, *A Instrument of Revival: the complete life of Evan Roberts 1878-1951*, (South Plainfield, NJ: Bridge Publishing, 1995).

Jones, Edna, 'Personal Letter from Edna Jones.' to W. K. Kay, (6 June, 2006).

Kay, William. K., *Prophecy*, (Mattersey, UK: Lifestream, 1991).
— 'Belief in God in Great Britain 1945-1996: moving the scenery behind classroom RE', *British Journal of Religious Education 20, 1*, (1997) *28-41*, 20, 28-41.
— 'Childhood, Personality and Vocation', in L. J. Francis and W. K. Kay (eds), *Joining and Leaving Religion: Research Perspectives*, (Leominster: Gracewing, 2000), pp.215-231.
— *Pentecostals in Britain*, (Carlisle: Paternoster, 2000).
— 'Society, Christian Beliefs and Practices: the large scale', in W. K. Kay and L. J. Francis (eds), *Religion in Education (3)*, (Leominster: Gracewing, 2000).
— 'Prosperity Spirituality', in C. Partridge, (ed), Encyclopaedia of New Religions: New Religious Movements, Sects, and Alternative Spiritualities, (London: Lion, 2004).
— and Leslie J. Francis, 'Suicidal Ideation among Young People in the UK: churchgoing as an inhibitory influence?', *Religion, Mental Health and Culture*, 9.2, (2006), pp.127-140.

Kendrick, Graham, G. Coates, R. Forster, and L. Green, *March for Jesus*, (Eastbourne: Kingsway, 1992).

Kiernan, K., 'Family changes: issues and implications', in M. E. Morgan (ed.), *The Fragmenting Family: does it matter?* (London: IEA, 1998), p.56.

Kuhlman, Katherine, *I Believe in Miracles*, (London: Oliphants, 1963).

Ladd, George Eldon, *Jesus and the Kingdom*, (London: SPCK, 1966).

Latourette, Kenneth S., *A History of the Expansion of Christianity*, (Grand Rapids: Zondervan, 1976).

Lawson, James G., *Deeper Experiences of Famous Christians*, (Anderson, Ind.: Warner Press, 1911).

Lee, Young Hoon, 'The Life and Ministry of David Yonggi Cho and the Yoido Full Gospel Church', in Wonsuk Ma and H-S. Bae. (eds.), *David Yonggi Cho: a close look at his theology and ministry*, (Goonpo / Baguio City: APTS Press/Hansei University Press, 2004).

Lenin, Vladimir I., *Materialism and Empirio-criticism*, (Moscow: Foreign Languages Publishing House, 1947).

Lie, Geir, 'T. Austin-Sparks: a brief introduction', *Refleks*, 3, (2004), pp.48-52.

Lloyd-Jones, Martin, *Knowing the Times,* (Edinburgh: The Banner of Truth Trust, 1989).

Lyne, Peter, *First Apostle, Last Apostles*, (Tonbridge: Sovereign World, 1999).

MacLaren, Duncan, *Mission Implausible: restoring credibility to the church*, (Carlisle: Paternoster, 2004).

Manwaring, R., *From Controversy to Co-existence: Evangelicals in the Church of England 1914-1980*, (Cambridge: Cambridge University Press, 1985).

Martin, David, *A General Theory of Secularisation,* (London: Harper Collins, 1979).

— *Forbidden Revolutions,* (London: SPCK, 1996).

— Pentecostalism: the World their Parish, (Oxford: Blackwell, 2002).

— 'Secularisation and the Future of Christianity', *Journal of Contemporary Religion*, 20, (2005), pp.145-160.

Marwick, Arthur, *British Society Since 1945* (3rd edn), (Harmondsworth: Penguin, 1996).

Matthew, David, 'Arthur Wallis, 1922-1988: a Tribute', in J. Wallis (ed.), *Arthur Wallis: Radical Christian,* (Eastbourne: Kingsway, 1988 in a book published 1991).

— *Apostles Today*, (Bradford: Harvest Time, 1988).

Maurice, Frederick D., *The Kingdom of Christ,* (London: J. M. Dent & Co., 1842).

Mayho, Stuart, '"Do not be hasty in the laying on of hands" (1 Timothy 5:22): The Role, Recognition and Release of Leadership in the New Testament and Their Relationship to Recruitment in the Church Today', (University of Wales, unpublished MTh Dissertation, 2006).

McGavran, Donald, *Understanding Church Growth,* (Grand Rapids, Mich: Eerdmans, 1985).

Meeks, Wayne A., *The First Urban Christians: the social world of the apostle Paul,* (Yale: Yale University Press, 1984).

Millard, Amos D., 'The Holy Spirit and Worship', *Paraclete*, Winter, 3.4 (1969), pp.14-19.

Miller, Jonathan, Missionary Zeal and Institutional Control: organizational contradictions in the Basel Mission on the Gold Coast, 1828-1917, (Grand Rapids, Mich: Eerdmans, 2003).

Millward, J. C., 'Chalk and Cheese? An account of the impact of restorationist ecclesiology upon the Baptist Union - with particular reference to those churches in joint fellowship with the Baptist Union of Great Britain and New Frontiers International', (University of Brunel, PhD Dissertation, 2003).

Moore, Stephen D., *The Shepherding Movement,* (London: T & T Clark, 2003).

Morgan, D. Densil, *The Span of the Cross: Christian Religion and Society in Wales 1914-2000,* (Cardiff: University of Wales Press, 1999).

Morton, Tony, 'Tribute to Arthur Wallis', *Insight,* vol. 4, (1988), pp.2-5.

— 'Tribute to Arthur Wallis', *Insight,* vol. 8 (1990), p.6.

Moynagh, Michael, *emergingchurch.intro*, (Oxford: Monarch, 2004).

Murray, Ian. H., *Dr Martyn Lloyd-Jones: the fight of faith 1939-1981*, (Edinburgh: The Banner of Truth Trust, 1990).

— *The Puritan Hope*, (Edinburgh: Banner of Truth, 1985).

Murray, Stuart, *Church after Christendom*, (Carlisle: Paternoster, 2004).

Neighbour Jr, Ralph W., *Where Do We Go From Here? A guidebook for the cell group church,* (Houston, TX: Touch Publications, 1990).

Noble, John, *Forgive us our Denominations,* (London: Team Spirit, 1971).

Ortiz, Juan Carlos, *Disciple,* (London: Lakeland, 1975a).

— with Jamie Buckingham, *Call to Discipleship,* Plainfield, NJ: Logos International, 1975).

O'Sullivan, Anthony, 'Roger Forster and the Ichthus Christian Fellowship: the development of a charismatic missiology', *Pneuma,* 16, (1994), pp.247-263.

Osgood, Hugh J., 'African neo-Pentecostal Churches and British Evangelicalism 1985-2005: Balancing Principles and Practicalities', (unpublished PhD, London University, [SOAS], 2006).

Packer, Jim I., *Honouring the People of God,* (Carlisle: Paternoster, 1999).

Patten, Chris, *Not Quite the Diplomat,* (Harmondsworth: Penguin, 2006).

Pawson, David, 'A mixed blessing', in D. Hilborn (ed), *'Toronto' in perspective: papers on the new charismatic wave of the mid 1990s,* (Carlisle: Acute, [an imprint of Paternoster], 2001), pp.75-87.

Penn-Lewis, Jesse with Evan Roberts, *War on the Saints: a textbook for believers on the work of deceiving spirits among the children of God,* (London: Marshall Brothers and Leicester, The 'Overcomer' Office, 1912).

Percy, Martin, *Words, Wonders and Power,* (London: SPCK, 1996).

Perriman, Andrew (ed.), *Faith: Health and Prosperity,* (Carlisle: Paternoster, 2003).

Pietersen, Lloyd, *The Mark of the Spirit?,* (Carlisle: Paternoster, 1998).

Poloma, Margaret, *The Assemblies of God at the Crossroads: Charisma and Institutional Dilemmas,* (Knoxville: University of Tennesse Press, 1989).

— *The Toronto Report,* (Bradford-on-Avon: Terra Nova Publications, 1996).

— 'Inspecting the fruit of the 'Toronto Blessing': a sociological perspective, *Pneuma,* 20, (1998), pp.43-70.

Prince, Derek, 'The Local Church: God's view vs man's view', *New Wine,* 14-18 May, (1973).

Putnam, Robert D., *Bowling Alone,* (London: Simon & Schuster, 2000).

Pytches, David, *John Wimber: his Influence and Legacy,* (Guildford: Eagle, 1998).

Randall, Ian, *Educating Evangelicalism,* (Carlisle: Paternoster, 2000).

Randall, Ian and David Hilborn, *One Body in Christ: the History and Significance of the Evangelical Alliance,* (Carlisle: Paternoster, 2001).

Robeck jr, Cecil M., *The Azusa Street Mission and Revival,* (Nashville, TN: Nelson Reference and Electronic, 2006).

Robertson, A. Ewen, 'An Evaluation of Apostolic Ministry in Today's Church, with Particular Reference to the Offshoots of Covenant Ministries International', (University of Wales in partnership with Regents College: unpublished MTh dissertation: June 2006).

Robinson, John A. T., *Honest to God,* (London: SCM, 1963).

Russell, Bertrand, *Has Man a Future?* (Harmondsworth: Penguin, 1961).

Sandbrook, Dominic, *Never Had It So Good,* (London: Little, Brown, 2005).

— *White Heat,* (London: Little, Brown Group, 2006).

Shakespeare, Tom, K. Gillespie-Sells and D. Davies, *The Sexual Politics of Disability: Untold Desires,* London: Cassell, 1996).

Smith, David, 'An Account of the Sustained Rise of New Frontiers International within the United Kingdom', *Journal of the European Theological Pentecostal Association*, 23, (2003), pp.137-156.

Spittler, Russel P., 'David Johannes Du Plessis', in Stanley M. Burgess, Eduard M. van der Maas (eds.), *New International Dictionary of Pentecostal and Charismatic Movements*, (Grand Rapids: Zondervan, 2002).

Stapleton, Ruth C., *The Experience of Inner Healing*, (New York: Thomas Nelson, 1977).

Stibbe, Mark, *Times of Refreshing*, (London: Marshall Pickering, 1995).

Taylor, Michael R., *Endtime Sonship from 1940-1985*, (London: University of London Press, 2004).

Thompson, Damian, *The End of Time: Faith and Fear in the Shadow of the Millennium*, (Vermont: University Press of New England, 1999).

— Waiting for the Antichrist: Charisma and Apocalypse in a Pentecostal church, (Oxford: Oxford University Press, 2005).

Thompson, Michael J., 'An Illustrated Theology of Churches and 'Sects',' (University of Kent at Canterbury, unpublished PhD Dissertation, 1996).

Troeltsch, Ernst, 'The Social Teaching of the Christian Church', in R. G. (ed.), *Theology and Sociology: a reader*, (London: Geoffrey Chapman, 1987).

Trudinger, Ron, *Cells for Life*, (Basingstoke: Olive Tree Press, Eastbourne, Kingsway, [originally 1979], 1983).

Trust, T. R., 'Successful Leadership through Groups of 12', in T. R. Trust (ed.), (Richmond, Surrey, UK: The Reachout Trust, 2006).

Tugwell, Simon, *Did You Receive the Spirit?* (London: Darton Longman & Todd, 1971).

— 'Is there a 'pentecostal experience'?' *Theological Renewal*, 7, (1977), pp.8-11.

Urquhart, Colin, *When the Spirit Comes*, (London: Hodder and Stoughton, 1974).

— *Faith for the Future*, London: Hodder and Stoughton, 1982).

— *From Mercy to Majesty: moving into revival*, (London: Hodder and Stoughton, 1985).

Versteeg, P., 'Draw Me Close: An Ethnography of Experience in a Dutch Charismatic Church', (Vrije Universiteit Amsterdam, PhD dissertation, 2001).

Virgo, Terry, *Restoration in the Church*, (Eastbourne: Brighton, 1985).

— *No Well Worn Paths*, (Eastbourne: Kingsway Publications, 2001).

— *Does the Future have a Church?* (Eastbourne: Kingsway, 2003).

— *The Tide is Turning*, (Eastbourne: Kingsway, 2006).

Wacker, Grant, *Heaven Below*, (Cambridge, Mass.: Harvard University Press, 2001).

Wagner, C. Peter, 'Third Wave', in S. M. Burgess and E. M., van der Maas (eds), *International Dictionary of the Pentecostal and Charismatic Movements*, (Grand Rapids: Mich, Zondervan, 2002) p.1181.

— (ed), *Church Growth: the state of the art*, (Wheaton, Il: Tyndale House, 1986).

— and F. Douglas Pennoyer (eds), *Wrestling with Dark Angels: Towards a Deeper Understanding of the Supernatural Forces in Spiritual Warfare,* (Ventura, CA: Regal Books, 1990).

Walker, Andrew, *Restoring the Kingdom (4th edn),* (Guildford: Eagle, 1998).

Wallis, Arthur, *In the Day of Thy Power: Structural Principles of Revival,* (Arlesford: Christian Literature Crusade, 1956).

— 'A Fresh Look at the Baptism in the Holy Spirit', *Theological Renewal,* 73, (1978), pp.29-36.

— *China Miracle,* (Eastbourne: Kingsway, 1985).

Wallis, Jon, *Arthur Wallis: Radical Christian,* (Eastbourne: Kingsway, 1991).

Ward, Peter, *Selling Worship: how what we sing has changed the church,* (Carlisle: Paternoster, 2005).

Warner, Rob, 'Fissured Resurgence - Developments in English Pan-Evangelicalism 1966-2001,' (Unpublished PhD thesis, King's College, London, 2006).

Watts, D. J. and S. H. Strogatz, 'Collective dynamics of 'small-world' networks', *Nature,* 393, (1998), pp.440-442.

Weber, Martin, *The Protestant Ethic and the Spirit of Capitalism,* (London: Unwin University Books, 1930).

Weeks, Gordon, Chapter Thirty Two - part of: a history of the Apostolic Church 1900-2000, (Barnsley: self-published, 2003).

Whitchurch, B., *The Journey,* (Oxford: Salt and Light Ministries, 2002).

Wilson, Brian R., *Sects and Society,* (London: Heinemann, 1961).

— 'A typology of sects in a dramatic and comparative perspective'. *Archives de Sociologie de Religion,* vol. 16, (1963), pp.4,9-63.

Wimber, Carol, *John Wimber: The Way It Was,* (London: Hodder & Stoughton Religious, 1999).

Wimber, John, *Church Growth Leadership: Wimber interprets Wagner,* (Anaheim: Vineyard Publishing, 1984).

— 'Revival Fire', in J. Wimber (ed.), *Revival Fire conference,* (Anaheim Conference Centre, Anaheim, California, 28 January, 1991).

— 'The Essence of Discipleship', recorded at, *Holy Trinity Brompton Focus Week,* Holy Trinity Brompton, London, 1995).

— 'Introducing prophetic ministry', in J. Wimber (ed), *Equipping the Saints,* (Anaheim, Calif.; Vineyard Ministries International, [UK edition] 1990).

— 'Revival fire', in J. Wimber (ed), *Equipping the Saints,* (Anaheim: Vineyard Ministries International, [UK edition], 1991).

Womersley, Harold, *Wm F. P. Burton: Congo Pioneer,* (Eastbourne: Victory Press, 1979).

Wright, Nigel, 'Restoration and the House Church Movement', in Stephen S Hunt, Malcolm Hamilton and Tony Walter (eds), in *Charismatic Christianity: sociological perspectives,* (Basingstoke, Hants.: Palgrave MacMillan, 1997).

— 'The nature and variety of restorationism and the 'House Church' movement', in M. Hamilton and T. Walter eds. S. Hunt (ed.), *Charismatic Christianity: sociological perspectives,* (Basingstoke, Hants.: Macmillan, 1997), pp.60-76.

Yinger, John Milton, *Religion, Society and the Individual,* (New York: Macmillan, 1957).

Young, Lawrence A. (ed.), *Rational Choice Theory and Religion,* (London: Routledge, 1997).

Websites

About Inventors, 2006, (accessed 31 August, 2006); available from <http://inventors.about.com/library/inventors/blvideo.htm>.

Alpha, London, (accessed 30 August, 2006); available from <http://alpha.org/welcome/whositfor/index.htm>.

Basingstoke Council, Basingstoke, 2005, (accessed 20 November, 2005); available from <http://www.statistics.gov.uk/census2001/pyramids/pages/24ub.asp>.

BBC/ Politics, 2006, (accessed 24 August, 2006); available from <http://news.bbc.co.uk/1/hi/uk_politics/4812822.stm>.

Campbell, Fiona, Sowing Seeds, (accessed 29 August, 2006), available from http://www.new-wine.org/resources/Sowing%20Seeds.htm>.

Churches in Communities International, 2006, (accessed 2 June, 2006); available from <http://www.cicinternational.org/CiC.htm>.

Churches in Community International, CICInternational, 2006, (accessed 2 June, 2006); available from <http://www.cicinternational.org/CiC.htm>.

Churches UK, 2003, (accessed 28 January, 2005); available from <http://www.churchesuk.co.uk>.

Christianity Magazine, 2006, (accessed 24 August, 2006); available from <http://www.christianitymagazine.co.uk/index.cfm>.

Cic International, 2006, (accessed 2 June, 2006); available from <http://www.cicinternational.org/CiC.htm>.

Contemporary Christianity, (accessed 2 June, 2006); available from <http://www.contemporarychristianity.org/lionandlamb/038/evangelism.html >

Crawley online, Inquiry Chapter 2 Crawley: Crawley online, 2005, (accessed 20 November, 2005); available from http://www.crawley-online.eurobell.co.uk/inquiry/chaptertwo.html>.

Daily Telegraph [Newspaper], August 2003, (accessed 14 September, 2006); available from http://www.telegraph.co.uk/news/main.jhtml?xml=/news/2003/08/25/nevang 25.xml>

Destiny Church, 2006, (accessed 9 May, 2006); available from http://www.destiny-church.com/index.htm>.

Dye, Colin, 'Colin Dye's Comments on G12 London, (accessed 12 April, 2006); available from http://www.cellexplosion.com/?p=why_principle_of_12>.

—*'2000 and Beyond, the Vision of the London City Church',* London: 2005, (accessed 8 July, 2005); available from http://www.revivaltimes.org/index.php/10.htm>.

—'*The Why Principle of 12*', 2006, (accessed 12 April, 2006); available from http://www.cellexplosion.com/?p=why_principle_of_12>.

Edwards, Joel (President EA), 'Evangelical Alliance's Website' 2006, (accessed 12 April, 2006); available from http://www.eauk.org/index.cfm>.

Electoral Commission on 31st December 2004, (accessed 24 August, 2006); available from http://en.wikipedia.org/wiki/Labour_Party (UK)>.

Find a Church Web Site, 2003, (accessed 28 January, 2005); available from <http://www.findachurch.co.uk/>.

Finney, John, Interview with John Finney Concerning the the Emmaus Course, 2006, (accessed 30 August, 2006); available from <http://www.chpublishing.co.uk/feature.asp?id=2389830>.

*Fresh Expressions, (*accessed 21 August, 2006); available from <http://www.freshexpressions.org.uk/section.asp?id=14>.

Fusion, 2006, (accessed 18 January, 2006); available from <http://web.fusion.uk.com/content.php?type=1&id=118&site_id=2>.

Gentry, Dale, Home Page, 2006, (accessed 04 January, 2006); available from <http://www.dalegentry.com/>.

Gott, Ken, Metro Church International, (accessed 12.04.06); available from <http://mci12.org.uk/mci/>

Government Statistics, 2006, (accessed 31 August, 2006); available from <http://www.statistics.gov.uk/cci/nugget.asp?id=822>.

Green Belt Web Site, 2006, (accessed 10 July, 2006); available from <http://www.greenbelt.org.uk/?s=9>.

Health Protection Agency, 2004, (accessed 2004); available from <http://www.hpa.org.uk/>.

Her Majesty's Prison Service, 2006, (accessed 22 August, 2006); available from <http://www.hmprisonservice.gov.uk>.

Heron, David and Kerridge, Peter, Premier Radio, 2006, (accessed 23 August, 2006); available from <http://www.premier.org.uk/engine.cfm?i=751>.

Ichthus Web Page, 2005, (accessed 06 October, 2005 and 02 May, 2006); available from <http://www.ichthus.org.uk/vision/>.

Kensington Temple, London, 2005, (accessed 9 July, 2005); available from <hhtp://www.kt.org/about>.

Kingsway International Christian Centre, 2005, (accessed 9 July, 2005); available from <http://www.kicc.org/about>.

Kress, Gunther, 2006, *Culture, Language and Communication, University of London: The Institute of Education*, (accessed 12 September, 2006); available from <http://ioewebserver.ioe.ac.uk/ioe/cms/get.asp?cid=4441&4441_0=5194>.

Kingsway International Christian Centre, 'London: KICC (Chamelion Net)', 2006, (accessed 2 June, 2006); available from <http://www.kicc.org.uk/network.asp>.

Lee, Steve, 'Where I Live: Hampshire: Faith Features: Miracle Street', Southampton: 15/09/2005, (accessed 13 July, 2006); available from <http://www.bbc.co.uk/hampshire/content/articles/2005/09/12/miracle_st_fe ature.shtml>.

Lifelink International Website, 2006, (accessed 9 May, 2006); available from <http://www.lifelinkinternational.org.uk/Default.aspx>.

Ministry Books, 'Living Stream On Line Ministries', (accessed 6 October, 2005); available from <http://www.ministrybooks.org/books.asp?id=19&chapterid=0&sectionid=1&pageid=1>.

New Wine Web Site, 2006, (accessed 2 June, 2006); available from <http://www.new-wine.org/>.

Noble, John, *Pioneer*, 2006, (accessed 21 August, 2006), available from <http://www.pioneer.org.uk/Mobile/default.aspx?group_id=10832>.

— *'Spirit Connect'*, 2006, (accessed 21 August, 2006); available from <http://www.spiritconnect.org/mainpage.html>.

—*(*accessed 21 August, 2006); available from <http://www.pioneer.org.uk/Group/Group.aspx?id=15853>.

Omnibus Survey, Office for National Statistics, 2006, (accessed 31 August, 2006); available from <http://www.statistics.gov.uk/statbase/Product.asp?vlnk=5672>.

Pioneer, (accessed 21 August, 2006); available from <http://www.pioneer.org.uk/Group/Group.aspx?id=15853>.

Reach out Trust, A Look at the G12 Richmond, Surrey, 2003, (accessed 12 April, 2006); available from <http://www.reachouttrust.org/articles/relatedsubjects/g12.htm>.

— *(post 2003), 'Successful leadership through Groups of 12', Richmond, Surrey.*

Rich and Poor, 2006, (accessed 31 August, 2006); available from <http://news.bbc.co.uk/1/hi/special_report/1999/10/99/information_rich_information_poor/466651.stm>.

Salt and Light, (accessed 22 August, 2006); available from <http://saltlight.org/>.

Saturday Home Language Schooling 2006, (accessed 12 September, 2006); available from <http://ioewebserver.ioe.ac.uk/ioe/cms/get.asp?cid=4441&4441_0=5194>.

Scanlon, Paul, *Abundant Life Website, Bradford: Abundant Life*, 2006, (accessed 7 June, 2006); available from <http://www.alm.org.uk/church/>.

Schools 2006, (accessed 16 June, 2006); available from <http://news.bbc.co.uk/1/shared/bsp/hi/education/03/school_tables/secondary_schools/html/931.stm>.

Scott, Martin, *Sowing the Seeds for Revival*, March 2004, (accessed 3 January, 2006); available from <http://www.wild-fire.co.uk/>.

Smith, Chuck, *The Philosophy of Ministry of Calvary Chapel*, 2006, (accessed 28 February, 2006); available from <http://www.calvarychapel.com/?show=Resources.Ebooks.thephilosophyofministryofcalvarychapel>.

Spinnaker Trust, a schools' charity, (accessed 2 June, 2006); available from <http://www.spinnakertrust.org.uk/>.

Spring Harvest Web Site, 2006, (accessed 20 May, 2006); available from <http://www.springharvest.org/mainevent.html>.

Steve, John Wimber, a blog with reference to The Los Angeles Times, (1972), (accessed 3 June, 2006); available from

<http://www.deepcallstodeep.sonafide.com/index.php/2004/05/27/john-wimber-a-leader-to-know.

Successful Leadership through Groups of 12 Richmond, Surrey: post 2003, (accessed 12 April, 2006); available from <http://www.reachouttrust.org/articles/relatedsubjects/g12.htm>.

Tax Payers' Alliance, 2006, (accessed 24 August, 2006); available from <http://www.taxpayersalliance.com/opinion/individual_opinion.php?opinion_id=35>.

The Church of England General Synod, The Church of England General Synod 2006, (accessed 26.06.2006); available from <http://www.cofe.anglican.org/about/gensynod/>.

Thompson, Hugh, Revival Times, 2000, p.158, (accessed 08.07.2005); available from http://www.revivaltimes.org/index.php/10.htm>.

Up My Street, 2006, (accessed 02 June, 2006); available from <http://www.upmystreet.com>.

Vineyard International Consortium: World of the Vineyard 2006, (accessed 29 June, 2006): available from <http://www.vineyard.org/>.

Vineyard Website UK, 2006, (accessed 3 June, 2006); available from <http://www.vineyardchurchesuk.com/>.

—*About Us: New Wine* 2006, (accessed 30 August, 2006); available from <http://www.new-wine.org/about_us/>.

Virgo, Wendy, Tribute to Simon Pettit, 2005, (accessed 5 May, 2005); available from <http://www.newfrontiers.xtn.org/magazine/volume2issue10/article_index.php?id=290>.

Interviews

William K. Kay interviewed: -

Stuart Bell, Lincoln: New Life Christian Fellowship, Lincoln, 5 December, 2004

Peter Butt and David Damp, Southampton, 11 January, 2006.

John Coles, London, 17 July, 2004.

Gareth Duffty, Coventry, 5 May, 2005.

Colin Dye, Kensington Temple, London, 16 January, 2004.

Colin Dye, London, (telephone) 22 September, 2005.

Roger Forster at Forest Gate, London, 12 December, 2003.

David Heron and Peter Kerridge, 13 January, 2004.

Dave Holden, Sidcup, 27 April, 2004.

Keri Jones, Bryn Jones's brother, Cardiff, 2 February, 2006.

Andrew McNeil, 27 February, 2006.

David Matthew, Castleford, 15 December, 2004.

Marlon Nartey, London, 10 December, 2003.

Wesley Richards by phone, in Slough, 9 March, 2006.

Spring Harvest leaders: Peter Broadbent, Steve Chalke, Ian Coffey, Ruth Dearnley, Alan Johnson, Gerald Kelly, Jeff Lucas and Rachel Orrell, 25 January, 2005

Alan Scotland, Bangor, 15 November, 2004.
Steve Thomas, Basingstoke: Salt and Light, 12 January, 2006.
David Tomlinson, London, 4 May, 2005.

Anne E. Dyer interviewed: -
Laura McWilliams, in Hull, 10 April, 2005.
Terry Virgo in Lincoln, 25 August, 2005.

Restoration **Magazine Articles**

Brand, Jean, 'Basingstoke Community Church', *Restoration*, January /
February, (1982), p.34.
Coombs, Barney, 'It All Fits Together', *Restoration*, no.1, April, (1975), pp.18,
19.
—'It All Fits Together', *Restoration*, no. 1, April, (1975), pp.18, 19.
Day, Roger (compiler), 'Help Africa', *Restoration*, March/April, (1986), p.12.
Day, Roger (ed.), 'Go Teams National Launch', *Restoration*,
September/October, (1985), p.25.
— 'Exciting Christian Growth in Bradford', *Restoration*, September/October
(1986), p.19.
— 'Help Africa', *Restoration*, July/August, (1986), pp.9, 24.
— 'Winning the World in This Generation- God's Strategy for Britain',
Restoration, November/December, (1987), p.17.
— 'Dayspring - Thousands Challenged to Active Evangelism', *Restoration*,
July-August, (1988), p.19.
— 'High Praise at Restoration 90', *Restoration*, November/December, (1990),
p.33.
— 'From Help Africa to Help International', *Restoration*, January/February,
(1992), p.38.
— 'A Voice to the World: Interview with B. and K. Jones, D. Mansell, D.
Matthew', *Restoration*, July/August (1992), p.35.
Jones, Bryn,
— 'Apostles for Today Tomorrow', *Restoration*, September/October, (1985),
pp.30-34.
— 'Apostles and Prophets -what's the difference?', *Restoration*, November
/December, (1985), pp.24-27.
— 'God Wants You to Prosper -Success Today', *Restoration*, September
/October, (1986), pp.2-4.
— 'Apostles and Prophets- What's the Difference?' *Restoration*, November
/December, (1985), pp.24-27.
— 'Apostles and Prophets -What's the Difference?' *Restoration*, November
/December, (1985), pp.24-27.
— 'God Wants You to Prosper.' *Restoration*, September /October, (1986),
pp.2-4.
— 'Life after Dales Bible Week', *Restoration*, July / August, (1986), p.22.
— 'Interview with Bryn Jones', *Restoration*, May / June (1989), p.39.
— 'The Middle East', *Restoration*, August, (1992), p.37.

Matthew, David (ed.), 'Editorial', *Restoration*, July /August, (1982), p.5.
— 'Focus: Circulation', *Restoration*, July /August, (1982), p.5.
— 'Chart of Church Decline over the Centuries', *Restoration*, November / December, (1983), p.40.
— 'Church History Chart', *Restoration*, November / December, (1983), p.40.
— 'Bible Weeks', *Restoration*, 1986, p.14.
— 'Life Changing Days', *Restoration*, November/December, (1986), p.14.
— 'Abundant Life Church', *Restoration*, November/December, (1987).
— 'Bible Weeks', *Restoration*, May/June, (1987), p.19.
— 'Future Leaders', *Restoration*, July/August, (1987), p.21.
— 'Help Africa', *Restoration*, November/ December, (1987), p.18.
— 'Mainstream Decline', *Restoration*, May/June, (1987), p.27.
Richards, Wesley, 'Everything You Always Wanted to Know About Bryn Jones but Were Afraid to Ask Part 1', *Restoration*, March/April, (1989), pp.28-34.
— 'Everything You Always Wanted to Know About Bryn Jones but Were Afraid to Ask Part 3', *Restoration*, July-August, (1989), pp.34-5.
— 'Everything You Wanted to Know About Bryn Jones and Were Afraid to Ask Part 2', *Restoration*, May/June, (1989), pp.38-42.
Ring, Nigel, 'Trends: Bible Weeks', *Restoration*, May/June, (1987), p.19.
Thompson, Hugh, 'Equipped for the Job', *Restoration*, May/June, (1985), p.39.
Tomlinson, David, 'Q:A: Some Burning Questions About Apostle', *Restoration*, November/December, (1981), p.19.
Tooze, Chris, 'National Women's Day- Just the Beginning', *Restoration*, September/October, (1986), p.19.
Various, 'Post Bag', *Restoration*, May / June, (1992), p.40.
Virgo, Terry, 'The Church: God's Only Answer' *Restoration*, November/December, (1978), p.13.
— 'The Puritan Hope', *Restoration*, January/February, (1980), p.11.
— 'An Apostle by the Grace of God', *Restoration*, September/October, (1985), pp.22-23; 30-34.
— 'Apostles Today', *Restoration*, September/October, (1985), pp.20-22.
Wall, Joy, 'Postbag', *Restoration*, June, (1992), p.40.
Wallis, Arthur, 'Springs of Restoration 2', *Restoration*, September/October, (1980), pp.6-9.

Other Primary Sources

Cornerstone, 'Minutes of Cornerstone Team Meeting', (Southampton, 1982-86).
Fountain Trust Advisory Council Minutes 13 April, 1972, (London: Fountain Trust, 1972).

Index

Studies in Evangelical History and Thought

(All titles uniform with this volume)
Dates in bold are of projected publication

Andrew Atherstone
Oxford's Protestant Spy
The Controversial Career of Charles Golightly

Charles Golightly (1807–85) was a notorious Protestant polemicist. His life was dedicated to resisting the spread of ritualism and liberalism within the Church of England and the University of Oxford. For half a century he led many memorable campaigns, such as building a martyr's memorial and attempting to close a theological college. John Henry Newman, Samuel Wilberforce and Benjamin Jowett were among his adversaries. This is the first study of Golightly's controversial career.

__2006__ / 1-84227-364-7 / approx. 324pp

Clyde Binfield
Victorian Nonconformity in Eastern England

Studies of Victorian religion and society often concentrate on cities, suburbs, and industrialisation. This study provides a contrast. Victorian Eastern England—Essex, Suffolk, Norfolk, Cambridgeshire, and Huntingdonshire—was rural, traditional, relatively unchanging. That is nonetheless a caricature which discounts the industry in Norwich and Ipswich (as well as in Haverhill, Stowmarket and Leiston) and ignores the impact of London on Essex, of railways throughout the region, and of an ancient but changing university (Cambridge) on the county town which housed it. It also entirely ignores the political implications of such changes in a region noted for the variety of its religious Dissent since the seventeenth century. This book explores Victorian Eastern England and its Nonconformity. It brings to a wider readership a pioneering thesis which has made a major contribution to a fresh evolution of English religion and society.

__2006__ / 1-84227-216-0 / approx. 274pp

John Brencher
Martyn Lloyd-Jones (1899–1981) and Twentieth-Century Evangelicalism

This study critically demonstrates the significance of the life and ministry of Martyn Lloyd-Jones for post-war British evangelicalism and demonstrates that his preaching was his greatest influence on twentieth-century Christianity. The factors which shaped his view of the church are examined, as is the way his reformed evangelicalism led to a separatist ecclesiology which divided evangelicals.

2002 / 1-84227-051-6 / xvi + 268pp

Jonathan D. Burnham
A Story of Conflict
The Controversial Relationship between Benjamin Wills Newton and
John Nelson Darby
Burnham explores the controversial relationship between the two principal
leaders of the early Brethren movement. In many ways Newton and Darby were
products of their times, and this study of their relationship provides insight not
only into the dynamics of early Brethrenism, but also into the progress of
nineteenth-century English and Irish evangelicalism.
2004 / 1-84227-191-1 / xxiv + 268pp

Grayson Carter
Anglican Evangelicals
Protestant Secessions from the Via Media, c.1800–1850
This study examines, within a chronological framework, the major themes and
personalities which influenced the outbreak of a number of Evangelical clerical
and lay secessions from the Church of England and Ireland during the first half
of the nineteenth century. Though the number of secessions was relatively
small—between a hundred and two hundred of the 'Gospel' clergy abandoned
the Church during this period—their influence was considerable, especially in
highlighting in embarrassing fashion the tensions between the evangelical
conversionist imperative and the principles of a national religious establishment.
Moreover, through much of this period there remained, just beneath the surface,
the potential threat of a large Evangelical disruption similar to that which
occurred in Scotland in 1843. Consequently, these secessions provoked great
consternation within the Church and within Evangelicalism itself, they
contributed to the outbreak of millennial speculation following the
'constitutional revolution' of 1828–32, they led to the formation of several new
denominations, and they sparked off a major Church–State crisis over the legal
right of a clergyman to secede and begin a new ministry within Protestant
Dissent.
2007 / 1-84227-401-5 / xvi + 470pp

J.N. Ian Dickson
Beyond Religious Discourse
Sermons, Preaching and Evangelical Protestants in Nineteenth-Century Irish Society
Drawing extensively on primary sources, this pioneer work in modern religious history explores the training of preachers, the construction of sermons and how Irish evangelicalism and the wider movement in Great Britain and the United States shaped the preaching event. Evangelical preaching and politics, sectarianism, denominations, education, class, social reform, gender, and revival are examined to advance the argument that evangelical sermons and preaching went significantly beyond religious discourse. The result is a book for those with interests in Irish history, culture and belief, popular religion and society, evangelicalism, preaching and communication.
2005 / 1-84227-217-9 / approx. 324pp

Neil T.R. Dickson
Brethren in Scotland 1838–2000
A Social Study of an Evangelical Movement
The Brethren were remarkably pervasive throughout Scottish society. This study of the Open Brethren in Scotland places them in their social context and examines their growth, development and relationship to society.
2003 / 1-84227-113-X / xxviii + 510pp

Crawford Gribben and Timothy C.F. Stunt (eds)
Prisoners of Hope?
Aspects of Evangelical Millennialism in Britain and Ireland, 1800–1880
This volume of essays offers a comprehensive account of the impact of evangelical millennialism in nineteenth-century Britain and Ireland.
2004 / 1-84227-224-1 / xiv + 208pp

Khim Harris
Evangelicals and Education
Evangelical Anglicans and Middle-Class Education in Nineteenth-Century England
This ground breaking study investigates the history of English public schools founded by nineteenth-century Evangelicals. It documents the rise of middle-class education and Evangelical societies such as the influential Church Association, and includes a useful biographical survey of prominent Evangelicals of the period.
2004 / 1-84227-250-0 / xviii + 422pp

Mark Hopkins
Nonconformity's Romantic Generation
Evangelical and Liberal Theologies in Victorian England
A study of the theological development of key leaders of the Baptist and
Congregational denominations at their period of greatest influence, including
C.H. Spurgeon and R.W. Dale, and of the controversies in which those among
them who embraced and rejected the liberal transformation of their evangelical
heritage opposed each other.
2004 / 1-84227-150-4 / xvi + 284pp

Don Horrocks
Laws of the Spiritual Order
Innovation and Reconstruction in the Soteriology of Thomas Erskine
of Linlathen
Don Horrocks argues that Thomas Erskine's unique historical and theological
significance as a soteriological innovator has been neglected. This timely
reassessment reveals Erskine as a creative, radical theologian of central and
enduring importance in Scottish nineteenth-century theology, perhaps equivalent
in significance to that of S.T. Coleridge in England.
2004 / 1-84227-192-X / xx + 362pp

Kenneth S. Jeffrey
When the Lord Walked the Land
The 1858–62 Revival in the North East of Scotland
Previous studies of revivals have tended to approach religious movements from
either a broad, national or a strictly local level. This study of the multifaceted
nature of the 1859 revival as it appeared in three distinct social contexts within a
single region reveals the heterogeneous nature of simultaneous religious
movements in the same vicinity.
2002 / 1-84227-057-5 / xxiv + 304pp

John Kenneth Lander
Itinerant Temples
Tent Methodism, 1814–1832
Tent preaching began in 1814 and the Tent Methodist sect resulted from
disputes with Bristol Wesleyan Methodists in 1820. The movement spread to
parts of Gloucestershire, Wiltshire, London and Liverpool, among other places.
Its demise started in 1826 after which one leader returned to the Wesleyans and
others became ministers in the Congregational and Baptist denominations.
2003 / 1-84227-151-2 / xx + 268pp

July 2005

Donald M. Lewis
Lighten Their Darkness
The Evangelical Mission to Working-Class London, 1828–1860
This is a comprehensive and compelling study of the Church and the complexities of nineteenth-century London. Challenging our understanding of the culture in working London at this time, Lewis presents a well-structured and illustrated work that contributes substantially to the study of evangelicalism and mission in nineteenth-century Britain.

2001 / 1-84227-074-5 / xviii + 372pp

Herbert McGonigle
'Sufficient Saving Grace'
John Wesley's Evangelical Arminianism
A thorough investigation of the theological roots of John Wesley's evangelical Arminianism and how these convictions were hammered out in controversies on predestination, limited atonement and the perseverance of the saints.

2001 / 1-84227-045-1 / xvi + 350pp

Lisa S. Nolland
A Victorian Feminist Christian
Josephine Butler, the Prostitutes and God
Josephine Butler was an unlikely candidate for taking up the cause of prostitutes, as she did, with a fierce and self-disregarding passion. This book explores the particular mix of perspectives and experiences that came together to envision and empower her remarkable achievements. It highlights the vital role of her spirituality and the tragic loss of her daughter.

2004 / 1-84227-225-X / xxiv + 328pp

Don J. Payne
The Theology of the Christian Life in J.I. Packer's Thought
Theological Anthropology, Theological Method, and the Doctrine of Sanctification
J.I. Packer has wielded widespread influence on evangelicalism for more than three decades. This study pursues a nuanced understanding of Packer's theology of sanctification by tracing the development of his thought, showing how he reflects a particular version of Reformed theology, and examining the unique influence of theological anthropology and theological method on this area of his theology.

2005 / 1-84227-397-3 / approx. 374pp

Ian M. Randall
Evangelical Experiences
A Study in the Spirituality of English Evangelicalism 1918–1939
This book makes a detailed historical examination of evangelical spirituality
between the First and Second World Wars. It shows how patterns of devotion
led to tensions and divisions. In a wide-ranging study, Anglican, Wesleyan,
Reformed and Pentecostal-charismatic spiritualities are analysed.
1999 / 0-85364-919-7 / xii + 310pp

Ian M. Randall
Spirituality and Social Change
The Contribution of F.B. Meyer (1847–1929)
This is a fresh appraisal of F.B. Meyer (1847–1929), a leading Free Church
minister. Having been deeply affected by holiness spirituality, Meyer became
the Keswick Convention's foremost international speaker. He combined
spirituality with effective evangelism and socio-political activity. This study
shows Meyer's significant contribution to spiritual renewal and social change.
2003 / 1-84227-195-4 / xx + 184pp

James Robinson
Pentecostal Origins
Early Pentecostalism in Ireland in the Context of the British Isles
Harvey Cox describes Pentecostalism as 'the fascinating spiritual child of our
time' that has the potential, at the global scale, to contribute to the 'reshaping of
religion in the twenty-first century'. This study grounds such sentiments by
examining at the local scale the origin, development and nature of
Pentecostalism in Ireland in its first twenty years. Illustrative, in a paradigmatic
way, of how Pentecostalism became established within one region of the British
Isles, it sets the story within the wider context of formative influences emanating
from America, Europe and, in particular, other parts of the British Isles. As a
synoptic regional study in Pentecostal history it is the first survey of its kind.
2005 / 1-84227-329-1 / xxviii + 378pp

Geoffrey Robson
Dark Satanic Mills?
Religion and Irreligion in Birmingham and the Black Country
This book analyses and interprets the nature and extent of popular Christian
belief and practice in Birmingham and the Black Country during the first half of
the nineteenth century, with particular reference to the impact of cholera
epidemics and evangelism on church extension programmes.
2002 / 1-84227-102-4 / xiv + 294pp

Roger Shuff
Searching for the True Church
Brethren and Evangelicals in Mid-Twentieth-Century England
Roger Shuff holds that the influence of the Brethren movement on wider evangelical life in England in the twentieth century is often underrated. This book records and accounts for the fact that Brethren reached the peak of their strength at the time when evangelicalism was at it lowest ebb, immediately before World War II. However, the movement then moved into persistent decline as evangelicalism regained ground in the post war period. Accompanying this downward trend has been a sharp accentuation of the contrast between Brethren congregations who engage constructively with the non-Brethren scene and, at the other end of the spectrum, the isolationist group commonly referred to as 'Exclusive Brethren'.

2005 / 1-84227-254-3 / xviii+ 296pp

James H.S. Steven
Worship in the Spirit
Charismatic Worship in the Church of England
This book explores the nature and function of worship in six Church of England churches influenced by the Charismatic Movement, focusing on congregational singing and public prayer ministry. The theological adequacy of such ritual is discussed in relation to pneumatological and christological understandings in Christian worship.

2002 / 1-84227-103-2 / xvi + 238pp

Peter K. Stevenson
God in Our Nature
The Incarnational Theology of John McLeod Campbell
This radical reassessment of Campbell's thought arises from a comprehensive study of his preaching and theology. Previous accounts have overlooked both his sermons and his Christology. This study examines the distinctive Christology evident in his sermons and shows that it sheds new light on Campbell's much debated views about atonement.

2004 / 1-84227-218-7 / xxiv + 458pp

Kenneth J. Stewart
Restoring the Reformation
British Evangelicalism and the Réveil at Geneva 1816–1849

Restoring the Reformation traces British missionary initiative in post-Revolutionary Francophone Europe from the genesis of the London Missionary Society, the visits of Robert Haldane and Henry Drummond, and the founding of the Continental Society. While British Evangelicals aimed at the reviving of a foreign Protestant cause of momentous legend, they received unforeseen reciprocating emphases from the Continent which forced self-reflection on Evangelicalism's own relationship to the Reformation.

2006 / 1-84227-392-2 / approx. 190pp

Martin Wellings
Evangelicals Embattled
Responses of Evangelicals in the Church of England to Ritualism, Darwinism and Theological Liberalism 1890–1930

In the closing years of the nineteenth century and the first decades of the twentieth century Anglican Evangelicals faced a series of challenges. In responding to Anglo-Catholicism, liberal theology, Darwinism and biblical criticism, the unity and identity of the Evangelical school were severely tested.

2003 / 1-84227-049-4 / xviii + 352pp

James Whisenant
A Fragile Unity
Anti-Ritualism and the Division of Anglican Evangelicalism in the Nineteenth Century

This book deals with the ritualist controversy (approximately 1850–1900) from the perspective of its evangelical participants and considers the divisive effects it had on the party.

2003 / 1-84227-105-9 / xvi + 530pp

Haddon Willmer
Evangelicalism 1785–1835: An Essay (1962) and Reflections (2004)

Awarded the Hulsean Prize in the University of Cambridge in 1962, this interpretation of a classic period of English Evangelicalism, by a young church historian, is now supplemented by reflections on Evangelicalism from the vantage point of a retired Professor of Theology.

2006 / 1-84227-219-5 / approx. 350pp

Linda Wilson
Constrained by Zeal
Female Spirituality amongst Nonconformists 1825–1875

Constrained by Zeal investigates the neglected area of Nonconformist female spirituality. Against the background of separate spheres, it analyses the experience of women from four denominations, and argues that the churches provided a 'third sphere' in which they could find opportunities for participation.

2000 / 0-85364-972-3 / xvi + 294pp

Paternoster
9 Holdom Avenue,
Bletchley,
Milton Keynes MK1 1QR,
United Kingdom
Web: www.authenticmedia.co.uk/paternoster